observations of deviance

observations of deviance

EDITED BY **Jack D. Douglas** UNIVERSITY OF CALIFORNIA AT SAN DIEGO

Random House, New York

Library of Congress Catalog Card Number: 76–121072

Manufactured in the United States of America.

Printed and bound by Halliday Lithograph Corp., West Hanover, Mass.

Typography by Hermann Strohbach

98765432

Preface

Probably the greatest need of any sociology course on deviance or social disorganization is for basic source material that will give students insight into the everyday lives of deviants. This kind of insight is of crucial importance to any student who wishes to know "what it's really like" and certainly to anyone concerned with arriving at a valid sociological theory of deviance.

Students come to most other sociology courses with an understanding of the subject matter gained from years of personal involvement with the relevant phenomena. But, obviously, this is rarely possible for the study of deviance. To get this crucial insight into the lives of deviants, students must rely primarily on carefully done case reports.

Like most other sociologists of deviance, I have often used novels in my courses on deviance to help develop this insight. But fictionalized accounts are, at best, not to be trusted very far. What we need above all else are careful participant-observer reports on deviant groups. We now have a number of excellent reports of this sort, but unfortunately they have always been very scattered and generally inaccessible for class use. In this volume I have tried to include the best of these studies to make them easily available in an inexpensive form.

The primary purpose of this volume, then, is to give students this crucial insight. But these case reports on deviance also provide the best available material for illustrating and evaluating the major contemporary theories of deviance.

It is my hope that this volume will stimulate sociologists and their students to do many comparable studies of deviance. If it does, this will surely be its greatest contribution.

J. D. D.

Contents

Preface   v

Introduction   3

part one   situational deviance

1 | **An Abortion Clinic Ethnography** | Donald W. Ball   15

2 | **Sexual Modesty, Social Meanings, and the Nudist Camp** | Martin S. Weinberg   28

3 | **Breakfast with Topless Barmaids** | Richard G. Ames, Stephen W. Brown, and Norman L. Weiner   35

part two   heterosexual styles of deviance

4 | **B-Girls and Prostitutes** | Sherri Cavan   55

5 | **Prostitution** | Wayland Young   64

part three   homosexual styles and ways of deviance

6 | **The Dynamics of Prison Homosexuality: The Character of the Love Affair** | David A. Ward and Gene G. Kassebaum   89

7 | **On Becoming a Lesbian** | William Simon and John H. Gagnon   107

8 | **On Being in the "Community"** | William Simon and John H. Gagnon 112

9 | **The Homosexual Community** | Evelyn Hooker 115

part four violence as a deviant style and way of life

10 | **Hell's Angels: Hoodlum Circus and Statutory Rape of Bass Lake** | Hunter Thompson 131

11 | **The Cherubs Are Rumbling** | Walter Bernstein 146

12 | **The Blackstone Rangers** | James Alan McPherson 170

part five lies, fraud, and theft as styles and ways of life

13 | **Types of Jockeys** | Marvin Scott 205

14 | **The Teen-age Shoplifter: A Microcosmic View of Middle-Class Delinquency** | Norman L. Weiner 213

15 | **The Hustler** | Ned Polsky 218

16 | **The Big-Con Games** | David Maurer 237

part six drugs as a deviant style and way of life

17 | **White-Collar Pill Party** | Bruce Jackson 255

18 | **The Drug Takers** | James Mills 266

19 | **Exiles from the American Dream: The Junkie and the Cop** | Bruce Jackson 272

20 | **Involvement in the Drug Scene** | James Carey 288

21 | **Heads and Freaks** | Fred Davis with Laura Munoz 301

22 | **The Hippie Ethic and the Spirit of Drug Use** | Sherri Cavan 314

23 | **Focus on the Flower Children: Why All of Us May Be Hippies Someday** | Fred Davis 327

observations of deviance

Introduction

No area of sociology has changed more rapidly or more creatively in recent years than that of deviance. After many years of slow development, deviance has become one of the major areas of development in sociology. A great amount of new research on deviant groups is being done today, especially by younger sociologists, and the theoretical developments in this area are already beginning to have a profound effect on general sociological theory. Because younger sociologists have found deviance such a fertile and exciting field for their own work, and because students share these feelings, deviance promises to become an even more important area of sociological research and theory in the coming years.

All sociologists have believed that careful and systematic observation of deviant groups and individuals is of tremendous importance to anyone concerned with gaining a valid understanding of deviance in our society. Even those sociologists who have made almost exclusive use of official statistics on deviance have agreed that case studies are very important; and, in fact, most of them have used case studies in some way. Even Émile Durkheim, for example, used certain case studies in his book, *Suicide,* though these studies were primarily literary. All of the better statistical theorists of deviance, like statistical analysts in other areas of sociology, have known that one must have valid case studies to determine the real meanings of the official statistics. Most statistical analysts of deviance have, indeed, considered it a great misfortune that there were not more good case studies available for their use. In fact, many people who have made exclusive use of official information on deviance have done so only because there were too few careful and systematic case studies, and because they would find it exceedingly difficult to do such studies themselves.

This age-old concern of sociologists with good case studies of deviance has grown dramatically in recent years. I believe it is in no way an overstatement to say that all sociologists of deviance today are aware of the many problems involved in using official information. Certainly there are great disagreements concerning the degree of bias involved in official information as well as the implications of such bias for our own research and theory on deviance. Many sociologists continue to use official information, though with increasing caution, whereas others reject such information entirely. Yet, even those sociologists who continue to do extensive analyses of official statistics on deviance are aware of the desirability of gaining more valid information through the use of participant-observer studies or, as we often call it, field research on deviance. It is apparent that most of these statistical analysts would prefer to use case studies because they are more subject to scientific controls than any official information could possibly be, but representative case studies are usually not available. While representative samples must lie far in the future—if, indeed, we are ever able to get such samples—the statistical analysts of deviance are beginning to rely increasingly on case studies to judge the bias involved in official information, so that they can adjust their studies accordingly.

There are many reasons why sociologists are deeply committed to doing participant-observer studies and using them to construct and test their theories of deviance. The most obvious reason, and the one we have been implicitly referring to so far, is that the sociologist has greater control over the methods of observation involved in getting information on deviance when he uses participant-observer studies, than when he uses information provided for him by nonscientists. While participant-observer studies of deviance are also subject to various problems of bias, such bias can be controlled by the sociologist, whereas the bias of official information, journalistic reports and so on are beyond our control. For this reason, if for no other, sociologists will undoubtedly do more studies of deviance by using participant-observer methods.

But there are other important reasons for making observational studies and using them as a primary source of information on deviance. Most importantly, only by getting inside deviant groups, and by experiencing things the way they do, can we ever come to see how deviants really view the world. Only in this way can we gain that all-important sense of their everyday realities. Only in this way can we ever be sure that we are not simply imposing our own preconceived biases about deviants onto them.

Even if we did not have these fundamental, scientific reasons for doing participant-observer studies of deviants, we would be interested in them because the things the deviants do and their moral conflicts with the rest of society are of intrinsic interest to us. And the fact that our students share this feeling also pressures us to do such studies and make use of them in teaching. While they certainly are of no greater social importance to us than such subjects as banking and accounting, subjects such as marijuana use and motorcycle gangs are of far greater interest to most of us. While it is only a coincidence that our scientific interests correspond with this emotional interest in deviants, it is a happy coincidence and, I believe, one that should be encouraged. It is this emotional involvement in the subject that provides us with the commitment necessary for producing significant work in any discipline.

Methods of Observing Deviants

There are many different methods of directly observing deviance, all of which are represented by the selections in this volume. At one extreme is the insider report—a report on deviance as observed by individuals who are themselves members of the deviant group. At the other extreme are the reports on deviance resulting from more journalistic forms of observation, especially those involving temporary relationships, such as a brief interview with the deviants. There are many degrees of involvement between these extremes.

The *insider reports* are among the most interesting and valuable, but they also pose some of the most difficult problems to the sociologist. Insider reports are often written as rhetorical justifications for one's way of life, or, even worse, as titillating reports on sinfulness written for meretricious purposes. For example, there are many books written by former criminals, such as the extremely interesting books by Caryl Chessman, which are largely attempts to justify to the general public what they did and did not do. There are probably even more volumes of the "I-Was-a-Madam-for-the-Mafia" type. These are books written only for money, not for understanding. Rather than providing us with any valuable understanding of what deviants are really like, reports of this sort can be tremendously misleading, resulting in a perpetuation of distorted views.

While these two types of insider reports are too blatantly distorted to be taken seriously by many sociologists and students of deviants, there is another more subtle kind of report that does mislead people at times. These are the *romanticized reports,* written by outsiders who have fallen victim to the common belief that any form of exciting life must be worthwhile and have its own beauty. Such romanticized insider reports are often written by "hangers-on"—people who are not really members of the deviant group themselves, but who simply hang out with the deviants and who feel that there is something especially beautiful about them. Because these individuals do know a lot about the deviants from their close observations and day-to-day involvement, they can give the appearance of having the "real dope" on the deviants. Their distortions are more a matter of interpretation than matters of fact. The facts become the bait, which lead the suckers to bite and get hooked.

Valuable insider reports are comparable to the diaries historians have used to gain a better understanding of what it was like to live in a given historical period. A sociologist has to know a lot about the nature of deviance and about the fronts that deviants use to mislead people before he can judge the adequacy of insider reports. Such insider reports sometimes literally take the form of a diary. Sometimes these insider reports take the form of recorded interviews in which the deviants willingly speak for themselves about their daily lives. One report of this sort included in this volume is that on "Breakfast with Topless Barmaids," which is a verbatim transcription of a taped discussion of three sociologists with several topless barmaids at a Los Angeles topless bar. While it would certainly be a mistake to assume that such an insider report tells one what the everyday lives of all such people are like, I believe that this insider report, along with a number of others available to sociologists, gives us a reasonably typical view of what it is like to do something that most members of society see as deviant or, at least, disreputable. Most important of all, it shows sociologists and students what the people who are stigmatized as deviants feel about that stigmatization, what effects it seems to have on their lives, and what they believe should be done about this. Although reading such insider reports will not necessarily make one become more sympathetic to the position of the deviants, and this is certainly not an avowed purpose of such sociological works, I think that any individual who has carefully studied such insider reports will have a more valid understanding of what the lives of deviants are like than if he has nothing more than his own imagination, Congressional testimony, or court testimony to use. This better understanding may also be conducive to wiser social policies for the society as a whole.

Closely related to these insider reports are the *insider participant-observer reports.* These are primarily reports on participant observation studies done by sociologists, or somebody working the way a sociologist would, which involve the sociologist's becoming a member of the group. Some of this research is done secretly: that is, the individuals being studied are not aware that they are being studied. As far as they know, the person we know as a sociologist is simply another member and they act toward him accordingly. There are many unresolved moral questions concerning this type of research and although we might prefer that it could be done otherwise, there are fundamental reasons why we must have *some* research of this sort. The participant-observer report can best show us whether the individual's awareness that he is being studied becomes such an important determinant of an individual's behavior that any research done in this way is inevitably too biased to be used. We need such secret research as a check, but, of course, we must provide our own checks against its abuse. As far as I know, individuals who have used this method have been careful to provide such checks. They always strive to maintain the anonymity of the individuals, groups, and places they have studied. Like all good journalists, they protect their sources; and this is essential if sociologists are to be accepted by any group in the society. It is also a moral requirement, as most of us would see it. In some instances sociologists involved in participant-observer studies unexpectedly become immediate observers of the deviant behavior. There is then a potential conflict between the laws concerning accessories to crime and the sociologist's moral obligation to protect the identity of his subjects. Yet sociologists would clearly not be able to see many things if they were not willing to face this conflict. We can see this conflict, for example, in Norman Weiner's excellent report on middle-class teen-age shoplifting (see Chapter 14) that he observed by accident. Yet, it would be extremely unlikely that any sociologist would be able to see exactly how a teen-age shoplifter manages the moral meanings of his action in his relations with his fellow teen-agers except by being involved with the individual *as* a fellow teen-ager. We have here a rare glimpse of the subtleties involved in managing moral meanings in everyday life, and I think we learn a great deal even from this brief glimpse.

Most insider participant-observer studies do not involve this kind of secrecy, but rather are done by individuals who at one time were members of the groups being studied and who later became sociologists. In going back to their former groups to do case studies they bring to such studies a wealth of common-sense understanding of the group. But they do not face the same kinds of problems encountered in doing secret research. Probably the best known example of this kind of insider participant-observer report is Howard Becker's study of jazz musicians. Becker was a jazz musician for many years. When he later became a sociologist he did his study of jazz musicians and their use of marijuana. Another example of this would be Ned Polsky's study of pool-hall hustlers. Polsky had spent a great deal of time playing pool with these people long before he became concerned as a sociologist with studying their behavior. This vast wealth of information undoubtedly proved valuable in gaining a sociological understanding of them.

There are also many kinds of participant-observer studies of deviants in which the sociologists doing the study are not exactly members of the group but are involved with them to a great degree in their everyday lives. These studies take a long time and involve close rapport with subjects. In most cases the sociologists and deviants know each other so well that the deviants no longer think much about what the sociologist is doing and do not even think of him as a sociologist. I suspect that in research of this sort the sociologist comes to have a kind of *fictitious membership* in the group. That is, the group knows he is not really a member, but for most purposes they can treat him as one. They trust him and they know he is not going to report them to officials. While it is sometimes hard to tell from the published reports of such studies which method of observation was used, I think Richard Carey's study of the college drug scene and Sherri Cavan's study of the hippies of the Haight-Ashbury are basically fictitious membership reports. In these studies the sociologist passes unobtrusively among the deviants in their everyday lives without his presence becoming a primary determinant of what can be observed. I believe that we can place far more trust in these kinds of reports than we can in those in which the sociologist's definition of himself as a sociologist is a more pressing circumstance for the deviants being studied.

We must always keep in mind that "deviants" are people who, by their very definition, have many enemies who can often harm them in some way. For this reason, deviants are wary of being observed by outsiders. Some deviant groups have carefully prepared an orchestrated *front* that they use to mislead outsiders, sometimes simply as a put-on, but sometimes to avoid being revealed. For these reasons, any sociologist doing participant-observer studies of deviants has to be extremely careful to win his subjects' trust. If the subjects do not trust the researcher, we cannot trust the researcher's report. Yet trust is very difficult to establish in some cases and in others, such as Hunter Thompson's study of Hell's Angels, it is very mercurial. Thompson did run with the gang for a whole year and he did appear to establish considerable trust with many of the members. Yet, at the end of that year he was badly "stomped" by a group of the Angels. Fortunately for the validity of the report, his study was done entirely before the beating.

It is because of this difficulty of managing the fronts of deviants and of establishing trust that we must constantly be critical of the methods used to study deviance and of the validity of findings on deviance. We must never assume offhand that the individuals doing the study were able to establish trust. To a considerable degree we have to rely on our previous knowledge of deviance to give us some clear idea of whether the researcher is being taken in by the fronts or is romanticizing the group. As pointed out earlier, we can use this prior understanding to gain a sense of how adequate his description and interpretation of the group are.

In spite of these problems, there are some excellent *outsider reports* on various deviant groups. The best of these are valuable for gaining greater understanding of deviants. At the very least, they provide us with the initial understanding that any sociologist needs in gaining the proper relations with such groups before doing more intensive studies.

Some of these outsider studies have involved considerable interaction with the deviants—interaction which sometimes has enabled them to establish trust from an early stage and, thereby, has given them reason to trust what they are told by the deviants. At their best, these outsider studies are like Alexis de Tocqueville's famous study of American society. Because De Tocqueville was an outsider rather than an American, he probably had considerable difficulties with the language and customs in various parts of American society. In some ways he was studying American society in order to better understand French society. Yet, he was able to arrive at vital understandings of American society which are still of great value to us.

An individual who already has a considerable background in the things he is going to study and who has the ability to empathize with the people he is studying can provide us with unique insights into their lives. David Maurer's studies of *The Big Con* are certainly excellent examples of this. Maurer spent a great deal of time discussing the big con games and professional thievery with former cons and thieves. While there are times when he comes dangerously close to romanticizing the big cons, he also provides us with knowledge of the details of their everyday lives that we cannot get from any other source. In the same way, a report such as Wayland Young's study of prostitution, which probably involved far less interaction with the individuals themselves, gives us a considerable understanding of their way of life.

There are some outsider reports on deviance that provide us with significant information, though they are not based on any extensive interaction with the deviants. In Bruce Jackson's report, "White-Collar Pill Party," for example, the interaction with the deviants was transitory. Yet, it enables us to see how middle-class people at that party were defining the drugs, and especially how matter-of-factly they treated them.

Deviant Situations, Styles, and Ways of Life

All the selections in this volume have direct bearing on fundamental theoretical issues in the sociology of deviance. This will be apparent to all sociologists and students of deviance. Some of the theoretical implications of the specific essays will, of course, be pointed out in the brief introductions to the selections throughout the volume. But the essays have not been arranged in terms of any theoretical structure.

Primarily, the essays have been selected because they are among the best available sources on deviance. These are the selections that the majority of sociologists and students of deviance will find most valuable as source material for any theoretical argument they are developing or testing. These sources can be used, not only as illustrations of such theoretical arguments, but also as material for partially testing such arguments. These are the materials that will provide the students with the basic facts about deviant behavior needed to judge the adequacy of any theory at least in a preliminary fashion. Such material is especially crucial in an area such as deviance in which most of us do not have much first-hand, common-sense experience that we can draw upon to judge the validity of sociological theories. This kind of material is essential if students are to be active participants in developing and testing theories of deviance, rather than simply assimilating them and then reproducing them on exams.

Rather than structure the volume in terms of a simple sequence of theoretical messages, I have structured it along two dimensions. First of all, I have tried to group the various essays in terms of the kind of deviance being dealt with. For example, the essays on sexual deviance are grouped together. Secondly, and importantly, I have structured the volume sequentially in terms of the general progression from *situational deviance* to *deviance as a way of life*.

Much of what is considered deviance in our society is highly situational; that is, behavior that is not usual for the individuals involved. These are one time, hit-and-miss forms of deviance which do not form a basic pattern in a person's life. Often, situational deviance is something the individual has to be shown how to do by experts in the deviance. For example, in the case of Donald Ball's study of an abortion clinic we see that the associates of the abortionist have to show the woman who is to receive an abortion how to go about doing it. An abortion, after all, is not something a woman is apt to have more than once. Situational deviance also constitutes only a small part of the person's life. That is, it may be something the individual is involved in at many different times, but it is not a part of the rest of his way of life. Nudists, for example, remain involved in nudism for long periods of time, but they are not usually nudists at any other time except when they go to nudist parks or nudist camps, which happens only once a month or once every two weeks, or what not. The nudists, in fact, are careful to isolate their involvement in nudism from the rest of their lives, so that it is relevant to them and to others only when they are taking part in it.

Styles of deviance involve more important parts of the lives of the deviants, yet do not constitute their basic identity or way of life. Homosexuality in prisons, for example, is only a style of deviance. Few homosexuals in prison remain homosexuals when they get out. Prison homosexuality is merely a stop-gap measure, as the prisoners see it. It is a style, not an identity, and yet it is something more than a situational involvement. It is a long-run situational involvement of great importance to them at the time.

Many deviants, on the other hand, are involved in deviance as a basic way of life. They identify themselves primarily in terms of that form of deviance. Homosexuals outside of prison, for example, see homosexuality as fundamentally important to what they are, who they are, and what their life is like.

Any such distinctions as this must not be taken as hard and fast distinctions. They are merely used as heuristic devices and should be treated as such. As heuristic devices, they should only be used to the extent that they help to throw light on the everyday lives of deviants. A primary purpose in this volume, after all, is gaining that immediate sense of what it is like to be involved in some form of deviance. Our purpose is not to solve all theoretical issues or to carve up deviance in neat topologies. Deviance is not like that, and it would be a grave distortion to pretend that it is.

Future Directions of Research on Deviance

There is little doubt that the field of deviance is moving increasingly in the direction of participant-observer studies and theories of deviance based on such research information. We are in the early stages of getting the information we need and in developing reliable methods for obtaining that information, but there are still vast gaps in our knowledge of deviance and of the best methods for getting the information we need.

At the same time, most of us feel very strongly that the participant-observer studies we already have, especially the kind presented in this volume, have shown us both the need for new directions in the study of deviance and how we can go about getting the information we need. The years ahead will undoubtedly bring fundamental changes in our theoretical orientation toward deviance and perhaps toward society in general, partly as a result of our changing theories of deviance. In so far as these theories are based on information derived from participant-observer studies, I believe we can be assured that these theories will constitute progress toward a greater understanding of deviance. And, I believe, this greater understanding of deviance will be of fundamental importance to our whole society in deciding what social policies toward deviance we should take or whether, indeed, we should have any policies toward some forms of deviance.

part one
situational deviance

1 | An Abortion Clinic Ethnography |
Donald W. Ball

Abortion is one of the most frequent forms of illegal behavior committed by middle-class and upper-class individuals in our society. There are probably between 200,000 and 500,000 abortions in the United States each year. No one knows exactly how many there are, but there are certainly enough abortions to support hundreds or even thousands of abortion mills in the major cities of the United States and, as illustrated in this study, along the Mexican border.

Abortion, homosexuality, and the use of various kinds of drugs are all illegal forms of behavior that are often the subjects of moral and political controversy in American society today. Edwin Schur and others have called these forms of behavior Crimes Without Victims *because they are crimes that do not necessarily harm other people. Such criminal behavior involves only consenting individuals and most resulting injuries are accidental or due to a lack of adequate medical knowledge and facilities, as in the case of abortions.*

Abortion, like most forms of sexual deviance, is situational or occasional, as Donald Ball points out in this essay; that is, the people who get abortions do so only once or, at most, a few times in their lives. Having an abortion is not something they want to do, but is rather the result of an unwanted pregnancy—something they would certainly have preferred to avoid in the first place. Abortion is also situational in that all of the individuals involved carefully isolate this activity from the rest of their lives and try to keep it secret, from both legal officials and other people.

The author has concentrated on showing how presentational devices are used by the abortionist to give the patient a feeling of confidence. Certainly we must be careful in inferring such intentions from what can be observed in the situation of deviance. Perhaps, if we were able to see things from the standpoint of the

From Donald W. Ball, "An Abortion Clinic Ethnography," *Social Problems,* 14, pp. 293–301; reprinted by permission of The Society for the Study of Social Problems.

abortionist, we would find that he gives somewhat different meanings to the things observed by the patients and by Donald Ball. Yet, the author's interpretations are very plausible, especially because they fit what we know about social actors from many other contexts, especially from those studied by Erving Goffman. *

Traditionally, the study of deviant behavior, however defined, has suffered from a lack of primary data. Materials available to students of various forms of deviance have usually been, in some degree, removed from the actual phenomena under investigation. Thus all too often reports dealing with unconventional social behavior and/or its organization have been based on official statistics produced by variously concerned agencies and on self-reports by the apprehended violators of formal rules and regulations. Neither of these sources is likely to produce an unbiased sample of deviant actors, their actions, and the social organization of these phenomena.[1]

An alternative method of pursuing the study of deviance, one rarely utilized, is to develop contacts with unapprehended deviants themselves, i.e. to go directly to unconventional actors and their subcultures; it is only with such procedures that the natural context of deviance can be studied without the skewedness typical of the usual sources of data.[2] The report which follows is an effort of this alternative: an attempt to utilize actual direct contact with deviant actors in their natural habitat—in this case an abortion clinic—in order to shed light on selected aspects of this relatively unstudied area of social life.[3]

More specifically, what follows is an effort to describe ethnographically certain aspects of a particular abortion clinic, especially as such data may illuminate the presentational strategies employed by an habitually deviant establishment in its dealing with a situationally deviant clientele.

For the clinic's staff, participation in an action legally defined as deviant, i.e. criminal abortion, is habitual; that is to say, it is regularly repeated on a routine, business-like basis. For patrons, however, participation is occasional, irregular, and frequently a once-in-a-lifetime engagement in this form of deviance. Most of them are members of

* I am grateful to Stanford Lyman for his critical comments on an earlier draft of this paper, to Theodore Ravetz for help at various stages of the project, and to Carma Westrum Coon for clerical assistance. I cannot adequately express my debt of gratitude to the anonymous contacts and informants who made this study possible. Portions of this material were presented to the panel on Medical Sociology, Pacific Sociological Association meetings, Vancouver, British Columbia, April 7, 1966.

otherwise law abiding cultures. Unlike the staff, their involvement in this deviant setting is not an aspect of a career, but an accidental consequence of an unwanted pregnancy.

In the context of the clinic, therefore, the deviant transaction ordinarily is enacted by two kinds of actors: those habitually involved in such exchanges, i.e. the staff; and those only situationally deviant, the otherwise conventional actors in their clinic-related roles as patrons. It becomes of some interest, then, to consider how the clinic manages and fosters impressions for this audience constituted of actors drawn from outside its habitually deviant, abortion-oriented sub-culture, and some of the characteristics of such strategies. Put another way, the focus herein will be upon techniques used by the clinic to key itself to the demands and expectations of a patronage drawn from the conventional culture.

Suffice to say, strictures of confidence prevent any elaborate discussion of method, problems of access, etc. Let it be noted, however, that the materials reported and interpreted herein are based upon: 1) sufficiently lengthy observation of a clinic's routine (exclusive of specifically medical procedures, which are not strictly relevant to the problem) to establish the patterns of its everyday functioning; 2) extensive interviews with a necessarily small number of patrons, some of whom were also observed within the clinic; and 3) limited discussions with some of the clinic's non-medical staff. Additionally, supplementary and confirmatory data have been drawn from interviews with individuals who have utilized other, similar facilities. Unfortunately, any more detailed methodological description would, not surprisingly, violate promises of anonymity guaranteed to the subjects involved; for similar reasons, no direct quotations will be presented.[4]

Background

The clinic studied is located, along with several like establishments, in a border town along the California-Mexico line. Its staff includes two practitioners or abortionists, ostensibly physicians, the younger of whom is in an apprentice relationship to the senior man; a practical nurse; a receptionist-bookkeeper; a combination janitress and custodian; a chauffeur-errand boy; and a telephone-appointments secretary.

As costs for such procedures go, the clinic is a relatively expensive one, with fees averaging $500 per abortion. The rate is somewhat less for other medical personnel and students, who are eligible for a discount; and more for persons desiring post-operative overnight observation, or else beyond the tenth week of pregnancy. In terms of finances, the clinic studied is probably representative of others catering to a middle and upper-middle class clientele.

In order to obtain a better picture of the establishment, a brief natural history of a typical involvement between clinic and patron is useful at this point.

Preliminarily, it should be recognized that the ideal-typical practitioner-patient model is not appropriate for the analysis of abortion. Like veterinarians and pediatricians, abortionists frequently have patients for whom financial, if not moral, responsibility is an aspect of the role of some other person, i.e. a client. For abortionists such clients include boyfriends, husbands, and parents. Along with persons such as accompanying friends, they comprise for the patient what might be classified as *supportive others:* persons attending the clinic along with the patient in order to provide psychological support and reinforcement in this crisis situation. Not surprisingly, it is rare for a patient to go to the clinic completely alone, without some morally supportive other. Thus, within the context of abortion, the typical practitioner-patient dyad usually becomes a triad, comprising practitioner, patient, and supportive other.[5]

After referral, usually by a physician, less often by friend or acquaintance, the patron makes original contact with the clinic by telephone. The typically tentative, noncommital, but implicitly urgent communication of the patron is immediately treated in a matter-of-fact manner by the telephone girl. In appropriate middle class speech patterns she asks the length of the pregnancy, extolls the skills of the staff, sets up a tentative appointment, and discusses the fee and its mode of payment. Treating as routine the patron's problem helps minimize anxiety inherent in such situations. Parallel to this is a "medicalization" of the situation, also helping to disarm the patron vis-à-vis the deviant nature of the proposed transaction; at all times, the terminology is that of conventional medicine and surgery. Later, ordinarily two or three days prior to the appointment, the patron again calls the clinic, this time to get confirmation of date and time.

Usually patrons spend the night before their appointment at a hotel or motel near the clinic. Early in the morning of the scheduled date they call the clinic once again, this time to get directions to the only then revealed place of rendezvous where they are picked up and transported to the clinic by one of the staff members in a large, late model station wagon.

It is at this time that patrons find that they are not alone in their dilemma as there are also several others picked up at the same time, filling the station wagon to capacity. Although propinquity might argue for it, there is little deliberate interaction among the patrons during the ride to the clinic, uncertainty effectively immobilizing them in this ambiguous situation.

Upon arrival at the clinic site, where the wagon and all related cars of the staff are hidden from street view, the patrons are ushered into a large, well furnished waiting room. The clinic itself resembles a roomy private home, both externally and internally in its non-medical areas, and is located in a prestigious residential neighborhood.

Once in, the patrons find seats for themselves and settle into a waiting period of hushed expectancy. Conversation is limited to patients and their respective supportive others, i.e. to those previously known to one another. After a short interval of perhaps five minutes, the receptionist appears and calls out the name of the first patient. The pair, patient and receptionist, then retire out of sight of the remaining patrons and into the medical wing of the clinic.

The first stop in the medical wing is an office. After first explaining the procedure in explicitly medical terminology, the receptionist shifts to her bookkeeper role and requests the fee (in cash or traveler's checks) from the patient, frequently finding that it is being held by an accompanying supportive other still in the waiting room. Following this discussion and collection of the fee, the patient is then sent to a bathroom, well appointed in terms of luxury rather than gynecology, to remove her street clothes and put on a surgical gown. Once gowned, the patient is directed to the room where the actual abortion will take place.

Those specifically involved in the procedure include, in addition to the patient, the two practitioners, senior and apprentice, and a practical nurse. Although an anesthetic is administered, at no time is the patient allowed to lose consciousness; a necessity born of the possible need for quick removal in the event of visitation by legal agents. Immediately upon completion of the procedure the patient leaves the table and is sent to another room to rest for fifteen minutes to an hour and a half. Finally, after receiving medication and instruction regarding post-operative care from the receptionist, the patient and any supportive others are returned to the site of the original rendezvous and thus to their conventional worlds.

Analysis

With this brief, oversimplified picture it is now possible to turn to more specifically sociological concerns: the aforementioned presentational strategies which make up what may be called, for the clinic, a *rhetoric of legitimization.*

Sociologically, a rhetoric is a vocabulary of limited purpose; that is to say, it is a set of symbols functioning to communicate a particular set of meanings, directed and organized toward the representation of a specific image or impression. Such vocabularies are not only verbal but also include visual symbols such as objects, gestures, emblems, etc.[6]

In the case of the clinic the rhetoric operates to subvert the conventional world's view of abortion, and to generate a picture of legitimate activity. Fundamentally, the question thus becomes: What techniques are utilized via this rhetoric to *neutralize* the context of deviance in which the clinic operates, so as to enhance parallels with conventional medical and social situations and thus derive a kind of "rightness" or legitimization?[7] How, in other words, are the setting and actions *qua* impressions manipulated to maximize the clinic's image over and above successful performance of its task and contradict the stereotypic stigma of deviance? Specifically, how does the clinic 1) minimize the possibilities of trouble with frightened or recalcitrant patrons; 2) generate the patron satisfaction necessary for referral system maintenance; and 3) present an image which will provide the most favorable self image or identity for the actors involved, whether patron or staff?[8]

For conceptual purposes, the clinic's rhetoric of legitimization may be treated by employing Goffman's delineation of *front* and its constituents of setting, appearance, and manner;[9] originally a framework for analyzing the presentation of self, it seems extendible to the strategies of establishments and institutions as well.

Essentially, front consists of those communications which serve to define the situation or performance for the audience: standardized expressive equipment including *setting,* the spatial/physical background items of scenery in the immediate area of the interaction; *appearance,* the sign-vehicles expressing the performer's social status or type; and those expressions which warn of a performer's demeanor, mood, etc., i.e. *manner.*

Examining each of these elements for evidence of how they are manipulated to make up a rhetoric will show the central themes and dimensions of the clinic's presentational strategies. Although the combination of the conceptions of rhetoric, neutralization, and front produces an admittedly loose theoretical scheme, the character of the data does not suggest the need for further rigor.

Setting. A paramount feature of the clinic's rhetoric is its physical and spatial characteristics. Especially important for patrons generally is the stereotype-contradicting waiting room, the first impression of the clinic itself—and the dominant one for supportive others. The waiting room is likely to be the only room in which the supportive others will be present during their entire visit to the clinic, save the possibility of a short interval in the office if they happen to be holding the fee, a frequent occurrence, especially if the other is also a client.

Spatially, the waiting room is L-shaped and extremely large; approximately 75 feet long and 50 feet wide at the base leg. Its size is accentuated by the fact that most of the room is sunken about three feet below other floor levels. Fully and deeply carpeted, well furnished with several couches, arm chairs, large lamps, and tables, the room speaks of luxury and patron consideration, also implied by the presence of a television set, a small bar, and a phonograph, in addition to the usual magazines present in waiting room situations.

Both the size of the room and the placement of the furniture function to provide private islands which need not be shared; space is structured so as to create withdrawal niches for each set of patrons. Couches and chairs are arranged along the walls of the room, maximizing distance between groupings and minimizing the possibilities of direct, inter-group eye-contact between the various patron-sets who, despite their shared problem and the recently experienced forced propinquity of the ride to the clinic, tend to keep their anxieties private. Thus, interaction among patrons in the waiting room is closed, confined to patients and their own accompanying supportive others only.

Turning to the medical wing: The picture is a far cry from the shabby and sordid image of "kitchen table abortion" drawn in the popular press; it is one of modern scientific medicine, and with it comes assurance to the patient. Once the patient has donned a gown, her next stop is the operating room, a designation used without exception by the staff. In addition to a gynecological table, the room contains familiar (to the lay patient) medical paraphernalia: surgical tools, hypodermic syringes, stainless steel pans and trays, bottles and vials enclosing various colored liquids, capsules, pills, etc.—props effectively neutralizing the negative stereotypes associated with abortion as portrayed in the mass media.

After the procedure has been completed, the patient is moved from the scientific arena of the operating room and back again into luxury. As is the waiting room, the rooms in which the patients spend their short period of post-operative rest are expensively furnished.

Ultimately, after resting, the patient returns to the waiting room and, for most, to supportive others, and receives a final post-operative briefing before being returned to the rendezvous site. Parenthetically it may be noted that throughout the entire episode piped-in music has pervaded every room in which patrons are present.

In terms of setting, the clinic presents itself as not unlike a small hospital albeit with a decorator-designed interior. For patient and supportive others the scenery and props have functioned to communicate an image of assurance and protection through the devices of cost and luxury along with scientific medicine, to minimize the deviant nature of the transaction, and to emphasize positive cultural values, thus efficiently counteracting the stereotypic image.

Appearance and Manner. A widespread device for visibly differentiating various social categories or types is clothing.[10] Items of dress may function as insignia or uniforms to label the persons so garbed as members of particular social groups, occupations, etc. Such institutionalized symbols act as both identifiers and identities; to be attired in certain ways is to be a certain kind of person, not only in the eyes of the audience, but also in terms of the actor's perception of himself. Dress is an integral aspect of social identity.

So it is with the staff of the clinic: practitioners, patient, nurse—all wear the appropriate symbols, from the layman's point of view, of dress for surgically centered roles. White tunics are worn by the practitioners; the patient is surgically gowned; the nurse and even the janitress wear white uniform dresses. This element of the rhetoric is highlighted at the beginning of the procedure when both practitioners ostentatiously don surgical gloves, visibly emphasizing their, and the clinic's, concern with the necessities of asepsis. This ritualistic activity also serves to forcefully identify these actors in their roles as defined by the rhetoric.

The medical model is further underscored by the pre-operative medical history which is taken and recorded upon a standard, multicarboned form (the destiny of these duplicate copies is unknown). Actions such as this, along with dress, provide major modes of stressing the medical legitimacy of the clinic, its staff, and its task.

From the receptionist on up through the clinic's hierarchy, behavior, particularly verbal, emphasizes medical and professional aspects of the clinic's operation. Nowhere is this more apparent than in the area of vocabulary; it is strictly medical, with no effort either made or implied to speak down to the less knowledgeable lay patron. It is also noteworthy that at no time is the word abortion used in the presence of a patron; rather, it is referred to as the operation, the procedure, or as a D and C (dilation and curettage). Similarly, as noted above, the room in which the procedure takes place is at all times designated by the staff as the operating room.

Other elements of staff behavior which further the medical impression are 1) the post-operative consultation and medication which effectively contrast with the popular view of abortion as an "off-the-table-and-out" procedure, and 2) the presence of an apprentice practitioner and its obvious analogy, at least to the medically sophisticated, with a teaching hospital. For the patient, the teaching aspects of the senior practitioner's role help to generate confidence in his skill, a matter which is verbally reinforced by other staff members in their interactions with the patrons.

As with appearance, the manner of the staff is essentially directed toward the medical elements of the clinic's rhetoric; their demeanor is professional at all times, with one exception. This exception is the receptionist-bookkeeper, whose role is, by definition, outside the strictly medical aspects of the clinic. As a result, freed of the obligations of professional mien, the receptionist is able to interact with patrons in a reassuring and supportive manner; in effect, her presentation of the rhetoric is through expressive strategies, while the manner of other staff members is more instrumentally oriented.[11]

Before turning to the central themes engendered among the patrons by the clinic's rhetorical strategies, it may be well to at least take note of some flaws in the presentation, even though they may escape the usual patron's attention. These may be considered under the general rubrics of pseudo-sterility and miscellaneous delicts.

Pseudo-Sterility. Although ostentation is the rule as regards the emphasis of aseptic and antiseptic precautions, there are also omissions less readily obvious. It will be recalled that measures apparently designed to minimize infection and also at the same time maximize parallels with legitimate medicine included the wearing of tunics by the practitioners, their donning of surgical gloves prior to the procedure, and the display of the tools and paraphernalia of medicine and surgery in the operating room.

It should be pointed out that, aseptically, tunics are no substitute for full surgical gowns, that full precautionary tactics would also include items such as face masks, caps, etc.; and that it is highly irregular for an operating room to lack an autoclave (for the sterilization of instruments) and changeable covering for the table, and for surgical instruments to stand on display, exposed to the air for long periods of time. Additionally, it may be noted that the portion of the preoperative medical history which is taken by the senior practitioner is recorded by him after his elaborate display of putting on the surgical gloves—a less than ideal practice for sterility.

These breaches of standard procedure suggest that much of what is passed to the lay patron as concern with aseptic and antiseptic practices is actually rhetoric, designed to communicate to the audience a standard of medical rigor which does not in fact exist.

Miscellaneous Delicts. Within this category are included additional practices at variance with the fostered impression.

Perhaps the most glaring of these is the lack of privacy afforded the patient in comparison with more conventional medical settings. The fact that patients are handled in groups, and moved and serviced in what in comparison with a hospital is a small and not systematically designed space, leads to a good deal of enforced contact between patients and staff involved in various stages of the process. Of necessity this leads to invasions of privacy, at least as perceived by patients accustomed to more traditional medical situations. Thus, for instance, the room used as an office also doubles as a resting room, and a patient lying there for post-operative rest may suddenly find herself witness to a financial transaction as a later-scheduled patron pays the fee; the resting patient is thus treated, in effect, as an object, becoming, in

Goffman's phrase, a nonperson,[12] i.e. an actor not accorded the usual deferences given as minimal acknowledgements of a person's moral worth simply by virtue of that person's being human.

Also of interest is the function of the music, piped into every room including the one for the procedure. When the patrons first arrive at the clinic the music is quiet, soothing, and relaxing in style; but with the entrance of the first patient into the medical wing, the tempo and timbre increase. The volume of the music then operates to drown out any untoward sounds which might emanate from the medical wing and alarm those patrons still in the waiting room.

Another delict involves the marked contrast in vehicles used in picking up and returning patrons to the rendezvous. In keeping with the symbolism of cost and luxury presented to the prospective patron, the station wagon which brings them to the clinic is an expensive late model. By contrast, for the return to the rendezvous, which is not done en masse as is the initial pick up, and by which time presentational strategies are less necessary, the car driven by the chauffeur-errand boy is an old, rather decrepit foreign sedan of low cost and questionable reliability.

Another item at variance with traditional medical procedures is the emphasis, especially by the practitioners, on the necessity of the patient's cooperation to assure the procedure's success. The patient is in effect invited, if not commanded, to become an active participant in the ongoing activity.[13] She is told, for instance, of the desirability of her concentrating on other matters, e.g. "think of something else and all will go smoothly and rapidly." This assigning an active role to the patient stands in marked contradiction to her objectification as regards matters of privacy, and implies expediency as a more central concern of the clinic's operation than is patient welfare.

Finally, it may be noted that though the practitioners are verbally represented by others on the staff as physicians, gynecologists in fact, no evidence of medical training in the form of certificates or diplomas is available for patron scrutiny.

Discussion

From this selective ethnographic description of various aspects of the clinic's front, two broad dimensions appear essential to its rhetoric of legitimization: 1) luxury and cost, and 2) conventional medical practices and procedures. It is these two themes which are emphasized in the clinic's efforts to neutralize its aura of habitual deviance before an audience of situationally deviant patrons drawn from the world of conventional culture. Thus, the rhetoric draws its vocabulary from meaningful and positive values of the patron's culture.

Within these two valued themes, four elements may be specified as contributing to the two broader dimensions of luxury and cost and conventional medicine: cleanliness, competence, conventionality, and concern for the patron.

Cleanliness and competence are both elements of the instrumental aspects of medicine. Albeit with significant flaws, unrecognized by most lay patrons anyway, the clinic's presentational strategies enhance these impressions, if not to the same extent their actualities. The obvious symbols of dress and equipment are presented to the patient in the medical wing of the clinic where anxiety and uncertainty are high. The symbols are readily recognizable and imply the conventionality of the situation; they provide, in effect, a set of familiar expectations drawn from past experience with legitimate medicine. In a similar allaying manner, the practitioner's skill and competence is repeatedly voiced by the staff from the time of the initial telephone contact until the beginning of the actual abortive procedure itself.

Conventionality here means a realization of the middle class values of most patrons. One of these values is, of course, a positive view of professional medicine, a view which the clinic attempts to exploit. Throughout the patron's experience with the clinic, parallels with this model are highlighted; but it is in another area that this element of the rhetoric functions most effectively.

This is the waiting room setting. The obvious expense, comfort, and general decor of this room are such as to disarm all but the most fearful and suspicious patron. This room and the first impressions it presents are such as to immediately link the clinic to the safe, known world of respectable middle class conventionality. In the process of this linkage, the clinic is, in the patron's perception, divorced from the usually illicit image conjured by abortion; if not rendered totally respectable, the clinic is at least brought within the context of the definitions and expectations of mundane, everyday experience. Because of its crucial location in the process, being the patron's first direct exposure to the clinic milieu, it is fair to say that this room is the most successful presentational strategy in the clinic's legitimizing rhetoric.

The comfort of the waiting room is but one of the forms of expression of concern for the patron which help to create a legitimitizing presentation. Other strategies include the telephone girl's supportive routinization of the patron's problem at the time of the initial contact; the similarly solicitous demeanor of the receptionist; and the post-operative consultation. This involves not only the dispensing of drugs to facilitate the patient's convalescence, but also a brochure specifically detailing an expected course of progress and steps to be taken in case of complications.

By demonstrating concern, the clinic affirms its subscription to the values of its patrons, and thus asserts its basically conventional nature, i.e. the congruence of its operation with the norms of those upon whom its income relies.

All of these factors combine to help construct a rhetoric of legitimacy: a set of presentational strategies which allows the clinic to minimize problems inherent in typically anxious and fearful patrons, and thus to function more effectively; and in addition to generate the reputation necessary for an establishment of its kind, dependent upon referrals from physicians.

Additionally, whether manifest or latent, the rhetoric also has consequences for the identities of the actors involved. Both habitual deviants, the staff, and situational deviants, the patrons, are able to partake of the rhetoric so as to enhance their own self images. The rhetoric helps the staff define their participation in the clinic's habitually deviant activities, despite the occasional flaws, as involvement in a professionally operating establishment with the trappings of conventional medicine. For patrons, though they too are admittedly involved in a deviant situation, the rhetoric blunts this hard truth. By accepting the presentational strategies as part of the clinic's image, the patron is allowed to define the situation through the symbols drawn from his conventional everyday experience. Thus, for both patron and staff alike, the rhetoric allows for a minimization of the threat to identity which is built into their illicit transaction.

Unfortunately, the confidential nature of this research does not allow one of the usual canons of science to be met, i.e. that regarding exact replication; and no claim regarding the typicality of the clinic described herein can be made. Hopefully, however, the materials have shed some light on a relatively little known area of social behavior. Given the incidence of abortion, it may be hoped that similar analyses can be conducted by others.[14] Additionally, it may be suggested that the concept of rhetoric provides a useful tool for examining the dramas of social life, whether deviant or conventional, spontaneous or routine, unusual or mundane.

NOTES

1 The sources of bias in official statistics are too well known to require citation, e.g. differentials in organizational actions, variances in definitions, etc.; to deal with apprehended violators only is to study the *technically unskilled* and the *politically unconnected*.
2 See the penetrating discussion of the ethical problems involved in this

method by Ned Polsky, quoted in Howard B. Becker, *Outsiders,* New York: The Free Press of Glencoe, 1963, pp. 171–172.

3 For a recent summary which demonstrates how little is known see Edwin M. Schur, *Crimes Without Victims,* Englewood Cliffs, N.J.: Prentice-Hall, 1965, pp. 11–16.

4 For those interested in procedural minutiae as criteria of validity, the only answer can be: Go out and replicate using your own design. Though precise comparisons would not be possible, such confirmation or refutation would be most desirable.

5 In this discussion the general label patron will be used in reference to patients, clients, and supportive others, unless reference is specifically limited to one of the roles in this category.

6 The concept of rhetoric as used herein is similar to but independent of the work of Kenneth Burke. As a theoretical point it should be noted that rhetorics are not necessarily the same thing as ideologies, although this may empirically be the case. The conceptual difference between the two is that rhetoric speaks to communication, both style and content, while ideology refers to perception and justification in terms of the ideologue's conception of the relevant portions of the world. It is quite conceivable that individual actors will utilize a rhetoric without any ideological convictions as regards its validity, but with a recognition of its pragmatic efficacy; and similarly, that ideological dedication does not automatically assume any developed rhetoric to attempt its maintenance or furtherance.

7 Compare Gresham M. Sykes and David Matza, "Techniques of Neutralization: A Theory of Delinquency," *American Sociological Review,* 22 (December, 1957), pp. 664–670, where the analysis is individual rather than institutional; also Matza, *Delinquency and Drift,* New York: John Wiley and Sons, 1964.

8 The second and third problems are, in effect, special cases of the first. Minimization of trouble is not motivated by fear of patron complaints to legal agents, which would involve the complainants in admitting complicity, but by desire to maintain referrals and enhance self images. Additionally, such minimization produces a smoother, easier work-flow for the staff; a similar rationale in conventional medical settings sometimes dictates the use of general anesthetics when, in terms of patient pain, locals would be adequate.

9 Erving Goffman, *The Presentation of Self in Everyday Life,* Garden City, N.Y.: Doubleday Anchor, 1959, pp. 22–30. This scheme formed the observational framework for data collection as well as a perspective for preparing the data.

10 Mary Ellen Roach and Joanne Bubolz Eicher (eds.), *Dress, Adornment, and the Social Order,* New York: John Wiley and Sons, 1965.

11 Excluded from this consideration is the telephone girl who is never in face-to-face interaction with the patrons but is also supportive in her demeanor.

12 Goffman, *The Presentation of Self, op. cit.,* pp. 151–152.

13 See the discussion of the patient as basically helpless and passive in Talcott Parsons, *The Social System,* Glencoe, Ill.: The Free Press, 1951, pp. 439–447. An alternative approach is indicated in Robert Leonard's work. See his several papers in James Skipper, Jr. and Leonard, *Social Interaction and Patient Care,* Philadelphia: J. P. Lippincott, 1965.

14 A step in this direciton is the dissertation (in progress) of Nancy L. Howell, "Information Channels and Informal Networks in the Distribution of Source Information," Department of Social Relations, Harvard University.

2 | Sexual Modesty, Social Meanings, and the Nudist Camp | Martin S. Weinberg

The majority of people in our society probably find nudism to be one of the more inexplicable forms of behavior. To most people, being nude in public would arouse intense feelings of embarrassment, guilt or, perhaps, sexual excitement. They find it almost impossible to understand how large groups of people can go around in the nude without experiencing the same emotions. Yet, there are perhaps several hundred thousand Americans who do devote a considerable amount of their time, energy, and wealth to carrying on nudist activities.

One of the values of this report on nudism is that it enables the student to see how individuals in this society can develop extremely different beliefs, patterns of feeling, and patterns of action from those shared by most of us. It will help the student to realize that not only are these patterns of behavior not inexplicable and not impossible, but that from the standpoint of the people involved they seem perfectly normal, healthy, moral, and controlled. In fact, of course, they are well controlled forms of behavior. The nudists have carefully isolated their nudism from the rest of their lives. They have built norms into their patterns of behavior both to maintain this isolation and to prevent any external forms of behavior, feelings, and beliefs from intruding into the nudist situation. By following these behavior patterns, the nudist avoids experiencing disruptive emotional and moral feelings. In this essay we can see how nudists are even able to maintain norms of "modesty" while going around in the nude.

The Nudist Camp

The ideology of the nudist camp provides a new definition of the situation regarding nudity, which in effect maintains that:

From Martin S. Weinberg, "Sexual Modesty, Social Meanings, and the Nudist Camp," *Social Problems,* 12, pp. 311–318; reprinted by permission of The Society for the Study of Social Problems.

1. nudism and sexuality are unrelated
2. there is nothing shameful about exposing the human body
3. the abandonment of clothes can lead to a feeling of freedom and natural pleasure
4. nude activities, especially full bodily exposure to the sun, leads to a feeling of physical, mental and spiritual well-being.

These definitions are sustained by nudists to a remarkable degree, illustrating the extent to which adult socialization can function in changing long-maintained meanings; in this case regarding the exposure of one's nude body in heterosexual situations. The tremendous emphasis on covering the sexual areas, and the relation between nudism and sexuality which exists in the outside society, however, suggests that the nudist definition of the situation might, at times, be quite easily called into question. The results of the field work and formal interviews indicate how the social organization of the nudist camp has developed a system of norms that contributes to sustaining the official definition of the situation. Since the major concern of this paper is modesty, we will restrict our discussion to the first two declarations of nudist ideology (i.e., that nudism and sexuality are unrelated, and that there is nothing shameful about exposing the human body). These are also the elements which lead to the classification of nudists as deviant. The normative proscriptions which contribute to the maintenance of this definition of the situation will be described.

Organizational Precautions. Organizational precautions are initially taken in the requirements for admission to a nudist camp. Most camps do not allow unmarried individuals, especially single men, or allow only a small quota of singles. Those camps that do allow male-singles may charge up to thirty-five per cent higher rates for the single's membership than is charged for the membership of an entire family. This is intended to discourage single memberships but, since the cost is still relatively low in comparison to other resorts, this measure is not very effective. It seems to do little more than create resentment among the singles. By giving formal organizational backing to the definition that singles are not especially desirable, it also might be related to the social segregation of single and married members that is evident in nudist camps.

An overabundance of single men is recognized by the organization as threatening the definition of nudism that is maintained. The presence of singles at the camp is suspected to be for purposes other than the "nudist way of life" (e.g., to gape at the women). Such a view may call into question the denied relation between nudity and sexuality.

Certification by the camp owner is also required before anyone is admitted on the camp grounds. This is sometimes supplemented by three letters of recommendation in regard to the character of the applicant. This is a precaution against admitting those "social types" which might conceivably discredit the ideology of the movement.

A limit is sometimes set on the number of trial visits which can be made to the camp; that is, visits made without membership in some camp or inter-camp organization. In addition, a limit is usually set on the length of time one is allowed to maintain himself clothed. These rules function to weed out those guests whose sincere acceptance of the "nudist" definition of the situation is questionable.

Norms Regarding Interpersonal Behavior. Norms regarding patterns of interpersonal behavior are also functional for the maintenance of the organization's system of meanings. The existence of these norms, however, should be recognized as formally acknowledging that the nudist definition of the situation could become problematic unless precautions were taken.

No staring. This rule functions to prevent any overt signs of "over-involvement." In the words of a non-nudist who is involved in the publication of a nudist magazine, "They all look up to the heavens and never look below." This pattern of civil inattention[1] is most exaggerated among the females, who manage the impression that there is absolutely no concern or awareness that the male body is in an unclothed state. Women often recount how they expect everyone will look at them when they are nude, only to find that no one communicates any impression of concern when they finally do get up their nerve and undress. One woman told the writer: "I got so mad because my husband wanted me to undress in front of other men that I just pulled my clothes right off thinking everyone would look at me." She was amazed (and somewhat disappointed) when no one did. . . . "Looking at" immodesty is controlled; external constraints prohibit staring.

> (Have you ever observed or heard about anyone staring at someone's body while at camp?)[2] I've heard stories—particularly about men that stare. Since I heard these stories, I tried not to, and even done away with my sunglasses after someone said, half joking, that I hide behind sunglasses to stare. Towards the end of the summer I stopped wearing sunglasses. And you know what, it was a child who told me this.

No sex talk. Sex talk, or telling "dirty" jokes, is not common in the nudist camp. The owner of one of the most widely known camps in the Midwest told the writer: "It is usually expected that members of a nudist camp will not talk about sex, politics, or religion." Or in the words of one single-male: "It is taboo to make sexual remarks here." Verbal immodesty was not experienced by the writer during his period of field work. Interview respondents who mentioned that they had discussed or talked about sex qualified this by stating that such talk was restricted to close friends, was of a "scientific" nature or, if a joke, was of a "cute" sort. Verbal immodesty . . . is not common to the nudist camp.

When respondents were asked what they would think of someone who breached this norm, they indicated that such behavior would cast doubt on the actor's acceptance of the nudist definition of the situation:

> One would expect to hear less of that at camp than at other places. (Why's that?) Because you expect that the members are screened in their *attitude for nudism*—and this isn't one who prefers sexual jokes.

> They probably don't belong there. They're there to see what they can find to observe (What do you mean?) Well, their mind isn't on being a nudist, but to see so-and-so nude.

Body contact is taboo. Although the degree to which this rule is enforced varies among camps, there is at least some degree of informal enforcement. Nudists mention that one is particularly careful not to brush against anyone or have any body contact, because of the way it might be interpreted. The following quotation illustrates the interpersonal precautions taken:

> I stay clear of the opposite sex. They're so sensitive, they imagine things.

One respondent felt that this taboo was simply a common-sense form of modesty:

> Suppose one had a desire to knock one off or feel his wife—modesty or a sense of protocol prohibits you from doing this.

When asked to conceptualize a breakdown in this form of modesty, a common response was:

> They are in the wrong place. (How's that?) That's not part of nudism. (Could you tell me some more about that?) I think they are there for some sort of sex thrill. They are certainly not there to enjoy the sun.

If any photographs are taken for publication in a nudist magazine, the subjects are allowed to have only limited body contact. As one female nudist said: "We don't want anyone to think we're immoral." Outsiders' interpretations of body contact among nudists would cast doubt on the nudist definition of the situation or the characteristics set forth as the "nudist way of life."

A correlate of the body contact taboo is the prohibition of dancing in the nude. This is verbalized by nudist actors as a separate rule, and it is often the object of jest by members. This indication of "organizational strain" can be interpreted as an instance in which the existence of the rule itself brings into question the nudist definition of the situation, i.e., that there is no relationship between nudism and sexuality. The following remark acknowledges this: "This reflects a contradiction in our beliefs. But it's self protection. One incident and we'd be closed."

Others define dancing in the nude as an erotic overture which would incite sexual arousal. Such rationalizations are common to the group. . . . It can be seen that incitements heightening latent sexual interest . . . are to some extent controlled by prohibiting body contact.

Alcoholic beverages are not allowed in American camps. This rule also functions in controlling any breakdown in inhibitions which could lead to "aggressive-erotic" overtures. . . . Even those respondents who told the writer that they had "snuck a beer" before going to bed went on to say, however, that they fully favored the rule. The following quotation is representative of nudists' thoughts:

> Anyone who drinks in camp is jeopardizing their membership and they shouldn't. Anyone who drinks in camp could get reckless. (How's that?) Well, when guys and girls drink they're a lot bolder—they might get fresh with someone else's girl. That's why it isn't permitted, I guess.

Rules regarding photography. Taking photographs in a nudist camp is a sensitive matter. Unless the individual is an official photographer (i.e., one photographing for the nudist magazines), the photographer's definition of the situation is sometimes suspect, especially when one hears such remarks as the following: "Do you think you could open your legs a little more?"

There may be a general restriction on the use of cameras and, when cameras are allowed, it is expected that no pictures will be taken without the subject's permission. Members especially tend to blame the misuse of cameras on single men. As one nudist said: "You always see the singles poppin' around out of nowhere snappin' pictures." In general, however, control is maintained, and any infractions which might exist are not blatant or obvious. Any overindulgence in taking photographs would communicate an over-involvement in the nude state of the alters and bring doubt on the denied connection between nudism and sexuality. . . . Like staring, it is controlled by the norms of the nudist camp.

The official photographers who are taking pictures for nudist magazines recognize the impression communicated by forms of immodesty other than nudity, i.e., for the communication of sexuality. . . . The following statement of an official photographer is relevant: "I never let a girl look straight at the camera. It looks too suggestive. I always have her look off to the side."

Accentuation of the body is suspect as being incongruent with the ideology of nudism. The internalization of the previously discussed principles of nudist ideology would be called into question by such accentuation. Thus, one woman who had shaved her pubic area was labeled as disgusting by those members who talked to the writer about it. Women who blatantly sit in an "unladylike" manner are similarly typed. In the words of one female nudist:

It's no more nice to do than when you are dressed. I would assume they have a purpose. (What's that?) Maybe to draw someone's attention sexually. I'd think it's bad behavior and it's one thing that shouldn't be done, especially in a nudist camp. (Why's that?) Because it could lead to trouble or some misfortune. (Could you tell me some more about that?) It could bring up some trouble or disturbance among those who noticed it. It would not be appreciated by "true nudists."

Unnatural attempts at covering any area of the body are similarly ridiculed, since they call into question the actor's acceptance of the definition that there is no shame in exposing any area of the human body. If such behavior occurs early in one's nudist career, however, it is responded to mostly with smiles. The actor is seen as not yet able to get over the initial difficulty of disposing of "outsiders'" definitions.

Communal toilets are also related to the ideological view that there is nothing shameful about the human body or its bodily functions. Although all camps do not have communal toilets, the large camp at which the writer spent the majority of his time did have such a facility, which was labeled "Little Girls Room and Little Boys Too." The stalls were provided with three-quarter length doors. The existence of this combined facility helped, however, to sustain the nudist definition of the situation by the element of consistency: if you are not ashamed of any part of your body, or of any of its natural body functions, why do you need separate toilets? Thus, even the physical ecology of the nudist camp is designed in a way that will be consistent with the organization's definition of modesty.

Consequences of a Breakdown in Clothing Modesty

In the introductory section of this paper it was stated that common-sense actors anticipate breakdowns in clothing modesty to result in rampant sexual interest, promiscuity, embarrassment, jealousy, and shame. The field work and interview data from this study, however, indicate that such occurrences are not common to the nudist camp. The social organization of the nudist camp provides a system of meanings and norms that negate these consequences.

Conclusions

Our results make possible some general conclusions regarding modesty: (1) Covering the body through the use of clothes is not a necessary condition for a pattern of modesty to exist, nor is it required for tension management and social control of latent sexual interests. Sexual interests are very adequately controlled in nudist camps; in fact, those who have visited nudist camps agree that sexual interests are controlled to a much greater extent than they are on the outside. Clothes are also not a sufficient condition for a pattern of modesty; the manipulation of clothes and fashion in stimulating sexual interest is widely recognized. (2) Except for clothing immodesty, which represents one cell of our typology of immodesty, all other forms of modesty are maintained in a nudist camp (e.g., not looking, not saying, not communicating erotic overtures). This suggests that the latter proscriptions are entirely adequate in achieving the functions of modesty when definitions regarding the exposure of the body are changed. (3) When deviance from the institutionalized patterns of modesty is limited to one cell of our typology (i.e., clothing is dispensed with), and the definition of the situation is changed, the typically expected consequence of such a breakdown in this normative pattern does not occur. Rampant sexual interest, promiscuity, embarrassment, jealousy, and shame were not found to be typical in the nudist camp.

NOTES

1 See Erving Goffman, *Behavior in Public Places,* New York: The Free Press, 1963, p. 84.
2 Interview questions and probes have been placed in parentheses.

3 | **Breakfast with Topless Barmaids** |
Richard G. Ames
Stephen W. Brown
Norman L. Weiner

Public nudity has been increasing at a very rapid rate in the United States over the last decade or two. A great moral and legal controversy has grown in response to the rapid increases in nudity —controversy which includes most segments of the society, all the way up to the Supreme Court.

One of the great leaps forward in public nudity was the topless barmaid movement which swept across California and then other parts of the country less than a decade ago. There has been a steady escalation in public nudity of various types as moral entrepreneurs and moral provocateurs have challenged the public morality and the laws by introducing new forms of behavior. Today most of the controversy over toplessness has subsided. The controversy in bars and nightclubs now centers around "bottomlessness." But, of course, most of the controversy over nudity and sexuality in public places today centers on the public showing of various sexual practices.

One of the most valuable aspects of this discussion with the topless barmaids is that it shows how they view the moral question. They are very aware of the various dimensions of the public controversy, and they have their own strong feelings about it. The article also shows how they handle the moral problems, both for themselves and for their families. It illustrates their moral counterattacks and their occasional attempts to conceal their occupation.

It is important to note that the girls have well developed fronts for managing their self-presentations to the people who come to buy beer and watch them. These fronts often take in the clients and, unfortunately, they sometimes take in the sociologists. It is apparent from the discussion that the girls do not feel quite as positive about all the clients as they appear.

This conversation is an excellent study in moral argument. It

This is an original essay prepared for this volume.

*demonstrates how individuals and groups can have different moral
ideas about the same patterns of behavior and can make a
plausible moral argument for their point of view.*

This article is an interview with four topless barmaids initially conducted for the purpose of preparing a survey questionnaire to study
this occupational category. For various reasons, among which was the
slow disintegration of the topless bar in the study area, the larger study
was never completed. However, the interview serves the useful function
of presenting a picture of an occupational group that has special
significance because it emerged as a part of the moral liberalization
that took place in the United States in the middle 1960s. Not only was
private sex behavior reported to be undergoing changes, but public
toleration of sex also became more liberal, and as it did, certain forms
of sex display became more public. One of the most controversial
activities in this sequence of liberalization was the emergence of the
topless barmaid. The question that we will raise later is the extent to
which the occupation of topless barmaid can be considered deviant.

Toplessness can be viewed as a social movement that swept California and made a few unsuccessful attempts in other states as well.
The forerunner of the topless craze was Carole Doda who captivated
the audiences at the Condor Club in the North Beach area of San
Francisco. Later she publicized Rudi Gernreich's monokini by taking a
topless dip in the Pacific surf. Once toplessness started, many of the
North Beach establishments, in an effort to meet competition, went
topless.

In Long Beach, California the topless beer bar was instituted at L'il
Abner's which had topless barmaids on a raised bar with low beer taps.
Customers flocked to the new topless bars, and toplessness became an
economic necessity for bars in Southern California. To illustrate the
economics involved, J. R. Leonard quotes the owners of L'il Abner's as
reporting that in one month of topless operation, sales jumped from 70
half kegs a month to 529.[1] At a conservative estimate of $85 profit per
half keg, this represents an increase in profit of approximately $40,000
per month. Toplessness had its financial advantages for the girls as
well as the owners. Going topless could easily double, triple, or even
quadruple any girl's wages. For this reason, many girls left routine jobs
to become topless waitresses. Surprisingly few non-topless barmaids
went topless.

The occupation of topless barmaid was permitted by law in some
areas, but its legality was constantly being challenged. The courts were

unable to accept the charge that toplessness was an outrage to public decency. Likewise, the charge that it was a health hazard failed to close the bars. Finally, the Los Angeles county government was able to enact a law requiring that all topless barmaids be registered and fingerprinted at the sheriff's office, a procedure usually reserved for the criminal subculture. This form of public stigmatization in an occupation where anonymity and propriety were values resulted in many of the girls leaving their jobs. Hence, many of the bars had to accept the dregs, or close down entirely.

The subjects were interviewed between 3:00 and 4:30 one morning over breakfast in a chain restaurant in Gardena, California. Participating in the interview were four barmaids and their manager from one of the famous topless bars in Los Angeles. Only two of the girls are specifically identified in the interview since they did most of the talking; their views are generally consistent and coherent. The reader should recognize the distinction between these two personalities. Georgie was a physically attractive girl who at 26 looked 19. She came from a broken home, grew up in a large city in the Midwest and then came to California. She had worked at many jobs ranging from assembly line work to being a Las Vegas showgirl at one of the better hotels. While in Las Vegas, she attended the local college but did not graduate. Her varied job history is typical of many of the girls. She is not afraid to comment, even where the comments showed her up in a bad light. Allison was another star of the same bar. She was quite unlike Georgie in that she was a Boston debutante who attended a large state university in the Northeast. Prior to becoming a topless barmaid, she was a secretary for the vice president of a well-known record company in Hollywood, a job she resumed after leaving the bar. Of Greek and Italian heritage, she was a proud and attractive girl.

For the sake of clarity, the authors have placed differing simultaneous conversations in sequence, eliminated extraneous conversations, and occasionally summarized sets of responses. Nonetheless, what appears here is reproduced verbatim with no changes in context. Comments are provided to help the reader where the need arises.

> **Richard G. Ames:** I was interested in the background of the girls. Where did they come from? What had they done before? What size town did they come from? Were they big city girls? Small town?
>
> **Georgie:** All over.
>
> **Allison:** I've been to college.
>
> **Girl 1:** This is an unusual collectionary of girls.
>
> **Ames:** Have many of the girls been to college?
>
> **Girl 1:** I have.
>
> **Girl 2:** I have.
>
> **Girl 3:** Yep.
>
> **Ames:** Are any of them college graduates?

Allison: Yeah, I am.

Girl 1: [Directed toward Allison.] Are you a college graduate?

Allison: Well, secretarial college.

Girl 1: Many of them are trained in other vocations, that's for sure.

Girl 2: Yeah, that's for sure.

Girl 3: It's the money. Let's face it, nobody works unless they want to.

Allison: I don't think any of us get a charge walking around without any clothes on. [Pause.] It's a fun job—at least you get to use your personality. Better than a secretary, and it's a respectable job. You work behind a nice big mahogany desk for $100 a week. Well, I'm not working because I want to be. And I enjoy this more than I do the other, because at least you get to use your personality, and something of yourself—more than there because all I did there was just type.

Ames: Have many of the girls had routine jobs and just been bored?

Georgie: Yes, I think so.

Girl 1: Some of them are in this because they can't get other jobs, because they don't have the training and skill, or if they do they're dissatisfied with their job.

Allison: A lot of girls do [work as topless barmaids] because they're married or they have to support their child, and where else can a girl, you know, in this situation, work and get good money—not being tied to anything?

Georgie: For many of them it's a means to an end, too.

Ames: What end?

Girl 1: Different types of jobs—where they can be their own boss. Or, uh, one where they can utilize the money they have to further their own personal career.

Ames: Another question I have is the effect of the job on people's personal private life. Is this a job which overwhelmingly dominates your life? All I can think of is the depiction of the reddle man in Thomas Hardy's *Return of the Native.*

Allison: Yeah, it sure does.

Georgie: To an extent it dominates you, yes.

Ames: More than you desire?

Georgie: It depends upon the individual.

Allison: There's friction in a lot of ways. Since you work at night you can't date a lot. And, you can't date anybody you meet on the job, because first of all it's a bad situation, you know.

Georgie: [Gives agreement to Allison.] Uh huh.

Allison: A lot of girls keep it separate. Only their immediate friends know, because a lot of people don't understand that you are doing a job and that you are doing it honestly. Just because you're making a lot of money they discredit the character of the job.

Ames: What about people's friends? Do they know about the job? Are they in favor of it or against it? Do the girls themselves feel that it's an illegal occupation?

Allison: I think it's legal, but I think you have to be a little careful who you tell because not everybody feels the same way you do about it.

Georgie: Personal friends that know you for yourself aren't going to think anything of it.

Allison: [Nods agreement to Georgie.] Right. [Pause.] Like Harry—the guy I date—I didn't tell him—at first. When I finally told him, he just laughed, thought it was a riot.

Georgie: You just can't beat the money.

Girl 1: I know one of my brothers got a big kick out of it.

Stephen Brown: I have a hot question: What do you do with all the money you make? [Puzzled silence.]

Georgie: You enjoy it! In any way you want to. Depending on how much money you make. The more money you have, the more you enjoy life.

Brown: What sort of philosophy do you have in mind to enjoy life?

Georgie: It takes money for everything.

Ames: What sort of rewards could you get out of participating in the study? [Referring to the larger planned study.] If we elicit some cooperation, what can we do for you? Is there anything—for instance, co-authoring publications, remaining anonymous—is this the biggest reward of all?

Allison: I don't think any one of us are really looking for a reward.

Georgie: The reward would be that more people would understand. People would know why, and if . . .

Brown: Are most of the girls who go into becoming topless waitresses or topless barmaids—are they from a wealthy background—middle class— low class?

Georgie: All different.

Allison: I think in the beginning we got a lot of lower class because they were the only ones who would do it, but then, you know, as it became more acceptable, more people realized that you just don't mix your business with your private life.

Ames: Incidentally, what is the exact title [of your job]?

Girl 1: Topless barmaid. We have to dance.

Allison: We're dancers at a topless bar.

Girl 2: What was the question?

Ames: Just what exactly was the title of the job?

Allison: To be or not to be . . .

Girls: [Laughs.]

Girl 2: That is the question.

Georgie: Whatever is right.

Allison: Would you believe . . . ?

Girls: [Laughs.]

Allison: Would you believe the truth?

Ames: Tell us a little about yourself, the job, how you got started, and especially where you expect to go from here. Is there any future goal that you are working for in particular?

Allison: I am going to open a nursery.

Ames: A nursery to take care of what? Not trees!?

Allison: Children!

Ames: How many of the girls are married?

Girl 1: None of us have ever been married. We're very exceptional.

Girl 2: Most topless barmaids have been married or are married and have children.

Ames: I was curious. Do the husbands concur with the job?

Georgie: Of course! The husbands see nothing wrong with it, because it's bringing in great money, they're not going out with anyone, they're getting paid to do their work, and they're not doing anything wrong.

Allison: A lot of husbands are low class, really. They're the kind of guys who don't care as long as their wives earn the money. Sometimes, you find just the opposite. You'll find an intellectual husband, you know, that realizes this is a job, and that it's going to bring in a lot of money. [Pause.] I'll tell you, you chose one of the two best places in the town to do the study.

Ames: What is the other one?

Georgie: The King of Hearts. [Near Los Angeles International Airport, hence near the aviation centers employing many young engineers.]

Ames: How many topless barmaids are there in Los Angeles?

Girl 1: Ask the police department, they'll know.

Girl 2: The security guards might know more than the police department, wouldn't they?

Girl 3: Where you're fingerprinted, the sheriff's department.

Ames: It's [topless bars] outlawed in Los Angeles city, right? It's only in the incorporated places outside the city?

[General agreement.]

Ames: You suggested that if we wanted to get the girls to fill out a questionnaire—[Pause.]—do you think they'll do this?

Allison: Most of them would. But there are a lot of stupid girls too who are going to think, "What's your gimmick, what's your gag?"

Georgie: That's for sure. They are going to think, "What's your story?" "Why are you doing this?"

Ames: What is the way to get around this?

Georgie: Pay them for it.

Ames: Pay them for it? You think that if they're used to doing anything for money then, . . .

Allison: No—I don't think so.

Georgie: If you walk up to a girl and say, "I am a professor and I am taking a survey and I wondered if you would fill out this little questionnaire," they are not going to say, "Well honey, have you got five dollars on you?"

Allison: If you tell them you won't use their real names, they'll fill it out and . . .

Manager: Get the assistance of the manager and get him to distribute the questionnaire to the girls—then they'll fill them out.

Brown: Do you think most managers would be cooperative and want to help?

Manager: Yeah, that's true.

Girl 1: Yeah, I do.

Girl 2: Yeah, I do.

Brown: I understand they're trying to outlaw [topless bars].

Georgie: Topless is here to stay, anyway, that's for sure.

Allison: Well, everybody's trying to get rid of it, and it's only people like the D.A.R. who have never been to a topless bar in their life, and have no conception at all what goes on, and they smell everything from their own little porch, and they sit there in their rocking chair and they find out, and they, you know, don't understand what goes on.

Girl 1: [To Ames.] Can you interview the customers?

Ames: This is a good question.

Girl 2: That's a good idea.

Ames: One of the things I was thinking about was what sort of customers do you get?

Allison: You get a lot of nice customers, who just come in to see the topless girls, but once they come in and get to know you and keep coming back to see you, it's all right because they're more interested in talking to you and getting to know your personality and everything.

Brown: I notice that each topless place has a different personality.

Girl 3: Different type bars, you mean?

Brown: Yes.

Girl 1: It's related to what the demand is in that particular area.

Allison: It's also in the girls, though. I've seen a lot of bars, you know, where everybody's sort of carrying on . . .

Brown: The girls over here always look so much younger, fresher, and more vibrant.

Girl 1: We are!

Brown: Is it [in reference to youth, freshness, and vibrancy] recruited, actually?

Manager: It's because the manager is younger, fresher, and more vibrant. [Laughter.]

Allison: Would you believe? [Laughter.]

Brown: Another thing would be the manager.

Manager: There would be a story!

Ames: What sort of people usually do manage these places? Are they people with a long history of managing bars, taverns, this sort of thing, or is it this something that's a first adventure?

Manager: I built racing engines before I came to work.

Brown: Do you know many of the managers?

Manager: One I know worked in construction. Another one I knew was a bartender.

Brown: I think of something that a lot of people think about, tell me— are any of the girls call girls or prostitutes?

Girl 2: What did you ask?

Girl 3: What did you say?

Georgie: There are these in any business or job that you'll find. Not professional prostitutes. Professional prostitutes—this is all that they do. They go to work at a certain hour, they come home at a certain hour, they live a respectable life—some of them—because I know some— but they are professional in their own way. It is strictly a job to bring in money. Then there are hookers, which is a different story—in this way not only are they making money plus their pay, but they are making extra.

Brown: It's a good way to make contacts then?

Georgie: Sure! Cause you're wide open to anything you want.

Ames: What sort of insulation do you girls build up to segregate your emotional reactions and the job—from your normal emotional reactions?

Georgie: That's very hard! After a while you act as if in a way you're hard because things don't affect you. I used to cry when people said things to me. Now I just smile like, "You're right, think whatever you want." Ha, ha!

Brown: What do you do if you have a rough customer? Is there a way of turning him off?

Girl 1: If we have the big security guy, we ring him, and if not—like we had the little one tonight—we yell for Cathy. [One of the other barmaids.] [General laughter.]

Brown: Girls, I was wondering if each of you girls would mind telling us a little about yourself.

Girl 2: Where do you want us to start?

Allison: You may think it funny, but you should hear me sing.

Ames: Do you sing pretty well?

Allison: No.

Georgie: [To the idea of telling a little about herself.] All right. Uh, I have done just about every kind of job. I've worked as a private secretary, cashier, a model, a showgirl, a dancer, a factory worker, a topless barmaid. Uh, I think that's all.

Brown: Where were you born?

Georgie: Missouri.

Ames: Small town, large town?

Georgie: St. Louis. [Pause.] And, each job I would take, after a while I wouldn't be satisfied with it, and I would want something with more money. This is why I covered such categories. I left Missouri when I was about sixteen, and I went back and forth from Los Angeles.

Brown: Brothers and sisters?

Georgie: Yes, a little brother and a sister.

Brown: Is there a floor manager? Is there a girl who is a boss girl?

Allison: Everybody's boss.

Ames: Do you generally get a feeling, though, of some sort of ranking among the girls? Don't you?

Georgie: No.

Girl 1: A little bit. Because we have to work together and if one girl isn't liked for one reason or another nobody's going to pay any attention to her, what she says or anything.

Allison: Everybody pretty much, you know, does their own job. The only thing we ever say to each other is, you know, it's your turn to dance, or it's your turn to collect for the jukebox.

Ames: Which gives you the most enjoyment on the job—talking with the customers or carrying on among yourselves?

Allison: Carrying on among ourselves.

Girl 1: Right! Definitely!

Brown: Are there many Negroes or Mexican Americans as topless waitresses?

Girl 1: No.

Girl 2: No.

Girl 3: Not many.

Brown: What about as customers?

Girl 1: Right! [Meaning yes.]

Girl 2: A lot of them.

Ames: A lot of them?

Girl 2: Yes.

Ames: What sort of social class differences do you see between yourselves and your customers? Is there a lot of social distance between yourselves and your customers?

Girl 1: Yes!

Girl 2: Definitely yes!

Girl 3: One that is not to be bridged!

Ames: One that is never bridged?

Girl 3: Some yes, some no.

Georgie: With the majority, I would say, they don't compare with us.

Ames: Uh huh.

Allison: No, not really. They're at the same level we are, it's just that we put ourselves above them because of the fact that we won't dance and we have to. Because they won't put us on their level, so we have to put ourselves above them. [Allison means that the one opportunity the girls had to put a customer down was to refuse to dance for him, even though they were supposed to dance as well as serve beer as part of their normal routine.]

Ames: Do you get many offers for dates?

Georgie: Yes, anyone in this kind of business does, whether it's topless or not. You know, it's funny, but you get a lot more respect and you're left alone, I would say, more as a topless waitress than you are as a regular one.

Allison: Cocktail waitress. Oh, yeah. You don't get pinched very much. Some of the customers pinch you and grab you . . .

Georgie: Can't help it. But when it happens, you just smile and see it through.

Brown: The guys who pinch you—are they mostly older? Younger? Richer? Poorer?

Allison: The worst guys in the world are those older guys, because they think they are wonderful.

Georgie: Right!

Allison: Because they're educated, and they have white-collar jobs, and they think they're so smart—and they're obnoxious! They're the first ones to grab you and the first ones to . . .

Georgie: The ones that don't give you the trouble are the ones that come in in the old work clothes and sit down, "Hi, how're you?"

Allison: Or, the 21- or 22-year-old guys.

Georgie: They're not the ones in the suits and everything who say—who stand and stare at you, and you say, "May I help you?" They say, "Oh-h-h yeah. Now that I think about it, you sure could." You say, "Well, uh, would you like a beer?" "Well, I really wouldn't care for a beer, but I guess I'll have one. I'd really like something else." It's all this line.

Girl 1: Our bar is also very exceptional because we get a lot of women in here.

Girl 2: Yeah.

Ames: Now this is a good question. What about these women, and especially couples? What about women customers?

Georgie: It's all in the individuals. I'd say, uh, like a lot of them, half of them, really don't care for it that much. They're going just to please their husbands.

Brown: Do they get embarrassed, or what?

Girl 1: Yes. You know, after they open up at our place, it doesn't phase them in the least.

Allison: In this place they're real nice.

Georgie: The majority of them are very nice to you. I mean, if they say anything at all, it's nice; otherwise, they keep their mouths shut. At [another bar], when I worked there, there was only a woman in there about three times in the whole six months. And each time she was with her husband, and she was sitting there and saying, "Don't look at her! What are you doing in a place like this? You know these girls are tramps!" And you're standing there and saying, "May I help you?" Smiling.

Ames: This is why I was curious what sort of mechanisms you girls have for insulating . . .

Allison: You just kind of laugh, because you know they're jealous.

Brown: Do people have any attitudes about competition [with other bars]?

Girl 1: No.

Brown: Do you have any attitudes about this? Any feeling pro? con?

Girl 2: About what?

Girl 3: No.

Ames: Competition with other bars.

Georgie: There is no competition whatsoever with our bar or any other topless bar, because we've got the best girls, and if they ask where any other bars are, we say "All around," and we'll tell them, because we have nothing to worry about.

Ames: What about feelings of jealousy among the girls? Is this something that's prevalent or something that's completely absent?
[General disagreement.]

Girl 1: [Joking.] Sorry about last night, Allison, really.
[Laughter.]

Georgie: A little bit, I imagine. Every girl has something to be jealous of a little.

Ames: But this isn't something that interrupts the job?

Georgie: Not really jealous. Maybe feel funny, but not really jealous.

Girl 1: Everybody has their own personality, and their own reasons for being liked and their own types of popularity.

Georgie: Everyone has their own little thing going for them. It's like, like Mousey. [A girl whose name derived from the fact that she had a picture of Mickey Mouse tattooed on her left breast.] You know Mousey? They make out a dance list. All right, now. Mousey gets up first, and say I get up second. Now, I'm not jealous of her, because I think she's a gas the way she dances, but I feel funny getting up after her because I can't dance, and it's not a jealous thing. It's an inferior type thing. You know.

Girl 1: After you're there for a little while, then you develop your own fans.

Ames: Your own what?

Allison: Your own fan club.

Georgie: And if you're gone for a week, they all miss you.

Brown: Who are the biggest tippers?

Allison: Orientals and Mexicans. And yet, they both give you the most trouble too, sometimes.

Georgie: Orientals? No, they don't really give you that much trouble, but at [another bar] when I worked there, Mexicans really gave you a lot of trouble.

Ames: Well, that's funny, because the Orientals—well, the Mexicans especially—probably earn less on the average than the rest of us.

Girl 1: This is where your outstanding tips come from.
[General agreement.]

Ames: Do a lot of them not tip?

Girl 1: Yes.

Girl 2: Yes.

Allison: Oh, yes.

Georgie: If we had a dime for every customer that comes in and doesn't leave a tip, think of the money we'd be making. Because in addition to that, your customers come from the work-a-day man who's a generally consistent tipper.

Ames: The person who might work in construction—is this what you mean?

Allison: Some day I want to walk up to one of these guys and say, "Why don't you leave a tip on the tray?" If they were going into a coffee shop they wouldn't think of leaving nothing as a tip. If they go into a topless place, they figure since they're paying so much for a beer they don't have to leave a tip or we're making so much money that they don't have to tip. Well, we're not making it if they're not tipping.

Georgie: Or, there'll be the type that sit down and they'll order a beer and everything, and they're trying to come on to you, you know, like, "What are you doing tonight?" and all this, and you think . . . Well, as for me, I don't go out with customers that I meet in the bar or anything. And I have my own life. They expect you to keep waiting on them. And you want to be nice to them. And you think, if you're nice to them, you expect they'll leave you something, because a waitress' job mainly depends as far as money upon their tipping. And they won't tip you and yet they want you to go out.

Allison: The people that try to date you don't tip.

Georgie: And you want to say, "Do you think you can afford to take me out?"

Brown: ". . . if you can't afford to tip."

Allison: You get better tips from the younger guys.

Georgie: You'd think if people can afford to pay 50¢, or 60¢ on weekends, for *one* beer, if they can afford that, then why can't they afford a small tip? it doesn't have to be a large tip.

Allison: A lot of people don't understand that though, George, [i.e., Georgie; it was very common for the girls to refer to each other with masculine names] because they've never worked at something like this.

Georgie: Even when I sit at a bar, I tip the bartender.

Allison: When you work in a field where you depend on your tips, you realize what they are, and then you remember to give them to others.

Brown: Aside from talking about people trying to pick you up, trying to proposition you, what else do customers talk about? Do they talk about politics with you?

Girl 1: No.

Girl 3: No.

Girl 2: You talk about your life or their life. They just talk about themselves, what they do, or what they're interested in. Anything.

Ames: Do they try to impress you?

Girl 1: They don't really care what they talk about, just so you bend over and talk with them.

Girl 2: They talk about your body a lot.

Georgie: They talk about your body a lot, which I don't mind. You know, somebody comes over and stares. I have to laugh. When you're taught all your life, you know, that you don't go around undressed, and then all these girls are running around nude, you can expect them to stare. Your body is an art, and you're making an honest living, but just the same, it's something that you've been taught against.

Brown: How many girls are nudists?

Girl 1: What do you mean?

Brown: Members of nudist camps.

Girl 3: No.

Girl 1: None of them.

Allison: Only one.

Girl 2: Maybe there are one or two.

Georgie: You can tell because we're working topless and the sun tan line looks funny.

Allison: I don't think it's funny, but I've got a place to do it now. Never did it before.

Georgie: Well, there's a difference between a nudist and working topless, because you don't want to run around seeing guys running around.

Ames: Makes a lot of difference?

[General agreement that it sure does.]

Manager: It has the same features.

Allison: I don't think there's anything wrong with it, though. If it's healthy . . .

Georgie: You don't knock it if you haven't tried it.

Brown: Do many guys tell about their wives?

Girl 1: Yes.

Georgie: Very much. Guys tell you about their wives, "If my wife was only like this, I'd be home right now. Why don't you go out with me? So what if I'm married?"

Brown: Do married guys proposition you more than single guys?

Georgie: Yes. Definitely!

Girl 1: Yes.

Allison: I don't know why. I think they just want to see if they're still desirable or something.

Georgie: Some men think it keeps their home together. It gives them a feeling of self-satisfaction, and when they're pleasant, they get along with their wives.

Brown: Do you find any people who are shy?

Allison: Yeah.

Georgie: [Disbelief.] Guys?

Allison: Yeah, there's a lot of guys that are really shy.

Ames: Are there more married guys or single guys that are shy?

Georgie: Single.

Allison: And they're younger.

Brown: Do you hear many dirty jokes?

Girl 1: No.

Georgie: Usually not, because they'll say, "Do you want to hear a joke?" and you say, "No."

Brown: What about the dirty-old-men type?

[Pause.]

Georgie: What about 'em?

Brown: Do they come in?

Georgie: Every night!

Allison: That's all we have, what do you mean?

Georgie: The type who say, "Why don't you dance? Get up there and . . . you know . . . !"

Allison: They're always right out with the quarters, too, when you take up a collection for the jukebox. Oh boy, they dig deep, but when it comes to leaving a tip, it's a different story.

Georgie: That's right. They want you to get up there and flop around. I had a guy say to me the other night, "I'll give you a quarter if you'll go up there and bounce your boobs."

Allison: Tell them for fifty cents we'll sit right there and bounce for them.

Georgie: I said, "For a quarter, I don't wanna." They bounce enough without any buying about It.

Brown: I can't understand why so many people don't tip. Because every time we've been there . . .

Girl 1: [To Ames and Brown.] What kind of tip did you all leave?

Allison: [Responding for them.] A quarter for beer. That's enough.

Brown: I've been leaving a quarter a beer all the time. Well, last night I walked out without tipping and felt very guilty yesterday.

Allison: When you think about it really 25¢ is a pretty big tip for a beer.

Girl 1: That's true.

Girl 2: That's over 50 per cent.

Georgie: After you arrive, you get stiffed [don't receive tips] so many times a night. Like, at the beginning of a night, when you start out at six, if you keep getting stiffed constantly, you get a bad mood, and you don't even want to wait on anyone; because you think they take advantage of you, because they're seeing us nude, we're serving them beer, and they're just expecting us to dance, do this, do that, and wait on them hand and foot, make sure their ashtrays are always clean, they're cleaned in front of them, and they've always got a beer. They don't want to tip us, you know. They think, "Well, it's your job, honey."

Brown: Would you say this is one of the worst things about your job?

Georgie: No.

Brown: What do you think the worst thing about your job is?

Georgie: Drunks! Conversation does the whole thing in. Because there's not that much physical thing as far as people trying to touch you. That's very seldom. There's not that much. But, its like the things that they say just add up. It just changes your whole attitude and everything after a while. Depending on how strong-minded you are.

Brown: Do you work six days a week? Get any vacation?

Girl 3: We don't know yet.

Girl 1: After you're there long enough, I guess. We haven't gotten one yet.

[Laughter.]

Allison: They're pretty good about it. You know, it's kind of informal. You know, if you want a week off or something, I mean, you can probably get it, because Ray's nice [The manager]. Or a day off for this or that. Like I called in a couple of times, because I wanted the night off for special reasons. You get it pretty readily, if they can rearrange the schedule, which is just fine.

Girl 2: They're honest about it.

Allison: Really, you couldn't ask for a better manager.

Girl 1: [To manager.] Don't you get a big head!

Girl 3: [Also to manager.] And, don't crack down either!

Brown: Do you know off hand if many of the managers are pimping?

Georgie: No. I'd say none.

Allison: Are you pimping, Ray?

Girl 1: [To manager.] Say, you aren't going to . . . ?!

Allison: I guess they could be if they wanted to. You couldn't do too much about it, I don't think.

Manager: Never happen!

Brown: Never happen?

Allison: Who'd want to pimp anyway?

Georgie: In the first place, they're making enough money without that stuff. I mean, in a small bar that isn't topless . . . (shrug) . . . but in a regular topless bar, they're making plenty of money.

Girl 1: And anyway, they're too busy in the first place.

Girl 2: And the changeover of girls is constant.

Brown: When a girl leaves a job does she usually go to another topless or does she go into something else?

Allison: It depends on why she left, how long she's been there, how much money she has . . .

Georgie: Generally, she'll go on to topless again, because she's so used to good money that it's a hangup to go back to a regular job and not make any money. It spoils you.

Girl 1: If you're at all smart, from here you only go up. You don't go down.

Brown: Where is up?

Allison: You've got to get out of the field, girl, because there's no where "up" to go.

Girl 1: That's right.

Allison: I mean, if you're working for something in particular, then you can go up, but if you're just working for money, you're not going up. There's no where you're going to go but topless.

Brown: Do you consider being a topless waitress higher than being a showgirl? That is, being a topless showgirl?

Allison: Not very much.

Georgie: No.

Brown: Which would be higher: a topless showgirl in Vegas or a topless waitress?

Allison: I'd rather be a showgirl.

Girl 1: More prestige.

Georgie: You're treated with respect, you're looked up upon. Never have a harsh word.

Allison: That's because you're in the entertainment business.

Georgie: Right.

Allison: We're not considered to be entertainment [here].

Girl 1: [To Allison.] Aren't we entertainers, huh?

Allison: Well, yeah, but nobody thinks we are.

Georgie: We're part of the entertainment class because we're dancers.

Brown: I'd like to get a sort of psychological background, biographical and psychological, of types of girls or the type of girl, the *typical* girl, who goes into this.

Georgie: I would say there's no typical girl.

Allison: I think what you find more of, than anything else, seem to be girls with different backgrounds.

Brown: Girls with what kind of backgrounds?

Ames: Different. Just a wide variety?

Allison: Yeah, I mean there's quite a big variety.

Ames: Is there much parental opposition, or do most of the girls . . .

Allison: My parents would probably disown me if they ever knew.

Girl 1: They wouldn't like it, but they wouldn't disown me.

Georgie: Well, they know, but . . .

Allison: Mine don't. My mother's Italian, for one thing, and sixty for another thing. Comes from a family of educated people. But she'd understand more than my father. He would just hit the ceiling. He would be crushed, because he would think of his reputation and his honor and all this kind of thing.

Georgie: But I know in my own mind that I'm not doing anything wrong, so . . .

Brown: What are the ages of the girls?

Girl 3: Over 21.

Allison: Well, now, isn't that intelligent? You have to be 21 to work in a bar. They go all the way up to 28.

Girl 1: Some of them aren't 21 though.

Girl 2: Majority are about 22 or 23.

Brown: Do you have many girls under age trying to get a job? [No answer.]

Brown: [To manager.] When you interview a girl, when you talk to a girl, how do you hire her? Experience, bust, beauty?

Manager: I look at 'em, if I like 'em, I hire 'em.

Brown: What about marriage? Are many of the girls who are single planning on getting married? Somebody in mind?

Allison: Let's say we're working on it.

[Laughter.]

Georgie: No. The majority, no.

Allison: The majority "no" what?

Georgie: The majority aren't planning on getting married.

Allison: [To Georgie.] What about you? You're not planning on getting married eventually? You don't *want* to get married eventually?

Georgie: Well, maybe *eventually,* but I mean *now,* you're talking about *now.* The majority, if they haven't been would say no. Whether or not they change their minds is one thing, but the majority, no.

Brown: Another thing that we hope to get into is the attitude of the girls towards the talk about outlawing topless places.

Allison: I see no reason why they should, because they have strippers who get up there and, you know, completely . . . Every movement is . . .

Georgie: Vile!

Allison: . . . suggestive! It's rank, and this is okay. But, you know, we're asked to get dressed from our heads to our feet. You know, because we do the same thing as a waitress would, a cocktail waitress would. And dancing, there's nothing suggestive about that. Everybody's just being themself and being nice to people. And I don't see any reason why they have anything against us.

Brown: Do you think, politically, most of the girls are more liberal or more conservative?

Georgie: Conservative, in the true sense of the word.

Allison: I don't know, I think probably a lot of us don't think too much about politics or any of that stuff. I don't myself.

Manager: I think a good point you should put down there, is that the topless bar is probably one of the safest bars in town, not only for the customers, but for the girls, too.

Allison: Yeah. You're very well protected.

Girl 1: That's true.

Manager: Everything's well protected.

Georgie: I mean, even after work you can get walked to your car. [Each topless bar was assigned a security guard who would walk a barmaid

to her car if she so requested. Such amenities were not available at
regular bars.]

Manager: You look at cocktail lounges. Where a male customer goes in
there, you know, I'd say a majority of the cocktail lounges around here,
they've got hustlers.

Brown: [To manager.] I guess some evidence is your coming along here
tonight. I assume this had some protective value.

Manager: They dragged me over.

[Laughter.]

Girl 1: We're protecting him!

At this point, breakfast finished and the interview ended.

However interesting the interview might be, to the sociologists it
serves simply as a data source. The question raised earlier, which we
wish to answer from these data, is to what extent can one consider the
occupation of topless barmaid a deviant occupation. We have prior
knowledge that the topless bar emerged as a part of a moral liberalization movement in the United States. Furthermore, we know that it was
semi-legal for the most part, especially in California. While it seemed to
fall just shy of the law, great pressure was placed on the lawmakers to
enact new laws that would eliminate the topless bar. Hence, its legal
status was constantly being challenged.

Legality, however, is an inadequate sociological definition of deviance. M. B. Clinard[2] has defined deviance as action "in a disapproved
direction, of sufficient degree to exceed the tolerance level of the
community." We can apply this definition of deviance to the occupation
of topless barmaid using the interview data. One index of the degree of
toleration of the community is the constant interplay of the definitions
and counter-definitions of the job given by the girls, their customers,
and by the larger society.

One of the first inferences we get in the interview of the girls' definition of the job is how they entered the occupation initially. Judging
from the lack of prior job stability, plus the lack of required training for
the job of topless barmaid, plus the lack of traditional goals such as
marriage and a family, one can infer that these girls drifted into this job
as haphazardly as they might have entered anything else. Since money
was not intrinsic to the particular job, their definition of the job was in
terms of ends, not means. As Allison says, "I don't think any of us get a
charge walking around without any clothes on."

Once engaged in the job, they presented an image to the outside
world which they felt had to be defended. Throughout the interview,
they referred to and reacted to hostile definitions of their occupation.
This included definitions of parents, close friends, their customers, the
customers' wives, and "the D.A.R." They could not date their customers "because it was a bad situation." They could not tell their
friends because they would not understand. They could not tell their

parents because the parents would "worry about their honor." The sheriffs fingerprinted them. Reformers were trying to outlaw the topless bars. They had to build an enhanced self-image as well as a hardness in order to have a barrier to counter the definitions ascribed by the customers: "You know these girls are tramps!" In short, the public definition of topless barmaids was unfavorable. That general public disapproval exceeded the tolerance level is shown in the constant attempts to outlaw topless bars. Thus, the occupation of topless barmaids may be seen as deviant behavior.

Given this negative definition of the job by others, how did the girls react? Throughout the interview, the theme is one of justification of what they were doing. Would they classify themselves as one type? No! Would they classify themselves as lower class? No!! Did they try to upgrade their status? Yes! They tried to view themselves as dancers rather than barmaids, they tried to pass as being better educated than they were, they objected to people discrediting the character of the job; they wanted people to understand that they were "doing a job and doing it honestly."

Another theme that runs through the discussion is that they tried to disavow being prostitutes, or the linkage of semi-nudity with promiscuity. They could not be bought, even if it was simply "bouncing your boobs for a quarter." They saw a good deal of difference between themselves and nudists, and between themselves and strippers. Strippers they considered to be vile. And yet, they perceived society as condoning strippers, but not them. Clearly, they could never see themselves cooperating with a manager who was pimping. Nor, did they see themselves as hookers who were making a little extra on the side. In short, the girls defined themselves as doing a job just like anybody else. They were not doing anything wrong, and just wished people would understand what they were doing and leave them alone.

From the perspective of what they were doing, rather than what people thought of them, walking around almost nude in public does violate norms of sexual modesty. As Georgie says, "It's something you are taught against." M. S. Weinberg points out, "sexual modesty is sexual reserve (or a communication of non-availability for sexual relations)."[3] Immodesty may be either verbal or non-verbal. One form of "non-verbal communication" is a "display of body." Toplessness carried with it public disapproval since it implied a lessening of the sexual reserve of modesty, and hence defined the girls as ones who would fulfill sexual desires. The expression of this is demonstrated in Allison's statement that, "You can't date anyone you meet in the bar" because they had a definition of the girl as one of loose morals. As a form of public ostracism, the girls were fingerprinted by the sheriff. A few allusions to vicarious sexual satisfaction appear in the interview

("Some men think it keeps their home together."), as well as general contempt for men.

These attitudes displayed by the girls are remarkably close to Harold Greenwald's report of the attitudes of prostitutes.[4] Especially important in this regard is the fact that they describe themselves as normal, and assign pimps, prostitutes, strippers, nudists, and dirty-old-men to the same "other" category. They alone were above the rest of the pack, although the general "they" who were the public assigned topless barmaids, strippers, prostitutes, and nudists to the same category. Yet, by all indications, the girls were not prostitutes. One of the themes running through the interview was that prostitution was something "nice girls don't do," and they defined themselves as nice.

What conclusion can be drawn from the issues bearing on our question of the extent to which the occupation of topless barmaid is a deviant occupation? Clearly, topless barmaids fall somewhere between prostitutes and barmaids in terms of a continuum of deviance. The bars were legal enough so that laws had to be manufactured for the purpose of opposing them. On the other hand, the fact that the laws were drawn up is indicative of an outraged public. Given the inability of the social structure to define the occupation of topless barmaid as illegal, qualities of deviance had to be sought at the level of the definition of the girls which took place at the level of personal interaction. Clearly, at the level of personal interaction the definitions by the girls clashed with those forced upon them by others. In fact, "definition and counter-definition" seem to describe the situation. For the most part, the girls refused to define themselves as deviant, and it is probably for this reason that many of the topless bars closed once the sheriffs' department, requiring them to be fingerprinted, treated them as deviant. Public stigmatization was simply too much to endure.

NOTES

1 Joe Robert Leonard, "Topless Beer," *FM Guide* (1966).
2 Marshal B. Clinard, *Sociology of Deviant Behavior,* 3rd ed. (New York: Holt, Rinehart, and Winston, 1968).
3 Martin S. Weinberg, "Sexual Modesty, Social Meanings, and the Nudist Camp," *Social Problems,* 12 (1965). [Ed. note: See Ch. 2 of this volume.]
4 Harold Greenwald, *The Call Girl* (New York: Ballantine Publications, 1958).

part two
heterosexual styles of deviance

4 | B-Girls and Prostitutes | Sherri Cavan

This selection from Sherri Cavan's book Liquor License *deals with the sale of sex in the setting of bars. The social definitions of bars make it easy for B-girls and prostitutes to carry on their activities there. B-girls use the "apparent promise of sex" to get bar customers to buy more drinks; and get a kick-back from the owners for the service. Prostitutes use the bar as a place to pick up customers.*

It is important to note that there is almost no consideration in this essay of the morality or immorality of the behavior described. Within the bar itself there is little disagreement over the morality of this behavior. Most of the patrons of her bar probably do not regard the behavior of B-girls and prostitutes as reputable or ideal. On the other hand, they don't consider it immoral or something that should be classified as illegal. The B-girl's activity is part of the everyday life of the bar and is accepted as normal.

B-Girls

The pickup is one form of sexually oriented exchange which may be transacted within the public drinking place, a form in which, at least ideally, neither participant expects any financial remuneration from the exchange. Sexually oriented exchanges can also be on a commercial basis, so that at some point in time one participant can expect, either directly or indirectly, a monetary payoff from the encounter. As one B-girl is quoted, "You really don't have to ask a guy to buy you a drink . . . just sit there and he'll send one over. I figured since guys were always making passes, why not collect on it?"[1]

Like the casual bar pickup, B-girls enter into sexually oriented encounters with strangers in the public drinking place. But unlike the casual pickup, for the B-girl the bar is a work setting and the flirtatious sociability in which she engages with the patrons is a source of financial remuneration. Although she sits at the bar like those who are

Reprinted from Sherri Cavan, *Liquor License: An Ethnography of Bar Behavior* (Chicago: Aldine Publishing Company, 1966); Copyright © 1966 by Sherri Cavan.

present as patrons, the B-girl, unlike the female patron, is not unconditionally open for interaction. Rather, she is available only to those who
are willing to pay for the encounter.

> Ginny (the B-girl) had one drink when she came on, around noon, and
> after that, Connie, the bartender, fixed her coffee. When a new man came
> into the bar, she would push the coffee cup away and sit twirling her
> empty glass, saying nothing unless the male offered to buy her a drink.
> Once a drink was bought for her, she would smile, laugh, and chat with
> the buyer until he either left or ceased buying her drinks.
> Although the drinks in the bar cost the patrons fifty cents, her drinks
> cost a dollar. Each time a patron bought her a drink, Connie would put
> a penny into one of the empty sections in the cash register. At 5 P.M.,
> when her husband came to pick her up, sixteen or seventeen pennies
> had accumulated. Just before she left, she and Connie went down to the
> end of the bar, where Connie handed her some folded bills. When I
> looked in the cash register later, the section where the pennies had been
> was empty again.
> When business was slow, Ginny would go out for periods of five or
> ten minutes. On one of these occasions she came back with a young
> man in tow. He bought her two drinks and stayed about half an hour.

One of the male field workers writes:

> There were two women sitting at the bar, each by herself. I came in
> and obviously avoided the empty stools to sit next to the blond. I im-
> mediately ordered a drink for myself and, after it came, said to the
> blond, "Why is it so lively tonight?"
> "All the dead end kids are here," she answered.
> "How can you tell which end is dead?"
> She just shrugged. About this time, one of the men at the entrance end
> of the bar bought a drink for himself and one of the male patrons seated
> at his left. The latter appeared to be a new acquaintance. When the
> blond saw this, she downed her drink, said *"C'est la vie"* to me, got up,
> and walked down and sat next to the patron who had bought the drinks,
> saying to him, "I'll have a drink, too. She ordered it from the bartender,
> who brought it and then indicated that the patron should pay. He took a
> dollar from the patron and rang up the drink. There was no change (al-
> though the patron's drinks cost only fifty cents) and he put a penny in a
> glass by the cash register to tally the drink. Before I left, the patron had
> bought the blond three drinks, each time at her request.

While the B-girl is present in the bar in the guise of a patron, in some
marketplace bars flirtatious sociability may be purchased by the drink
from women who are explicitly employed in the establishment, such as
cocktail waitresses, barmaids, and entertainers. While such bar func-
tionaries are, in fact, expected to carry out the tasks that are associated with their occupational role, in the marketplace bar they are also
present to provide cross-sex sociability for patrons who are willing to
pay for it by the purchase of a drink.

> I answered an ad for a cocktail waitress, no experience necessary. The
> ad and the address had been in the paper about every two to three
> months for over a year.

The bar was located on skid row. It was a very small place, with perhaps twenty to twenty-two seats along the bar and two booths in the back, but these were piled with beer crates and miscellaneous items and apparently were not used. When I asked the bartender why he needed a cocktail waitress, he said, "If these guys walk by and see me behind the bar, they don't want to come in and talk to me. . . . All you have to do is serve soft drinks and beer and talk with the guys—you know."

A similar example comes from the notes of one of the male field workers:

I had been buying drinks and talking with one of the strippers for about twenty minutes or so. When she said she had to leave to do her act, the bartender suggested to Lolly (one of the other strippers sitting next to the first girl) that she move down and sit with me, which she did.

I bought Lolly a couple of drinks and we talked for a while. At first she allowed me to suggest buying her a drink, but after a while she became increasingly aggressive about suggesting that I buy her a drink, finally asking me outright. At one point she offered me a cigarette. It was her last one and she said that I would "have to" buy her more. I did so at the cost of fifty cents.

About this time I was running out of money and told her I would have to leave. As I excused myself, she requested that I go out and buy some mints for her, saying that she could not leave the place.

Whether the B-girl is in the bar in the guise of a patron or whether she is available for cross-sex encounters in addition to other duties, her problem of working efficiently (by maximizing the number of drinks purchased for her) is aggravated by the fact that all present, whether they are there as patrons or employees, are defined as open for interaction to anyone, regardless of whether a drink has been bought for them or not. Defined by the patrons as unconditionally open and by her employer as conditionally open, her solution usually rests upon making overtures with promises. She uses her open character either to instigate a conversation or to permit a conversation to be instigated with her, but once she has shown her interest in an encounter, she makes herself unavailable, either physically or socially, to continue the encounter without the purchase of a drink.

The following examples come from the notes of two male field workers:

I had been at the bar for twenty minutes or so when one of the girls sat down two stools from me. I watched her for a few minutes and then introduced myself. I did not offer to buy her a drink.

"My name's Bruce. What's yours?"

"Janie."

"I'm from Fresno."

"Oh." She turned her head away.

"Not much to do down there," I said.

"I imagine not," she said, turning her head away again.

> The conversation continued in this manner: question or statement by me and a brief answer, with her turning her head away or using some other gesture of avoidance. Finally I asked her if she would like a drink.
>
> "Yes, thanks. What do you do for a living?"
>
> Once the drink was bought for her, she seemed much more willing to enter into a conversation with me.
>
> I picked up my drink and moved down to the other end of the bar where the brunette was sitting. When I sat down I said to her, "Why so sad?"
>
> She answered, "I need a drink. Want to buy me one?"
>
> "I'm short on funds this week. How much is it going to cost?"
>
> "A dollar."
>
> "That's a little high. Can't I buy you a fifty-cent drink?"
>
> "No."
>
> "Can you go down to the V——— Club with me? It's a little livelier there."
>
> "Sorry, I have to stay here. Do you like the V——— Club?"
>
> "It's Okay. Tonight's the first time I've ever been there."
>
> At this point she got up and went behind the bar, where she fixed a straight pineapple drink for herself. Then she picked up a newspaper, seated herself at the far end of the bar (moving about three stools away from me), and began reading.

Similarly, ongoing encounters with the B-girl are characteristically viable only so long as drinks are forthcoming from the male. Thus one of the male field workers writes,

> I had bought Nancy two drinks. When the bartender came around for the third drink I told him that I wanted no more. Nancy cut off the conversation and became very restless. I could no longer keep a conversation going. Finally she said that she had to get ready for her act, and she prepared to leave. At this point I asked her if she would like another drink. She accepted and talked for another ten minutes or so.

Similarly, while I was working as a barmaid, as long as the patron was buying drinks for me there would be no other duties that I had to attend to. However, once my drink was finished and no other offer was made to me by the patron, the bartender would typically find an assortment of minor tasks that needed my attention, tasks which could be immediately dropped if the patron offered me another drink.

Many who buy the services of B-girls do so with full realization that they are, in fact, buying the cross-sex encounter as a commodity,[2] and that they are getting no more than they are paying for, although they may well demand that they get at least as much as they pay for.

> Marv said that last night he went to the T——— (a bar just a few doors away from this one) and "dropped" five dollars with May, one of the B-girls. "It was sort of a waste," he said, "because she drank it so fast that I couldn't even talk to her."
>
> Lunt said that Julie (another B-girl at the same bar) "at least left the drink in front of her long enough for you to know that she had got it."
>
> Marv and Lunt then started discussing the merits of the various girls

along the street, and Kenny joined them with some of his own experiences. The consensus appeared to be that the girls who drank their drinks too fast were not only unsatisfactory, but unfair as well: if a fellow was paying for conversation he was entitled to it. Lunt said, "If I just wanted to look at her I could do it for free."[3]

Where the purchase of sociability is taken as a normal pattern for cross-sex interaction, there is no stigma attached to being a buyer and like the Don Juan in an arena of noncommercial sex, the exploits of heavy buyers may be treated as though they were feats of a culture hero.

> After Marv, Lunt, and Kenny were finished with their evaluations of the B-girls along the street, there was some general conversation about the men who patronize them as well. Everyone had some story to contribute, mainly about how much various people had dropped with the girls on one occasion or the other.
>
> Connie, the bartender, told a very long, elaborate story about a horse trainer from Colorado who dropped almost $3,000 in the various bars along the street one night. Connie said that at one point in the evening the horse trainer had asked him to bring some fresh girls in, not because he was tired of the ones that were there, but because he wanted to pass the money around to all the girls equally.
>
> Everyone laughed at the stories, but it did not appear that they were laughing at the men involved in them.

In addition to those for whom transactions with the B-girls are a matter of course, there are also customers who may treat the interaction as something different or something more than what it is expected to be from the standpoint of the B-girl. Thus, there are those who may enter into an encounter with a B-girl believing it to be a noncommercial bar pickup, and those who may enter into an encounter believing it to be a commercial encounter, but one which offers more than mere sociability. In either situation, such patrons may make trouble for the B-girl and the bartender as well, the former because the patron must be made to pay for what he believes he is getting free and the latter because he feels he is not getting as much as he believes he is paying for. The complaints that are made to the official agencies about B-girls' activity may come from either source.

Prostitutes

Just as the public drinking place may be used as a setting where flirtatious sociability can be purchased, so, too, may such places be used as settings where arrangements for commercial sexual relations outside the bar can be transacted. In this way, the public drinking place may be, and frequently is, used as a locale within which professional and part-time prostitutes can be found.

In Worktown, a town in which strangers are not common and whose transient population is small, prostitution does not flourish; the full-time prostitute is a rarity. The small band of them that exists is to be found in a few town centre pubs. They circulate within this limited orbit of a few hundred yards. One of these pubs in particular is regarded as their head-quarters.[4]

There are a number of cocktail lounges and restaurants which are known haunts of call girls, but the solicitation here is usually not direct. In these places the management encourages the trade of call girls. They usually sit at the bars, drinking by themselves; occasionally introduction is made by the bartender or manager where the potential client is not very adventurous and asks aid. The more adventurous clients will ap-proach the girl themselves, in which case the encounter frequently takes on the appearance of an ordinary barroom conversation. It is then im-portant for the call girl to display her skill in negotiation so that she can obtain the promise of a fee without being too crudely commercial in her negotiations, as many men find such an attitude dampening to their ardor.[5]

In some establishments, the relationship between prostitution and the public drinking place is one in which prospective "tricks" are merely channeled through the establishment, to make contact with the prostitute at some other location. Thus, some bars may be known as places where information about prostitution may be obtained, even though the women themselves may not be found on the premises. In other establishments, either with or without the knowledge of the management, women may work as cocktail waitresses primarily for the purpose of making arrangements with patrons for after-hours employ-ment. But in most situations, the prostitutes have no contractual agreement with the establishment of any kind; they are simply there and available.[6]

A young man came in with two rather nicely dressed young women. He motioned them toward the bench across from the bar and then went up to the bar. When he returned, he had a drink for himself and for one of the women, but nothing for the second one. The three of them sat for a few minutes talking, and then the woman with the drink wandered off.

There was a man, probably in his fifties, standing a few feet away from them, for all practical purposes simply eyeing the women who were present. The young man looked over at him, said something indistinguish-able to the remaining woman he was with and then went up to the older man, saying to him, "Are you busy?"

"No."

"Would you like to meet a girl?"

"Yes."

"Are you violent?"

"Oh, no. I'm very pleasant."

"What's your name?"

"Stan."

"Okay, Stan, wait a minute."

The young man then returned to the girl and there were a few minutes of huddled conversation between them, while Stan stood paying no attention to them, and fidgeting in what appeared to be a rather anxious manner. Every so often he would surreptitiously look over at them.

Finally the young man went over to Stan, took him by the arm and brought him over to the woman, introducing her as Louise. After the introduction, Stan said, "Let me buy you a drink." He went to the bar and came back with a drink for himself, the young man, and the woman. The young man then moved over so that Stan could sit next to the woman, but once Stan sat down, the young man disappeared.

P. C. noted that the young man seemed to know most of the hookers at the bar and went from one to another, chatting with them. At one point, one of them started to pay for her drink and the young man said to her, "Put that away," which she did, and then the man seated next to her offered to buy it for her.

One of the male field workers writes of another establishment:

A middle-aged woman (Rita) was sitting a few stools away from me. Her "escort" was amorously rubbing her buttocks every now and then, but not appearing to make too much headway otherwise; Rita kept saying, "No!"

A second woman (Daphne) came in, sat down at the far end of the bar for about twenty minutes, and finally walked down to where I was sitting, saying, "Don't you remember me? Don't you still love me?" I said yes and we hugged. Then one of the other male patrons asked her to dance, and the two of them stood in the middle of the floor, moving a little to the music but mainly hugging one another. All this time Daphne had an overnight case in her hand and her coat on and buttoned up. When the "dance" was finished, she came back to where I was sitting, saying to me, "Nobody's at home. They're out probably having a ball and I'm here in San Francisco, broke and no place to stay."

About this time Rita asked me to explain to Daphne what a "French job" was, because her "boyfriend" was interested in one and she was not about to accommodate him, but perhaps Daphne would be interested. However, the fellow that Rita was with moved over to Daphne to do his own talking.

Rita then said to me, in a rather loud voice (although no one paid any attention to her), "He wants it kissed and he wants to kiss a pussy. . . . She [indicating Daphne] is a pro who would come on the floor." This last part of her statement was addressed more to everyone at the bar than it was to me.

The bartender came over to me and introduced himself about this time, saying he was just an extra for the night. I asked him where I could get a girl "who's not my mother" (since most of the women were in their late forties or older) and he answered, "They're in and out of here. . . . There's a blond named Marcie, but I haven't seen her here tonight." Then both of us looked up and down the bar to see if we could spot anything.

Not infrequently, professional and part-time prostitutes can be found in the same public drinking places that are used, and known to be used, for noncommercial heterosexual pickups. The presence of what the professionals call "those who give it away" has little effect on their own opportunities, since it appears that the market for the noncommercial pickup and the market for the professional prostitute have little overlap. As one patron in such an establishment said,

> A guy comes in here and he picks up with one of the prostitutes and he knows in the end that he's going to get what he wants. It might cost him the same [as a noncommercial pickup] and probably it will cost him less to go with the prostitutes. And in the end they won't say no. You take one of these office dollies out of here and take her to dinner, that's thirty bucks; and then some place else to drink and that's another twenty bucks; and then you take her home and she says "Good night." . . . They know they can get a nice night out of any guy here and never have to put out.

Insofar as the dalliances between strangers in the bar are absolved of the consequences which they can be anticipated to engender in more serious settings, the bar provides a locale where such activity can routinely and, so to speak, "inexpensively" take place. With the expectation that the participants will not find themselves committed to a later course of action of a particular kind or find themselves later accorded a reputation of a particular kind, bar pickups take on the character of open possibilities. But at the same time, if the bar generates an indeterminate outcome for the sexual encounters of some, this indeterminate outcome may also permit those who offer guarantees to work the setting profitably, since there may be others who are interested in guarantees.

NOTES

1 *San Francisco Chronicle,* April 27, 1953. There is, in many respects, a good deal of similarity between the B-girl and the taxi dancer. Of the taxi-dance halls, Cressy writes, "Young women and girls are paid to dance with all comers, usually on a fifty-fifty commission basis. Half of the money spent by the patrons goes to the proprietors . . . while the other half is paid to the young women themselves. The girl employed in these halls is expected to dance with any man who may choose her and to remain with him on the dance floor for as long a time as he is willing to pay the charges. Hence the significance of the apt name 'taxi-dancer' . . . like the taxi-driver with his cab, she is for public hire and is paid in proportion to the time spent and the services rendered" (Paul G. Cressy, *The Taxi-Dance Hall* [Chicago: University of Chicago Press, 1932], p. 3).
2 Analogous situations exist for the patrons of the taxi-dance hall as well. See Cressy, *op. cit.,* pp. 109 ff.
3 It might be noted that one of the typical items of "evidence" that ABC agents and the police put forth in support of a charge that a woman is engaged in B-girl activities is the speed at which she consumes her drinks. For example, one agent is quoted as testifying that a girl "drank eight champagne cocktails at $1.50 each in 33 minutes." (*San Francisco Chronicle,* June 6, 1953.)

4 "Mass Observation," *The Pub and The People* (London: Victor Gollancz, Ltd., 1943), p. 266.
5 Harold Greenwald, *The Call Girl* (New York: Ballantine Books, 1960), p. 22.
6 Although to my knowledge there is nothing comparable to the B-girl in the homosexual market place bar, there are gay bars which are known as places for finding male prostitutes. *Cf.* Gordon Westwood, *A Minority* (London: Longmans, Green & Co., 1960), p. 73, as well as examples in C. Wright, *The Messenger* (New York: Farrar, Strauss & Co., 1963), and John Rechy, *City of Night* (New York: Grove Press, 1963).

5 | **Prostitution** | Wayland Young

This essay on prostitution by Wayland Young begins by putting prostitution in its general context. Prostitution is not only almost universal in human societies, which would indicate that it is very much related to certain basic individual or social needs that cannot be met by other social means, but it also has a very long and detailed history in each Western society. In the West most prostitutes are members of a deviant subculture, not in the sense that they have any group structure, but in the sense that they have many shared beliefs, values, and techniques that are transmitted from one generation of prostitutes to another. As will be very obvious in this essay, prostitutes also share common fronts, which they use to manipulate the public.

In American society today there is a very clear distinction between prostitutes who are primarily "streetwalkers," who occasionally work out of a house of prostitution, and the "call girls." Call girls work at the middle- and upper-class levels. They are primarily a result of the technological innovation of the telephone and changes in laws over recent years. The laws of evidence and rulings against entrapment make it almost impossible for the police to prove prostitution against call girls as long as they use only the telephone and a safe clientele. The American call girl today is a far cry from most of the prostitutes described in Young's essay. She, herself, is generally middle-class and lives by middle-class standards in most respects.

As this essay demonstrates, prostitutes and call-girls can exist only because generally law-abiding citizens are willing to pay for their services, but it is the prostitutes who are socially stigmatized through arrest, conviction and, sometimes, imprisonment for the activity. The customers (or "Johns") are almost never revealed or, if revealed, are not stigmatized. This is the common situation for crimes without victims and while it may certainly be a more efficient way to control such deviance, it does raise serious moral questions.

All women are sitting on a fortune, if only they realized it. ■ *Prostitute's saying*

There are in our society now two great classes of people excluded from the web of the normal because of their sex lives: whores and homosexuals. Of these the whore will better repay study in the context of this book because she is wholly excluded, all round the clock, whereas the homosexual is only excluded *as* a homosexual; he is accepted in working hours, the whore is not.

There are societies without prostitution; one of them is described in Verrier Elwin's book, *The Muria and their Ghotul*.[1] But they are very rare. It flourishes almost everywhere, and certainly in all Christian and post-Christian societies. In the Hellenic world it was part of the slavery-pederasty-prostitution triangle, the unruffled toleration of which so sharply distinguishes that world from ours, and so sharply contrasts, in our view, with the philosophic and artistic excellence we find in it. In other cultures, prostitution has been religious in motivation, or at least ritual. In some cultures there have been prostitutes by profession, who are set apart for that work. In others, the occasional act of prostitution has been something permitted to any woman; the function is not localized in this or that person but spread throughout society. Only five hundred years ago, Anglo-Saxon society was one of the latter sort. When Pope Pius II was in Berwick on Tweed as a young man, he was surprised to find that all the Englishmen locked themselves up in a tower at night, for fear of Scottish robbers, but left the women outside, thinking no wrong would befall them, and "counting outrage no wrong." Two young women showed Aeneas Silvius, as the future Pope was then called, "to a chamber strewn with straw, planning to sleep with him, as was the custom of the country, if they were asked." But he ignored them, "thinking less about women than about robbers," and took the fact that no robber came in the night as a reward for his continence.[2]

The custom whereby a man lends his wife or daughter to a guest is a form of prostitution; in return for her kindness the family or the clan expect to receive his good will, or even sometimes the good will of the gods, expressed in fertility of crop and of people. But the wife or daughter does not thereby become a prostitute.

In our society now, prostitution is specialized, mercenary, and reprobated. We confine the function to individual women who become a class apart, and whose characters become formed by their condition and experience. We pay them for exercising their function. We also despise them and penalize them. They are extruded from the body of society, as we like to conceive it, and live a life of their own according to their own values and customs. We know little of what these values and customs are, because we fear the prostitute. We fear her because we fear our own need for her, which conflicts with our formulated ideal of the relation between the sexes. We also project onto her our own guilty desires; because our accepted values declare us low and beastly when we go to her, we feel that she is herself low and beastly. Because we desire her when we go to her, we also feel that she desires us. We punish and blame her with one hand, and pay her handsomely with the other; we see her with one eye as a baited trap, and with the other as a golden haven of rest and warmth. Meanwhile, as Aretino said, she laughs with one eye and weeps with the other.

A whore is a woman who fucks for money. If you pay her enough, she pretends to come.

Let us take, as texts for this definition, first the words of a seventeenth-century pornographer (using the word in the strict sense: a writer about whores), and second those of a London whore today.

Writing in Venice in the 1630's, Ferrante Pallavicino advised the whore to handle her clients as follows:

> Let her go along with the humor of these people, and speak as they wish, even though she hold them in scorn. Let her expressions be in general common ones, as my dear, my own heart, my soul, I am dying, let us die together, and such like, which will show a feigned sentiment, if not a true one. Let her add panting, and sighing, and the interrupting of her own words, and other such galantries, which will give her out to be melting, to be swooning, to be totally consumed, whereas in fact she is not even moved, but more as if she were made of wood or of marble than of flesh. It is certain that the whore cannot take pleasure in all comers, . . . She must nevertheless give pleasure through her words, if not her deeds, and let her put into operation what she can, authenticating her words by closing her eyes, by abandoning herself as if lifeless, and by then rising up again in full strength with a vehement sigh as if she were panting in the oppression of extreme joy, though in fact she be reduced and languid. These lies can be singularly useful, although they are discredited by too common feigning, and often obtain little credence.[3]

And here is a contemporary London prostitute:

> There's some of them lies still as stones, they think it's more lady-like or something, but I say they don't know which side their bread's buttered. Listen, if you lie still the bloke may take half the night sweating away. But if you bash it about a bit he'll come all the quicker and get out and away and leave you in peace. Stupid to spin it out longer than you need, isn't it? I learned that from Margaret. Wonderful actress, that girl. I learned from her in exhibitions when I first was on the game. She wasn't the first girl I did an exhibition with, that was a coloured girl who used to pitch near me. I was dead scared of any of that at first, and then one night this coloured pallone comes up to me and says: "Bloke here wants an exhibition; will you help me out? Three pounds each." I was scared, but she said do it just to help her, so I said, "Do we have to go turn and

turn about?" but she said she'd lead all the time. Was I grateful! Anyhow, like I say, this Margaret and I used to do exhibitions after that; wonderful actress. Of course you know they're all faked, exhibitions are. We keep our hands down there all the time, which is why I used to shit myself laughing when I saw her pretending to pull hairs out from between her teeth afterwards. It was her I learned to grunt and groan from.

And another thing; when I'm with a client I always put the rubber on him very gently, you know, stroking him and spinning it out as long as I can. "You ought to have been a nurse," they say. That's always what it makes them think of. And then with a bit of luck they come before they even get into me. When they do I look ever so loving and gentle and say: "Traitor!" Well, I'm not paid just to be a bag, am I? I'm paid to make them feel good. It's easy for me, so why not? That's how I see it.

Mark that she learned to "grunt and groan" not from herself, not from a man, but from another whore. And that one word "Traitor!" sums up the whole structure of pretense which is whoring.

The pictures on the wall? I cut them out of a German phornographic book. I don't use photos much. There's some likes them and occasionally it helps to get a bashful client started. I don't know much about who makes them. I did a day's photographic work yesterday, but that wasn't phornographic. I've been asked to, though. Bloke rang up once and offered me fifty pounds for an afternoon's work. Said he'd find the male model. Said he'd take my head out too and put someone else's in, but I didn't believe him. And anyhow, I don't do that.

Here is a poem by a London prostitute.

The Game

Last night
A rather trite
Thought occurred to me. Exactly what pleasure
Is there in being a "Lady of Leisure?"
One has to submit (and grit one's teeth) to a great many men who, when
   the "fun" is at an end
Pretend
They've "never done this before."
And it's really such a bore
To listen enthralled
As they tell you about having called
At the furriers to buy coats for their spouses
(Made from mouses)
And, while wrapped in gorilla-like embraces,
You lie making faces
At your big toe over a beefy shoulder,
And he becomes colder

Because you do not respond as he breathes garlic,
Or worse, alcoholic
Fumes over your pretty neck
And you fervently wish that he'd break his . . .
There are of course so many different types:
Like the one who wipes
His hands all over your bedspread, and though you are very sweet to
   him
And entreat him
Not to do it again, he does—when you turn your back.
And you're just dying to whack
The man who is so "thoughtful" and feels he really ought to give you
   "pleasure" too because you're really far too "good"
For this life. (As if he could!)
And have you ever met the one who is just longing for sex,
But only ever pays with perfectly good cheques?
So when you're fool enough to agree—
(If you wish, he'll meet you at the bank next day, long before three)
You find he's hopped it—
And stopped it!
And how about the pound-of-flesher who insists
On being kissed
All over the place, and wants you to remove every bit of your clothes,
   including those nylons you spent your last pound on this afternoon,
Which will so soon
Be in shreds.
I'm forgetting the "slave":
On bended knee he'll crave
To be allowed to clean your lavatory,
And when you've stripped him
And whipped him
Mercilessly,
Asks: "Do you get many like me?"

What is the pattern of the whore's own desires and pleasures? Here
are several glimpses from different London girls:

> I think I have come; I'm not sure. Twice in my life I've thought to my-
> self, now maybe this is what they talk about. That was before I was on
> the game. I couldn't bear the sight of the man afterwards. He couldn't
> get out quick enough for me.

> I get my kicks from dancing, Latin American dancing mostly. I don't
> know, there's something about the movements. My first man was after a
> dance; I didn't know where I was. And the father of my child was after a
> dance too. It's always dancing with me.

I'm rather abnormally built. You see, my clitoris is very high—I'm not embarrassing you by talking like this?—it's a long way round, and so it gets a bit left out in a straight fuck. My womb's high up too; I guess everything's a bit far apart with me. I can only come if the man goes down. Well, there's only one man in ten that I even want to go down, and only one in ten of those that thinks of it. I can't ask them, can I? They're not there for my pleasure, I'm there for theirs. That's how the game is. I tell you, it's not all ninepins.

I don't know why I like girls. It feels safer, somehow. And I'm not talking about pregnancy. I think everybody agrees now—take Kinsey—that the clitoris is where women get their pleasure.

The man in the Boat's my mascot. As a matter of fact it's every woman's mascot, though there's not many men'll recognize it.

You know, the young men's pricks seem to be getting bigger and bigger. It must be the Welfare State. I hate it, though; it splits me.

Sandra would be no good on the game. She likes men and she enjoys fucking.

Perhaps what is most striking about these casual remarks is the feeling they all give of "I'm different; I'm not so well off as some; I can't; I don't; I can't." They suggest a temperament which is already in some way reduced, depleted, disabled, lacking, and that this temperament is a necessary condition of being able to be a whore at all.

It is very difficult to discover how whores become whores. It is difficult to do from a sociological or criminological standpoint, or by observing certain cafés or night clubs, because it is not a thing you *see* anyone doing. They don't enroll through an employment agency, and you don't see thousands of them trooping to work when the whistle blows. It's also difficult to do by asking prostitutes at firsthand. If a whore feels guilty about her trade, feels that the majority society is right to condemn her for it, as many do, then she will naturally have surrounded the memory of how she commenced with a cloud of inhibitions, and may even have suppressed it altogether. On the other hand if she stands up for herself she is likely to have put in some hard thought on what prostitution really is, and to take off into Shavian arguments to the effect that there is no dividing line anyhow, no hard and fast occasion, no key moment. She may throw the question back at you; Is fucking for pity prostitution? For a job? For an apartment? And then of course—for three pounds. Whether she feels guilty or whether she feels defensive or even defiant, she has every interest in slurring over the moment of change. Her present way of life demands it; she could hardly continue to function if she was to admit to herself that at one moment she was one sort of creature, morally speaking, and at the next another.

One of the best of a very small number of good books on prostitution is *Women of the Streets,* by Rosalind Wilkinson.[4] In her account of how girls get on to the game, she lays stress on a preliminary period of vague, floating promiscuity, of what she calls elsewhere "increasing irrelation to society." This is something different from maladjustment, which she sees as a deformed relationship, a warped and impracticable relationship, but one which may be as strong as any other. "Irrelation" is an absence of all relationship. The girl comes to London—most London whores come from provincial industrial cities—and bums around, living with this man or that, and perhaps frequenting one of the drinking clubs the easy establishment of which has recently caused new regulations to be brought in. Or perhaps she finds work as a "hostess" in a night club. There are one or two night clubs which seem to be simply highroads into the game. This intermediate phase is the one when the girl is called a *mystery:* is she going to take to the game or not? Generally speaking, nobody pushes her. This is an important point; the popular conception of well-organized recruiting agencies is a mistaken one. The motive for entertaining the illusion is fairly clear; the more a respectable man idealizes women, and the higher the value he sets on the merits of conventional society, the less will he be willing to believe any girl capable of abandoning it except under pressure or devious corruption. To such a man, all whores will be "poor unfortunate girls," and his imagination will people Soho and Paddington, the main prostitute districts of London, with dope-pushers, razor-slashers, and so forth.

One way on to the game is often open before the girl comes to London. A girl who has been an "easy lay" at school—not usually so much because she likes fucking as because she wants to find out if it isn't possible to like it more—takes work as a waitress or chambermaid at a provincial hotel. She sleeps with the odd traveling salesman, and one day one of them gives her a pair of nylons. The next one gives her a pound to buy her own, and the penny drops. She has been paid for it. Next stop London and the big money.

Here is the commencement of a prostitute, as seen by the man in the story:

> I met this girl at a party one night; she'd been sleeping around for some time with all sorts of people. I gave her a lift home after the party and as she was getting out of the car I asked her to have dinner with me a day or two later. She kind of paused, and then she said:—Look that dinner's going to cost you about three pounds. Why don't you just give me the three pounds and come along in and do me now?—So I did.

One does not often hear of the penny dropping so clearly.

But perhaps the commonest way on to the game is by the urging of a friend or elder sister. "Wake up, girl; how much longer are you going to *exist* on eight pounds a week? Why don't you come on out and *live?* You leave things to me, and I'll see you're getting a hundred a week before you know where you are."

Here is a fairly usual "life story." Until the recent law, which cleared most of the prostitutes off the London streets, Dorothy was a street-walker; she charged three pounds. A pound more for stripping, but she'll do it all the same if the client can't raise the extra. Hates kissing. Undertakes most kinks if she's feeling like it, but no buggery. Buggery is grounds for money back and throw them out. She was illegitimate, and brought up without a father. When she came home after school she would find her mum smooching away in the corner with some man. When she was twelve and thirteen the neighborhood kids used to say to her: "Had your R.C. yet?" She did not know what it meant, but shook her head, and they said: "All right, you can stay with us." R.C. meant "red change," or first period. She had her R.C. one day during an exam at school. She fainted, and was carried by the invigilator to the Head-mistress, who said "Are you ill?" "I don't think so." "Well, I mean, er, have you eaten anything?" Yes, she had steadied her nerves by guzzling Rowntrees Clear Gums, and to this day feels sick at the sight of them. So much for sex education.

At sixteen she had her first man, and at nineteen bore a child to an American soldier. While she was carrying the child she took up with a medical student and learned for the first time that she had a thing called a womb. He also taught her hygiene.

> And I may say most of the girls don't know a thing about it. They just put some soap on their fingers and tickle themselves. But he taught me to use a douche, and not more than once a week, otherwise it hurts your insides.

She believes masturbation gives you a bellyache. When her mother asked her who the child's father was, she said she really didn't know. She had passed out at a party and didn't know what had happened to her. Her mother legally adopted the child, a girl, and Dorothy never sees either of them. She blames her mother for her own upbringing, and fears her own child may be brought up the same way, but it's nothing to do with her, it's miles away now.

After the birth of the child she went to London and took work as a barmaid. She went concurrently with a well-off married man every third Sunday, and with the manager of the hotel in the afternoons. One night in a clipjoint she got drunk and started telling the manager of the joint what was wrong with the place; the pattern of the wallpaper was too small, the place was dirty, the girls were badly dressed. This manager took her on the spot as his girl friend and co-manager, and she lived with him for four years. Then it broke up, and she was underfed and began hitting the bottle. (This is the "period of increasing irrelation.") She had a taste for "pretty things and bright lights," as well as for liquor; one night she got drunk at a party and the next morning found she'd been laid and paid for it. (The same story she'd told her mother about the baby.) So there she was, a whore. She began walking the street, though she didn't stand yet.

Before the law virtually put an end to the street trade in London, standing was the end of irrelation; the mystery was accepted. Some older whore invites the walker to share her pitch and makes friends with her. There might be a Lesbian arrangement, and there would probably be something of a team about it. "With your looks and youth you could earn well, that is if you consent to profit by my experience." Perhaps they would do exhibitions together. The older woman might get a rake-off in return for her patronage. The arrangement would be a fleeting one, like everything in the underworld.

Here is another life story, one from the other end of the social scale; prostitution, like everything else in England, is all shot through with class values. Mary was a successful call girl, and occasionally reached the maximum possible earnings, up to fifty pounds for an all night fix. When she was twelve, she was "the only girl without a title" at a snobbish Roman Catholic boarding school run by nuns. Her parents were kindly, but cold. The father was blind, and the mother, having had a total hysterectomy, cut out love not only from her bed but from her whole life. Then, within a year, three things happened. She found papers on her mother's desk which taught her she was the illegitimate daughter of the illegitimate daughter of a housemaid; her true mother had put her in an orphanage when she was three years old, and she had been adopted by the people she thought were her parents on medical advice to compensate for the death of their own, physically irreplaceable, son. She had her first period at school, didn't know what was happening, feared disease, and was told to take an aspirin and think about the Virgin Mary. And thirdly, perhaps not surprisingly, she created a scandal at school by refusing to believe in the Virgin Birth. Her adoptive parents were sent for and she was told to have faith.

At seventeen she wanted to go to a university, but was taken to Cyprus instead by a relative of her adoptive parents. She was not allowed to learn Greek, or to take a job there. She quarreled with the relative, returned to London and took work as a hotel receptionist. Her adoptive parents died, and she set to work to trace her true family. She found her grandmother first, herself the illegitimate daughter of an illegitimate woman; there hadn't been a marriage in the family for generations. The grandmother was not interested. Later she found her mother. This last door slammed in her face with a particularly horrible twist when she learned that her mother had put her away when she was three because she was pregnant again. She had preferred the unborn child to the child of .three, and had in fact brought the second child up.

Mary committed suicide at the age of thirty.

A staple of conversation among whores is the "kinkies." Until recently you could see the ads in Soho shop windows: Miss Du Sade; Miss Du Cane; Miss De Belting (Flagellation). Strict governess: Corrective Training; Corr. and Disc., (the sado-masochistic procedures in general). Miss Kiki This and Kiki That (anything). Lady's black mackintosh for sale. Boots, high-heeled shoes, plastic raincoats for sale (all with the girls inside them). Fifi or Froufrou gives French lessons; recently back from France, French and English conversation (which means *gamming,* from the French *gamahucher,* or *blowing,* or *plating,* or *noshing,* from the Yiddish *nosh,* to nibble, or eat between meals). . . .

The code for kinks is well known to those who need to know it; not many people apply to these girls for French lessons. The code for prostitution itself is more fluid, and it depends what medium is used for the ad. No London newspaper would take an ad for a photographic model, followed by her measurements, but many will take ads for fur coats, and that naturally means that the whore has to contend with a lot of people who really want fur coats. From time to time some paper or other will carry the biggest chestnut of them all: "Demolition agent for temporary erections," until a startled building contractor calls back.

The whole topic of unusual requirements, of perversions, or kinks, is a repulsive one to many people. When the "normal citizen" reads or hears kink stories he may be tempted to consider them as myths, as products of an inflamed imagination which keep on going the rounds out of some sort of unhealthy fascination, but which don't actually happen. Or he may think that all that is old hat; it is all in Krafft-Ebing, and that is where it should stay. But it is a determining condition of the whore's life that she is engaged day by day in enacting the myth, in living through the silly dream, in assuaging the unusual desire. These are not amazing, disgusting or funny stories to her; they are part of her day-to-day work, as real and as normal as dressing wounds is to a nurse; something for which she is paid, and in which she takes a wry pride.

Blowing generally counts as a kink, or a sort of semi-kink, and costs a bit extra. Some girls confine themselves to blowing when they have the curse. Others let the curse make no difference; they plug themselves up and bash right ahead, draining between clients.

> Well, as for kinkies, it depends on what I'm feeling like. If I'm feeling cheeky, all right, and good luck to them. But you can't do it every day. When I was working ——'s [a restaurant] the manager said to me one

night: "See that fellow over there? He's a member of parliament. Go and see what you can do for him." So I went over and he said: "Listen, have you got manacles and anklets?" I said: "No darling, but I can get them." So I arranged to meet him there a week that day. What he wanted me to do was manacle him and all and then drop candlegrease on his prick. Course I never did it. There he was next week, but I wasn't feeling the same, and I didn't even go over to him.

Beatings are usually a pound a stroke, either way.

Client came to me one night and offered me three quid for three. Fine, said I. So he got into the drag—had it with him in a suitcase, and for me too: black nylons and high wedge shoes and all. He said he was a servant girl called Millie and I was his mistress. They often want that. I had to say: "Where were you last night, Millie?" And he said he'd been out with a boy. And I had to say: "Now it was clearly understood between us when you came to work for me, Millie, that there was to be none of that." He was licking my shoes all the time. "And I think you deserve a beating, don't you, Millie?" "Oh yes, Madam, I do, I do." So then I gave him the three he'd paid for. But I don't know what it was; I was just feeling like it, I suppose, but I suddenly lost my temper, oh, not only with him, with everything and everybody. So I gave him four more and took another four quid off him and chucked him out. I really lit into him; he loved it. And yet people ask me why I like cats.

And then another time there was a client took me back to his place. I had to tie him up, you know all the girls have to know how to tie a bloke up to a chair properly. I did him really well, couldn't move an inch. And then I had to strap his prick up against his belly with elastoplast. I was feeling the same way that night, I suppose, because there was some elastoplast over so I put one piece across his mouth and another across his eyes. "There's for you, you bastard," I thought. "You asked to be strapped up, and you get strapped up." He'd told me earlier he had a cleaner come in every second morning. I hope she did, that's all I can say. That was two months ago.

Quite a common one is the client who gets the whore to dress up as a nurse, powder his bottom, put diapers on him and tuck him up with a bottle.

After all, every man has had his first orgasm somewhere or other, hasn't he? But most of them don't get like that. I often wonder about it. And what about women, anyhow?

I was taken back to his place by this bloke. And as soon as I got inside the door he gave me thirty pounds. Ah-ah, I thought; what's coming? But in those days thirty pounds was quite a lot—as a matter of fact it still is. He made me undress and sat me right across the room from him. I had to open my legs, and he took a lot of cream buns from a paper bag and threw them at me. Not a bad shot, he was, either, once he'd got his aim. Then he put marmalade on my breasts and stuffed iced cherries up my cunt and licked the whole lot off. It *was* embarrassing; I didn't know whether I was allowed to wash afterwards.

A variant of this from another girl.

> A client used to come to me quite regularly. I had to undress and stand with my arms above my head. He took six kippers—he had them in pairs wrapped in cellophane, you know the things—and threw them at me one by one. If one of them missed he came trotting across the room and picked it up and tried again. Afterwards there was a pine scented foambath waiting for me. He went back to South Africa in the end. I was quite sorry. I used to get fourteen pounds a time.

And again:

> A client took me back to his place, and as soon as I got in the door there was a dirty great coffin standing open. He put me in a white nightie with a rosary in one hand and a Bible in the other and a wreath of roses on my head. Then I had to lie down in the coffin. I thought: "Is this a gag to get my money?" But I had my bag in the coffin with me. Then he started nailing the lid down and all the time he was shouting out: "You're dead now, God damn you to hell." He'd told me his wife had died. He'd given me a big spanner to knock the lid up with, but I tell you I was wondering whether I'd ever get out again. I did though, and when I looked round he'd gone.

The Street Offences Act of 1959 cleared the girls off the London streets overnight, as it had been meant to. They went indoors into pubs and clubs, and on to the telephone. Some put up fluorescent red bell-pushes; some hustled by standing at open doors and windows. So much as a nose or a finger in the air space of the street was illegal. Some advertised in the press, and many in shop windows. One put up a neon sign saying: "French Lessons."

Before the Act, the penalty for soliciting in the streets had been two pounds. There was a working agreement with the police that it should not be exacted more than fortnightly, and often a girl could go six months or a year without being booked. There was sometimes a rota system, and the greatest grievance against the police was: "It's not my turn." The routine appearance In the Magistrate's Court and the routine branding as a "common prostitute" played some part in forming the underworld-like pseudo-criminal personality of the prostitute, but the fine itself was fiscal in effect, not punitive or deterrent.

The new Act raised the fine to thirty pounds, with prison on third conviction. Nevertheless, within a year the girls began to come back on the streets. They were forced to by the prosecution of the clubs they used, and of a magazine called *The Lady's Directory,* in which they published their telephone numbers. (The title took up that of a similar publication in the eighteenth century.) The £30 fine works both ways. The girls defend themselves in court, which they had not done against the £2 fine, and this means the policemen who book them have to spend a whole day there instead of half an hour. They, and their superiors, can think of better things for an undermanned police force to do, and so the girls are back on many of the streets. They simply come out later, and close the bargain with less haggling, so as to be less conspicuous.

Among the call girls, one is in a different world. Take the word *whore.* The street and club girls use it quite naturally. It is the simple, obvious word for what they are. The phrase, almost a signature tune, "whoring it along the Dilly" [Piccadilly] has a fine generous ring to it. An occasional highbrow whore who quotes Proust and keeps up with the sexual oddities of the eminent will use the word about herself with a conscious, open-eyed feeling, in the same way that Bernard Shaw used to call himself "an old entertainer." But the call girl uses it to imply all that she is not. She uses it as synonymous with *slack,* which is the call girl's word for a street girl.

> I don't look like one, do I? You wouldn't ever know, would you? Not ever? Would you? Would you?

The call girl is tremendously nice. The flat where she lives, and also her gaff where she works, if she has a separate place, are spotless; dusted, shiny, warm, welcoming. The taste will be contemporary, aware of fashion.

> The first thing you must realise is that I'm not a whore. I have my friends, but I don't take just anybody. Like for instance if a man rings up and says he's been given my number by so and so, I don't just leave it at that. I put him through it. When did you last see so and so? How was he? Where did you meet? Has he shaved his beard off? He said he was going to. Oh, there are all sorts of ways to find out if they're on the square. All right, then he comes round. Maybe I don't like the look of him. "Ooooh, I'm so sorry. It's really too bad. She's just gone out. Would you believe it; isn't that just too bad." And even afterwards, if I haven't liked him I tell him I'm going off the game, or I'm going away on holiday; he'd better not come again.

> You know, half my work's what we call social work. That is, say some friend of mine has someone come to London to visit his firm, and he gives him my number. I have connections with a lot of good firms. All right, he takes me out; dinner, a show, perhaps a party. I go down on his expense account, or something. It may lead to sex, it may not. Often it doesn't. I don't mind. In fact, I'm pleased.

Again:

> It's a hell of a life. You know, I imagine the slack is afraid of disease, and afraid of the sex maniac who thinks it'd be fun to strangle her. Well, that's not what we're afraid of. The trouble in this game is when you're afraid you're slipping. Some days you sit and sit by the telephone smoking and smoking, and nobody rings, and you think: "Look out, kid, you're slipping. What have I done? WHAT HAVE I DONE? Are they telling each other I'm no good?"

The London prostitute comes in all colors and sizes of temperament, but there is enough in common to make it worth saying something about the not so obvious ways in which she differs from other women. She has no sense of time, because her life is without routine. Time is divided into day and night and that's all. She has a sense of obligation, but it is shakier than other people's. It works in an immediate way, because she is used to payment on the spot. If she says she will meet you somewhere in half an hour, she will. Tomorrow, or next Tuesday, is another matter. If you take her to a public place, say a restaurant, she is a little awkward or embarrassed, or by contrast flamboyant, coming in and going out; everybody is looking at her, but can they tell? Once settled, she relaxes at once. She is an excellent listener; listening, next to fucking, is the thing she does most of. Her own favorite topics are the wealth and eminence of her clients, the sexual hypocrisy of our culture, king stories, money, clothes, interior decoration, bars, coffee bars, night clubs. She prefers the pageant of life to vicarious involvement through the arts, but she is blind to politics and the organization of society in general. She notices and comments on the women round her more than the men, partly because she is comparing herself to this mysterious competitor the wife, but often also out of straight Lesbian interest. She is probably a fairly heavy drinker. When she is watching her words and thinking what she should say next, she will tell you that she went on the game with a conscious decision, for the loot. She realized she was sitting on a fortune, and made up her mind. She continues on the game because it's interesting, and she's used to it.

When she is relaxed and talking without care or discretion, the picture changes. She is afraid, like all outlaws. She is afraid of disease. Few whores go to a doctor or a V.D. clinic for a regular check-up. On the other hand many seem to believe they are gifted with second sight about their clients' health.

> Well, I have a good look at him, and if he looks a bit poxy or anything, out he goes.

This particular bit of professional vanity often coexists with a perfectly sound knowledge of the fact that infectiousness is not related to visible signs. She is also afraid of infecting a client's wife, or even his unborn child, a running, uncheckable fear which she may allow to prey on her and to carry other guilts on its back. She is afraid of the sex maniac who may want to kill her; that is why she may keep a dog or, if she can afford it, a maid. If she has no ponce,[5] she may take care to live in a house where the neighbors will accept her and her occupation, then she can shout for them in an emergency. She is afraid of being nicked; however often it has happened (and Mrs. Wilkinson cites a Belgian woman who was arrested 219 times), the appearance at Marlborough Street or Bow Street is always a humiliation. Now, under the new Act, she is afraid of prison.

Above all, she is afraid of old age. The older whores will say quite simply: "There is no way out." The younger ones will keep their chins up and pretend to themselves they're not like the rest. Nobody ever went on the game for keeps.

> Of course I'm only in it for five years.
> For a few years.
> Until I'm bored with it.
> For five years.
> For five years. I've got it all worked out.
> Then I'll—
> Buy a shop.
> Go into partnership with a friend who has a garage.
> Buy house property and let rooms.
> Buy a coffee bar.
> Buy a restaurant.
> Club together with one or two other girls and buy a hotel.
> Get some old sucker to marry me.
> Put my savings into. Put my savings into.
> Put my savings into.

Not one in a hundred can save. The ability to save goes with a retentive personality, with foresight, caution, affective momentum, narrow affections. The whore is all on the surface, mercurial, shortsighted, chaotic, frigid.

What often happens is that they go on and on, into their fifties and even sixties. They pass downward into a class called the four-to-sixers, who go on the streets and into the joints before dawn, when the clients are so drunk they don't care what they're getting. Some become maids to younger women, which is probably the happiest conclusion. Then there is a saying, "End up drinking red biddy in the Docks."

The elderly whore, the old-timer, often has delusions of social grandeur. She has missed the few possible escape lines, and gets attached in a half-light of unreality to the idea of what she might have been. She cannot deny that she is a whore, so she may sideslip into denying that she is something else that she is. If she is Jewish, she may take pleasure in proving that she is not, and in looking down on the Jewish client. If she is poor she may try to prove that she is rich; if Irish, English; and, over and over again, if she is dark she will pretend to be fair. Conversely, she may try to prove that the innocent little woman in the flat above *is* a whore.

> One of these old-timers asked me to tea the other day. I went along, and there were just the two of us. She poured out the tea with her little finger crooked and told me how she'd been asked to Buckingham Palace.

> Afterwards she entertained me by playing Gounod's *Ave Maria* on the piano.

Some whores do get married, or set up what is meant to be a permanent liaison with a man. He may be a former client or not. If he does not even know his wife has been a whore, the situation is emotionally hopeless. If he does know, it may last, conceivably. But if a woman is capable of sustaining a regular relationship, why didn't she do it at first instead of going on the game? They usually come back, the ones who marry; not because of the attractions of whoring, but because the marriages don't work. When they do come back, they are naturally welcomed with open arms; their return justifies the others.

Consider what it is like for a whore to try to construct a marriage, even in favorable circumstances. Wherever they go together—street, pub, parties, job-hunting, home-hunting—the slightest flicker of interest, of attention, from some man brings back that which has to be forgotten. The man might simply be thinking: "Now where have I seen that girl before?" It might even have been waiting in a movie line. But she knows her husband does not know where it was. If anything goes wrong—some people who are coming to dinner cry off at the last moment, a job falls through—have they found out? There is no defense against the suspicion. Laughter at one's own groundless suspicions is the most mirthless there is.

All right, one may say: London is a great big easygoing metropolis, who cares? Why don't they publish and be damned? Surely so many people would be on their side. . . . But picture turning up at someone's house who *knows.*

> I shall probably be the first tart they've ever had in their house. They'll be so damned nice, they'll be curious, with that terrible curiosity of conscious liberalism. They only want to know. They'll observe my dress, my turns of speech, my gait.

That is what the whore who gets married has to face with other people. What she has to face in bed with her husband is easily imagined. It can be done, and it is done, but it's no wonder it is not often done.

The way off the game is feet first.

In 1959 a committee of inquiry chaired by Sir John Wolfenden reported on prostitution in Britain and recommended changes in the law. During the parliamentary debates on the Wolfenden Report, which did in fact lead to the new and more restrictive law, Mr. R. A. Butler, then Home Secretary, promised stiffer penalties against living on immoral earnings as a "consolation." It was not clear what for. Mr. Edwards, the Member for Stepney, a prostitute area, referred to ponces[6] as the "dirtiest, filthiest lot in creation." Another member spoke of "monarchs of the industry." Until 1948, ponces could be flogged. Whenever there is a discussion on prostitution in the press many people write saying this or that about the prostitutes, but end up: ". . . and reserve the really heavy penalties for the ruffians who batten on these unfortunate girls."

The very word *ponce* suggests *pounce;* fifty years ago ponces were called *bullies,* which sounds even fiercer. Try consulting your own feelings about the ponce. There he is, this unspeakably debased male, lurking in doorways and pouncing on his unsuspecting prey, tearing her hard-earned three pounds out of her pathetic clutch, and roaring away in his gangster-type limousine to the next girl, whom he threatens with a razor. He spends the night going round twenty or thirty of his hundred and fifty girls, or perhaps his section of the big syndicate administered by his super-boss, slashing his girls, doling out shots to the junkies, coshing a client or two, and squaring four or five detective inspectors. Toward dawn he goes, surrounded by henchmen, to the girl he has chosen for himself that night and, little recking that her flaccid flesh is still reeking from the forty or fifty slavering lechers who have been before him, enjoys her.

It is quite rare for a London prostitute to have a ponce at all. If she does, it is because she feels she needs someone to kick her out on the street at nightfall, to make sure she has the rent ready on rent day, to keep her off the bottle, to tell her what clothes she looks nice in and, perhaps most important of all, to help her see if she can't build up some sort of a sex life of her own.

The ponce in London today is usually neither more nor less than the whore's husband. He provides stability for her, a bit of discipline, someone to listen to her adventures. He fucks her as much for her sake as for his own, and takes trouble over it. He is also a gauge of her prestige. If she keeps him well in handmade shoes and black silk shirts, then her credit goes up among the whores, and his among the ponces.

"Mine's a good earner. Just look at this shirt."

Economically and in prestige values, he corresponds to the wife of the normal citizen, and the fact that he is living on her earnings and not she on his is only of secondary importance to either of them.

It often arises like this. A man is earning ten pounds a week, and he takes up with a girl who is earning a hundred. His self-respect may lead him to keep his own job for a bit, but then one day she is ill, or perhaps her child is ill, or she is picked up and he wants to go to court with her. He stays off work and loses his job. Their earnings drop from a hundred and ten to a hundred a week. So what the hell? He's a ponce: all right, so he's a ponce. There are plenty of others.

Mrs. Wilkinson published figures showing that about forty per cent of those *convicted* of poncing in England have also been convicted of other crimes. It cannot of course be known what proportion of ponces are never convicted either of poncing or of anything else. But the whore is herself usually a criminal—we make her one with our laws—and she develops a modified form of the criminal personality. It is not surprising that she takes up with others for company. Moreover, minorities against whom the majority discriminates will also seek each other out, and this is the main reason for the apparently disproportionate number of colored men among ponces in London.

> I used to live in Knightsbridge when I first went on the game. It was terrible. I didn't seem to be real; you know, it was as if nobody could see me. But since I moved over here among the colored people I'm—well, you know—I feel kind of at home. I don't have to pretend any more.

Some share a ponce with another whore, or even with two others, but this arrangement is exceptional in London. It does not arise because the ponce is able to subject two or three reluctant but silly women for his own gain; it arises because in the world of prostitution, as in all other minority worlds which are at once defined and discriminated against by the majority world, like the criminal world proper, the Negro world, the world of the arts and, in former days, the worse-off working class—in such worlds monogamy is not the rule. Add to this that in the world of prostitution chastity is by definition something which does not come in, and that many whores are at least a bit Lesbian, and the multiple ponce becomes comprehensible.

Then there are the call house madams, or switch-bawds. These, in London, are women with a two or three-bedroom flat, and a list of twenty or thirty telephone numbers. The client gives his order; she calls the most suitable girl, he meets her at the flat. He pays the madam, and the madam passes on a proportion—always alleged by the girls to be too low—to the girl. Or she allows the client to go to the girl's flat, and the girl passes on the rake-off. The call house madam is of course just as criminal as the male ponce, but society is not somehow so angry with her. After all, she's a woman, she's probably a superannuated whore herself, and women are never so frightening anyhow.

There has only been one large organization in London since the war, the famous Messina Organization. I cannot vouch for the truth of the following account of it, but it is what is generally believed among the whores.

The five Messina brothers used to buy the best girls out of the, then legal, brothels in France, Belgium and Italy for a down sum, marry them to sailors for fifty pounds, and bring them to London. This was, of course, a white slave traffic, and sounds terrible. But for the girls themselves it was a merciful deliverance. In the closed houses of the Continent, they would be taking fifty men a day and getting anything down to twenty cents a go for it. How they got there is another matter, but once there, there is no doubt that the Messina brothers were so many St. Georges. To come to London was the dream of all of them. In London they were set up two by two in shared flats and provided with "gaffs" (apartments) elsewhere to work in. They were run on Service lines. They paid over their entire earnings each week, and were given spending money. What was left of the earnings after the organization rake-off was then banked for them in a deposit account. They were supplied with an issue of the most destructible clothing, nylons and so on, and with food, and a bottle of wine a day would be sent to their living flats. One of the brothers or their agents would inspect their pitch nightly to see that standards of dress were satisfactory. Other girls who reached this standard were allowed to pitch there too, but anybody who did not was rushed off by the Messina girls themselves. If any girl earned outstandingly well she was given a bonus, typically a mink coat. Medical inspection was provided weekly and hospital treatment when necessary. They were given a return ticket home each year, but, naturally, were not allowed to take any of their savings with them. When they were finally judged unemployable, their savings were released to them and they were sent home. If a girl wanted to get off the game while she was still employable, it was made extremely difficult for her, but she could do it at the expense of a large proportion of her savings. The Messinas would never have English girls in the organization, and the English girls looked at it all between envy and contempt. Envy for the safety and regularity, contempt for the discipline and spoon-feeding; the same mixed feelings that they have for the idea of licensed brothels. The brothers were mostly imprisoned or deported in 1951, but a remnant of their girls remained for some years Their price dropped from five pounds to three, and badly dressed slacks were no longer hustled off.

Apart from this, allegations in London that so and so is "running a string of girls," generally turn out to mean only that he gives them a cut rate on his string of taxis, or lets rooms to them, but in no sense controls them.

So why then are we so hot against the ponce? To begin an answer to this, we must first ask what we feel about the whore herself. We are all in touch with her, or in touch with her image in our own minds. She has been around for millennia. Every man has thought of going to her, even if he hasn't been. Every woman has thought of her husband or her son going to her. It is enough to ask yourself if you're a man, or your closest man if you're a woman, under what circumstances you would go to her. You go to her when you want a fuck. But if there was a woman by you who loved you and was going to come when you came, you could not possibly go to a whore. Even if there was a woman by you who did not love you, but was still going to come, out of animal spirits and general good will, you could not go to a whore. Even if she was a complete stranger, at a party say, and you didn't know whether it was going to be a good lay or not, you still could not prefer a whore, because if you did you would be paying for the certainty of pretense instead of taking the chance of reality free. By now we are pretty low down the scale, if a complete stranger at a party, whom you think about in terms of "a good lay" is still preferable; we are pretty far away from love. Perhaps the only circumstance in which a man who has experienced love, or even a casual fuck in friendship, could go to a whore would be if he was completely alone in a strange city and had the most terrible stone-ache, like millions of men every day, on military service or traveling one way or another.

So who does go, apart from soldiers and travelers? Kinkies, first. Men who can only come if they're allowed to dress up as this or that, or use the cat, or throw cream buns about; men who have associated the experience of orgasm with something which most people find irrelevant to it. If any moralist wanted to reduce prostitution and the flagellation market in England he could do it by breaking the chain of corporal punishment in the schools. Kicks are infectious; if the teacher likes it, the child will too.

Then the physically deformed; not directly because they are deformed, but because the shyness born of deformity may prevent them ever learning the experience of love. If the whore has a useful social function, as many people say she has, it is with the kinkies and the deformed.

> If I have a hunchbacked client, I always keep my eyes on his face while he's undressing. I can't look at his hump, and I can't look away from him; he'd notice it at once and feel it. I keep my eyes fixed on his. I had one the other day, and we turned the light out. Afterwards he said: "Would you mind not turning the light on?" I said: "Of course not, darling. I never do." He said, as quick as lightning: "Why's that?" I said, "I don't like it. I always like to get at least into my bra and pants first."

> I had one with an amputated leg, too. There he was unstrapping his wooden leg; I kept my eyes on his face, in the same way. Can you imagine what it's like to feel a man's stump going against your thigh? I don't know what I felt. I think I loved him, or something. I tell you, it takes it out of you.

Then there are the men who want to avoid trouble and complication, who simply want the "sneeze in the loins" without any responsibility, emotional contact, give-and-take, or indeed any involvement whatever; the duckers.

> They know *I'm* not going to ring up and tell them I'm lonely, or write them long letters or go whining to them with this or that.

Lastly there are all the men, all the millions of men in England and America, who feel that sex is something apart from the society they live in, and wrong. They may be simply burning for a blow, or to do it dog-fashion, and daren't turn their wives round. They may be unmarried, and terrified by the thought of having a girl friend. They may never have found out that women come too. All these will end up with the whores, because they have been twisted out of sight of their own natures by the society they grew up in. If once you get to believe it's dirty, regrettable, unmentionable, something you wish to spare a refined woman, then there's not much reason why you shouldn't buy it. And if you've never found out that women come, you may find the whore's pretense of coming quite irresistible, and it may make you feel a hell of a fellow. She hopes it will.

And so back to the ponce. The whore has done her little turn, and you have paid her for it. It probably does not cross your mind that you could have something ten times as good with a real girl if you got up and took it, so you don't worry too much about the money. But the thought that the first thing she does when your back is turned is to hand the money over to someone else, and that someone else a man, and that man fucking her for free, and for all you know sneering with her at your peculiarities—why, it's absolutely revolting. It makes you bust with rage. If ever you laid hands on such a man, you'd beat the life out of him, because he is living proof that what you've had was counterfeit. He is your disillusionment. Into prison with him, and let the illusions flourish. And if two years isn't enough, let him have seven, and that will be some consolation to us all.

In unpublished evidence for the Wolfenden Committee, Mrs. Wilkinson wrote (and kindly allows me to quote):

> The society formed by prostitutes and their associates, though not hereditary, is continuous; it has a fairly permanent structure and composition. It exists because it absorbs asocial or antisocial personalities; it is economically dependent on the expression of an antisocial tendency in members of ordinary society. Its cohesion is strengthened by the attitudes of the general public towards the prostitute, her guilt feelings which prevent her return to ordinary life by causing her to exaggerate and anticipate critical attitudes towards her, and by attitudes within the society itself towards its members who try to break away.

The whore world is like a little gearwheel meshing with a big one; it goes round faster, and in the opposite direction. You could see it until recently on the pavements of Piccadilly; the whores standing still and the men pouring past, looking, considering, pausing to haggle, passing on to the next. The countersociety or underworld, like the society or overworld from which it is excluded, is classridden, intolerant, but free from oppression. As to the rest of us, we cherish and pay it with one hand and belabor it with the other. That's how it gets as it is. When we cherish the whore, she feels like a necessary safety valve, warm, trustworthy and useful. When we belabor her, she feels like a criminal.

> If that's how it is, I thought, I'll bloody well live up to the image—I'll buy a Rolls and get a Nubian chauffeur in a leopard-skin jockstrap and hustle with all the lights on and a cigarette-holder a mile long. And three Afghan wolfhounds on golden leashes trotting behind. And scythes on the wheels.

The overworld views the whore as a social problem or a social service, according to the amount of use it makes of her. The whore judges the overworld by what she sees. First, she sees the client, whom she holds in contempt for his gullibility and in respect for his purse. Through him she sees his wife who, he inevitably tells her, is cold. To the English whore, England is a country of women as frigid as she is, or more so, but who don't even try to pretend.

> Ask me, the only difference between me and some of these wives is that they don't keep the bargain and I do.

The overworld and the underworld depend on each other, their characters are complementary, and yet ignorance prevails. If it did not, the two worlds would probably fuse, and that would be an end of prostitution. The ignorance itself is preserved by the fear, and the fear is the result of the exclusion of fucking from the realm of the normal. The whore incarnates the Extruded.

I headed this chapter with the whore's catchphrase to sum up her feelings about other women; her bewilderment that they are not whores like her. Let us conclude with a remark made by a girl who had grown up in a prostitute district of London, and who had been much solicited to go on the game because of her looks. To her friends who were whores and ponces, she was "sitting on a fortune." But her answer was: "I don't see how you can, not if you know what love is."

NOTES

1 Oxford University Press, 1947.
2 *The Commentaries of Pius II,* "Memoirs of a Renaissance Pope," London, 1960 (New York, 1961), p. 35.
3 *La Retorica delle Puttane,* Cambrai, 1642, pp. 115–116.
4 London, 1955.
5 See note 6 below.
6 In England a distinction is made between the *ponce* who runs the girl's life in general, and the much rarer *pimp* who actively solicits men to go to her. In America the word *pimp* covers both classes. Perhaps the American *sweet daddy* is the closest to British ponce, but it is more colloquial.

part three
homosexual styles and ways of deviance

6 | The Dynamics of Prison Homosexuality: The Character of the Love Affair |
David A. Ward and Gene G. Kassebaum

Criminologists have learned in recent years that homosexuality is the rule rather than the exception in prisons. Homosexuality in prisons is a situational form of behavior for the vast majority of the prisoners who take part in it. Relatively few of the prisoners are homosexuals in the outside world and all prisoners make a clear distinction between those who are homosexuals by general preference—that is, regardless of the situation—and those who are homosexuals only because of the situational pressures. This is a very important moral distinction and they treat individuals of different types in very different ways.

Situational homosexuality is a clear indication of the ways in which social situations created by the larger, more powerful society create deviance as defined by that larger society. Certainly American society in general did not intend to create this form of homosexuality and, indeed, most members of our society are still not aware that it is a common practice in prisons. Yet, by creating prisons, putting people in prison for various crimes, and preventing prisoners from having normal heterosexual relations (as is often possible in other Western societies), American society did produce a situation in which homosexuality was almost inevitable. Since homosexuality is itself a crime, we can see that in this case the members of the society in general have responded to crime in such a way as to produce another crime. This resulting behavior is what Lemert and other sociologists have called secondary deviance.

There is general consensus among staff and inmates that homosexual affairs generated in prison are temporary and situational.[1] The distinction between jailhouse turnouts and *true* homosexuals suggests that the prospects for continuing a prison affair in the free world are not good. The recognition of the temporary nature of prison homosexuality is especially problematic for butches who have made a more definite and dramatic commitment to homosexuality. They cannot count on holding the affection of the femme,* not only because of separation by staff or parole, but also because femme jailhouse turnouts do not have a long-term commitment to the gay life. This lack of commitment is a major source of internal strain in institutional love affairs and it results in the use of mechanisms of self-protection which give many of the love affairs the character of a contest in which the affectional commitment of femmes is subjected to several kinds of testing. These tests are principally employed by butches who because of their greater invest-ment in homosexuality as a way of life must insure themselves against the short-lived and unstable character of prison love affairs. Both the exploitation of femmes for material goods and housekeeping services and *giving up the work* help keep the butch in control of her own emotional involvement and the course of her love affair.

I Love You for Commissary Reasons

A pattern reported in several accounts of life in women's prisons [and alluded to in the previous chapter] involves the practice whereby butches exact tribute in the form of goods and services as manifesta-tions of the love and loyalty of their femmes.[2] In addition to the practice of gift-giving used by femmes to gain the initial attention and interest of a butch, many butches use gifts in the process of rushing new inmates. However, the effort of these butches is to secure the affection of these femmes and then demand tribute in terms of goods and services in exchange for assurances that they [the butches] will not *play* with any other femme. Such demands are described by a femme in the following review of her relationship to the butch who turned her out:

> She played with other girls. She told me if I had been with another girl she wouldn't have been interested in me . . . If you don't buy them [butches] cigarettes they won't play. She said, "If you don't buy them, somebody else will—you don't want that do you?" She asked me to *be with* [become homosexually involved] another girl to get pills—the girl worked in the hospital. She asked me to play up to this girl to any point and I told her [the girl] that my friend and I were broken up. As soon as I got the pills I handed them to my friend. I was so happy just to see the smile on her face.

* [Ed. note: A "butch" is a lesbian who plays the role of the male in a sexual relationship. A "femme" is a lesbian who plays the role of the female.]

This girl also reported that to demonstrate her willingness to get scarce items to please her lover she prevailed upon her brother-in-law to bring benzedrine into the prison when he visited her.

The butch appears to be strongly motivated to enhance the control and asymmetry of the relationship to prevent exploitation of her own emotional involvement. In either case, whether she is sought by a femme or whether she initiates the affair, the butch is the recipient of material goods and housekeeping services.

Giving Up the Work

Another mechanism of self protection is evident in the actual sexual relationship between some butches and femmes. Our interviewees indicated that in about one-third of the homosexual relationships at Frontera the butch refuses to let the femme touch her or reciprocate sexually. Some butches remain completely clothed during such sexual activity. This would appear not only to maintain the facade of masculinity that non-feminine dress affords, but also, of course, to conceal distinguishing female sex characteristics. The role of the femme in these cases is one of complete passivity while the butch *gives work,* i.e., engages in cunnilingus (referred to as *giving some head*), manual manipulation of the clitoris, and breast fondling. While the butch gives work, the denial of sexual gratification for herself is called *giving up the work.* Giving up the work calls for a number of adjustments and accommodations between the partners as to role responsibilities, as indicated in the following statement by one femme jailhouse turnout:

> **Q:** Can you tell me about "giving up the work?"
>
> **A:** You mean definition? Well, that means who's gonna do who. I mean, which one of you are going to commit the sexual act on the other one. Well, it's usually the one that's the aggressor and doing the love-making, is the one that's giving up the work. [Note the butch is *giving* work at the same time she is giving *up* reciprocal sexual interaction.] The other one isn't giving up anything, she's receiving. It usually refers to the stud broad and usually the stud broad will be very modest and strict about who knows if she's been receiving any work or not.
>
> **Q:** Why do you think that is?
>
> **A:** Well, I guess it's because it's kind of publicly giving up a little of her masculinity. She doesn't like to do this, you know. Like, say if it was me and my friend—if I was giving her some work too, she wouldn't want me to tell anybody about it because she prefers to be masculine. You can tell this by her appearance.
>
> **Q:** Does this suggest that in playing the masculine role they feel that men do not receive satisfaction?
>
> **A:** No, I think it's more that they realize a woman is satisfied by a man, as a rule, this is the natural rule, and that they want to satisfy you as

much as a man would, if not more. They want to get this certain edge over you, this certain control over you. But being aware in the back of their minds that they're a woman too, they know that it's just as possible for you to get control over them, and I think that they fight this more than they misunderstand what a man gains from the sexual act, because in their minds their main goal is to satisfy and control you—keep you.

Q: And do you think by participating their control is lessened?

A: Yeah. There's a chance that they might end up being controlled instead, and it has happened. It's happened to me. This one particular girl, I guess it was a challenge because she'd never been touched, they just call them the "untouchables." And so I just started this little mental game with her and it wasn't so much a desire for her because I didn't love her, it was just that I wanted to prove she was a woman as much as I was. Since I knew she was trying to control me but never would, I wanted to see if I could control her instead, kind of turn the tables on her and then tell her about herself. I don't know why, I guess because I'm evil in some ways or something, but this was my game at the time.

Q: In your own relationship now, do you feel that you have the control you talk about, or is there reciprocity in sexual activities?

A: No. She has the control. She has the control mainly because I've given it to her. This is true. I've let her know me, my weaknesses and my ways, and this has given her control over me, but I've been aware that this control is there but I want this control from her and I like the way she controls me because I know it's not for selfishness.

The butch partner of the respondent quoted above was interviewed on the same day and asked to describe her reasons for wishing to have a relationship characterized by giving up the work:

Q: You said you want to be protective and you want to be aggressive and that one of the things the butch wants to do is to be aggressive sexually but not have it returned. Is giving up the work the usual way on the streets as well as in here?

A: Yeah, it's the usual. Well, for me it's the usual. Most of your butches are the same way. They enjoy making love to somebody but they don't especially want somebody making love to them. But after they've been together for a while then usually it's returned, but it's after you've grown to trust somebody and love somebody and want to please them too. But when I make love to a girl that's all I want to do—I just want to make love to her and I don't want it returned—at all.

Q: Why is that? Why is it, do you think, that many of the girls don't want it returned?

A: In myself—the only desire I have is to make love and not have love made to me. I don't feel the need for it or the desire for it. The desire for it can be aroused and has been—I'm not saying that a girl hasn't made love to me—but it's very few and far between that I want somebody to make love to me. I want to do the work, and that's the way I get my pleasure, by making love to her, a woman. When I make love to a woman I like the power of being able to satisfy her. It gives me a good feeling to know that she responds to me and that I can satisfy her desires. And this is where I get my enjoyment. I feel a sense of power. Maybe this isn't right, but this is what I feel. This is what most of the other butches feel. When I refer to the butches I mean my friends on the streets because they're the only real butches that I know. But this is what they want—to satisfy a woman—this is their main worry. And I guess if I couldn't satisfy her when I made love to her it would hurt me—I like being gentle. I don't want her to do any of the work.

Q: When you talk about satisfaction for yourself, is this satisfaction in terms of orgasm, or is it satisfaction in other terms?

A: It's a satisfaction more or less mentally, and not really—it's a physical satisfaction but merely because I know I've done a good job, or I hope I have, and I'm satisfied with knowing that I've pleased her and I'm just relaxed through the whole act. Otherwise, no, I don't reach a climax. I have, but it's very seldom that I do. I don't lose myself that much, I don't like to lose that much control. I like to keep my mind as clear as I can so I'm aware of exactly what I'm doing, and I'm aware of my timing, and I'm aware of the girl—if she's responsive at a certain time then I know that's what she likes, and then if she's not responding then I can do something else. Where, if I was just lost in passion I don't recognize any of these things, and I don't feel that I would satisfy her as fully as if I didn't lose myself all that much and kept concentrating on her, watching her—that's what I do. And then when the act is over I'm tired and that tiredness brings on a satisfaction in itself. And it gives me a form of release, the tension sort of releases after I've made love to somebody. But I don't reach a climax —not generally. I have, but—well, I have real strong desires for women, it's not—there's no other desires for men or anything like that. I don't know, I've talked to a lot of butches, and they say, "Yeah, I reach a climax," and I talk to other butches and they're the same way that I am. They don't really reach a climax but they're satisfied all the same. And then there's a lot of butches that just— "Yeah, I want my old lady to make love to me too, then I reach a climax." I guess there's all kinds of different ways of doing it, but that's my way.

Q: You suggested that it's frequent that after you've been with somebody a while, I think you used the word "trust," then you ask for the tables to be turned, so to speak.

A: Well, usually *they'll* ask for it.

Q: Has that been your own experience or that of other girls that you know who have had a more lasting relationship with a girl?

A: Yes. Well, all my friends that I know on the streets that have had a more or less lasting relationship—anything over two years to me is lasting—and their women will make love to them and they'll enjoy it, or even if they don't enjoy it they'll do it because they love the girl and the girl wants to do it. This was my case. When I was with this girl for about three of four years, she wanted to make love to me merely because it was a challenge. I didn't want her to, but then after she made love to me—she would every once in a while want to make love to me—and I'd let her if she wanted to.

Q: It wasn't what you wanted but what she wanted—is that it?

A: Yes, more or less, yes. I loved her, so I let her. But it's not something that I really want. All my desires are for making love *to* somebody, not to have love made to me.

Some femmes, however, become dissatisfied at what they view as the butches' taking unfair advantage in the relationship due to their refusal to permit reciprocal sexual behavior. In the following, a femme jail-house turnout calls into question the degree of involvement of the butch and indicates that she is well aware of the tactics and emotions that are involved in *giving up the work:*

> **A:** The code that a lot of the butch broads stand by, a few of them any-way, is that they are always the aggressor, never the receiver. This puts them in a pretty nice position because this means that if I'm with a butch broad I never get to her, she's never weak, I never break her down by this physical thing at all. So, therefore she's strong all the time. She's always irritable, she's always the man. It's just a big front as far as I'm concerned. But I can see why they do this. This is something that took me a long time to figure out. They won't con-cede this. All the butch broads who say that they never do this— why, they wouldn't even think of letting their people work on them or "give them any work" is the term. But this is what's behind it.
>
> **Q:** You're saying then that they are getting physical satisfaction and not letting themselves become emotionally involved with a femme?
>
> **A:** No, they don't even receive physical satisfaction. They just give, that's all. But, as a receiver, as the femme, I would never be allowed to do anything like this. So naturally this is a thing of human nature. If you and I don't have anything intimate going or if the intimate thing is only one-sided, man, of course I'm more involved than you are. It's just an obvious thing to me. But they maintain that this is a matter of strength, just a principle they live by, which is baloney.
>
> **Q:** Are you saying then that, for example, they don't allow themselves to be caressed?
>
> **A:** Yes.
>
> **Q:** Then the femme really has to be passive?
>
> **A:** Oh yes, and I don't go for this type of affair at all. I didn't have this type of affair. And I don't think I'd hold still for it a minute because there's something in the relationship that I would have to fear then. You've got this—why do you need this strength to hold it over me? Probably it means you're going to do some hurting of me in the end, so no, I couldn't go along with anything like that, but there're a lot of people who do. And at the same time there are a lot of femmes who do not want to. It's repulsive to them, to have anything physical to do with another woman, but they're perfectly willing to be the receiver.
>
> **Q:** Then they ought to fit in pretty well with the butches?
>
> **A:** Yes. Damn near an ideal setup, in many respects. I have a good friend, another one, she's never turned out. She's had eyes for this one girl for a long time, but she won't have anything to do with the girl because all this time she thought that she would have to do something along the physical sense. She finally found out that she didn't—why she's been dismally disappointed because she's wasted all this time when she could have physical satisfaction and not have to do anything. It's somewhat like turning a trick, I guess, in a way.

While there are apparent similarities between a prostitute receiving the attentions of a customer and a femme receiving a butch who gives work, there are major differences implicit in the rationale for the latter. The male customer of the prostitute, while an active sex partner and to some degree the aggressor, is not viewed as being in danger of becoming emotionally involved with her. The action of the active and aggressive butch, however, is specifically directed toward preventing herself from becoming more deeply attached to her partner. For many women who assume the butch role because they were unsuccessful in heterosexual relationships, there is the danger of becoming emotionally involved and then rejected again by femmes who are promiscuous or who want only a temporary substitute for a man. The passive sexual role played by the femme is similar to that of the prostitute except that the primary object of this activity for the femme is *her* sexual satisfaction. Participation in this non-reciprocating role may be the basis for the charge by butches and nonhomosexuals that many femmes are promiscuous or *chippy around*.

The attitude of the butch, however, is not a peculiar or distinctive one in love affairs. In describing heterosexual affairs Waller and Hill have described individuals who

> . . . treat every courtship as tentative, and often attempt to remain mentally ready to accept its disruption; they want to be prepared to save face when the break occurs and to have the means of rationalizing the shock to their own egos. Therefore, they commonly hide the extent of their own involvement from themselves and others in order that they may not suffer too keenly from a severance of the relation. They try not to show jealousy; they feign indifference until the other is committed.[3]

It is thus evident that giving up the work can be a safety device in which the butch maintains distance from someone who might reject her.

The need for this protection is often acute and of conscious concern. We interviewed a severely masculine-appearing butch who had been recently hurt by a break-up with her femme. She claimed that she did not want to be "touched" by anyone, male or female, and said she did not want sexual reciprocity. That this was not an entirely natural demeanor was suggested by her further comment, however, that "you've really got to hold back, you can't let yourself go." Giving up the work for her was clearly a protective device but one that required considerable will power on her part. She concluded by saying that the one thing she wanted was a baby because "a baby can be called your own." She felt she could only count on a completely dependent person as a secure love-object.[4]

In practice, for most of those affairs where giving up the work is operative, it seems to characterize the beginning or courtship stage of the relationship. Presuming that there is mutual attraction to begin with, it seems to be difficult to have such intimate contact without, over time, developing more intense affectional ties. Since the trial period may serve to more deeply involve the femme, giving work can be an effective means of total seduction in which the femme who is resistant or feeling guilty is brought along slowly. (An important piece of homosexual folklore in this regard is that the femme will never leave the woman who has turned her out.)

Therefore, in many cases the major test of affectional commitment comes when the butch asks the femme to reciprocate sexually. In some cases the femme wishes to take the role of an active sexual partner and the opportunity for her to give work consummates the union. In other cases, an affair is ended, as is described below, when the femme refuses to actively participate in sexual interaction:

> **Q:** Is the phenomenon of giving up the work something that you've heard discussed or that you know about?
>
> **A:** Like I said, with the two people that I know—I've heard them talk, and they talk very freely about their sexual activities. One in particular has said, "Even on the streets I will never undress in front of my old lady [her femme]—she'll never lay a hand on me." And some that give the work themselves they also like it in return. Not all the time, just when the mood hits them. And *then* is when they turn out the little femme that has never done it before. Say this butch started going with a girl that had never played before—and usually they like this best, because it's a challenge to them to win them over to their side. So, she makes it with the little girl and she makes mad, passionate love to her. Now the girl is madly in love with her and will do anything for her. She's known on the campus, this butch being her people. Now she's got a name, she's got a reputation, she's got a place in the community, she's one of the few that are really together and she doesn't want to let go of this easily, and she won't. She'll fight for it if necessary. But one day, if the butch happens to be this kind, like the kind that was a prostitute, at times she pulled this on my friend— my friend was telling me how she worked up to it. She said, "You know it's not very often that I want anybody to make love to me, but I love you so much that I want you to." And the girl went around for days like in a daze—she didn't know what to do, didn't want to lose her, but she didn't want to do it either. She didn't mind receiving it and then the little butch threw this up to her. She said, "You would let me do it but then you don't love me enough to do it to me." And the girl was frantic, so another girl and myself talked to her and said she should just try staying away from her for a week because if she loved you she would be content with the way things are. "How come she didn't tell you this in the first place?" So anyway, it went on and on and on—many hassles and scenes and loud talking So finally, the girl says, "I just can't, I'm sorry. If that ends our relationship, it just ends it." And it ended it, right there. But then there are some that this doesn't end it, because they reciprocate.

Enough women refuse to participate in reciprocal sexuality to confirm the fears of their partners and the testing process continues.

The behavior of butches, generally speaking, in regard to giving up the work and the apparent exploitation of femmes for material goods should be viewed as defenses against deep emotional involvement and subsequent loss of the affection of these women as they leave prison. It can be seen that the butch goes through a series of steps by which she seeks to protect herself. She picks a new inmate who is likely to be lonely and thus receptive. She tries to take advantage of the emotional attachment which accompanies sexual involvement. She refuses to let the femme reciprocate physically in order to keep the femme from affecting her emotionally. The initial period during which the femme remains passive in sexual relations serves the important function of screening out women who are *chippying*. As one butch said: "You check them out, to see if she's gonna stay."

Giving up the work literally means keeping someone at arm's length. The lack of involvement it symbolizes is functional for the butch in protecting her self-image as the power holder of the relationship and in preventing the pain of loss if her femme is really only playing.

Prison love affairs then, like new heterosexual affairs, are subject to internal strain as the partners subtly seek to control their own emotional commitment and thus the direction of the relationship. The questions of power and dependency seem to be especially important in homosexuality where, for one partner at least (the butch), the dominant role is a new and unfamiliar one. In discussing masculine aspirations in women, Ovesey has asserted that the relative strength of the motivations of dependency and power determine the configuration of the homosexual relationship. The power motivation leads to a dramatization of masculinity and the "husband" role, and dependency motivation underlies the assumption of the "wife" role.[5]

While power-dependency motivation may operate in disposing women to play one or another homosexual role, it is clear that the question of power, in terms of controlling the course of the relationship, is explicitly recognized by participants. In the terms of our respondents, control of the relationship means that one partner attempts to get a greater emotional commitment from her partner than she gives to the relationship. The purpose is twofold. The dominant member makes an effort to restrict her own commitment in the event that her partner is only temporarily or spuriously involved and at the same time she tries to elicit greater emotional commitment from the partner. Matters of power and control are overemphasized for the role requiring extensive overt manifestations—the pseudo-masculine role.

In some cases the femme is in fact exploiting the butch by receiving sexual favors until she is asked to reciprocate and "go all the way" herself. Women experiencing considerable guilt over the source of their sexual satisfactions are especially likely to refuse such requests which symbolize to them the assumption of a homosexual role. The attitude of these femmes is similar to that of the young male delinquents studied by Reiss who permit male adults to perform fellatio on them but who do not think of themselves as homosexual. The boys define themselves and each other not on the basis of homosexual behavior per se, but on the basis of non-participation in the role which is perceived as the homosexual role, that of the fellator.[6] It should also be noted that a similar self-conception is held by tough adult male prisoners who permit effeminate homosexuals to perform fellatio on them or on whom they commit sodomy.

At this point a number of differences between patterns of homosexuality among male and among female prison inmates can be discerned and these differences again suggest the significance of latent social identities and pre-prison experiences in accounting for prison behavior.

Patterns of Homosexuality Among Male and Female Prisoners

There are several apparent differences between homosexuality in prisons for men and women. For one thing, no inmate at Frontera reported, nor was there any other evidence of, any inmate (or group of inmates) using physical force to exact sexual favors from another. In most men's prisons the use of physical coercion, although infrequent, is not unknown. For example, at a federal correctional institution for young men studied by one of the authors, new inmates were pressured to become sexual partners who play a role similar to the femme, called the *kid.* If the new inmate does not immediately demonstrate his masculine self-image by fighting, the pressure continues until he either takes a stand or succumbs. In some instances, new inmates are forcibly sodomized by several other inmates.

Another aspect which appears to differ between men and women is the use of sexual favors as a means of discharging debts. In a state prison for men, we observed the following exchange between an inmate who had tried to escape from the prison and a staff member, who was aware that the inmate had a growing indebtedness. The debt started with four cartons of cigarettes and had grown to thirty cartons through high interest:

> **Staff member:** You're never gonna get away from those guys. I wish we could promise you that everything would be okay if you told us who is bothering you, but we can't. The debt will probably follow you to [another state prison]. Has anyone asked you to bend over yet?
> **Inmate:** No.
> **Staff member:** It won't be long before you'll be grabbing your ankles over this debt.

Later the inmate admitted he had been pressured to *punk* and that is one of the reasons that he wanted to escape—". . . not just to avoid payment of debt, but to avoid homosexual pressure."

It has been observed in a number of penitentiaries housing long-term, recidivistic male inmates that some *wolves* (the masculine homosexual role corresponding to the female butch) ply the prospective *punk, kid* or *lamb* (the male counterpart of femme) with gifts and favors over periods as long as a year before making the demand for a payoff in terms of sexual favors.

There was no report at Frontera of inmates being coerced into paying off debts with sexual favors. The limited gambling and merchandising of contraband found in the women's prison does not make for indebtedness that is sanctioned by force. Sexual favors are occasionally used at Frontera by butches to gain some scarce or desirable material goods, but most transactions with femmes involve an exchange of commissary items for continued interest and loyalty, not sex. The role of material goods in homosexual affairs at the women's prison is similar to that in the men's prison in at least two respects: (1) in the beginning of a relationship goods may be used in the process of seducing homosexually uninitiated inmates, and (2) when the inmate is committed and indebted to the seducer, goods can be demanded as the price of loyalty. However, if such goods are not forthcoming in the women's prison the dominant partner threatens to withdraw affection, not impose physical punishment. Particularly in the cases when the femme is not *giving work* she must substitute material goods and personal services for sexual reciprocity in an effort to make the relationship continually rewarding for the butch. The male *punk,* however, often gives goods to appease inmates threatening physical abuse. Butches accumulate material goods because they constitute symbols of their status as desirable affectional objects and persons in command of the relationship. The male *wolf* accumulates material goods because they are status symbols of wealth and power.

Some male prisoners do fall in love with each other and some women like to accumulate material goods, but in the main, the roles played by males and females in the larger society make themselves manifest in the character of homosexual relationships in the prisons of either sex. Men in prison are more concerned with material goods as a medium of exchange, more likely to impose physical sanctions, and more often represent the significance of the homosexual relationship in terms of physical satisfaction.[7] The women are more concerned with sexual relationships which are seen as symbolic of affectional ties. Few women are in homosexuality, so to speak, for the money. As we have noted, there are relationships among the women in which only one participant derives sexual satisfaction; but even in these relationships the partners are intimately bound up with the emotional needs of each other.

Unlike most male prison wolves and the young delinquents described by Reiss, the majority of female jailhouse turnouts have genuine love affairs with their sexual partners, and have repeated contact with the same person.

The importance of the emotional component of homosexual relationships is a fundamental distinction between the self-image and role behavior of butches and wolves. These distinctions are apparent in Sykes' description of the wolf:

> The stress on the "masculinity" of the *wolf's* role is reinforced by the fact that many inmates believe his part in a homosexual relationship to be little more than a search for a casual, mechanical act of physical release. Unmoved by love, indifferent to the emotions of the partner he has coerced, bribed, or seduced into a liaison, the *wolf* is often viewed as simply masturbating with another person. By this stripping the *wolf* of any aura of "softness," of sentiment or affection, his homosexuality loses much of the taint of effeminacy which homosexuality often carries in the free community. His perversion is a form of rape and his victim happens to be a man rather than a woman, due to the force of circumstances.[8]

Although the butch plays a role similar to the wolf, unlike the latter she does not receive sexual satisfaction, and while the action of butches and wolves is designed to inhibit the emotional involvement, the butch, unlike the wolf, defines herself as homosexual.

Among women one did not hear of homosexuals being kept as punks by an inmate who considered herself heterosexual. In men's prisons this is often the self-definition of the inmate who obtains occasional sexual release through fellatio or sodomy with a punk or *queen* whom he rejects as an object of legitimate emotional and sexual attention. The wolf disclaims emotional involvement because it conflicts with his masculine self-image rather than because he fears losing the affection of his homosexual partner.

The homosexual pairings of both male and female prisoners are unstable for similar reasons such as staff intervention, parole of one partner, and the lower degree of commitment to homosexuality as a way of life after prison. Among the population of both sexes the inmates with the greatest commitment are those homosexuals who assume the role of the opposite sex—the male queen and the female butch. The male role in our society carried over into the prison setting, however, means that those playing this role—the wolves and the butches—act from a position of strength and thus appear in the position of exploiters of the more dependent feminine role partner.

Homosexual and Heterosexual Love Affairs

The course of the homosexual love affair in the prison setting does not run smoothly despite the positive function it serves. However, since the same abstract statement has been made in regard to heterosexual affairs, we shall briefly compare some features of heterosexual and homosexual love affairs.

In some senses, prison homosexuality resembles normal heterosexuality both in its positive and negative aspects. Each relationship can be sought to assuage loneliness, give sexual satisfaction, provide meaning or purpose to daily life, and give status from the association with another person. It can also engender disenchantment and great unhappiness. Fears of desertion, lack of complementarity, jealousy, personality defects, sexual incompatibility, differing interests, and decreased intimacy over time can also characterize the homosexual affair.

A particularly relevant analogy is the adolescent love affair. In each of these types of affairs the emotional and sexual involvement is subject to a delay, if not a prohibition, against formal recognition of the relationship as a social unit. Both adolescent and prison lovers are subject to the control and scrutiny of others. Both are accused of being only infatuated and not being seriously in love. In another context, Waller and Hill have observed that "young people must carry on their courtships without the guidance and support of community groups and standards and that each party must guard himself against exploitation by the other while he learns to seek thrills in the body of the other."[9] These features apply with equal force to homosexual couples.

Much of the folklore about homosexuality is to the effect that physical, sexual experience between homosexuals is far more satisfying than the sexual relationship between men and women. One jailhouse turnout found her affair so satisfying that she divorced her husband and put her child up for adoption.

> I'm planning to live with a woman on the outside. I find the physical relationship much more satisfying than with men. A woman can't tell a man she wants to be kissed or touched in a certain way and women start slowly—with other women you don't have these problems.

On this latter point the women have the support of Kinsey and his associates:

> It is not generally understood, either by males or by females who have not had homosexual experience, that the techniques of sexual relations between two females may be as effective as or even more effective than the petting or coital techniques ordinarily utilized in heterosexual contacts . . .
>
> . . . two individuals of the same sex are likely to understand the

anatomy and the physiologic responses and psychology of their own sex better than they understand that of the opposite sex. Most males are likely to approach females as they, the males, would like to be approached by a sexual partner. They are likely to begin by providing immediate genital stimulation. They are inclined to utilize a variety of psychologic stimuli which may mean little to most females . . . Females in their heterosexual relationships are actually more likely to prefer techniques which are closer to those which are commonly utilized in homosexual relationships.[10]

Henry concurs:

Much can be learned from study of the affectionate relations of sex variants which might contribute to the success of heterosexual unions. The sex variant is more likely to continue with the romantic aspects of affectionate unions and he or she makes full use of erogenous areas which, through ignorance or indifference, are often neglected by the heterosexual.[11]

Some of our interviewees perhaps used sexual satisfaction as a justification or a rationalization for homosexuality, but in many cases, particularly those where the respondent had been a prostitute, there appears to be a basis in fact. While comments were made by our interviewees about the lack of ability and lack of finesse of most of the males they had encountered compared to an experienced homosexual, there is nothing intrinsic to homosexual relationships which makes them more satisfying than sexual relations between males and females. Most of the women felt that men could be better sexual partners if they (men) so desired, but they were not optimistic about finding many men who would devote the time, attention, understanding and skill that their homosexual partners practiced.

Despite the sexual satisfaction to be gained in some homosexual relationships, it may be that these affairs, particularly in an institutional setting, lack some of the attributes that are asserted to characterize successful intimate relationships. These have been discussed in detail by George Bach.[12] Persons defined as psychologically intimate enjoy what he has termed "existential freedoms." Few of these are present in the relationships we have outlined. Bach has stated that intimacy brings to the participants a freedom from exploitation of one partner by the other; in heterosexual intimacy, the studied tactics of seduction and the orientation to the manipulation of the masculine or feminine sexual image as a commodity diminish; the need to maintain a favorable balance in the distribution of favors characterizes much homosexual behavior. Pure intimacy is free from collusion with irrational, ego-alien tendencies, free from rigid role-playing, and free to allow role-reversal. In butch-femme relationships, we have found what might be termed "type-casting" where the butch is frozen into a strict caricature of male bravado, and where role reversal is antithetical to the practice of giving up the work. Bach has discussed intimacy in terms of the absence of "zero-sum" competitiveness (where one partner's gain is the other partner's loss), an absence of manipulative power struggles, and a consequent freedom to trust the other with knowledge about oneself. These features also involve freedom from the fear of replacability and the anxiety of separation. The structural elements of prison life do little to encourage these qualities. Finally, intimacy may be said to involve a freedom of genuine self-assertion and spontaneity and freedom to display the intimacy as a social unit. In the case of homosexual relationships, these freedoms are expressly prohibited by social attitudes and institutional regulations.

The Transition from Prison Homosexuality to the Gay Life

In addition to the defects inherent in homosexual relationships and the difficulties in carrying on a prison love affair outlined in the preceding pages, there is a strain upon most relationships when lovers give serious consideration to the prospects of continuing their affair in the free world.

Homosexuality is not fully approved even in the prison, but it is safer and easier to engage in it when one's family and friends are absent. Escape into institutional deviance can be rationalized on the basis of "they aren't around" or "they won't know," even though legal and emotional ties to significant others in the free world have not been voluntarily severed; rather they have been interrupted by imprisonment.

Institutional deviance can be justified as appropriate, considering the circumstances. However, the implications of continuing to play a homosexual role outside of prison are so serious and so socially stigmatizing that most women appear to return immediately upon release to their roles as mothers, wives and girlfriends.

Release from prison means, in most cases, that inmates are leaving, not entering an environment where a deviant sexual role is supported and encouraged by a deviant subculture. Female homosexuality in a large metropolitan area can of course be supported by membership in an organized deviant group which provides a receptive environment and justifications for one's behavior.[13] Such membership, however, requires not only the interest of the parolee but an introduction to such a group. Women leaving Frontera might get such references from the true homosexuals, but we were told of no such interest by either prospective parolees or true homosexuals. The latter who regard most of the turnouts as unauthentic homosexuals apparently are not motivated to bring these women into the gay life. The jailhouse turnout as she prepares for release is thus unfamiliar with the world of the homosexual outside of prison. When she leaves Frontera it is without her partner and the inclination to reassume the familial and friendly ties she had before confinement is likely to be strong. Upon release, she is usually picked up at the prison by parents, husbands, boyfriends or friends and is given little opportunity to try to make her way alone while waiting for the release of her prison lover.

This is not to say that many jailhouse turnouts are not seriously conflicted about the kind of relationship they want to have upon release. Giving up a lover is never an easy matter. Imminent parole, however, usually prompts the first serious consideration of the implications of continuing to play a homosexual role in the free world. The majority of jailhouse turnouts we have said are femmes and for the most of them the butch substitute cannot provide in the free world the recognition or social status that a man does. Prisoners who are mothers (more than half of the population) are reluctant to bring up children without a father and they realize that with increasing age children will realize the abnormal character of the relationship they see at home. For childless women, a homosexual marriage precludes the possibility of ever playing the maternal role. Women who continue in homosexual relationships thus must be prepared to give up their status in the conventional community for membership in the homosexual community.

An additional post-release concern for many women, and an excuse for some of them, is that there are risks to be taken in living in the free world in a homosexual relationship with one's prison lover. While there is considerable variation in reporting practices among parole agents and within the parole districts of the state, the official policy of the Department of Corrections is that parole may be revoked in cases where parolees are living in a homosexual relationship. Grounds for revocation in these instances include association with another inmate and engaging in immoral behavior. Since almost all Frontera inmates are released on parole and are thus subject to official control and supervision in the community, the pressure of families and friends on the inmate to return to a conventional heterosexual role is supported by the threat of imposition of punitive sanctions by the parole division.

It should be noted incidentally that the granting of a parole date also has important implications for prison adjustment. By the time a date is given most inmates have learned much about how to live in prison. Methods of combating the pains of imprisonment that were unknown in the early months are now familiar. The need for information, advice, interpersonal support and encouragement which initially prompted many femmes to seek support from a butch are less important to the experienced prisoner—particularly the prisoner who knows how much longer she will be confined. As parole approaches, the inmate's thoughts turn to the outside world and serving time becomes a matter of secondary concern.

Our final point in regard to the transition from prison to the community is that when the inmate is paroled she usually faces different problems of adjustment than those she encountered in the prison.[14] Her problems in the community have to do with her reintegration into her family and her social acceptance by friends, associates, and employers. In many cases, this adjustment is made easier because, in making the transition from prisoner to citizen, she receives the very things she did not get while moving from the status of citizen to prisoner—the advice, encouragement, affection and support of family and friends. Finally, the character of other deprivations and restrictions of imprisonment are changed or removed. Material deprivations are the result of less money, not prohibitive rules. Prison restrictions on heterosexual contact, freedom of movement and individual autonomy are removed.

Although there are prison love affairs that continue after the release of both partners, these instances are infrequent. In most cases, the granting of a parole to one partner seems to signal the beginning of the end of the affair before either partner is released. Many of the women who have turned out in prison thus leave Frontera with an unhappy experience behind them which in effect assists them in reassuming heterosexual relationships. As these women leave, however, a continuing supply of prospective femmes and butches are beginning the reception process.

NOTES

1 The situational character of prison love affairs has been noted by the superintendent of another prison for women. See Elizabeth M. Kates, "Sexual Problems in Women's Institutions," *The Journal of Social Therapy,* 1 (October, 1955), p. 191.
2 See Elizabeth G. Flynn's poem, "Commissary Love," in *The Anderson Story* (New York: International Publishers, 1963), p. 202.
3 Willard Waller and Reuben Hill, *The Family: A Dynamic Interpretation* (New York: Dryden Press, 1951), pp. 147–148.
4 Rowland has described attachments which developed in a mental hospital between a catatonic and another patient termed homosexual by the staff. The mechanism used by the homosexual seems similar to that employed at Frontera: "There is undoubtedly an unconscious sexual factor entering into certain cases but this can be viewed only as a partial explanation. It would be equally plausible to regard this type of relation in a different light. The catatonic is a non-responding object and as such he is an ideal object for a strong affect attachment. A patient who has considerable affect and little insight meets many rebuffs in the hospital environment. When this affect is directed toward a nonreacting object, the individual becomes relatively happy. The quality of such a relationship is similar to that between a master and a dog, or between a mother and baby." Rowland, "Friendship Patterns in a State Mental Hospital," *Psychiatry,* 2 (August 1969), p. 366.

5 Lionel Ovesey, "Masculine Aspirations in Women," *Psychiatry,* 19 (November, 1956), p. 351. The question of dependency and power in homosexual relationships in prisons for males is discussed by George Deveureux and Malcolm C. Moos, "The Social Structure of Prisons, and the Organic Tensions," *Journal of Criminal Psychopathology,* 4 (October, 1942), p. 323, and by Jack L. Ward, *op. cit.,* p. 306.

6 Albert J. Reiss, "The Social Integration of Queers and Peers," *Social Problems,* 9 (Fall, 1961), pp. 118–119.

7 Situational homosexuality among male prisoners as reported by Dinerstein and Glueck has the same characteristics as that of the female jailhouse turnout—permitting an overt homosexual to perform fellatio or masturbation, engaging in sexual activities in prison which were viewed as matters of convenience and expedience, and resumption of heterosexual activities upon release from prison. Russell H. Dinerstein and Bernard C. Glueck, Jr., "Sub-Coma Insulin Therapy in the Treatment of Homosexual Panic States," *The Journal of Social Therapy,* 1 (October, 1955), p. 184. Similar views are expressed by Herbert A. Block, "Social Pressures of Confinement Toward Sexual Deviation," *The Journal of Social Therapy,* 1 (April 1955), p. 122; Robert M. Lindner, *Stone Walls and Men* (New York: Odyssey Press, 1946), pp. 458–462; Donald R. Clemmer, ed., *The Prison* (New York: Holt, Rinehart, and Winston, 1961), pp. 260–262.

8 Gresham M. Sykes, *The Society of Captives* (New Jersey: Princeton University Press, 1958), p. 97.

9 Waller and Hill, *op. cit.,* p. 133.

10 Alfred C. Kinsey, Wardell B. Pomeroy, Clyde E. Martin, and Paul H. Gebhard, *Sexual Behavior in the Human Female* (Philadelphia: W. B. Sanders Co., 1953), pp. 467–468.

11 George W. Henry, (New York: Hoeber, 1948), p. 1027. An opposing position is taken by Cory who asserts: "Whatever form the physical expression may take, the sex act is more likely to be frustrating for homosexuals even for those who reach a climax, than a heterosexual act is for heterosexuals. This is because of physical obstacles to a satisfactory relationship (lack of biologically complementing fit) and because for many of these people homosexuality is not a search for but a flight from something unknown . . . Their imperious desires for male-male relationships are actual vicarious and substitutive diversions from other desires and therefore leave unanswered and unresolved the basic needs of the individual. It is for this reason that the astonishingly frequent partner-changing and the short-lived character of homosexual relations must be viewed not as healthy variedism and freedom from puritanical codes of artificial fidelity but as a revolt against the partner with whom sex has been consummated and as an unending search for an ideal and unobtainable total gratification." Donald W. Cory, "Homosexuality," in Albert Ellis and Albert Arbarbanel (eds.), *Encyclopedia of Sexual Behavior,* Volume 1 (New York: Hawthorne Books, 1961), p. 489.

12 George Bach, *Intimate Enemies* (New York: Doubleday and Company, in press).

13 For a discussion of deviant careers and the implications of membership in an organized deviant group on such careers see Howard S. Becker, *Outsiders* (Glencoe: The Free Press, 1963), pp. 25–39. See also Maurice Leznoff and William A. Westley, "The Homosexual Community," *Social Problems,* 3 (April, 1956), pp. 257–263 and Hooker, *op. cit., passim.*

14 The dependent status of women in prison is seen by some practitioners in the field of corrections as carrying over into the post release period. Some parole officials see the prison as providing protection and security for the inmate, and regard her problem as that of adjusting to the rigors of the life in the free world. See Bertha J. Payak, "Understanding the Female Offender," *Federal Probation,* 27 (December, 1963), p. 10 and Margaret A. Teachout, "Problems of Women Parolees," *National Probation and Parole Association Journal,* 3 (January, 1957), p. 31.

7 | On Becoming a Lesbian |
William Simon and
John H. Gagnon

One of the most important aspects of this essay is its treatment of the process of commitment to deviance. The deviant is commonly imagined as an individual facing the clear choice between moral and immoral behavior. This common-sense picture depicts deviants as people who make a choice for evil—a very clear and distinct choice made with free will. This is very far from the truth. On the contrary, in most cases, individuals "drift" into deviance by a slow process. In Delinquency and Drift *David Matza has argued that there is a specific phase, the* drift *phase, which individuals enter before they become deviants. In this phase they are available for deviance but are not completely committed to it. Most of their lives are still taken up with perfectly legitimate activities and their deviance does not involve an identity change at that stage.*

One note that ran through all the interviews was a sense of how totally feminine was the mode of discovery or entry into a homosexual career. One of the strongest findings to emerge from the initial research of Kinsey and his associates was the relatively early development of sexuality among males and the striking contrast this had to the experience of females.[1] Clearly, the organizing event in male sexuality is puberty, while the organizing event for females is that period of romantic involvement that culminates for most in marriage. For males, then, a commitment to sexuality, or at a minimum, the reinforcing experience of orgasm, occurs early in adolescence and for females late in adolescence or in the early adult years. One might say that for females the "discovery" of love relations precedes the "discovery" of sexuality while the reverse is generally true for males. For the lesbians

From pp. 251–255 in *Sexual Deviance,* edited by John H. Gagnon and William Simon. Copyright © 1967 by the Institute for Sex Research, Inc. Reprinted by permission of Harper & Row, Publishers, Inc.

we interviewed this appears as a rather consistent pattern. The discovery of their homosexuality usually occurred very late in adolescence, often even in the years of young adulthood, and the actual commencement of overt sexual behavior frequently came as a late stage of an intense emotional involvement. Indeed, in many instances their first emotional attachment, which began to generate in them a recognition of their special sexual inclination, involved only the most preliminary forms of sexual activity, unmarked by anything as unambiguously sexual as genital contact.

This romantic drift into sexual behavior was typified by one lesbian who described the beginning of her first homosexual affair in the following way:

> The fall after graduation from high school I started at [a residential school]. I met a girl there who was extremely attractive. She had a good sense of humor and I was drawn to her because I liked to laugh. Many of the girls used to sit around in the evenings and talk. As our friendship grew, our circle narrowed and narrowed until it got to be three or four of us who would get together at night and talk. Then there was only three. Then two—us. And maybe after a couple of months of this our relationship developed into something more. Starting out by simply kissing. Later petting. That type of thing. It didn't actually involve overt sexuality [genital contact] until February.

Clearly, for the woman in question there was only a vague sense of what was associated with such behavior. There was little awareness of what a lesbian is and what she does.

> [*When was the first time you began to talk about yourself using terms like "lesbian" or "homosexual"?*] Even when I was involved with her for five or six months, we didn't talk about it. We didn't give ourselves names. We spoke about how much we cared for one another. But we didn't discuss it. I may have thought it, but I don't know.

A second lesbian described a situation that was very similar. In this case there actually was some mild homosexual play during midadolescence, though with no apparent recognition of a homosexual inclination.

> It was at home with my cousin. It was like a game we played in bed at night. It really wasn't to the fullest extent, sex. It was caressing, fondling. It was, as I said, something we did last night . . . we never talked about it.

However, her strongest emotional attachment was to come several years later. Between the first relation with the cousin and this second attachment, there was no sexual involvement, and the second "affair" was itself overtly sexual only to a limited degree.

> We met at the [a residential hotel for women]. We started out just being friends and then it became something special. She taught me a lot of

things. I love music and she taught me how to listen to it and appreciate it. She liked things I liked, like walking. We read a lot together. We read the Bible, we read verses to each other. We shared things together. We caressed each other and kissed. I think it was a need to have someone there. And I was there and she was there and we just held on to each other. [*Did you ever become sexually involved on a more physical level?*] Not to the fullest and when I say not to the fullest extent I mean we didn't take off our clothes and lie in the nude with each other. I enjoyed being with her. I got something from her without going through the actions of sex.

Yet, although the young woman in question went on to become involved in several overt homosexual affairs, the above-described relationship and the woman involved became, for her, a model of what an ideal relationship and love object should be like.

It is not uncommon for lesbians to report that the realization of their own homosexuality appeared early in adolescence or even during childhood. Typically, one lesbian reported an acute "shock of recognition" upon encountering a dictionary definition of homosexuality during very early adolescence. Another reported a sense of tentative recognition in childhood.

I always had this fantasy about being a cowboy or Robin Hood. And then I realized they always had a girl friend, a Maid Marian. So in my fantasies I began to have my girl friends.

However, the amount of existential distortion in such recall remains an unknown quantity. One must remember that such retrospection occurs after an identity has been refashioned to contain an active homosexual component, and that it is not uncolored by an understandable desire to establish a sense of continuity with the past.

What is interesting in both these cases of early recognition (as was true for others like them) is that active involvement in sexual behavior did not occur until the subjects were in their early twenties. For them, apparently, a commitment to a socially deviant choice of sexual objects was not a necessary, immediate stimulus to alienation from other socially ordered aspects of sexual career management. Most lesbians, apparently, are not exempt from the constraints and norms that regulate the development of female sexuality in general. This appears to be particularly true of the timing or phasing of entry into active sexual roles, as well as of the quality of relationships required to facilitate that entry.

While the pattern described above has the suggestion of modality, in this—as in most things—human behavior is complex and tends to present itself as a range. One does encounter modes of entry that were immediately sexual and that occurred earlier in adolescence. In one case, though there are surely numerous others, early homosexual activity was associated with sexually segregated, institutional arrangements. Such environments have historically been charged with generating unusually high proportions of homosexuals. One might keep in mind, however, that the operating mechanism may involve more than little opportunity for heterosexual activity; a question to be considered is the alienative effects of the process that brings the adolescent girl to this type of institution in the first place.

Our limited number of interviews yielded only one example of a young woman who actively sought a test of her lesbian impulses.

> I've had these tendencies ever since I can remember. In high school I'd look at this or that girl and I'd have the desire to talk to her, get to know her better. I was never aroused by just any girl, I always had to have a special attraction to her. I just didn't want her, I'd want her to want me. I didn't want to be the aggressive one. . . . I started dating boys when I was twelve and a half and just stopped a month ago. I had light petting when I was thirteen or fourteen, I had intercourse when I was sixteen or seventeen. I'm not a tramp or anything. I don't like having sex with a guy, I just did it to cooperate when they got too pushy. I've never enjoyed it, I never had an orgasm with a guy. [*How did your homosexuality become sexual?*] Through this guy I was going with. He wasn't satisfying me and so I told him how I felt. That I had this attraction for girls. I heard that there were lesbian bars and I told him I wanted him to take me to one so I could find out if this was what I wanted. And he went along with it thinking that after I found out I might go back to guys. So he asked a friend who knew about these things and got an address. He took me there and left me. I met a girl there and went home with her.

The number of homosexual careers characterized by an experience comparable to this is hard to determine. We suspect that the proportion may not be too large, perhaps no larger than the proportion who have as extensive a history of sexual activity during adolescence as did this girl. What might be necessary, in order to be able to articulate a sexual need as this young woman did, is the deinhibition that often follows extensive sexual activity.

Curiously, the experiences that follow for this respondent fell into an essentially feminine pattern despite the seemingly "masculine" and detached character of her pursuit of the lesbian experience. In short succession she had brief contact with three females, all of whom left her as unsatisfied as did her previous encounters with men. It was only the fourth contact, which had a more extended and intense emotional content, that provided the respondent with her first, positive sociosexual experience as well as her first orgasm. Possibly, the process of development that constrains the female in our society to become trained in the rhetoric of love prior to the rhetoric of sex can be discarded only with a more total rejection of feminine identification than most lesbians are capable of.

What was missing in the interviews was one of the most popular representations of the introduction into homosexuality provided us by modern fiction: seduction by an older woman. While there were some instances in which the initial partner was an older woman, in most cases there was advance evidence of movement away from conventional heterosexual patterns. In several of these cases the older woman was the object of seduction rather than the seductress. This is not to say that this cannot occur. There is the likely possibility that we missed lesbians for whom seduction by an older woman was the mode of entry into homosexuality and, more importantly, the cause of detachment from more conventional patterns, but the size of such a group is probably not very large. The real social importance of the image of the older seductress, an imagery providing the basis for many popular "explanations" of the "causes" of homosexual behavior, lies in its function of reducing a sense of guilt and shame. Suddenly, as the image of the corrupt and corrupting seducer appears on the scene, the need to examine relationships and processes closer to home is considerably reduced.

NOTE

1 A. C. Kinsey, *et al., Sexual Behavior in the Human Female,* Philadelphia, Saunders, 1953, pp. 642–689.

8 | On Being in the "Community"
William Simon and John H. Gagnon

In the last chapter we saw how individuals moved through the process of becoming deviants. In this selection Simon and Gagnon try to show how the individual's identity changes as he becomes increasingly involved in the deviant community.

We have here a clear example of individuals who are going from deviance as a style of life to deviance as a way of life—from deviance as primarily situational to deviance that involves a personal identification of oneself as a deviant.

For both male and female homosexuals one can talk about the existence of a community, at least in most relatively large cities. As for many ethnic or occupational groups, which also can be said to have a community, this subcommunity does not require a formal character or even a specific geographical location. It is, rather, a continuing collectivity of individuals who share some significant activity and who, out of a history of continuing interaction based on that activity, begin to generate a sense of a bounded group possessing special norms and a particular argot. Through extensive use such a homosexual aggregate may identify a particular location as "theirs," and in almost all large cities this includes one or more taverns that cater exclusively to a particular homosexual group. In these bars the homosexual may more freely act out his self-definition as compared with less segregated situations. Recently, several homophile social and service organizations have appeared, which offer a more public image of the homosexual. These various kinds of social activity reinforce a feeling of identity and provide for the homosexual a way of institutionalizing the experience, wisdom, and mythology of the collectivity. A synonym for this community, one not untouched by a sense of the ironic, is the "gay life."

For the individual homosexual the community provides many functions. A major function is the facilitation of sexual union; the lesbian

From pp. 261–263 in *Sexual Deviance,* edited by John H. Gagnon and William Simon. Copyright © 1967 by the Institute for Sex Research, Inc. Reprinted by permission of Harper & Row, Publishers, Inc.

who finds her way to the community can now select from a population that, while differing in other attributes, has the minimum qualification of sharing a lesbian commitment. This greatly reduces what is for the isolated lesbian the common risk of "falling for a straight girl," i.e., a heterosexual. The community provides a source of social support; it is a place where the lesbian can express her feelings or describe her experiences because there are others available who have had feelings and experiences very much like them. It is an environment in which one can socialize one's sexuality and find ways of deriving sexual gratification by being admired, envied, or desired, while not necessarily engaging in sexual behavior. Lastly, the community includes a language and an ideology which provide each individual lesbian with already developed attitudes that help her resist the societal claim that she is diseased, depraved, or shameful.

While all the lesbians interviewed were part of a community to one degree or other, a larger proportion of lesbians avoid such communities than is the case for male homosexuals. This possibly occurs because the lesbian has less need for the community, since her homosexuality is not as immediately alienating from the conventional society. The lesbian may mask her sexual deviance behind a socially prepared asexuality. Not all categories of women in our society are necessarily defined as sexually active, as, for example, the spinster. In line with this, the image of two spinsters living together does not immediately suggest sexual activity between them, even when considerable affection is displayed. The same is not true for men. The bachelor is presumed to be even more sexually active than the married man, and the idea of two males past young adulthood rooming together strikes one as strange indeed. It is possible that the same techniques of repression that lead to differences between males and females in age of initiating sexual activity also allow the female to handle later sexual deprivation more easily. More female homosexuals than male homosexuals, then, should be able to resist quasi-public homosexual behavior that increases the risk of disclosure, as well as resist relations that involve only sexual exchange without any emotional investment.

One lesbian, who had previously avoided the community (during a long period of heterosexual marriage followed by a period of no sexual activity) and now was involved with the community only on a fairly marginal basis, expressed resistance to "the gay life" and its tendency to reinforce lesbian commitments at the expense of greater alienation from conventional society.

> No, I didn't consider myself part of the gay world and I consider myself fortunate. [Why?] From what I've seen of the gay world, not the elite, but kids who hang around the bars get too . . . involved. Particularly the young girls. It drains all of her energy, all of her time, and her money. I see

an awful lot of girls who have a lot of potential and ability which has never been used and will probably never be used because they waste all those good years. They hang around the bars and just because they're homosexual the gay life becomes everything.

Another lesbian, who had spent eight years defining herself as a homosexual and had experienced three fairly long homosexual affairs before she encountered the homosexual community, represented one of the positive aspects of the community. She came initially from a working-class background and had previously worked at a fairly low status, semiskilled occupation. Her affairs, initiated largely on the basis of adventitious meetings, were conducted with the most limited awareness of other lesbians and with lovers who were drawn essentially from similar social backgrounds. Entry into the gay world for this young woman provided her the first sustained interaction across social-class lines. The very salience of sexuality provided a basis for her transcending many social barriers in this community. In rather short order her aspirations in many other areas of life began to rise. She became dissatisfied with her present occupation and started training for one that paid more, possessed higher prestige, and required greater skill. Her commitments to art, music, and eating, and the very style of her life began a rapid transformation. Clearly, for some persons the homosexual community represents a new kind of opportunity structure, while for others it is a resource that is paid for by withdrawal from the larger community.

9 | The Homosexual Community
Evelyn Hooker

This essay begins with a consideration of some of the problems and methods involved in using participant-observer methods to study a deviant community. It shows clearly the tremendous problem any researcher faces in understanding and dealing with the deviant fronts—in this case, the "homosexual mask." It also demonstrates how the researcher established trust and gained the cooperation of the deviants that she wanted to study.

As Evelyn Hooker argues, most individuals who commit homosexual acts do so only as a situational activity. She shows the difficulty of distinguishing between those of this category and those who practice homosexuality as a way of life; that is, those who are members of the homosexual community for the "gay life."

This report illustrates how highly developed the common understandings are in such a deviant culture and how effective such common understandings can be in screening their community life from the larger society which they see as their enemy.

The article also explains how important it is for the members of such deviant subcultures to have a setting in which they can carry on their common public activities. Too, it shows many of the reasons (including economic) why individuals are willing to operate such public settings as the "gay bars," even when they are not members of the community. It is often a great mystery to individuals in our society as to why there should be such deviant settings in which illegal activities are contracted. Certainly the police and other officials know where these deviant settings are. They know almost all the gay bars in any city, but again, the laws of evidence and the laws concerning freedom of assembly, etc., which are intended primarily to protect our general civil rights, make it illegal to arrest anyone for suspicion of illegal activity simply because he is found in such a setting. It is probably also true that many police believe that such methods of enforcement

From Evelyn Hooker, "The Homosexual Community," in John H. Gagnon and William Simon, eds., *Sexual Deviance* (New York: Harper and Row, 1967), pp. 167–184. Reprinted by permission.

would not stop something such as this and would, in fact, only lead to more "secondary deviance." For most individuals who have established a clear homosexual identity, any attempts at enforcement—short of methods that most of us would consider inhuman, such as permanent isolation in prisons—lead only to further alienation from society and further deviance.

In view of its socially tabooed character, it is not difficult to understand why homosexuality as a collective phenomenon in urban settings has rarely been subjected to scientific investigation.[1] The necessity of escaping the penalties of social or legal recognition impels many homosexuals to lead a highly secret private life. Only when caught by law enforcement agents, or when seeking psychiatric help, are they usually available for study. Gaining access to secret worlds of homosexuals, and maintaining rapport while conducting an ethnographic field study, requires the development of a non-evaluative attitude toward all forms of sexual behavior. Social scientists tend to share the emotional attitudes of their culture, and thus do not find this an easy task. Most psychological studies of homosexuality are clinical in orientation and largely concerned with individual psychodynamics.[2] I know of only one sociological study of a homosexual community in an urban setting (Leznoff & Westley, 1956).

The present investigation of the homosexual community in metropolitan Los Angeles is part of a large project, on which I have been engaged for seven years, which also includes a study of the multiple developmental routes by which males travel to self-identification as homosexuals, and an analysis of adult personality structure and adjustment (Hooker, 1956, 1957, 1958, 1959). It has become increasingly clear that these aspects of the problem must be viewed as functionally interrelated: the homosexual community or world and the kinds of persons who travel those paths and live in that world cannot be treated as independent of each other. The relations between personality variables and homosexual subculture variables in determining the commitment to, and patterns of, adult homosexuality are complex. For many, the stability of the commitment appears to be a function of the interaction of both sets of variables.

My methods for studying the homosexual community are essentially those of an ethnographer: interviewing its members about the institutions and activities and participating in those activities whenever possible, with subsequent recording of my observations. Full participation is impossible for two reasons; my gender—I am studying a male community[3]—and my research role. My objective is to see the homosexual world through the eyes of research subjects as the only way in which to know what is really going on; to look with the subject at his world as he knows it. Only if I can achieve and maintain an attitude such that non-evaluation is constant, and that whatsoever I hear or see is simply a matter of sheer interest, will I be able to establish the necessary conditions of trust for complete frankness. The homosexual mask in the presence of a representative of the dominant culture is so firmly set, the expectation of moral disapproval so constant, and the distrust and suspicion of motives so ready-to-be-alerted, that the researcher must prove his trustworthiness again and again. Only if the genuineness of the researcher's interest in simply understanding what he sees and hears is conveyed by his total attitudes of feeling and behavior, is it possible to enlist the full cooperation of the subjects. They must become, in effect, research assistants in the enterprise, seeking to learn as much for themselves about the community in which they live as for the researcher, and to enlist others as well.

My original access to the community was not deliberately sought for research purposes, but developed quite accidentally in the course of normal processes of social interaction with a group of friends to whom I had been introduced by a former student—a highly successful businessman. After a period of testing my capacity to accept their behavior in a non-judgmental way, while divesting themselves of their protective masks, they made an urgent request that I conduct a scientific investigation of 'people like them.' By 'people like them,' they meant homosexuals who did not seek psychiatric help, and who led relatively stable, occupationally successful lives. They had read clinical literature on homosexuality and felt that much of it was irrelevant to an understanding of their condition. With their offer to supply unlimited numbers of research subjects, and to provide entrée into homosexual circles and public gathering places, I accepted the research opportunity. Thus, the original relationship was not that of researcher to research subject, but of friend to friend. With the expansion of contacts through networks of mutual friends, the research role became more clearly defined and separated from its social origin. Independent contacts with official homosexual organizations led to other social strata in the community. Participation in the community and deliberate efforts to locate representative members of varying sectors of it, such as male prostitutes, bisexuals, bartenders and bar owners, adolescents and the aged, produced ultimately a wide cross-section.

There are no unique features of Los Angeles which are necessary conditions for the development of a homosexual community since one exists in every large city in the United States, and, indeed, probably in the western world. Only the roughest estimates can be made of the numbers of practicing homosexuals in Los Angeles. The Kinsey estimates of 4% of the white male population as being exclusively homosexual throughout their lives would give an approximate figure of 26,631, age 20 or over, on the basis of the 1960 census. Exclusive homosexuals, however, account for a small proportion of the total. If we accept the Kinsey estimates, the incidence of those having some overt homosexual experience between adolescence and old age reaches 37 percent. The largest proportion will have had heterosexual experiences as well. Thus, the suggested figure does not even begin to encompass the total white homosexual population in Los Angeles—to say nothing of non-Caucasians of whom there are many.

That portion of the homosexual population which forms a loosely organized society, world, or collectivity having a unified character, as distinguished from a mere aggregate of persons, is not a community in the traditional sense of the term, as it has been used by sociologists, in that it lacks a territorial base with primary institutions serving a residential population. If, however, one is permitted to use the term to refer to an aggregate of persons engaging in common activities, sharing common interests, and having a feeling of sociopsychological unity, with variations in the degree to which persons have these characteristics, depending on whether they constitute the core or the periphery,[4] then it is completely germane to homosexuals. Although homosexuals as a total group do not have a bounded territorial base, they are, nevertheless, not randomly distributed throughout the city, nor are the facilities of institutions which provide needed services and functions as focal gathering places. Mapping the residences of persons known to us, or known to subjects who have supplied us with their addresses, and noting the residential areas in the city described by them as having heavy concentrations of homosexuals results in large cluster formations. In these sections, apartment houses on particular streets may be owned by, and rented exclusively to, homosexuals. Single streets of individual dwellings may have only one or two non-homosexual families. The concentrated character of these areas is not generally known except in the homosexual community, and in many instances by the police. The population is also distributed widely throughout the city and its suburbs since other factors than association affect the choice of residence. Buying of tract houses by 'married pairs' has become sufficiently common to be referred to as 'homosexual suburbia,' the term referring to style of living and not the character of the neighborhood.

An adequate description of the 'gay life,' that is, the homosexual community life or 'scene' as the member knows it, depends on whether it satisfies the conditions of our being able to tell a person how to act, think, and feel as the homosexual does as he 'makes the scene.'[5] That scene, as the community member knows it, is essentially a round of activities utilizing a particular set of institutions, facilities, or areas and governed by common expectations, beliefs, and values. It is important to distinguish between the visible, or public community activities in which only a small portion of the total homosexual population appears to participate, and the invisible, private community activities which go on in friendship cliques. A commonplace, but relevant, analogy is the iceberg in which only the top of a very large mass is visible. A stranger to the community may enter it via its public institutions, provided he knows where they are, or its private clique structure, provided he can manage a social introduction. Experienced homosexuals who are strangers to a particular community have no difficulty using either entrance since the community map is fairly standard from one city to another in the United States. The most favorable entrance for the researcher is via the clique structure since it leads inevitably to the public community, whereas the reverse is more difficult.

In the present account of the community, however, I shall begin with the public institutions, facilities and areas used by homosexuals in their round of activities. Because most homosexuals make every effort to conceal their homosexuality at work, and from heterosexuals, the community activities are largely leisure time or recreational activities. The most important of these community gathering places is the 'gay' bar ('gay' is a synonym for homosexual as used by many members of that community), but there are also steam baths catering almost exclusively to homosexuals, 'gay' streets, parks, public toilets, beaches, gyms, coffee houses, and restaurants. Newsstands, bookstores, record shops, clothing stores, barber shops, grocery stores, and launderettes may become preferred establishments for service or for a rendezvous, but they are secondary in importance.

In the Los Angeles area, there are at present count, 60 'gay' bars. Since their continued operation is subject to surveillance by police and alcoholic beverage control authorities, it is difficult to keep the list current. They are not randomly distributed over the city even in areas which permit the licensing of establishments for the dispensing of liquor. A map of the city on which the locations of 'gay' bars is plotted shows that like the residential areas, there is a clustering effect. Bars tend to be grouped in a given area in part because of the bar-going habits of their clientele. An individual seldom spends an entire evening in a particular bar, but usually makes the rounds of bars in a particular area, going from one bar to another, seeking sexual contacts or social partners. There is, therefore, a large turnover of personnel in a given evening. Bars nearby can capitalize on this fact. The areas in which the clusters of bars occur in Los Angeles are characterized by one or more of the following determinants: proximity to 1. residential areas with heavy concentrations of homosexuals, 2. beaches or other places of homosexual group recreation or leisure time activity, 3. public entertainment districts—theatres, etc., 4. areas of high tolerance for and relative permissiveness toward other forms of deviant behavior. In Los Angeles there are five regions in which 'gay' bars are located. The location of any given bar, however, within a general region depends on multiple factors too complex for elaboration in this presentation.

I begin the account of the community life with 'gay' bars for a number of reasons: 1. In them, the public aspect of 'gay' life is to be encountered—any stranger may enter. 2. Here, the 'gay' and 'straight' (heterosexual) worlds intersect: the 'gay' world can become most visible to the 'straight' world or to representatives of the 'straight' world—the police, newspapers etc. 3. On behalf of these institutions in the 'gay' world, the legitimacy claim is most often made by protagonists such as lawyers in the 'straight' world. 4. Here, one will find the largest, and widest representation of types, socioeconomic levels, and social strata in the homosexual world—if one goes from bar to bar, as the homosexual does. It is estimated that on a Saturday night between the hours of 10 and 2 A.M., a thousand men will pass through the doors of one of the largest and most successful bars. 5. Here, one may observe one of the most standardized and characteristic patterns of social interaction in the 'gay' world: the meeting of strangers for the essential purpose of making an agreement to engage in sexual activity known as the 'one night stand.' 6. For many homosexuals the 'gay' bar is a social institution, where friends are met, the news of the homosexual world is to be heard, gossip exchanged, invitations to parties issued, and warnings about current danger spots and attitudes of the police given.

I conceive of homosexual bars as free markets which could only arise under a market economy in which buyers and sellers are governed by rules whereby the right to enter in is determined by whether the buyer has the wherewithal. The term market as applied to bars has two meanings: 1. As a business enterprise in which leisure is accomplished via the market: gain from the sale of liquor and entertainment is legitimate. 2. As a metaphor to conceive of transactions between homosexuals, a set of terms relating to the negotiation of an exchange of sexual services.

While individual bars are relatively unstable and may be short-lived, the bar system is relatively stable, although subject to the constant surveillance of appropriate authorities of the repressive agencies. Its stability may be accounted for by the following facts: 1. Bars are highly lucrative for the owners and despite harassment and closing of individual bars, licenses are constantly sought to re-open under new ownership or to establish ones in new locations. 2. They meet the expectations and needs, and are geared in an integral way to the behavior patterns of a large homosexual population. 3. Authorities unofficially believe that elimination of the system is both undesirable and impossible: 'that kind of person has to have someplace to go and at least they are with their own kind, and you don't lose 'em; you just move 'em around a little.'

The successful operation of a 'gay' bar is a highly skilled performance requiring a knowledge of tastes and behavior of homosexual clientele, and the ability to create the kind of atmosphere which will attract large numbers, as well as the ability to successfully control behavior within the limits which law enforcement officers, behaving as willing objects of the cruising game, and thus passing as ordinary clientele, cannot make the subject of legal objection.

I turn now to the second meaning of the term market as applied to 'gay' bars, that is, as a sexual market: a place where agreements are made for the potential exchange of sexual services, for sex without obligation or commitment—the 'one night stand.' If one watches very carefully, and knows what to watch for in a 'gay' bar, one observes that some individuals are apparently communicating with each other without exchanging words, but simply by exchanging glances—but not the kind of quick glance which ordinarily occurs between men. It is said by homosexuals that if another catches and holds the glance, one need know nothing more about him to know that he is one of them. The psychological structure of that meeting of glances is a complex one, involving mutual recognition of social, but not personal, identity, sexual intent and agreement. Many men in the bar, then, are not engaged in conversation, but are standing along a wall, or by themselves at a vantage point in the room so that they may be seen as well as see, and are scanning faces and bodies. Occasionally, we may see a glance catch and hold another glance. Later, as if in an accidental meeting, the two holders-of-a-glance may be seen in a brief conversation followed by their leaving together. Or, the conversation may be omitted. Casually and unobtrusively, they may arrive at the door at the same time, and leave. If we followed them, we would discover that they were strangers, who by their exchange of glances had agreed to a sexual exchange. The terms of the exchange remaining to be settled will be the place and the nature of the sexual act. A few minutes, or a few hours later, one or both men may appear in another bar to begin the same procedure all over again, or they may stay together for the night, and the next night seek a new partner. What I have described is one form of 'cruising.' While the agreements resulting in the 'one night stand' occur in many settings—the bath, the street, the public toilet—and may vary greatly in the elaboration or simplicity of the interaction preceding the culmination in the sexual act, their essential feature is the standardized expectation that sex can be had without obligation or commitment. Irrespective of persons, time, place, and from city to city, in the United States at least, this is a stable, reproducible, standard feature of the interaction.

What stabilizes this pattern of expectation and regularized course of conduct? That is the big question to which I have only partial answers. The promiscuity of the homosexual has been attributed to his psychodynamic structure; among other things, to his primary narcissism. I do not believe that the answer to the question is to be found only in psychodynamic explanations but requires that the system effects of the community be taken into account.

That system, as a sexual market, grows out of the 'market mentality.' Riesman (1954) comments: 'In a market situation pervaded by what Karl Polanyi has termed the "market mentality" . . . control of the economy will carry with it, to an unusual degree, control of the ethical regime' (p. 60). He suggests that all values are subjected to the market, and are transformed by it; and, further, 'it is not the genuine self that is put on the market . . . but the "cosmetic" self . . .' (pp. 59–60). Nothing is more conspicuous in the 'gay' bar market than the emphasis on appearance: on dress, manner, and body build. To furnish a genuine self in the exchange of partners, biography and prospects would be essential. In this meeting of strangers, the disengaged character of activities from any ascriptive characteristics is promoted. The pressures toward maintaining secrecy, with respect to work and personal biography in homosexual encounters, are derived in part from the functional consequences of their being revealed. The legal, occupational, and personal hazards of identification as a homosexual in our society are amply documented. The risk of information leakage from the 'gay' world to the work world is high.

But if the market mentality pervades society, and if it is the cosmetic self that is put on the market, why should sexual exchange in the relations of male to female be exempt from the characteristics of the 'one night stand'—sex without obligation or commitment? The heterosexual world is *not* exempt, but anything other than monogamous, legally sanctioned, obligated relations is a departure from strongly sanctioned norms, whatever the actual practice may be. That these norms are so strongly sanctioned in the heterosexual world, may be in part a function of the fact that sexuality means more to the female than to the male.[6] Women have more to lose by divesting sexuality of rights, obligations, and commitment because their value in the competitive marriage market partly depends on it as bargaining power, and because their role as child-bearers and child-rearers requires psychological and economic support. The relative absence of women in the homosexual world, the negative sanctions of society against homosexual relationships, the pressures toward secrecy and the risks of revealing one's own personal identity as a homosexual, and the market character of the bar setting in which meetings occur, combine to produce the kind of sexual exchange which we have described as a stable feature of the 'gay' world.

'Gay' bars also serve other important functions for the community. It is estimated by bartenders that 50% of the patrons on any given evening will be habitués, who come at least once a week, and, frequently, three or four evenings a week. Every bar has its clusters of friends who gather to exchange gossip, to look over the new faces, and to spend a social evening in an atmosphere congenial to them where the protective mask of the day may be dropped. Bars are, therefore, communication centers for the exchange of news and gossip, and for the discussion of problems and hard luck stories. Practical problems such as finding a job, or a place to live, or a lawyer, may be solved with the help of friends or newly met acquaintances. The opening of the newest bar in town, or a place which has recently become 'hot,' or whether there is a party going on that evening to which one might be invited are topics of conversation. They are also, paradoxically enough, security operations. While arrests are made in bars, and the presence of vice-squad officers or alcoholic bevarage control authorities in plain clothes is an ever present possibility, the bartender, or bar owner will warn the patrons of their presence, if their identity is known—and it frequently is. Warnings will also be passed about particular patrons who are known to be 'dirt,' that is, who are likely to rob or demand money or possessions, or to beat up the sexual partner after the consummation of the sexual act. News travels quickly from bar to bar of harassment activities of the authorities.

Bars also serve as induction and training, and integration centers for the community. These functions are difficult to separate. The young man who may have had a few isolated homosexual experiences in adolescence, or indeed none at all, and who is taken to a 'gay' bar by a group of friends whose homosexuality is only vaguely suspected or unknown to him, may find the excitement and opportunities for sexual gratification appealing and thus begin active participation in the community life. Very often, the debut, referred to by homosexuals as 'coming out,' of a person who believes himself to be homosexual but who has struggled against it, will occur in a bar when he, for the first time, identifies himself publicly as a homosexual in the presence of other homosexuals by his appearance in the situation. If he has thought of himself as unique, or has thought of homosexuals as a strange and unusual lot, he may be agreeably astonished to discover large numbers of men who are physically attractive, personable, and 'masculine' appearing, so that his hesitancy in identifying himself as a homosexual is greatly reduced. Since he may meet a wide cross-section of occupational and socioeconomic levels in the bar, he becomes convinced that far from being a small minority, the 'gay' population is very extensive indeed. Once he has 'come out,' that is, identified himself as a homosexual to himself and to some others, the process of education proceeds with rapid pace. Eager and willing tutors—especially if he is young and attractive—teach him the special language, ways of recognizing vice-squad officers, varieties of sexual acts and social types. They also assist him in providing justifications for the homosexual way of life as legitimate, and help to reduce his feeling of guilt by providing him with new norms of sexual behavior in which monogamous fidelity to the sexual partner is rare.

In the bar world the initiate soon acquires a body of knowledge which includes a set of common understandings[7]—'what everybody knows.' 'Everybody knows' that: sex can be had without obligation or commitment; it is a meeting of strangers, and the too familiar face may not make out in the sexual market; one can't afford to be seen too frequently or one is counted out of the cruising competition—after the initial newcomer phase; preferences for sexual acts may be specialized and congruence of sexual interests between partners is always problematic; discrepancy between expected sexual behavior and appearance is not a surprise; success in the sexual market will be increased by 'masculine' appearance and the appearance of youth; life in the bars for sexual purposes is time limited: older persons (35 or more) may not make out unless they pay for partners; although the potential supply of partners is large, 'making out' may be difficult because everyone in the 'gay' world may be afraid of rejection and the criteria of selection may be highly specific.

Earlier I described the homosexual community with the analogy of the iceberg phenomenon, in which the visible part of the community— visible to those who seek it out—is to be found in a round of activities in public institutions, facilities, and areas. I believe, as do homosexuals I have interviewed, that this is a very small part of the total community, and that submerged or hidden, the secret and private activities of the world of social friendship cliques are fundamental to an understanding of the whole. In this world are to be found persons who have established long-term living relationships with another homosexual, and who rarely if ever go to bars or other public establishments because of their sexually predatory and competitive character. They may have had a period of bar going but now have come to dislike the bar activites or to fear them because of their threat to the stability of an established relationship. Others, especially those of high occupational or socioeconomic status, may restrict their community life to private social cliques because of the fear of exposure or arrest. Others may not enjoy drinking, or may find sufficient sexual and social companionship in homosexual groups, whether they are living alone or in an establishment with another homosexual. There are, of course, many homosexuals who are isolates on the margin of both parts of the community.

The organization of the homosexual world outside of the bars, but linked with it by members common to both, is a loosely knit extended series of overlapping networks of friends. The forms of these networks vary greatly. The three most common are: 1. tightly knit clique structures formed from pairs of homosexually 'married' persons, or singles, many of whom are heterosexually married, 2. larger groups with one or more loose clique structures as sociometrically central and a number of peripheral members; and 3. loose networks of friends who may meet only on the occasion of parties. Clique structures and pairs, as well as loose networks of friends, cut across occupational and socio-economic levels, although particular professions or occupations such as teaching, medicine, interior decoration, and antique dealers may form association in-groups which have social gatherings. Police exposés of homosexual circles or rings frequently reveal the widespread occupational and age ramifications of such groups. Although the networks are overlapping, the population is so large that nothing occurs like the rapid communication in the criminal underground. For example, in comparing two lists of friends, one of 250 names made by a man of 40 and the other of 35 names made by a man of 23, I found only one name common to the two lists although the modal age and range, and the occupations were strikingly similar. The unity of this social world does not consist of close friendship bonds which link person to person throughout the total network, but of common activities, common sexual interests, and a feeling of a common fate which makes them interdependent.

In the cliques, groups, and networks of friends, social occasions, such as evening parties, dinners and cocktail parties are frequent, ranging from the simplest to the most elaborate, and from the most intimate to the large, spur of the moment affairs. 'Wedding' anniversaries, birthdays, and other special occasions, much as in the heterosexual world, call for celebrations. Some groups make special efforts to maintain social relations with heterosexual couples, usually ones who are 'wise,' that is, are aware of and at least partially accept their homosexuality. These, in my experience, are very rare except in literary, other artistic, or highly sophisticated circles. In the main, members feel uncomfortable in the social presence of heterosexuals, and prefer social occasions in which the guest list is made up of homosexuals so that they can, as their phrase puts it, 'let down their hair'—that is take off their protective masks, use their in-group language, discuss intimate details of their sexual lives, and 'camp.'

Although the forms of behavior involved and the definitions of camping given by homosexuals vary widely, we shall not distort too greatly, perhaps, by describing it as usually involving some aspect of the feminine, dramatically displayed in gesture or speech—whether in serious or caricatured form. For example, it is a common practice to use feminine nicknames in homosexual circles, and in the diminutive form. An interchange at a party between two homosexual males in which nicknames are used with effeminate gestures would be a form of what the writer, Christopher Isherwood, has called 'low camp.' The social-psychological implications of camping are complex. Some homosexual cliques or groups will not tolerate such behavior, and make every effort to behave in such a way as to minimize any indication of characteristics which would identify them as homosexual.

As contrasted with the 'one night stand' of the 'gay' bar world, there is constant seeking for more permanent relationships in the social world outside the bars. Indeed, the hope of many who engage in the 'one night stand' round of activities is that a particular encounter may lead to a more permanent arrangement. Some long-lasting relationships do begin in the bars but the total system operates against them, as we have seen. In these relaionships, sometimes called marriages, complex problems of role management and practical problems of domestic establishments must be solved since they are subject to the strains of a hostile heterosexual society, as well as those of the homosexual world. That many do survive these pressures is well established in my data. Accurate estimates of proportions are impossible since I am not engaged in a survey. In the limited time, I cannot undertake an adequate description of these relationships; of the variety and complexity of their patterns. I want to comment only on one characteristic feature of sex and gender role in relationships in the homosexual world as I have observed them. Contrary to a widespread belief, these are not dichotomized in a clear-cut fashion into masculine and feminine. One does observe pairs with well-defined differentiation but they appear to be in the minority. The terms active or passive partner, masculine or feminine role, as distinguishing members of a pair may be inapplicable to the greater number of these pairs. Instead, the variety and form of the sexual acts between pair members, the distribution of tasks performed, and the character of their performance do not permit such a differentiation. New solutions appear for which the old terms are inapplicable. In part, the emergence of new solutions may be attributed to the changing culture of the homosexual world. In what appear to be large sectors of that world, the stereotype of the effeminate is fought. In some, the result is a caricature of masculinity. The motorcycle crowd, or the leather set, with its affectation of the symbols of tough masculinity, is one form of caricature. In others, the insistence on being men, despite the homosexuality, results in a deliberate effort to develop patterns of behavior which are indistinguishable from the heterosexual, except, of course in the sexual sphere, and here the dominant-submissive pattern is consciously resisted.

One of the important features of homosexual subcultures is the pattern of beliefs, or the justification system. Central to it is the explanation of why they are homosexuals, and involves the question of choice. The majority of those whom I have interviewed believe that they were born as homosexuals, or that familial factors operating very early in their lives determined the outcome. In any case, it is a fate over which they have no control, and in which they have no choice. It follows as a consequence that the possibility of changing to a heterosexual pattern is thought to be extremely limited. To fight against homosexuality is to fight against the inevitable since they are fighting against their own 'nature' in its essential form, as they experience it. They believe that homosexuality is as 'natural' for them, as heterosexuality is for others. Such belief patterns are widely shared by those who identify themselves as members of the community, and who participate in the round of activities we have described. I must reiterate that not all who engage in homosexual practices have accepted this identification, and share these beliefs.

In conclusion, I have attempted to describe some features of a homosexual community in a large urban setting: its ecological distribution; its visible, public institutions which have been conceptualized as market settings for the exchange of sexual services, and as induction, training, and integration centers for the community; its invisible world of friendship cliques and group structures in which more stable patterns of relationships are likely to develop; the common understandings and shared beliefs. In the time allotted I have not been able to discuss other important features of the community, such as the formal leadership structure, the language patterns, the special humor, the management of impressions by community members in interaction with heterosexual society, and the problems of trust and secrecy within the community. I have tried to show that once an individual enters the community, and begins to enter into its round of activities, he is subject to the beliefs, understandings, and norms of that world. The patterns of behavior which develop, as a consequence, may be as much a function of the system-effects of the community, as of need-predispositions which play an important role in shaping the entry routes of some of the members. It is highly probable that it is at least as accurate to speak of the homosexual community as a 'deviant community' as to describe it as a 'community of deviants.'

NOTES

1 The brevity of this paper on a problem of such broad dimensions is due to the fact that it was written for oral presentation (1961) within specified time limits. It is highly over-simplified and fragmentary, especially in the description of complex social phenomena and the development of a theoretical framework to account for them. A radical and complete revision in greatly expanded form would be required to fully correct these and other inadequacies and to bring it up to date.

2 This statement refers to studies at the human level and is a rough generalization about the relative proportion of publications in which the content focuses on etiology, personality patterns and psychodynamics, or treatment of homosexuality in individuals (or aggregates of individuals), as contrasted with those in which the focus is on social patterns in groups, societies, or collectivities.

3 A study of the total homosexual community would, of course, include homosexual women. The relations between homosexual men and women in private social gatherings, in bars, and in homosexual organizations are not discussed in this brief paper, but are, of course, important features of the total project—although the focus is on the collective aspects of male homosexuality.

4 For the concept of the 'community' as outlined in this sentence, I am indebted to Johnson (1955).

5 For this concept, I am indebted to Harold Garfinkel. My very large indebtedness to Dr. Garfinkel in the development of the concepts used in this paper cannot be explicitly and adequately documented.

6 Suggested by Erving Goffman in a personal communication.

7 For the term 'common understandings,' I am indebted to Harold Garfinkel. The meanings of the term as he uses it are to be found in his 1964 paper.

REFERENCES

1 Garfinkel, H. The routine grounds of everyday activities. *Soc. Prob.,* 1964, *11,* 225–250.

2 Hooker, E. A preliminary analysis of group behavior of homosexuals. *J. Psychol.,* 1956, *42,* 217–225.

3 Hooker, E. The adjustment of the male overt homosexual. *J. proj. Tech.,* 1957, *21,* 18–31.

4 Hooker, E. Male homosexuality in the Rorschach. *J. proj. Tech.,* 1958, *22,* 33–54.

5 Hooker, E. What is a criterion? *J. proj. Tech.* 1959, *23,* 278–281.

6 Johnson, R. The nature of the minority community: internal structure, reactions, leadership, and action. Unpublished doctoral dissertation (Cornell University), 1955.

7 Leznoff, M., and Westley, W. A. The homosexual community. *Soc. Prob.,* 1956, *3,* 257–263.

8 Riesman, D. *Individualism Reconsidered.* Glencoe, Ill.: The Free Press, 1954, p. 529.

part four
violence as a deviant
style and way of life

10 | Hell's Angels: Hoodlum Circus and Statutory Rape of Bass Lake |
Hunter Thompson

*The Hell's Angels are undoubtedly one of the most notorious
gangs in the history of the United States. In California and
throughout the nation they have captured many headlines, especially for violence. Shortly before Hunter Thompson spent a
year with the Angels and wrote his book entitled* Hell's Angels,
*the attorney general of the state of California published the Lynch
report which was a gory account of innumerable instances of
violence and rape among the Angels.*

*While Thompson found a great deal of violence, especially that
associated with sex, he also found ample evidence that the Lynch
report was highly fallacious and sensationalistic. The report is an
excellent example of the ways in which law enforcement officials
and deviant groups view each other as total enemies and, therefore, construct highly distorted pictures of each other which then
become the basis for ineffective action against each other.*

*While in some ways the Angels apparently are "enemies of
society," they are by no means unprincipled or simply wild men.
Like all groups of deviants, the Hell's Angels do have some shared
norms which they enforce as a community. But these shared
norms are very different from those of the general society and
often lead them into open conflict with the larger society. Their
norms on sex, for example, lead to styles of action that most
members of our society would see as deviant. But, as Thompson
argues, we would find it hard to agree on just what the legal
ramifications of some of their actions are.*

**The fact that people are poor or discriminated against doesn't necessarily
endow them with any special qualities of justice, nobility, charity or
compassion.** ▪ **Saul Alinsky**

To squelch any possibility of the Angels roaring drunkenly out of camp during the night, Baxter and the Highway Patrol announced a ten-P.M. curfew. At that time, anyone in camp would have to stay, and nobody else could come in. This was made official just after dark. The deputies were still trying to be friendly and they assured the Angels that the curfew was as much for their protection as anything else. They kept talking about "bunches of townspeople, coming through the woods with deer rifles." To forestall this, the police set up a command post at the point where the Willow Cove trail joined the highway.

Meanwhile, a mountain of six-packs was piling up in the middle of camp. This was in addition to the original twenty-two cases in my car. By the time it got dark the car was half empty, so I put the rest of the beer in the back seat and locked my own gear in the trunk. I decided that any symbolic alienation I might incur by securing my valuables was worth the risk of having them all lost—which they probably would have been, for it was not long before the camp became like an animal pen. A reporter from the *Los Angeles Times* showed up the next day and said it "looked like Dante's Inferno." But he arrived about noon, when most of the outlaws were calm and stupefied from the ravages of the previous night. If the midday lull seemed that awful, the bonfire scenes might have permanently damaged his mind.

Or perhaps not, for the ten-o'clock curfew had a drastic effect on the action. By driving all the fringe elements out of camp, it forced the Angels to fall back on their own entertainment resources. Most of those who left were girls; they had seemed to be enjoying things until the deputies announced that they would either leave by the deadline or stay all night. The implications were not pleasant—at ten the law was going to pull out, seal off the area and let the orgy begin.

All afternoon the scene had been brightened by six or ten carloads of young girls from places like Fresno and Modesto and Merced who had somehow got wind of the gathering and apparently wanted to make a real party of it. It never occurred to the Angels that they would not stay the night—or the whole weekend, for that matter—so it came as a bad shock when they left. The three nurses who'd picked up Larry, Pete and Puff earlier in the day made a brave decision to stay—but then, at the last moment, they fled. "Man, I can't stand it," said one Angel as he watched the last of the cars lurch off down the trail. "All that fine pussy, just wasted. That wiggy little thing with the red shoes was all *mine!* We were groovin! How *could* she just split?"

It was a rotten show by almost any standards. Here were all these high-bottomed wenches in stretch pants and sleeveless blouses half unbuttoned . . . beehive hairdos and blue-lidded eyes . . . ripe, ignorant little bodies talking horny all afternoon ("Oh, Beth, don't these bikes just drive you kinda wild?"). Yeah, baby, wild for the open road

. . . and off they went, like nuns hearing the whistle, while the grief-stricken Angels just stood there and watched. Many had left their own women behind, fearing trouble, but now that the trouble was dissipated, there was not going to be any strange ginch either.

Among the hardest hit was Terry the Tramp, who immediately loaded up on LSD and spent the next twelve hours locked in the back of a panel truck, shrieking and crying under the gaze of some god he had almost forgotten, but who came down that night to the level of the treetops "and just stared—man, he just looked at me, and I tell you I was scared like a little kid."

Other Angels rushed off to the beer market when the curfew was first announced, but their hopes for a party with the tourists were dashed when the place closed right on the dot of ten. There was nothing to do but go back to camp and get wasted. The police were lenient with late arrivals, but once in, there was no getting out.

The hours between ten and twelve were given over to massive consumption. Around eleven I ducked into the car and worked for a while on the tape, but my monologue was constantly interrupted by people reaching through the back windows and trying to wrench the trunk open. For hours there had been so much beer in camp that nobody worried about seeing the end of it, but suddenly it all disappeared. Instead of one beer at a time, everybody who reached into the car took a six-pack. The stash had begun. It was like a run on a bank. Within minutes the back seat was empty. There were still twenty or thirty six-packs piled up near the bonfire, but these weren't for stashing. The cans were clipped off one at a time. Nobody wanted to start a run on the public-beer stock. It would have been very bad form . . . and if the hoarding became too obvious, those who planned to drink all night might get violent.

By this time various drug reactions were getting mixed up with the booze and there was no telling what any one person might do. Wild shouts and explosions burst through the darkness. Now and then would come the sound of a body plunging into the lake . . . a splash, then yelling and kicking in the water. The only light was the bonfire, a heap of logs and branches about ten feet wide and five feet tall. It lit up the whole clearing and gleamed on the headlights and handlebars of the big Harleys parked on the edge of the darkness. In the wavering orange light it was hard to see faces except those right next to you. Bodies became silhouettes; only the voices were the same.

There were about fifty girls in camp, but nearly all were "old ladies"—not to be confused, except at serious risk, with "mamas" or "strange chicks." An old lady can be a steady girl friend, a wife or even some bawdy hustler that one of the outlaws has taken a liking to. Whatever the connection, she is presumed to be spoken for, and unless she makes obvious signs to the contrary she will usually be left alone. The Angels are very solemn about this, insisting that no member would think of violating the sanctity of another's liaison. This is true, but only up to a point. Unlike wolves, old ladies don't mate for life, and sometimes not even for a month. Many are legally married, with several children, and exist entirely apart from the general promiscuity. Others are borderline cases who simply change their minds now and then . . . They switch loyalties without losing rank, establishing just as firm a relationship with one Angel as they previously had with another.

These can be very shifting sands. Like beauty and honesty, promiscuity is in the eyes of the beholder—at least among the Angels. An old lady who changes her mind once too often, or perhaps only once, will find herself reclassified as a mama, which means she is common property.

There are mamas at any Angel gathering, large or small. They travel as part of the troupe, like oxpeckers,[1] fully understanding what's expected: they are available at any time, in any way, to any Angel, friend or favored guest—individually or otherwise. They also understand that the minute they don't like the arrangement they can leave. Most hang around for a few months, then drift on to something else. A few have been around for years, but this kind of dedication requires an almost preterhuman tolerance for abuse and humiliation.

The term "mama" is all that remains of the original expression "Let's go make somebody a mama," which was later shortened to "Let's go make a mama." Other fraternities have different ways of saying it, but the meaning is the same—a girl who's always available. A widely quoted section of the Lynch report says these girls are called "sheep," but I have never heard an Angel use that word. It sounds like the creation of some police inspector with intensely rural memories.

The mamas aren't pretty, although some of the newer and younger ones have a sort of demented beauty that erodes so fast that you have to see it happen, over a period of months, to feel any sense of tragedy. Once the girls have developed the proper perspective, it's easy to take them for granted. One night in Sacramento the Angels ran out of beer money and decided to auction off Mama Lorraine in a bar. The top bid was twelve cents, and the girl laughed along with the others. On another occasion, Magoo was packing Mama Beverly on a run to Bakersfield when he ran out of gas. "Do you know," he recalls, "I couldn't find a single gas-station attendant who would give me a free gallon of gas for a go at her." The public prints are full of testimony by men who take pride in having "sold their talents dearly," but people who understand that their only talent is not worth fifteen cents or a gallon of gas are not often quoted. Nor do they usually leave diaries. It would be interesting to hear, sometime, just exactly what it feels like to go up on the auction block, willing to serve any purpose, and get knocked down for twelve cents.

Most mamas don't think about it, much less talk. Their conversation ranges from gossip and raw innuendo, to fending off jibes and haggling over small amounts of money. But every now and then one of them will rap off something eloquent. Donna, a stocky, good-natured brunette who came north with the exodus from Berdoo, once put the whole thing in a nut. "Everybody believes in something," she said. "Some people believe in God. I believe in the Angels."

Each chapter has a few mamas, but only Oakland maintains as many as five or six at a time. Among other outlaw clubs the situation varies. The Gypsy Jokers are not as mama-oriented as the Angels, but the Satan's Slaves are so keen on the practice that they take their communal women down to the tattoo parlor and have "Property of Satan's Slaves" etched permanently on the left rump-cheek. The Slaves feel that branding gives the girls a sense of security and belonging. It erases any doubt about peer-group acceptance. The branded individual is said to experience powerful and instantaneous sensations of commitment, of oneness with the organization, and those few who have taken the step form a special elite. The Angels are not given to branding their women, but the practice will probably catch on because some of them think it "shows real class."[2]

"But it takes the right girl," said one. "She has to really mean it. Some girls won't go for it. You know, like who wants to go to the baby doctor with a big tattoo sayin your ass belongs to the Satan's Slaves? Or what if a girl wants to cop out sometime and get married? Man, imagine the wedding night. She drops her nightie and there it is. Wow!"

There were about twenty Slaves at Bass Lake, but they didn't do much mixing. They staked out a small corner of the clearing, parked their bikes around it and spent most of the weekend lying around with their women and drinking their own wine. The Gypsy Jokers were less inhibited, but their behavior was oddly subdued in the presence of so many Hell's Angels. Unlike the Slaves, few of the Jokers had brought girls, so they were spared the constant worry that some pill-crazed Angel might try to move in and provoke a fight that the Angels would have to win. In theory the Hell's Angels confederation is friendly with all other outlaws, but in practice the half-dozen Angel chapters clash frequently with various clubs around their own turf. In San Francisco the Jokers and the Angels nurse a long-standing enmity, but the Jokers get along famously with other Angel chapters. A similar situation prevailed for years in the Los Angeles area, where the Berdoo Angels had sporadic rumbles with the Slaves, Comancheros and Coffin Cheaters. Yet these three clubs continued to speak well of every Hell's Angel in the state except those dirty bastards from Berdoo, who kept muscling in on other people's turf. All this was changed, however, by the Monterey rape, which resulted in such overwhelming heat that the Berdoo Angels were forced into desperate coexistence with the Slaves and other L.A. clubs, who were not much better off.

The Satan's Slaves are still a power in outlaw circles, but they have lost their slashing style of the early 1960s.[3] Other outlaws say the Slaves have never recovered from the loss of Smackey Jack, their legendary president, who had so much class that even the Angels held him slightly in awe. Smackey Jack stories still circulate whenever the clan gets together. I first heard about him from an easygoing Sacramento Angel named Norbert:

"Man, that Jack was outta sight. Sometimes he'd run wild for three or four days on pills and wine. He carried a pair of rusty pliers around with him and we'd sic him on strange broads. Man, he'd jerk em down on the ground and start pullin their teeth out with those goddamn pliers. I was with him in a place one time when the waitress wouldn't give us any coffee. Jack climbed right over the counter and took out three of her front teeth with his pliers. Some of the things he did would turn your stomach. Once he pulled out one of his own teeth in a bar. People couldn't believe it. A lot of em ran out when they saw he was serious. When he finally got the thing out, he laid it down on the bar and asked if he could trade it for a drink. He was spittin blood on the floor, but the bartender was too shook up to say anything."

Smackey Jack's turbulent three-year reign came to an end in 1964. Few of the outlaws seem to know what happened to him. "I heard he took a real bad fall," said one. "He pushed his luck about as hard as a guy could." Motorcycle outlaws are reluctant to talk seriously about former buddies who came to a bad end; the implications are too depressing. Smackey Jack, with his penchant for free-lance dentistry, was not the type to retire peacefully. Whatever happened—whether he was jailed, killed or forced to flee anonymously—he exists in outlaw legend as a rollicking, unpredictable monster who always prevailed. His loss was a demoralizing blow to the Satan's Slaves, whose spirit was already faltering under continued police pressure. By the end of 1964 the club was on the verge of disbanding.

The Slaves, along with several of the Hell's Angels chapters, were saved from extinction by the Lynch report and the nationwide infamy that followed. It gave the outlaws something to live up to, but they could never make it big unless they stopped fighting among themselves. Barger was among the first to realize this, and the other clubs were not far behind. Their long struggle for equality was suddenly rendered futile. The publicity breakthrough gave the Angels such prestige that the other clubs had no choice but to get on the bandwagon or perish. The process of consolidation took most of 1965, and it was only in the first stages at the time of the Bass Lake Run. Of the dozen or so functioning outlaw clubs in the state, only the Jokers and the Slaves felt confident enough to show up at Bass Lake in significant strength. Individual Angel chapters might have lost their supremacy, but when all of them got together, there was no question about who had the action. All things considered, it was a nervous time for the Slaves to show up with their women, who tend toward a wispy, blondish prettiness—a tempting sight for any Hell's Angel brooding drunkenly on the whys and wherefores of an unjust sex ratio.

By eleven it was plain that every girl in camp was not only spoken for, but taken. Off in the bushes there were sounds of giggling and groaning and twigs snapping, but the hundred or so outlaws who remained around the bonfire were discreetly oblivious. Many had worked off excess energy in the traditional war games. On some earlier run they had formed two secret battle societies: The Lodge and U-Boat 13. At any moment, at the sound of a prearranged signal, the U-Boat mob would rush on some hapless Lodge partisan, crushing him under a pile of bodies. Other Lodgers would then come to the rescue, adding to the pile-up. It looked like a scramble for a loose ball in a game between the Chicago Bears and the Green Bay Packers, except at Bass Lake the human heaps involved fifty or sixty people. I remember seeing Puff, who weighs about 225, sprint for about twenty yards and dive headfirst into the pile with a beer in each hand. For some reason there were no injuries. The outlaws are not athletic in the sense that any are ex-lettermen, but nearly all of them stay in good shape. They don't work at it, but the way most of them live they don't have to. What work they get paid for is usually physical anyway, and when they're not working they exist on hamburgers, donuts and whatever else they can hustle. Many swell up with beer, but the swelling bears little resemblance to the stylish pot of the desk-bound world. Even the few fat Angels are built more like beer barrels than water balloons.

There are those who claim the outlaws don't need food because they get all their energy from pep pills. But this is a bit far-fetched. The substitution doesn't work, as anyone who ever tried it can tell you. There are drugs to stimulate latent energy, but they are worthless and enervating unless the energy is there in the first place. Taken in excess on an empty stomach, pep pills induce a kind of nervous stupor characterized by fatigue, depression, chills and soaking sweats. The Angels deal freely on the black market, and if any pill really worked as a substitute for food they would use it in large quantities, for it would vastly simplify their lives. As it is, they take their nourishment wherever they can. Girls cook for them, waitresses give them "credit" at greasy diners, and there are always the married men, whose wives rarely balk at feeding five or six of the brethren at any hour of the day or night.

According to the code, there is no such thing as one Angel imposing on another. A hungry outlaw will always be fed by one of the others who has food . . . and if times are lean all around, a foraging party will hit a supermarket and steal everything they can carry. Few clerks will try to stop a dangerous hoodlum rushing out the door with two hams and three quarts of milk. The outlaws are not apologetic about stealing food, even though it goes against their pride. They prefer to think they don't have to—but whenever they do, they aren't sneaky. While one is gathering hams or steaks another will create a disturbance to draw the clerks. A third will fill a rucksack full of cans and vegetables on the other side of the store . . . and then they will all flee at the same time through different exits. There is nothing difficult about it. All it takes is gall, a threatening appearance and a surly disregard for whatever the neighbors might think. As for the police, by the time they reach the scene of the crime the food is already being cooked, twenty blocks away.

The outlaws are not articulate when it comes to the strengths and weaknesses of the world they function in, but their instincts are finely honed. They have learned from experience that some crimes are likely to be punished, and some aren't. A Hell's Angel who wants to make a long-distance call, for instance, will usually go to a pay phone. He will deposit enough money for the first three minutes, acknowledge the operator's signal at the end of that time and talk for as long as he wants. When he finally finishes, the operator will tell him how many coins he should put in the black box . . . but instead of paying, he laughs, spits obscenities into the phone and hangs up. Unlike the normal, middle-class, hard-working American, a motorcycle outlaw has no vested interest in the system that is represented by the voice of a telephone operator. The values of that system are completely irrelevant to him. He doesn't give a damn, and besides, he knows the phone company can't catch him. So he completes his call, abuses the operator and goes off to get happily wasted.

. . . .

rapere: to seize, enjoy hastily . . . ■ *Latin dictionary*

The Fresno Angels don't make news very often, but when they do, it is usually for something outlandish, some genuinely wretched affront to everything the squares hold dear. One of these was a brutal "rape" in a little town called Clovis, near Fresno, in the Central Valley. When the story hit the papers, the citizens were outraged for miles around.

A thirty-six-year-old widow and mother of five claimed she'd been yanked out of a bar where she was having a quiet beer with another woman, then carried to an abandoned shack behind the bar and raped repeatedly for two and a half hours by fifteen or twenty Hell's Angels and finally robbed of $150. That's how the story appeared in the San Francisco newspapers the next day, and it was kept alive for a few more days by the woman's claims that she was getting phone calls threatening her life if she testified against her assailants.

Then, four days after the crime, the victim was arrested on charges of "sexual perversion." The true story emerged, said the Clovis chief of police, when the woman was "confronted by witnesses. Our investigation shows she was not raped," said the chief. "She participated in lewd acts in the tavern with at least three Hell's Angels before the owners ordered them out. She encouraged their advances in the tavern, then led them to an abandoned house in the rear . . . She was not robbed, but according to a woman who'd accompanied her, had left her house early in the evening with five dollars to go bar-hopping."

This incident did not appear in the Attorney General's report, but it is as valid as any that did and it is one of the classic Hell's Angels stories. The O. Henry gimp in the plotline gives it real style. Somebody should have done a public opinion survey in Fresno, getting one set of reactions after the first version of the "rape" appeared, and another when the worm did a full turn. Like the Monterey rape, the Clovis outrage was one of those cases where the prosecuting attorneys would have fared better if their witnesses *had* been intimidated into silence.

The Clovis story is amusing not because of what happened, but because of the thundering disparity between accusation and reality. Here was the *rape mania,* the old bugaboo, one of the big keys to the whole Hell's Angels phenomenon.

Nobody is objective about rape. It is a horror and a titillation and a mystery all at once. Women are terrified of being raped, but somewhere in the back of every womb there is one rebellious nerve end that tingles with curiosity whenever the word is mentioned. This is even more terrifying, for it hints at basic depravity and secret lusts too dangerous to even think about. Men speak of rapists with loathing, and talk about their victims as if they carried some tragic brand. They are sympathetic, but always aware. Raped women have been divorced by their husbands—who couldn't bear to live with the awful knowledge, the visions, the possibility that it *wasn't really rape.* There is the bone of it, the unspeakable mystery. Everybody has heard the joke about the lawyer who used a quill and an ink bottle to get his client acquitted on a rape charge. He told the jury there was no such thing as rape, and proved it by having a witness try to put the quill in the bottle—which he manipulated so deftly that the witness finally gave up.

That sounds like one of Cotton Mather's jokes, or the wisdom of somebody very much like him—somebody who never had his arm bent up between his shoulder blades. Any lawyer who says there's no such thing as rape should be hauled out to a public place by three large perverts and buggered at high noon, with all his clients watching.

California averages more than 3,000 reported cases of forcible rape every year—or almost three a day. This would be a menacing statistic if it were not meaningless. In 1963, an average year, 3,058 forcible rapes were reported. But only 231 of these cases were brought to trial, and only 157 rapists were actually convicted. There is no way of knowing how many rapes were actually committed. Many went unreported or were hushed up by victims who feared the publicity and possible humiliation of a public trial. Rape victims concerned for their reputations often refuse to press charges, and few prosecutors will compel them to testify. A rapist who confines his lust to middle- and upper-class ladies is on pretty safe ground. But he is taking his life in his hands when he preys on women to whom the rape stigma has little meaning. Given a victim willing to testify in open court, an articulate prosecutor can re-create the "attack" in such vivid, carnal detail that even the meekest defendant will appear to the jury as a depraved Hun. The small percentage of rape cases that come to trial would indicate that the state only tries those it feels sure of. Despite this, only seven out of ten California rape trials end in conviction, while the figure for all other felony trials is eight out of ten.

The rape mania is such a complex phenomenon that it will eventually have to be dealt with by Presidential fiat. A blue-ribbon commission will have to probe it, along with logrolling and the fatback syndrome. Meanwhile, the Hell's Angels will continue to be arrested for rape with monotonous regularity. It has come to be known as one of their specialties—particularly gang rape, the most painful and degrading kind of sex assault. Although most of the membership has been arrested for rape at one time or another, in fifteen years less than half a dozen have been convicted. The outlaws insist they don't rape, but police say they do it continually. Convictions are hard to get, the cops ,say, because most women are reluctant to testify, and those few who are willing usually change their minds after the Angels—or some of the mamas—threaten to cut them up or "turn them out" for the whole club.

In July 1966 four Angels went on trial in Sonoma County for the forcible rape—at an Angel party—of a nineteen-year-old San Francisco model. Nineteen Angels were charged, but the county attorney narrowed it down to four—Terry, Tiny, Mouldly Marvin and Magoo II[4]—and went into court with no doubt in his mind that he would get four convictions. Two weeks later, after three Angel defense attorneys had cross-examined the victim, a jury of eleven women and one man voted for acquittal. They needed less than two hours to reach a unanimous verdict.

There is a certain amount of truth in the intimidation charges, but not nearly enough to explain why the Angels are so often charged and seldom convicted. The biggest part of the truth lies in the problem of defining an act of rape in terms of what actually happened. Obviously, if a woman is jerked off the street and forced to commit fornication against her will, that is rape. Yet the Angels say this never happens.

"Why take a chance on a fifty-year rape rap?" said one. "Hell, rape's no fun anyway—not if it's real—and we get all the action we can handle just by standing around. Christ, I've had women proposition me at stoplights, I've had em open my fly in bars without even saying hello, and if nothing happens by accident I just call around and find out who's horny."

"Sure, we'll take whatever we can get," said another. "But I've never yet heard a girl yell rape until it was all over and she got to thinking about it. Let's face it, a lot of women can't make it with just one guy at a time, they can't get their jollies. But the trouble is that sometimes a girl wants to stop before we do, or maybe while she's taking on fifteen guys in the back of a pickup truck somebody heists a few bucks from her purse—so she flips her lid and brings the heat down on us. Or maybe we get rousted and there she is all naked in the middle of a bunch of Hell's Angels, so suddenly she's been raped. What can we say? It's an automatic bust. But all we have to do is get a lawyer in her ear, tell her all the stuff that'll come out in court, and she decides to drop charges. Most of our rape raps never even get to court."

There are stories even in police records of girls who freely admitted to making it with two or three Angels and then trying to call a halt. What does a jury make of testimony to the effect that the first hump was for love, the next two for kicks and all the others were rape? An alleged rape victim in Oakland came to a bar one evening with an Angel she had met the night before and proceeded to do him on a pool table in a back room. One of the others looked in, saw what was happening, and naturally stood by for seconds. The girl protested, but when her true lover threatened to punch her she saw the light. After the third go she realized what she was in for and became hysterical, causing the bartender to summon the law.

Another girl rode a motorcycle up from Los Angeles and insisted on joining the club. The Angels told her she could, but only after she showed some class. "Man, what a nutty broad," said one. "She came to the party the next night with a big St. Bernard dog, and what an *act* she put on! I tell you it damn near blew my mind." He smiled wistfully. "After that, she took on everybody. Christ, what a bitch she was! She went right out of her gourd when she realized we weren't gonna let her join the club. She called us all kinds of shit, then she went out to a phone booth and rang for the cops. We all got busted for rape, but we never heard nothin more about it, because the broad split the next day. Nobody's seen her since."

Whenever the word "rape" comes up, Terry the Tramp tells the story about the "off-the-wall broad who rolled up to the El Adobe one night in a taxicab—a really fine-lookin chick. She paid the cabbie and just stood there for a minute, lookin at us . . . and then, man, she walked across the parking lot like she owned the place and asked us what the hell we were starin at. Then she started laughin. 'All right!' she yelled. 'I fuck, I suck and I smoke a lot of dope, so let's get started!' Wow! We couldn't believe it. But by God, she wasn't lyin. We put her in the back of that old panel truck we had then, and damn if she wasn't still yellin for more when the bar closed. We had to take her out to the country."

The Angels are full of stories about girls who seek them out. They tend to embellish both the action and the girls, but few of the stories are made up out of thin air. After dozens of long nights with the outlaws, I don't recall many when there wasn't at least one girl going down for the crowd, or whoever felt the sap rising. Usually they were mamas, but now and then what the Angels call "a strange broad" or "new pussy" would show up. Most of these seemed to be under the impression that they were "with" one of the Angels, and sometimes it worked out that way. The new pussy would dance a bit, drink a few beers, then roar off into the night with her Shane. Other girls, however, were taken into the panel truck and not seen again for many hours. With a few rare exceptions, the fact of some gang action in a nearby truck or back seat does not cause much of a stir. Of the thirty or so outlaws at the El Adobe on a weekend night, less than half would take the trouble to walk across the parking lot for a go at whatever ginch is available. A girl might be kept humping for hours, but only because a group of ten or so will take several turns each. Any outlaw whose old lady is around will gallantly ignore the sex action. The wives and steady girl friends won't stand for it. They don't actively resent the mamas, but they observe a rigid social barrier. One of the Oakland old ladies, a pretty, dark-haired girl named Jean, thinks mamas are pretty sad people, born losers. "I just feel sorry for girls like Mama Beverly," she says. "They think they have to put out and do anything at all just so they can be around guys like the Angels. But there are a lot of girls like that. One time at a party in Richmond a girl nobody had ever seen came in and started showing around a nude picture of herself. Then she went in the back room with half a dozen guys. Man, you ought to see the girls who flock around when the Angels are on a run, and just because they're Angels. If any girl claims she was raped by the Angels, it was most likely because she came up and asked for it."

That sounds a bit harsh. Invariably, the girls who pursue the Hell's Angels are in the grip of some carnal urgency, and some are deranged sluts, but few really look forward to being gang-raped. It is a very ugly experience—a fact the Angels tacitly admit by classifying it as a form of punishment. A girl who squeals on one of the outlaws or who deserts him for somebody wrong can expect to be "turned out," as they say, to "pull the Angel train." Some of the boys will pick her up one night and take her to a house where the others are sitting around with not much else to do. It is a definite ceremony, like the purging of a witch: the girl is stripped, held down on the floor and mounted by whoever has seniority. The punishment is administered in a place where everyone can watch, including the mamas and old ladies, although most of the Angel women are careful to avoid these shows. Not all the outlaws go for them either. The purging is usually done by the wronged Angel and a handful of others with a taste for this kind of discipline. Every chapter has a few gang-bang aficionados; they are usually the meanest of the lot . . . not the toughest, but the ones who are unpredictably hostile, day and night, in all kinds of situations.

At a party many months after I first met the Angels, when they were taking my presence for granted, I came on a scene that still hovers, in my mind, somewhere between a friendly sex orgy and an all-out gang rape. It was not an Angel party, but they had been invited, and twenty or so showed up for what turned into a two-day bash. Almost immediately several of the outlaws located a girl, the ex-wife of another guest, who agreed to make the beast with two backs in a small building set apart from the main house. Which she did, and happily so, with the chosen trio. But word quickly spread of the "new mama," and soon she was surrounded by a large group of onlookers . . . drinking, laughing and taking a quick turn whenever some vacancy occurred.

I keep a crumpled yellow note from that night; not all of the writing is decipherable, but some of it reads like this: "Pretty girl about twenty-five lying on wooden floor, two or three on her all the time, one kneeling between her legs, one sitting on her face and somebody else holding her feet . . . teeth and tongues and pubic hair, dim light in a wooden shack, sweat and semen gleaming on her thighs and stomach, red and white dress pushed up around her chest . . . people standing around yelling, wearing no pants, waiting first, second or third turns . . . girl jerking and moaning, not fighting, clinging, seems drunk, incoherent, not knowing, drowning . . ."

It was not a particularly sexual scene. The impression I had at the time was one of vengeance. The atmosphere in the room was harsh and brittle, almost hysterical. Most people took a single turn, then either watched or wandered back to the party. But a hard core of eight or ten kept at her for several hours. In all, she was penetrated in various ways no less than fifty times, and probably more. At one point, when the action slowed down, some of the Angels went out and got the girl's ex-husband, who was stumbling drunk. They led him into the shack and insisted he take his own turn. The room got nervous, for only a few of the outlaws were anxious to carry things that far. But the sight of her former old man brought the girl out of her daze just enough to break the silent tension. She leaned forward, resting on her elbows, and asked him to kiss her. He did, and then groggily took his turn while the others cheered.

Afterward the girl rested for a while and then wandered around the party in a blank sort of way and danced with several people. Later she was taken back for another session. When she finally reappeared I saw her trying to dance with her ex-husband, but all she could do was hang on his neck and sway back and forth. She didn't even seem to hear the music—a rock-'n'-roll band with a very swinging beat.

What would a jury make of that one—presuming they could know all the facts, circumstances and ramifications? If the girl was raped why didn't she protest or ask somebody for help? The Angels were vastly outnumbered, and it was not the sort of party they would have wanted to break up for the sake of a would-be mama. There was plenty of action around, and if anybody had protested the gang-bang the outlaws would have called it off. But nobody seemed bothered, and one or two of the non-Angel guests finally joined in. The girl had several chances to leave the party and call the police, but that was out of the question. Girls who get turned out at Hell's Angels parties don't think of police in terms of protection.

But sex is only one aspect of rape's broader definition. The word derives from the Latin *rapere,* "to take by force"; and according to Webster, the contemporary translation ranges from (1) "the crime of having sexual intercourse with a woman or girl forcibly and without her consent" to (2) "the act of seizing and carrying away by force" or (3) "to plunder or destroy, as in warfare." So the Hell's Angels, by several definitions, including their own, are working rapists . . . and in this downhill half of our twentieth century they are not so different from the rest of us as they sometimes seem. They are only more obvious.

NOTES

1 Webster defines oxpeckers as small, dull-colored birds that feed on ticks which they pick from the backs of infested cattle and wild animals.
2 In early February 1966, Terry and a Frisco Angel named George Zahn were arrested for "contributing to the delinquency" of a fifteen-year-old girl who had "Property of Hell's Angels" tattooed across her back at the shoulder-blade level. She also had the clap, which worries the Angels about as much as bad breath.

3 The Slaves returned to prominence with a vengeance in the summer of 1966, when thirty of them ransacked an apartment house in Van Nuys, a suburb of Los Angeles. On the morning of Saturday, August 6, three Slaves were served with eviction notices and forced to leave an apartment they had occupied for only a week. On Saturday night the three evictees returned to the building with a noisy raiding party and wreaked havoc for several hours. The terrified occupants locked their doors while the outlaws smashed sixteen windows and threw thirty pieces of furniture into the swimming pool. The Slaves threatened their ex-neighbors with further attacks if anyone called the police—which somebody finally did, but not until the motorcyclists had roared off into the night, seeking new nadirs, etc.

4 Another Magoo—not the one from Oakland.

11 | **The Cherubs Are Rumbling** |
Walter Bernstein

*This essay provides us with rare insight into the everyday lives of
what appears to be a typical urban gang. While the article is
written largely from the standpoint of the gang worker, it provides
valuable information on the situation and values of gang boys in
America's urban slums. In particular, it points out the reasons why
gangs become involved in fights or rumbles.*

 *The gangs are generally not formed for overtly aggressive pur-
poses, but rather as a means of protection. Just as national
governments have standing armies to protect them from other
nations, so gang boys form themselves into a standing army to
protect themselves from foreign forces. In fact, gangs often develop along national lines in the large, ethnically heterogeneous
slums of American cities. Just as nations go to war partly because
they share so few understandings and values with their neighboring nations, so do the boys. And, just as nations can often find
some compromise solution to their conflicts when they negotiate
them, so do the boys. It would appear that gang workers serving
as negotiators for gangs have been very successful in the last few
decades in eliminating most serious gang wars.*

One Saturday night a few weeks ago, I attended a dance at a Y.M.C.A.
in Brooklyn given by the Cherubs, a street gang with about thirty-five
members, all between the ages of fourteen and seventeen. The Cherubs
are not good boys. They regard the police as their natural enemies, and
most policemen who have come to know them reciprocate this attitude—with some justification. The Cherubs fight other gangs, using
knives, baseball bats, and guns; they have been known to steal; they
occasionally commit rape, though usually of the statutory kind; many of
them are truants; a few of them take dope; and while they fear the law,
they do not admire or respect it. The prospect that the Cherubs, if left

to themselves, will grow into model citizens is not at all bright. Their normal activity, though organized, is rarely social, and for this reason I was interested to learn that they were about to give an organized social dance. I heard about it from a friend of mine named Vincent Riccio, who knows the Cherubs well. He lives in their neighborhood and teaches physical education at Manual Training High School, in South Brooklyn, where some of them are reluctant students. Before becoming a teacher, in 1955, Riccio spent five years as a street-club worker for the New York City Youth Board, an agency dealing with problems of juvenile delinquency. His job was to go into a neighborhood that had a street gang known for particularly vicious habits, try to win the confidence of its members, and then, if possible, guide them in the direction of healthier pursuits. He is generally considered to have been the most successful street-club worker the Youth Board has ever had. "In his day, the Youth Board in Brooklyn *was* Riccio," a present Youth Board worker told me. Riccio has almost total empathy with young people— especially the delinquent kind—and they trust him. He speaks their language without patronizing them. Like most of the delinquents he has worked with, he comes from a rough, semi-slum background; his parents were immigrant Italians, and they had twenty-one children, six of whom have survived. As a boy, he did his share of gang fighting and thievery, though he claims to have been interested in stealing food rather than money. His specialty was looting the Mrs. Wagner pie trucks. His youthful experiences have convinced him that, except for the relatively rare psychotic cases, no delinquents are beyond help— that all are responsive to anyone they feel really cares for them. Riccio cares very deeply; he may even care too much. He had good reasons for switching to teaching as a career—among other things, he had a family to support—but he has a strong sense of guilt about having quit the Youth Board, and feels that it was a betrayal of the boys he had been working with.

For all practical purposes, Riccio hasn't quit. He has a name among the young people in his part of Brooklyn, and they are still likely to come to him for help with their problems, seeking him out either at home or at the school. He takes pride in this, and does what he can for them. He was particularly enthusiastic about the Cherubs' dance—as I could see when he asked if I'd like to attend it with him—because one of the gangs he had worked with when he was employed by the Youth Board was the forerunner of the Cherubs. That gang was also called the Cherubs, while the gang now known as the Cherubs was called the Cherub Midgets. Today, although a few of Riccio's former charges are in jail, most of them are respectable young men, gainfully employed and, in some cases, married. They are no longer bound together in a gang, but, Riccio explained, they take a collective avuncular interest in the current lot. In fact, they had helped organize the dance, and some of them were to act as chaperons. "They're trying to steer the kids straight," he said. "Show them they can get status by doing something besides breaking heads."

Riccio had asked me to meet him in front of the Y.M.C.A. at about nine o'clock on the night of the dance, and when I arrived he was already there, looking like an American Indian in a Brooks Brothers suit. A swarthy, handsome man of thirty-eight, he has a sharply angular face, with a prominent hooked nose and high cheekbones. He is not tall but he is very broad; his neck is so thick that his head seems small for his body, and his muscular development is awesome. He used to be a weight lifter, and still has a tendency to approach people as though they were bar bells. Whenever I shake hands with him, I have an uneasy feeling that I will find myself being raised slowly to the level of his chest and then, with a jerk and press, lifted effortlessly over his head. Actually, Riccio's handshake, like that of many strong men, is soft and polite. He is essentially a polite man, anxious to please, and he has a quick, warm smile and a trust in people that might seem naive in a less experienced person. I shook hands with him warily, then followed him inside the building and into an elevator. "The kids were lucky to get this place," he said as the door slid closed. "The last club dance held here broke up in a riot." We got out at the fourth floor and walked into a solid mass of music. It roared at us like water from a burst dam, and the elevator man hastily closed his door and plunged down again before he was flooded. A table stood by the elevator door. Seated importantly behind it was a boy of about sixteen, with long black hair carefully combed back in the style known as a ducktail and wearing a wide-shouldered double-breasted blue suit. He was a good-looking boy, with regular features, and he had an innocent look that did not seem quite genuine. His face lit up when he saw Riccio.

"Man, look who's here!" he said. "It's Rick!"

Riccio smiled and walked over to the table.

"Man, where you been keeping yourself?" the boy asked.

"You come to school once in a while, Benny, you'd know," Riccio said. He introduced me as his friend, and I felt for my wallet to pay the admission fee of a dollar that was announced on a piece of paper tacked to the table.

Benny reached across and put his hand on mine. "You're a friend of Rick's," he said reprovingly.

Riccio asked Benny how the dance was going. "Man, it's *crazy!*" the boy replied. "We got two hundred people here. We got Red Hook, Gowanus, the Tigers, the Dragons." He counted them on his fingers. "We got the Gremlins. We got a pack from Sands Street. We even got a couple of the Stompers."

"I thought the Stompers and Red Hook were rumbling," Riccio said.

"They called it off," Benny said. "The cops were busting them all over the place. They were getting *killed.*" He laughed. "Man, the law busted more heads than they did."

"Well, I'm glad it's off," Riccio said. "Whatever the reason, it's better off than on. Nobody gets hurt that way."

"It'll be on again," Benny said. "You don't have to worry about *that.* Soon as the cops lay off, they'll swing again."

Leaving Benny, we went through a door into the room where the dance was being held. I was astonished to see that all the music came from four boys, about fifteen years old, who were seated on a bandstand at one end of the room. They were small but they looked fierce. They were playing trumpet, guitar, piano, and drums, and the room rocked to their efforts. It was a large room, gaily decorated with balloons and strips of crepe paper. Tables and chairs ringed a dance floor that was crowded with teen-age boys and girls—including a few Negroes and Puerto Ricans—all wearing the same wise, sharp city expression. The usual complement of stags, most of them dressed in windbreakers or athletic jackets, stood self-consciously on the sidelines, pretending indifference.

I followed Riccio over to one corner, where two boys were selling sandwiches and soft drinks through an opening in the wall. Business appeared to be outstripping their ability to make change. As we came up, one of them bellowed to a customer, "Shut up a minute, or I'll bust you right in the mouth!" Watching all this tolerantly were two husky young men—in their early twenties, I guessed—who greeted Riccio with delight. He introduced them to me as Cherub alumni, who were helping chaperon the dance. One was called Louie, and the other, who limped, was called Gimpy. The boys at the refreshment window saw Riccio and immediately yelled to him for help. He went over to them, and I stayed with Louie and Gimpy. Louie, it developed, had been a paratrooper in the Army until only a few days before, and was nervous about resuming civilian life. He said he would never have been able to get into the Army if it had not been for Riccio. He had been on probation when he decided to enlist, and Riccio had persuaded the probation officer to let him sign up.

"Believe me," Gimpy said, "we owe a lot to that Riccio."

I asked what else Riccio had done for them, and Gimpy said, "Well, he was looking out for us. We needed a job, he'd try to get us a job. He'd try to keep us out of trouble."

"It ain't exactly what he did," Louie said. "We just didn't want to louse him up."

"Well, he did a lot, too," Gimpy said. "A kid might be sleeping in the subway, scared to go home. He'd be scared maybe his old man would beat him up, like Mousy was that time. Well, Rick fixed it so Mousy could go home and his old man wouldn't beat him up."

"Oh, he did a lot," Louie said. "That's what I mean. A guy that's doing a lot for you, you don't want to louse him up. I mean, we'd start thinking of something to do. What are we going to do today? Break a few heads? Steal a few hubcaps? We'd be talking about it, and then somebody would say, 'What about Rick? What's Rick going to think about this?' So then we wouldn't do it." He stopped, looked over at the refreshment window, where Riccio was helping the two boys make change, and added, "Well, a lot of the time we wouldn't do it."

A small boy came up to Louie and whispered in his ear. "Excuse me," Louie said, and headed determinedly toward the door.

Riccio returned, and we stood watching the dancers, who were doing the cha-cha. He seemed pleased with what he saw. "Notice the Negro kids and the Puerto Ricans?" he said. "Two years ago, they wouldn't have dared come here. They'd have had their heads broken. Now when a club throws a dance any kid in the neighborhood can come—provided he can pay for a ticket." A pretty little girl of about twelve danced by with a tall boy. "She's Ellie Hanlon," Riccio told me, nodding in her direction. "Her older brother was a Cherub—Tommy Hanlon. He was on narcotics, and I could never get him off. I was just starting to reach him when I left the Youth Board. Two weeks later, he was dead from an overdose. Seventeen years old." Riccio had told me about Tommy Hanlon once before, and I had suspected that, in some way, he felt responsible for the boy's death.

The Hanlon girl saw Riccio and stopped dancing to run over to him. He picked her up and kissed her on the forehead. As soon as he had put her down, she started to pull him out onto the dance floor. "Hey, I'm too old for that kind of jazz," Riccio said, but he allowed himself to be pulled. He turned out to be an excellent dancer—graceful and light on his feet. When the dance ended, he returned the girl to her partner and came back, panting a little. "Man, am I out of shape!" he said.

Louie rejoined us, shaking his head. "Look what I took away from a kid at the door," he said. He showed us a blackjack.

"You know the kid?" Riccio asked.

Louie said he thought it was one of the Sands Street boys.

"That's a rough crew—Sands Street," Riccio said.

The demon band was really sending now. The trumpet player had put on a straw sombrero that came down to the bridge of his nose. He looked as though he had lost the top part of his face, but it didn't hamper his playing. The notes shrieked from his horn, desperate to escape. The boy on the drums seemed to be going out of his mind. On the floor, the dancers spun and twisted and shuffled and bounced in a tireless frenzy. "Man, I get pooped just looking," Riccio said.

Benny, the boy who had been collecting admissions, pushed his way through the crowd to us, his eyes wide with excitement. "Hey, Louie!" he said. "The Gremlins are smoking pot in the toilet."

"Excuse me," Louie said, and hurried away to deal with the pot, or marijuana, smokers.

"Them stinking Gremlins!" Benny said. "They're going to ruin our dance. We ought to bust their heads for them."

"Then you'd really ruin your dance," Riccio told him. "I thought you guys were smart. You start bopping, they'll throw you right out of here."

"Well, them Gremlins better not ruin our dance," Benny said.

I asked Riccio if many of the boys he knew smoked marijuana. He said that he guessed quite a few of them did, and added that he was more concerned about those who were on heroin. One trouble, he explained, is that dope pushers flock to neighborhoods where two gangs are at war, knowing they will find buyers among members of the gangs who are so keyed up that they welcome any kind of relaxation or who are just plain afraid. "You take a kid who's scared to fight," Riccio said. "He may start taking narcotics because he knows the rest of the gang won't want him around when he's on dope. He'd be considered too undependable in a fight. So that way he can get out of it." He paused, and then added, "You find pushers around after a fight, too, when the kids are let down but still looking for kicks." Riccio nodded toward a boy across the floor and said, "See that kid? He's on dope." The boy was standing against the wall, staring vacantly at the dancers, his face fixed in a gentle, faraway smile. Every few seconds, he would wipe his nose with the back of his hand.

"Man, that Jo-Jo!" Benny said. "He's stoned *all* the time."

"What's he on—horse?" Riccio asked, meaning heroin.

"Who knows with that creep?" Benny said.

I asked Benny if any special kind of boy went in for dope.

"The creeps," he said. "You know, the goofballs." He searched for a word. "The *weak* kids. Like Jo-Jo. There ain't nothing the guys can't do to him. Last week, we took his pants off and made him run right in the middle of the street without them."

"You wouldn't do that to Dutch," Riccio said.

"Man, Dutch *kicked* the habit," Benny said. "We told the guy he didn't kick the habit, he was out of the crew. We were *through* with him. So he kicked it. Cold turkey."

Louie returned, and Riccio asked him what he had done about the offending Gremlins. Louie said he had chased them the hell out of the men's room.

I kept watching Jo-Jo. He never once moved from his position. The music beat against him, but his mind seemed to be on his own music, played softly and in very slow motion, and only for him.

As the dance continued, Louie and Gimpy and several other chaperons policed the room with unobtrusive menace, and there was no further trouble; everyone seemed to be having a good time. At eleven-thirty, Riccio said to me, "Now is when you sweat it out." He explained that the last half hour of a gang dance is apt to be tricky. Boys who have smuggled in liquor suddenly find themselves drunk; disputes break out over which boy is going to leave with which girl; many of the boys simply don't want to go home. But that evening the crucial minutes passed and it appeared that all was going well.

A few minutes before midnight, the musicians played their last set, and proudly packed their instruments. The trumpet player took off his sombrero, and I saw that he already had the pale and sunken face of a jazz musician. As the crowd thinned out, Riccio said, with some relief, "It turned out O.K." We waited until the room was almost empty, and then walked to the doorway. Benny was standing at the entrance of a make-shift checkroom near the elevator. "Good dance, Ben," Riccio said, "You guys did a fine job." Benny grinned with pleasure.

Just then, a boy came out of the checkroom. He seemed to be agitated. Riccio said, "Hi ya, Mickey," but the boy paid no attention to him, and said to Benny, "I want my raincoat. I checked it here, it ain't here."

"Man, you checked it, it's here," Benny said.

"It ain't here," Mickey repeated. Benny sighed and went into the checkroom, and Mickey turned to Riccio. He was a small boy with a great mop of black hair that shook when he talked. "I paid eighteen bucks for that raincoat," he said. "You can wear it inside and out."

"You'll get it back," Riccio said.

"It's a Crawford," Mickey said.

Benny came out of the checkroom and said, "Somebody must have took it by mistake. We'll get it back for you tomorrow."

"I don't want it tomorrow," Mickey said.

"Man, you'll get it tomorrow," Benny said patiently.

"I want my raincoat," Mickey said, his voice rising. Some of the boys who had been waiting for the elevator came over to see what was happening.

"You're making too much noise," Benny said. "I don't want you making so much noise, man. You'll ruin the *dance.*"

"There ain't no more dance," Mickey said, "The dance is over. I want my raincoat."

More boys were crowding around, trying to quiet Mickey, but he was adamant. Finally, Riccio pulled Benny aside and whispered in his ear. Benny nodded, and called to Mickey, in a conciliatory tone, "Listen,

Mick, we don't find the raincoat tomorrow, we'll *give* you the eighteen bucks."

"Where the hell have you got eighteen bucks?" Mickey asked suspiciously.

"From what we made on the dance," Benny told him. "You can buy a whole new coat, man. O.K. You satisfied? You'll shut up now and go home?"

"I don't want the eighteen bucks," Mickey said.

"Oh, the hell with him," one of the other boys said, and turned away.

"I want my raincoat," Mickey said. "It's a Crawford."

"You can buy another Crawford!" Benny shouted at him, suddenly enraged. "What are you—some kind of a wise guy? You trying to put on an act just because Rick's here? What do you think you are—some kind of a wheel?"

"I want my raincoat," Mickey said.

"And I don't want you cursing in here!" Benny shouted. "You're in the Y.M.C.A.!"

"Who's cursing?" Mickey asked.

"Don't *curse*," Benny said grimly, and walked away. The other boys stood about uncertainly, not knowing what to do next. In a moment the elevator arrived, and Riccio asked the operator to wait. He went over to Mickey and spoke a few soothing words to him, then came back, and the two of us got into the elevator. Two boys from the crowd got in with us.

"What do you think of that creep, Rick?" one of them asked.

"Well, it's his coat," Riccio said. "He's got a right to want it back."

"I think he stole the coat in the first place," the boy said as the elevator reached the ground floor.

Riccio and I walked through the lobby, already dimmed for the night, and out into the street, where he saw Louie and Gimpy getting into a car. They offered us a lift, but Riccio said he had brought his own car, so they waved and drove off. At that instant, a couple of boys dashed out of the building, looked wildly around, and then dashed back in. "Now what?" Riccio said.

We followed them in, and found perhaps a dozen boys bunched near the entrance. I could see Mickey in the middle, red-faced and angry and talking loudly. Benny, who was standing on the edge of the group, told us, "Now he says one of the Stompers took his coat. Man, he's *weird!*" He waved at Mickey in disgust and went outside.

Riccio pushed his way into the center of the crowd and separated Mickey from several boys who were arguing with him heatedly. A few of these wore jackets with the name "Stompers" stitched across the back. "Come on, now," Riccio said to Mickey. "We got to get out of here."

"He says we robbed his lousy coat, Mr. Riccio," one of the Stompers said.

"It's a Crawford!" Mickey yelled at him.

"The coat was probably taken by mistake," Riccio said calmly. "You'll get it back tomorrow, Mickey. If you don't get it back, you'll get the money and you can buy a new one. You had a good time, didn't you?" He was speaking to all of them now, his arm around Mickey's shoulder as he guided the boy gently toward the door. "You ought to be proud, running such a dance. You want to spoil it now? Hey?"

Mickey was about to say something when a boy burst in through the door, shouting, "Hey, Benny and one of the Stompers are having it out."

Everyone rushed for the door. When I got outside, I saw Benny and another boy swinging desperately at each other on the sidewalk. Benny hit the boy on the cheek, the boy fell against a car, and Benny moved in and swung again. The boy went into a clinch, and the two of them wrestled against the car. I heard a click near me and turned to see one of the Stompers holding a switch-blade knife in his hand, but before he or any of the other boys could join in, Riccio was down the steps and between the fighters, holding them apart. The boy with the knife turned suddenly and went back into the building, and then I saw what he must have seen—a policeman walking slowly across the street toward us. Riccio saw him, too. "Cut out!" he said, in a low voice, talking to the whole crowd. "Here comes the law! Cut out!" He pushed the fighters farther apart as two of the Stompers ranged themselves alongside Benny's opponent. "Beat it!" Riccio said, in the same low voice. "You want to end up in the can? Cut out!" The Stompers turned and started to walk away, but the rest of the boys continued to stand around the steps of the Y. The policeman, now at the curb, looked curiously at Riccio and Benny, and then at the boys. Everyone appeared casual, but the air was heavy with tension. The policeman hesitated a moment, and then went on down the block.

"All right," Riccio said, with a tone of finality.

"He started to rank me," Benny said, meaning that the Stomper had been taunting him.

"Now, forget it," Riccio told him. "You want a ride home?"

Benny shook his head. "I'll grab a bus," he said, looking up the street, where the Stompers could still be seen walking away. Then he turned back to Riccio and said defiantly, "Man, what did you *want* me to do? Punk out?" He straightened his jacket, ran his fingers through his hair, and set off across the street with several other Cherubs. We watched them until they got to the corner. The other Cherubs kept walking straight ahead, but Benny turned down the side street. "You see how it can start?" Riccio said. "One minute they're having a dance, and the next minute they're having a war."

We went down the block to where Riccio's car was parked. I got in beside him, and he drove to the corner, where he stopped for a red light. I found that my hands were shaking. The light changed, but Riccio did not move. "I got a feeling," he said reflectively. "If you don't mind, I want to go back for a minute." He drove around the block until we were in front of the Y again, and then he turned the corner where Benny had left the others. And there was Benny, caught in the glare of our headlights, held down on his knees in the middle of the street by two boys while a third boy savagely hit his bowed head. The headlights fixed the scene like a movie gone suddenly too real—Benny kneeling there and the boy's arms rising and falling—and then Riccio had slammed on the brakes and we were out of the car, running toward them. By the time we reached Benny, the other boys were gone, lost in the dark; all that was left was the echo of their footsteps as they ran off into the night, and then there was not even that—no sound at all except the soft, steady ticking of the motor in Riccio's car. Benny was getting slowly to his feet. "You O.K.?" Riccio asked helping him up. Benny nodded, and rubbed his neck. "I figured something like this," Riccio said to me, and then, turning back to Benny, he asked, "You sure you're all right? Maybe we ought to stop by the hospital."

"Man, I'm all right," Benny said. "They didn't hit me hard."

After looking the boy over, Riccio took him by the arm and led him back to the car, and the three of us got into the front seat. We drove in silence to a housing project near the waterfront, where Benny got out, still without speaking. We watched him enter one of the buildings, and then Riccio drove me to a subway station. "Now you know about these kids," he said as we shook hands. "They can blow up while you're looking at them." Riding home, I kept thinking of Benny as he had knelt there in the street, his head bent as though in prayer.

One afternoon a few weeks later, I got a telephone call from Riccio. "I thought you might be interested," he said. "The Cherubs are rumbling. They just put Jerry Larkin, from the Stompers, in the hospital. Caught him out of his neighborhood and left him for dead. He'll be all right, but they beat him up pretty bad. I think they worked him over with one of those iron tire chains." He said that there was now a full-scale war between the Cherubs and the Stompers, and that he had been talking with members of both gangs, trying to get them to call it off. Then he told me he was going to try to mediate again that night, and asked if I would like to go along. I said I would, and we arranged to meet at his house at seven o'clock.

Riccio lives in a small apartment on the top floor of an old brownstone in the Park Slope section of Brooklyn, with his wife and two children—a girl of eight and a boy of eleven. From the steps of the house, one can see the Statue of Liberty, like a toy in the harbor. When I arrived, the children were watching a Western movie on television.

Riccio and his wife, an attractive blonde named Evelyn, have fixed up their apartment with modern furniture and abstract paintings, some of the latter the work of Riccio himself. He has done a lot of painting, and once considered a career as a commercial artist, but decided that it would be too insecure. As we were about to leave, Mrs. Riccio came out of the kitchen with a dish towel over her arm, and her husband kissed her goodbye. She looked worried. I recalled that one reason Riccio had quit the Youth Board was his wife's fear that he might be beaten up himself. But now she just told him not to stay out late, because he had to get up early the next morning.

"There's a lot going on tonight," Riccio said as he and I walked downstairs. "Some kid shot another kid with a zip gun, and the heat's on." He went on to explain that this shooting had nothing to do with the rumble between the Cherubs and the Stompers. The boy who was shot had not belonged to any gang; he had simply not wanted to go to school, and had asked a friend to shoot him in the arm, so he would have a good excuse to stay home. The friend had obliged, using a homemade gun, but the wound had been a little deeper than planned. The injured boy's parents had taken him to a hospital, where the bullet was removed. The police were notified, as a matter of routine, and now they were searching for the friend and the gun, both having disappeared.

We got into Riccio's car, and he started to drive slowly through the neighborhood. "We ought to find some of the Stompers hanging around these corners," he said. At first, no boys were to be seen. The part of Brooklyn we were riding through was not quite a slum. The streets were lined with old and ugly brownstones, but they seemed in good repair. The whole effect was dispirited, rather than poor; it was a neighborhood without cheer. As night fell, the houses retreated gradually into shadow, but they lost none of their ugliness. The street lamps came on, casting pools of dirty-yellow light. "The Stompers used to have a Youth Board worker assigned to them," Riccio said. "But he was pulled off the job and sent up to the Bronx when all that trouble broke up there. I guess these kids won't get another worker until they kill somebody." He said this without rancor, but I knew he felt strongly that the best times to do any real good with a gang are before it starts fighting and after it stops.

Ahead of us, a boy appeared from around a corner and walked rapidly in our direction. "One of the Stompers," Riccio said, and drew over to the curb. He called out to the boy, and when the latter paid no attention, he called louder. "Hey, Eddie, it's me! Riccio!" The boy stopped and looked at us warily, and then, reassured, came over to the car. His face was bruised and he had a lump under his left eye. "What happened?" Riccio asked. "You get jumped?"

"The cops busted me," Eddie said. He was about fifteen, and he was wearing a leather jacket with spangles on the cuffs that glittered in the light from a street lamp. His hair was blond and wavy and long. "They just let me out of the God-damned station house," he added.

"Why'd they pick you up?" Riccio asked.

"For nothing!" Eddie said indignantly. "We were just standing around, and they picked us all up. We wasn't doing a thing." He paused, but Riccio didn't say anything, and after a moment he went on, "You know *them.* They wanted to know did we have zip guns like what shot that stupid kid. I told them I didn't have no gun. So they banged me around." He laughed. "You think they banged *me* around. You should have seen what they done to Ralphie." Riccio asked where the other Stompers were now, and Eddie replied that he thought they were hanging around a nearby grammar school. "But not me," he said. "I'm going home."

"Good idea," Riccio said.

"I got to get my gun out of the house," Eddie said, "I don't want them coming around and finding it."

"Why don't you give it to me?" Riccio said.

"No, sir," Eddie said. "I paid three bucks for that piece. I'm going to leave it over at my uncle's house. Maybe I'll see you later." He waved and walked off.

I asked Riccio how teen-agers could buy guns for three dollars, or any amount. He shrugged wearily and told me that salesmen of second-hand weapons periodically canvass sections where gangs are known to be active. A good revolver, he said, costs about ten dollars, but an inferior one can be bought for considerably less.

"Well, anyway, now I know Eddie's got a gun," Riccio said as we started up again, heading for the grammar school. "That's important—that he told me about it. Every time a kid tells you he's got a gun or he's going to do something bad, like break heads or pull a score—a robbery, I mean—he's telling you for a reason. First, he wants your attention. Maybe nobody has been giving him attention. You know—at home or in school or with the gang. He knows the way to get it is to do something real bizarre. And when he tells you, he knows this is one way to get you to stop and listen to him. You know—talk to him, pay him a little attention. But at the same time he's saying to you, 'Show me how I don't have to do it. Show me a way out.' But it's got to be a way that will let him save face. That's the big thing. It's all a question of status. Show him a healthy way out, in terms of his social setup, not yours—show him a way out that will make it possible for him to preserve his status with his friends—and he'll grab it in a minute. But first you've got to reach him. If you haven't reached him, he won't listen to your way out. Some of them you can reach, and some of them you can't reach.

Some of them you know you ought to be able to reach, but then you find you just can't." He paused, and I imagined that he was again thinking of the Hanlon boy's death from an overdose of drugs. "You try, but you can't really reach them. They're too disturbed, or you're not going about it right. So you give up on them. You turn your back, and they go down the drain." I remarked that he could hardly hope to help them all, but he said, as if he hadn't heard me, "You can't turn your back on them."

In a minute or two, the grammar school loomed up before us in the darkness with a solid, medieval look, and we saw a group of boys lounging under a street light—hands in pockets, feet apart, and, as they talked, moving about in a street-corner pattern as firmly fixed as that of the solar system. Riccio parked the car, and we got out and walked over to them. They froze instantly. Then one of them said, "It's Rick," and they relaxed. Riccio introduced me, and I shook hands with each of them; their handshakes were limp, like those of prize-fighters. There were eight of the boys—all with long hair and wise little faces. They said they had been picked up, like Eddie, and questioned about the recent shooting, and they laughed about their experiences at the station house, taking for granted their relationship with the law—the obligation of the police to hunt them down and their own obligation not to cooperate in any way. There was little bitterness and no anger, except on the part of the boy named Ralphie, who felt that he had been hit unnecessarily hard.

Riccio suggested that they all go into the school, where they could talk more comfortably, and led the way inside. Walking down a corridor, he asked the Stompers about Jerry, the boy who had been beaten up. They said he would be out of the hospital in a couple of days. "They thought he had a fractured skull," Ralphie said, "but all he had was noises in the head."

"I was with him when it happened," one of the other boys said. "There were four of them Cherubs in a car—Benny and that Bruno and two other guys."

"That Bruno ain't right in the head," another boy said.

"I got away because I was wearing sneakers," the first boy said. "That Bruno came after me with that chain, I went right through the sound barrier."

Riccio pushed open a pair of swinging doors that led into the school gymnasium, and as I followed him in the dank, sweaty smell hit me like an old enemy; I had gone to a school like this and hated every minute of it. The windows were the same kind I remembered—screened with wire netting, ostensibly as protection against flying Indian clubs but actually, I still believe, to keep the pupils from escaping. Out on the floor, several boys were being taught basketball by a tall young man in a sweatsuit. Riccio went over to talk with him, and, returning, indicated some benches in a corner. "He says we can sit over there," he said. We moved over to the corner, where Riccio sat down on a bench while the boys grouped themselves around him, some on benches and others squatting on the floor and gazing up at him.

"All right," Riccio said. "What are you guys going to do? Is it on or off?"

The boys looked at Ralphie, who seemed to be the leader. "We ain't going to call it off," he said.

"They started it," one of the others said.

"They japped us," a third boy said, meaning that the Cherubs had taken them by surprise. "You want we should let them get away with that?"

"All right," Riccio said. "So they jap you, they put Jerry in the hospital. Now you jap them, maybe you put Bruno in the hospital."

"I catch that Bruno, I put him in the cemetery," Ralphie said.

"So then the cops come down on you," Riccio went on. "They bust the hell out of you. How many of you are on probation?" Two of the boys raised their hands. "This time they'll send you away. You won't get off so easy this time. Is that what you want?" The boys were silent. "O.K.," Riccio said. "You're for keeping it on. That's your decision, that's what you want. O.K. Just remember what it means. You can't relax for a minute. The cops are looking to bust you. The neighborhood thinks you're no good, because you're making trouble for everybody. You can't step out of the neighborhood, because you'll get jumped. You got to walk around with eyes in the back of your head. If that's what you want, O.K. That's your decision. That's how you want things to be for yourself. Only, just remember how it's going to be."

Riccio paused and looked around him. No one said anything. Then he started on a new tack. "Suppose the Cherubs call it off," he said. "Would you call it off if they do?"

"They want to call it off?" a boy asked.

"Suppose they do," Riccio said.

There was another silence. The basketball instructor took a hook shot, and I watched the ball arc in the air and swish through the net without touching the rim. The room echoed with the quickening bounce of the ball as one of the players dribbled it away.

"We ain't going to call it off," Ralphie said. "They started it. We went to their lousy dance and we didn't make no trouble, and they said we stole their lousy coat. Then they jumped Jerry, and that Bruno gave him that chain job."

"They say you guys jumped Benny after the dance," Riccio told them.

"He started it," one of the boys said.

"Don't you see?" Riccio said. "No matter who started what, you keep it up, all it means is trouble. It means some of you guys are going to get sent away. You think I want to see that happen? Man, it hurts me when one of you guys get sent away."

"We ain't calling it off," Ralphie said.

"Suppose they want to call it off," Riccio said.

"They're punks," Ralphie said. He stood up, and then others stood up and ranged themselves behind him. They looked like a gang now, with their captain out in front to lead them. Riccio sat where he was, looking up at one face after another.

"Just because they had a dance," Ralphie said. "You know what? We were going to have a dance, too. And not in the lousy Y.M.C.A. In the American Legion."

"Why didn't you?" Riccio asked.

"They took away our worker," one of the other boys said. "They wouldn't give us the American Legion hall unless we had a worker."

"You'll get the worker back," Riccio told them. "He'll come back in a week or two, and then you can have your dance."

"He said he was coming back last week," Ralphie said bitterly.

"I'll tell you what," Riccio said. "I'll talk to the people down at the Legion. Maybe if they know I'm working with you, they'll give you the hall."

"We were going to have an eight-piece band," one of the boys said.

"I'll see what I can do," Riccio said. "But you know how it is when it gets around that you're swinging with another crew. You'll have trouble getting the hall. And even if you do, who wants to come to a dance when there might be trouble? The girls won't want to come—they'll be too scared."

"You sure the Cherubs said they want to call it off?" a boy asked.

"I'm going over there right now," Riccio said.

"They want to call it off, let them call it off," Ralphie said. He stood there for a moment, a young Napoleon, and then turned and started for the door. The others followed him, some of them waving to Riccio and calling goodbye. Then they were gone, leaving only Riccio and me and the basketball players. The ball bounced off the backboard and over to the benches, and Riccio caught it and, still seated, took a one-handed shot at the basket. He missed, shook his head ruefully, and stood up.

We walked out to his car, and when we were driving through the streets again, he said, "I'm glad they told me about the dance. It gives them a reason for calling it off." I remarked that the boys hadn't sounded to me as if they wanted to call it off. "If they didn't want to call it off, they wouldn't have listened to me," he said. "They wouldn't have hung around that long. They want to call it off, all right—they're scared about what happened to Jerry. Only, they don't know how. They don't want to be accused of punking out."

We drove past the housing project where Benny lived. "The Cherubs hang out in that candy store down the block," Riccio said. He pulled up in front of the shop, which I could see was crowded with youngsters, and said, "Wait here while I take a look." He went inside, came out again, and got back in the car, saying, "The Cherubs aren't here yet, so we'll wait." We both settled back and made ourselves comfortable. It was only nine-thirty, but the neighborhood was deserted. The candy store was the only shop in sight that was open, and ours was the only car parked on the dark street. Above and behind the tops of the brownstones rose the great bulk of the housing project, like some kind of municipal mausoleum, but dotted here and there with lights as evidence that life persisted inside. Two boys came down the street and were about to enter the candy store when Riccio called out, "Hey, Benny!" They turned and walked over to the car, and Riccio said, "Get in. It's too jammed in there." They slid into the back seat, and Riccio, turning to face them, said to me, "You know Ben, don't you?" and introduced me to the other boy—Bruno, the one who had used the tire chain on Jerry. He was very thin, and had enormous eyes. "I've just been over with the Stompers," Riccio said, without preamble. "I think they'll call it off if you'll call it off."

"We won't call it off," Bruno said.

"Not even if they do?" Riccio asked.

"Man, they *ruined* our dance," Benny said.

"Nobody ruined your dance," Riccio said. "Your dance was a big success. You had one of the best dances around here." He went on to give them the same arguments he had given the Stompers. They listened restlessly, shifting in their seats and looking everywhere but at him. "Well, how about it?" Riccio said, finally.

"We call it off, what else are we going to do?" Bruno asked.

"There's other things to do besides breaking heads," Riccio said, and then I jumped as the car shook from a violent bang against its left side and the head of a policeman suddenly appeared in the window next to the driver's seat.

"Out of the car!" the policeman said. "All of you! Out!"

"Boy, you scared me, Officer," Riccio said.

"Get out of the car!" the policeman repeated. *"Now!"*

"We're not doing anything wrong," Riccio said. "We're just sitting here talking."

"Get out of that car!" the policeman said, and with that we found ourselves staring at a gun, which he was pointing straight at Riccio's head. It looked as big as a cannon.

"Jesus, Rick, get out of the car!" Bruno whispered from the back seat. "I'm on probation. I don't want to fight with the law."

"I'm getting out," Riccio said. He opened the door on his side and the policeman stepped back, but not quickly enough. The door hit his hand and knocked the gun to the pavement.

"Oh, Christ!" Benny said. "Now he'll kill us all!"

I shut my eyes, then opened them. The policeman had dived to the ground and recovered his gun. "O.K.—all of you," he said tightly. He motioned with his gun, and we all got out of the car and stood beside Riccio. "Face the car and lean against it with your hands on the top," the policeman said. We did, and he ran his free hand down the sides of our clothes, searching for weapons. Finding none, he said, "O.K., turn around." We turned around, and he said to Riccio, "This your car?" Riccio nodded, and the policeman asked for his license and registration. Riccio handed them over, and the policeman peered at them and then went around to compare the number on the car's license plates with the one on the registration. When he saw that the numbers matched, he said to Riccio, "Open the trunk." Riccio opened the trunk, and the policeman looked inside. Then he closed the trunk.

"Satisfied?" Riccio asked.

"Shut up," said the policeman.

"We didn't do anything," Riccio said. "What right have you got subjecting us to all this humiliation?"

"I'll crack this thing over your head," the policeman said, but his voice now betrayed a lack of conviction. "You're pretty old to be hanging around with kids. What the hell do you do?"

"I'm a teacher at Manual Training High School," Riccio told him.

"Well, why didn't you say so?" the policeman said. He put the gun back in his holster, and Benny exhaled slowly. "How the hell am I supposed to know who you are?" the policeman went on. "It's a suspicious neighborhood."

"That's no reason to treat everybody in it like criminals," Riccio said.

"Here," the policeman said, handing Riccio his license and registration. He seemed glad to get rid of them. Riccio and the rest of us climbed back into the car. "You see some guys in a car with some kids, how the hell are you supposed to know?" the policeman asked.

Riccio started to answer, but Benny, from the back seat, broke in, "Hey, Rick, let's cut out of here, man. I got to get home."

"Sure, Ben," Riccio said over his shoulder, and then drove off, leaving the policeman standing in the street. As soon as we were well away, the boys started talking excitedly.

"Man!" Benny said. "You could of got your head kicked in!"

"Did you see that gun?" Bruno said. "A thirty-eight. He could of blowed you right apart with that gun!"

"Man, I thought we were *gone!*" Benny said. "And we weren't even doing anything!"

The idea of their innocence at the time appealed to the boys, and they discussed it at some length. They both got out at the housing project, still talking. "I'm setting something up with you and the Stompers," Riccio said. "Just two or three guys from each side to straighten this thing out. All right?"

"Did you think that cop was going to shoot you, Rick?" Bruno asked.

"He was just jumpy," Riccio said. "Now, look. I'll get a place for us to meet, and we'll sit down and talk this thing out. O.K.?"

"Man, I thought we were *all* going to be busted," Benny said. "And for *nothing!*"

They drifted away from the car, laughing, and Riccio let them go. "I'll be in touch with you, Ben," he called. Benny waved back at us, and we watched them as they disappeared into the depths of the project.

I asked Riccio if he was always that tough with policemen, and he looked surprised. "I wasn't trying to be tough," he said. "That guy's job is hard enough—why should I make it any harder? I was making a point for the kids. I always tell them, when you're right, fight it to the hilt. I thought we were right, so I had to practice what I preach. Otherwise, how will they believe me on anything?"

Riccio invited me to go home with him for coffee, but I said I'd better be getting along, so he drove me to the subway. As I got out, he said, "I'm going to try to get them together this week. If I do, I'll let you know." We said good night, and I went down the subway stairs. On the way home, I bought a newspaper and read about a boy in the Bronx who had been stabbed to death in a gang fight.

I did not hear from Riccio again that week. The following week, I called him one night at about ten o'clock. His wife answered the phone, and said to me he was out somewhere in the neighborhood. She sounded upset. "It used to be like this when he was working for the Youth Board," she said. "He'd go out, and I'd never know when he was coming back. Three in the morning, maybe, he'd come back, and then the phone would ring and he'd go right out again. I told him he'd get so he wouldn't recognize his own children."

The next day, Riccio called me. He sounded discouraged. "They had another rumble," he said. "The Stompers came down to the housing project and broke a few heads. I got there too late." Fortunately, he added, it hadn't been too bad. A few shots had been fired, but without hitting anyone, and although a Cherub had been slashed down one arm with a knife, the wound wasn't serious, and nobody else had been even that badly hurt. Riccio told me he was going out again that night, and I could hear his wife say something in the background. He muffled the phone and spoke to her, and then he said to me, almost apologetically, "I've got to go out. They don't have a worker, or anything. The newspapers have raised such a fuss that the Youth Board's got its workers running around in circles, and it hasn't enough of them to do the job anyway, even when things are quiet. If somebody doesn't work with these kids, they'll end up killing each other." Then he told me he still had hopes of a mediation meeting, and would let me know what developed. Ten days later, my telephone rang shortly before dinner, and it was Riccio again, his voice now full of hope. He said that he knew it was very short notice, but if I still wanted to be in on the mediation session, I should meet him at eight o'clock in a building at an address he gave me. "I got it all set up at last," he concluded.

By the time I reached the building—a one-room wooden structure in an alley—it was five minutes after eight. Riccio was already there, together with three Cherubs—Benny and Bruno and a boy he introduced to me as Johnny Meatball.

"I was just waiting until you got here," Riccio said. "Now I'll go get the Stompers." He went out, leaving me with the three boys. The room had a fireplace at one end, and was furnished with a wooden table and several long wooden benches. It was hard for me to believe that I was in the heart of Brooklyn, until I read some of the expressions scrawled on the walls. I asked Benny who ordinarily used the place, and he replied, "Man, you know. Them Boy Scouts."

Bruno said he had gone to a Boy Scout meeting once, because he liked the uniforms, but had never gone back, because the Scoutmaster was a creep. "He wanted we should all sleep outside on the ground," Bruno said. "You know—in the woods, with the bears. Who needs that?" This led to a discussion of the perils of outdoor life, based mostly on information derived from jungle movies.

It was a desultory discussion, however. The boys were restless, and every few minutes Benny would open the door and look out into the alley. Finally, Bruno said, "The hell with them. Let's cut out."

"I'm down for that," Johnny Meatball said.

"They ain't coming," Bruno said. "They're too chicken."

"I give them fifteen minutes," Benny said.

All three became quiet then. I tried to get them to talk, as a way of keeping them there, but they weren't interested. Just before the fifteen minutes was up, the door opened and Riccio walked in, followed by two Stompers—Ralphie and Eddie, the boy we had met going home to hide his gun. They held back when they saw the Cherubs, but Riccio urged them in and closed the door behind them. Though the Cherubs had bunched together, looking tense and ready to fight, Riccio appeared to pay no attention, and said cheerfully, "I went to the wrong corner. Ralphie and Eddie, here, were waiting on the next one down the street." He pulled the table to the center of the room. "You guys know each other," he said to the five boys. Then he pulled a bench up to each side of the table and a third bench across one end. He sat down on this one, and motioned to me to sit beside him. The boys sat down slowly, one by one—the Cherubs on one side and the Stompers on the other.

"There you are," Riccio said when everybody was seated. "Just like the U.N. First, I want to thank you guys for coming here. I think you're doing a great thing. It takes a lot of guts to do what you guys are doing. I want you to know that I'm proud of you." He smiled at them. "Everybody thinks all you're good for is breaking heads. I know different— although I know you're pretty good at breaking heads, too." A couple of the boys smiled back at this, and all of them seemed to relax a little. "All right," Riccio went on. "What are we going to do about this war? You each got a beef against the other. Well, what's the beef? Let's talk about it."

There was a long silence. The boys sat motionless, staring at the table or at the walls beyond. Riccio sat as still as any of them. They sat that way for at least three minutes, and then Bruno stood up and said, "Ah, let's cut out of here."

"Man, sit down," Benny said. He spoke calmly, but his voice carried authority. Bruno looked down at him and he looked up at Bruno, and Bruno sat down. Benny then turned to the two Stompers across the table. "You tried to ruin our dance," he said.

"Your guy said we stole his lousy coat," Ralphie said.

"You jumped Benny on the street," Johnny Meatball said. "Three of you guys."

"He started a fight," Ralphie said.

"Man, that was a *fair* one!" Benny said.

"You started it," Ralphie said.

"There was just the two of us," Benny said.

"You were beating the hell out of him," Ralphie said. "What did you want us to do—let you get away with it?"

The logic of this seemed to strike the Cherubs as irrefutable, and there was another silence. Then Eddie said, "You beat up two of our little kids."

"Not *us*," Benny said. "We never beat up no little kids."

"The kids told us some Cherubs caught them coming home from the store and beat them up," Eddie said.

"Man, we wouldn't beat up *kids*," Benny said.

"You got that wrong," Johnny Meatball said, backing Benny up.

"Those kids were just trying to be wheels," Bruno said.

The Cherubs were so positive in their denial of this accusation that the Stompers appeared willing to take their word for it.

There was another pause. Riccio sat back, watching the boys. They were now leaning across the table, the two sides confronting each other at close quarters.

"Remember that time at the Paramount?" Ralphie asked. "When me and Eddie was there with two girls?"

"Those were *girls?*" Bruno asked.

"Shut up," Benny said.

Ralphie then said to Benny, "Remember we ran into eight of your crew? You ranked us in front of the girls. We had to punk out because there was so many of you."

"You want we should stay out of the *Paramount?*" Benny asked incredulously.

"It wasn't right," Ralphie said. "Not in front of the girls. Not when you knew we'd have to punk out."

After thinking this over, Benny nodded slowly, acknowledging the justice of the argument.

Ralphie pressed his advantage. "And you been hanging out in our territory," he said, naming a street corner.

"Man, that ain't your territory," Benny said. "That's *our* territory."

"That ain't your territory," Ralphie said. "We got that territory from the Dragons, and that's our territory."

The argument over the street corner grew hotter, and after a while Riccio broke it up by rapping on the table with his knuckles and saying, "I got a suggestion—why don't both sides give up the territory?" He pointed out that the corner had nothing to recommend it, being undesirable for recreation and difficult to defend. After debating about that for a minute or two, both sides agreed to relinquish their claim to the corner. Riccio had what he wanted now; I could feel it. The boys had lost the sharp edge of their hostility. Their vehemence became largely rhetorical; they were even beginning to laugh about assaults each side had made on the other.

"Hey, Ralphie," Bruno said. "You're a lucky guy, you know that? I took a shot at you the other night and missed you clean."

"You took a *shot* at me?" Ralphie asked.

Bruno nodded. "The night you came down to the project. I was waiting with a thirty-two, and you came down the street and I took a shot at you."

"I didn't even hear it," Ralphie said.

"There was a lot of noise," Bruno said. "I was right across the street from you."

"You must be a lousy shot," Eddie said.

"It was dark out," Bruno said.

"You know, you could have killed him," Riccio told Bruno.

"I wasn't looking to kill him," Bruno said.

The other boys proceeded to kid Bruno about his marksmanship—all except Ralphie, who had become subdued. After a few minutes, Riccio looked at his watch and said, "Hey, it's ten o'clock. We got to get out of here before they close the place." He stood up, stretched, and said casually, "I'm glad you guys are calling it off. You're doing the smart thing. You get a lot of credit for what you're doing."

"You took a shot at me?" Ralphie said again to Bruno.

"What's past is past," Riccio said. "There's no reason you can't get along from now on without breaking heads. If something comes up, you do what you've been doing tonight. Mediate. Get together and talk it over. Believe me, it's a lot easier than breaking heads."

"What if we can't get together?" Bruno asked. "Suppose they do something, and they say they didn't do it and we say they did it?"

"Then you have a fair one," Eddie told him. "We put out our guy and you put out your guy. We settle it that way. That's O.K., ain't it, Rick?"

"It's better not to do any bopping at all," Riccio said.

"I mean, it ain't wrong," Eddie said. "It ain't making any trouble."

"Suppose we have a fair one and our guy gets beat?" Bruno asked.

"Man, you don't put out a guy who's *going* to get beat," Benny said.

The boys were on their feet now, all mixed together. A stranger might have taken them for a single group of boys engaged in rough but friendly conversation. "Listen, we got to break this up," Riccio said. He told them again how proud he was of them, and then he advised the Cherubs and the Stompers to leave separately. "Some cop sees the five of you walking down the street, he'll pull you all in," he said. So the three Cherubs left first, with Benny in the lead. They said goodbye very formally, shaking hands first with Riccio, then with me, and then, after a little hesitation, with the two Stompers. When they had gone, Ralphie sat down again on his bench. "That crazy Bruno," he said. "He took a shot at me."

A few minutes later, the Stompers stood up to go. Riccio said he would be around to see them and help them plan their dance. They thanked him and left. Riccio looked around the room. "I used to come here when I was a kid," he told me. "I got my name carved on the wall somewhere." He looked for it for a moment, without success, and then said, "Well, we might as well run along."

We went outside and got into Riccio's car. "Evelyn said if it wasn't too late, she'd have coffee and cake for us," Riccio told me, and I said that would be fine. He drove to his house and, after parking, leaned back in the seat and lit a cigarette. "I want to slow down a little before I go upstairs," he said. We sat there quietly for a few minutes. I could hear the whistles of ships down in the harbor. "Benny and Ralphie," Riccio said finally. "Those are the two to concentrate on. Maybe Eddie, too. But that Bruno—I don't know how far you could get with him. He's a disturbed kid. But you have to try. You have to try to reach him. That's the whole trick—reaching them. If I could have reached Tommy Hanlon, he wouldn't be dead now. I was just starting to reach him when he died. The last real talk we had, he told me he was scared to get a job. He'd quit school very early, and he couldn't read or write very well. He was scared if he got a job they'd make him do arithmetic and he'd look stupid. He was scared that they might send him over to Manhattan on the subway and he wouldn't be able to read the station signs. He'd never been out of Brooklyn. This was a kid there wasn't anything anti-social he hadn't done. Short of murder, there wasn't a thing. He broke into stores, he broke into cars, he molested girls. And, of course, he was on narcotics. I tell you, I used to look at this kid and think, How the hell can you defend a kid like this to society? And I'd think, How the hell can I help him? What can I do? This is too much. At the same time, he was such a nice-looking kid, I mean, he had a very nice face. Never mind what came out of his mouth—he had the dirtiest tongue I ever heard on a kid. But I worked with him, and he was starting to come around. He was starting to trust me. I don't think he'd ever trusted anybody in his whole life. I was his father. I was his mother. I was his best friend, his father confessor. I was all the things this kid had never had. And he was starting to move a little. The gang ran a dance, and he volunteered for the sandwich committee. You know what that meant? The kid was participating socially for the first time in his whole life. And he worked twice as hard at it as anybody else. I was starting to reach him. And then I quit the Youth Board."

Riccio fell silent again. "I had to quit the Youth Board," he said presently. "I had a wife and two kids, and I wasn't making enough to support them. I was spending more time with these kids than with my own. So I quit. The day I quit, I went down the street to tell the kids. They were in the candy store and Tommy Hanlon was with them, and he looked at me and said, 'What did you quit for?' I told him I had to, and tried to explain why. 'You know, I'm on the stuff again,' he said. And I said, 'Yes, Tommy, I heard you are, and I'm very sorry.' And he said, 'What do I do now?' And I said, 'Tommy, I'll always be around. We can still talk. You can still come and see me.' Then some other kid called me over to talk to him, and when I looked around Tommy was gone. Two weeks later, he was dead."

Riccio paused, this time for a long while. His cigarette had gone out, and he looked at it blankly and threw it out the window. "I know," he said. "The kid destroyed himself. He was a disturbed kid. If he wasn't disturbed, he wouldn't have been on narcotics in the first place. I went to the funeral and I looked in the casket and saw him laying there in a suit, with a decent haircut and his face all washed—and looking like a little old man. And I watched that kid's father getting drunk with that kid laying there in the casket. And I wanted to get up there at the funeral and, everybody who was there, I wanted to shout at them, 'You're the people who caused it! All you big adults! All you wise guys on street corners that feel sorry for the kid! Now you throw away your money on flowers!' I wanted to grab them by the throat."

He paused again, and then said, his voice low, "We hear about the soldier, a normal guy, who goes through all the tortures of war and all this brainwashing—takes everything they throw at him—and comes home a hero. Well, here was a kid that had everything thrown at him, too. Only, he was all mixed up, and still he took everything anybody could throw at him for seventeen years, and that was all he could take, so he collapsed and died."

Riccio abruptly pushed the car door open and got out. I got out on my side, and we went into the house together. Mrs. Riccio was both surprised and relieved to have her husband back so early. She asked if things had gone well, and Riccio assured her that things had gone very well. She went into the kitchen to make the coffee, and Riccio and I watched a quiz program on television until she came back. The three of us chatted awhile over our coffee and cake, and then, just before saying good night, I asked Riccio if Mickey had ever found the coat he lost at the dance. Riccio said that he hadn't but that the Cherubs had given him the eighteen dollars and he had bought a new one.

Riccio called me a few days later to tell me that the Cherubs and the Stompers were observing their armistice but that the enmity between Ralphie and Bruno had become so pronounced that they had decided to settle it with a fair one. Both gangs had gone to Prospect Park one night to watch the two of them have it out. A squad car had happened along, and the policemen had run the whole bunch of them in. Riccio was on his way to court to see what he could do for the boys.

12 | **The Blackstone Rangers** |
James Alan McPherson

Although the Blackstone Rangers depart from the traditional picture of slum gangs, they do have many things in common with the gangs described in the previous selection. They share some of the same patterns of violence, sociability, funmaking, and, certainly, a common desire for protection. In order to protect themselves from the people they see as their enemy, the Blackstone Rangers have become highly organized. This enmity is reinforced by the tremendous alienation of their community from the police and other law enforcement officials.

Unlike most earlier gangs, the Blackstone Rangers like many other gangs in America's big cities today have become politicized. Political activity is not new among the gangs of America's big cities. Earlier ethnic gangs, especially Irish and Italian groups, were involved in politics, but these earlier gangs were made up of older men and were not nearly as violent or revolutionary as the Blackstone Rangers appear to be. There is little similarity in this respect between the Blackstone Rangers and the streetcorner gangs of Italian Boston studied by William Foote Whyte in his famous work on Streetcorner Society *(Chicago: University of Chicago Press, 1943). But the Blackstone Rangers' political activities also differ because in this day of federal social welfare programs, political gangs, even gangs with violent tendencies, can receive government financing which may affect the development of the gang itself. The Blackstone Rangers have, in fact, become a national political issue.*

Since the revolution in race relations in the United States has now moved out into the high schools and junior high schools, it seems likely that the general pattern of politicization that can be observed in the history of the Blackstone Rangers will be repeated many times over in the years ahead. Whereas gangs were once involved more specifically in group criminal violence, they may become more involved in group political violence.

Sometime between 1961 and 1963, according to evidence presented to a Senate subcommittee chaired by John McClellan of Arkansas last July, an unknown number of black young men, who lived in the general area of Sixty-sixth Place and Blackstone Avenue in the Woodlawn area of Chicago's South Side ghetto, organized a street gang. Like most street gangs, it was formed to protect its members from intimidation by other gangs in the South Side area. The most formidable enemy of this new group was a gang called the Devil's Disciples, which claimed part of the neighboring Kenwood area. In the years which followed, the Disciples became the traditional enemies of the Woodlawn youths, who called themselves Blackstone Rangers.

At first the Rangers were interested only in protecting their territory and their membership from attacks and retaliations by the Disciples, but by 1965 there were an estimated 200 of them in the group, and they were breaking with traditional gang patterns. They were organizing in Woodlawn. And this organization caused some public concern, and even fear, because it began during a period of violent rivalry between the Rangers and the Disciples. During these formative stages the Blackstone Rangers seemed to have placed the running feud between the Disciples and themselves secondary to their primary goal: organization. Soon their influence in Woodlawn caused minor, less influential, less powerful gangs to join them. And they came from all over the South Side: the Maniacs, the Four Corners, the Lovers, the V.I.P.'s, the Pythons, the Warlocks, the F.B.I., the Conservatives, the Pharaohs. At present there are anywhere from 3500 to 8000 boys and men who identify with the Blackstone Rangers and who have affixed the Ranger name to the names of their own gangs. Such is the organizational structure and size of the Blackstone Rangers today that they call themselves a Nation. The Ranger Nation is headed by a group of young men called the Main 21. Until 1968 the president of the organization was Eugene "Bull" Hairston, the vice president was Jeff Fort (also called "Angel" and "Black Prince"), and the warlord was George Rose (also called "Watusi" and "Mad Dog"). The Rangers' spiritual leader was Paul "The Preacher" Martin, and the rest of the Main 21 was made up of leaders of the minor gangs who had joined with the Rangers. Each individual gang, it seems, maintained its own organizational structure with its own officers; but collectively all of the gangs made up the Blackstone Nation, which is presently incorporated to do business under the laws of Illinois.

Since the emergence of the Ranger Nation, individual members have been charged with murder, robbery, rape, knifings, extortion of South Side merchants, traffic in narcotics, extortion and intimidation of young children, forced gang membership, and a general history of outright violence, especially against the Disciples who never joined the

Rangers. On the other hand, the Ranger Nation has been credited with keeping the South Side of Chicago "cool" during the summer of 1967 and the spring of 1968, following the assassination of Dr. Martin Luther King. It has been said that they have kept drugs, alcoholics, prostitutes, and whites hunting for prostitutes out of their neighborhoods. They have also been credited with making genuine attempts to form lasting peace treaties between themselves and the Disciples in order to decrease the level of gang fighting on the South Side. They have been alternately praised and condemned by the national press, their community, the United States Senate, the local police, and Chicago youth organizations to such an extent that, if one depends on the news media for information, it is almost impossible to maintain a consistent opinion of the Blackstone Rangers.

Some of the Chicago papers have been quick to report any charges of violent activity against a Ranger. In newspaper accounts, the name of the gang takes precedence over the individual arrested and charged with crimes. Many of the charges are accurate; many of the young men who identify with the Rangers are guilty of various crimes. But much of the information passed on to the press is shown to have no substance upon thorough investigation. Still, the adverse publicity serves to keep the Chicago communities, both black and white, in a state of apprehension over the Blackstone Ranger organization, as opposed to the individuals in it.

There has been, and presently still is, a cry for a massive police crackdown on the Rangers. To accomplish this, the Chicago Police Department, following a general order issued by former Chicago Superintendent of Police O. W. Wilson, formed the Gang Intelligence Unit in March of 1967 to learn more about the Rangers and to decrease forcibly the level of gang violence in all areas of Chicago generally, and in the South Side area in particular. The stated purpose of the Unit was to eliminate "the antisocial and criminal activities of groups of minors and young adults in the various communities within the city."

In early June of 1967, The Woodlawn Organization (T.W.O.), a grass roots community association made up of one hundred or so block clubs, and civic, religious, and business organizations in the Woodlawn area of the South Side, received a $957,000 grant from the Office of Economic Opportunity to set up a special kind of youth project in the Woodlawn area. The purpose of the program was to utilize the existing gang structures—the Blackstone Rangers and the Devil's Disciples—as a means of encouraging youth in the gangs as well as nongang youth to become involved in a pre-employment orientation, motivational project. The project was to include eight hundred out-of-school unemployed youths. And the entire program was to operate through four job-training centers which were to be set up in the home territories of the Rangers and Disciples. Reverend Arthur Brazier, president of The Woodlawn Organization, was responsible for bringing the interest of OEO to the proposed program, which was admitted to be a "high-risk venture."

The money from OEO went directly to The Woodlawn Organization. It did not go through city agencies, although one of the conditions of the grant was that the mayor was to be "invited" to concur in the selection of a project director for the program. There is some opinion that the mayor's office was not pleased with this. In fact, the full operation of the program was delayed over two months because of the inability of the T.W.O. people and Mayor Richard J. Daley to come to an agreement on a director for the program. By the time the program officially began in September, a project director had not been hired, and the Rangers and Disciples had, apparently, lost much of their enthusiasm for the program.

In September of 1967, The Woodlawn Organization opened four training centers in the Woodlawn area: two for the Blackstone Rangers and two for the Devil's Disciples. One of the Ranger Centers was located in the First Presbyterian Church, a church in the Woodlawn area headed by Reverend John Fry, a white Presbyterian clergyman. The Xerox Corporation was hired to formulate the curriculum; the Chicago Urban League was hired to do job development; and Arthur Andersen & Company was hired to give T.W.O. monthly reviews. In addition, a Monitoring Unit with the Chicago police was set up to have two meetings a month with T.W.O. people and representatives from the two gangs, which had attempted to deescalate the level of their violent rivalry since the new program had been announced.

The trainees were paid $45 a week to take five hours of instruction a day for five days a week, in addition to travel expenses. The instructors in the program, or Center Chiefs, were not professionals but gang leaders who were supposed to be under the supervision of professionals because, as Reverend Brazier stated before the McClellan Committee, "many of these youth do not relate to professionals because the professionals with middle-class attitudes do not relate to them." Eugene Hairston, president of the Rangers, was hired as an assistant project director at a salary of $6500 a year. Jeff Fort, Ranger vice president, became a Center Chief and received $6000 a year. And many of the other members of the Main 21 occupied, at one time or another, salaried positions in the project. Apparently, there was not much public opposition to the hiring of gang leaders by the program. Rather, there seems to have been a reversal in public attitude toward the Rangers because of their performance in the year before the program began.

One of the activities which helped their public image was the production of a musical review called *Opportunity Please Knock,* which was sponsored by Oscar Brown, Jr., the jazz pianist, and performed by groups of Rangers and students from the Hyde Park High School. The show, which was eventually taken over by the Rangers, ran for six weeks in May and June of 1967. An estimated eight thousand people went to the First Presbyterian Church during the first weeks of its performance, and it received very favorable nationwide publicity. Subsequent performances were given in various suburban communities around Chicago, and parts of the show traveled to Watts to perform. Some members of the troupe appeared on the Smothers Brothers show, and *Ebony* featured a large color story of the production in its August, 1967, issue.

A second instance of positive Ranger activity, which also gained them favorable publicity, was their willingness to be bussed out of town on August 12, Bud Billiken Day (named for a mythical folk hero created by the Chicago *Daily Defender,* a black newspaper). All past major conflicts between the Rangers and the Disciples had taken place during the Bud Billiken Day Parade and picnic in the South Side's Washington Park. In 1966 the city of Chicago had financed an out-of-town picnic for the Rangers through the Boys' Club, although there is some evidence that it considered the picnic idea a kind of blackmail exacted by the Rangers. In 1967, however, The Woodlawn Organization requested from OEO permission to use $5000 of its funds to take six hundred Rangers to an out-of-town picnic at Valparaiso University. The Rangers made the decision to leave town, it is said, because of rumors of a brewing riot and the public expectation that they would cause or at least participate in it.

The Ranger vice president, Jeff Fort, had been jailed on July 30 on murder charges and was still in jail on Bud Billiken Day. There are conflicting statements about whether or not Fort threatened to start a riot. Policemen have testified that he stated that if he were arrested, "the city would burn," while other sources reported that he cautioned the Rangers, after his arrest, not to riot. In any case, he remained in jail until early September of 1967, and there was no riot. The Rangers attended their picnic, and there were few incidents during the day. Whether or not the Rangers and Disciples actively contributed to the calm remains an open question. But a safe assumption can be made that when the T.W.O. project began in September, the Blackstone Rangers were enjoying a good deal of favorable press coverage and community support.

A final incident in the fall of 1967 helped their image in the city. In the Kenwood district, which adjoins Woodlawn, the police dispersed a black-power rally on September 15. The crowd then moved to a local high school, where bottles were thrown and two shots were fired by a sniper. The situation seemed to have been too tense for the police, when Herbert Stevens, leader of the Four Corners Rangers and a member of the Main 21 (known as "Thunder"), was said to have stood before the crowd and said, "All you who are willing to die, step up now. Otherwise, let's go home." And as he turned to leave he said, "When I come back, I don't want to see anybody on the streets. I want these streets cleared." When he returned in five minutes, the story goes, the crowd had broken up.

The Blackstone Rangers wanted to play a major role in determining how the OEO-Woodlawn project should be run, and there were meetings throughout the summer of 1967 between the gang leaders and representatives of T.W.O. to determine the extent of their voice in the project. These meetings were kept under surveillance by detectives from the Gang Intelligence Unit.

The public favor enjoyed by the Rangers during the summer of 1967 dropped off severely when the president and vice president were arrested in late September of 1967 for soliciting three juveniles— Marvin Martin, fifteen, Sanders Martin, fourteen, and Dennis Jackson, also fourteen—to murder a narcotics dealer named Leo McClure. Mc-Clure was in fact one of three men who were shot. Though he was not, it emerged, the prime target, he was the only one of the three who died. Dennis Jackson was alleged to have done the actual shooting. Hairston, the Ranger president, was kept in jail without bond, and the newspapers printed so many stories about a Teen-age Murder, Inc., and so many details of the case against Hairston, that the first courtroom case ended in a mistrial.

During the same period the activities of Reverend John Fry and the First Presbyterian Church, which served as one of the T.W.O. training centers, were called into question. The church was said to be an arsenal for the Rangers to store their guns and a place where they sold and smoked marijuana, had sexual activity, and held their secret gang meetings. Then Jeff Fort was arrested in October and charged with murdering a Disciple. Both his arrest and the earlier arrest of Hairston encouraged the press to give extensive adverse publicity to The Woodlawn Organization because of their employment by the project. Soon afterward, three of the Main leaders, also members of the T.W.O. staff, were indicted for rape. The detectives of the G.I.U. made extensive visits to the training centers and found, according to their reports, no actual training taking place, the falsification of time sheets, gambling, and evidence that marijuana was being smoked on the premises. Finally, a Disciple was shot in one of the two Disciple Centers with a shotgun. The shooting was said to have been an accident, but the G.I.U. detectives who investigated the shooting found evidence that "light narcotics" (Robitussin) were being used at the Disciple Center. It was about this time that Senator McClellan's Permanent Subcommittee on

Investigations of the Committee on Government Operations began to gather evidence in its planned investigation of The Woodlawn Organization's "high-risk" project.

The investigation began on June 28, 1968, in Washington. There was nationwide television coverage as all those who had connections with the project, official or otherwise, testified before Senators Jacob Javits, Carl Curtis, Fred Harris, Edmund Muskie, Karl Mundt, and of course, Chairman John McClellan, who asked most of the questions.

Reverend Arthur Brazier made a desperate attempt to defend his project, explaining how participation of gang members was necessary for its success and charging that harassment from the Gang Intelligence Unit and explosively adverse news publicity had made it almost impossible for the project to develop as anticipated. Members of the Gang Intelligence Unit testified that they had made extensive visits to the training centers during the period of their operation and had found very little, if any, instruction going on. They also testified to the long list of crimes said to have been committed by gang members while under the sponsorship of T.W.O., especially the murder which was said to have been solicited by Eugene Hairston and Jeff Fort.

Perhaps the most damaging testimony against the program, if not against the Rangers themselves, came from George Rose, a former warlord of the Rangers who had defected from the organization, and a Mrs. Annabelle Martin, a black mother of ten who claimed to have had a very close relationship with the gang. The two Martin boys allegedly solicited by Hairston to commit the murder of Leo McClure were her sons.

Rose testified that the Rangers were involved in the sale of narcotics; that trainees in the program were forced to kick back to the organization from $5 to $25 each week; that the Rangers, from the start, had no interest in job training and that the program was used only to increase the gang's membership and its treasury; and that the First Presbyterian Church and its people—Reverend John Fry, Charles Lapaglia, and Anne Schwalbach, all white—were attempting to control and direct the gang through influence over Jeff Fort.

According to Rose's testimony, Reverend Fry had actually written the proposal for the OEO grant and had turned it over to Reverend Brazier; the church was used for the sale of narcotics, the storage of guns, and a convenient place for the Rangers to engage in sexual activity. He also told the Committee that Lapaglia had taken some of the Main 21 leaders on a trip to Michigan to purchase guns and on another trip to Philadelphia to attend a black-power conference where the murders of certain nonmilitant civil rights leaders were plotted. He said that the Rangers had made it known to Reverend Brazier that they considered the OEO money theirs and would not let outsiders—school dropouts who were not Rangers—into the program. And, according to his testimony, Brazier consented to this without informing OEO officials. Rose told the Committee that many of the gang leaders who had been hired as instructors or Center Chiefs had fifth- or sixth-grade educations and that Jeff Fort, who served as a Center Chief, could not read or write. Finally, he stated that students from regular schools were forced to drop out in order to join the program and the gang, and that those who refused were beaten, shot in the arms, forced to keep off the streets, or killed. In this way, he said, the Rangers induced "a couple hundred" students to leave public schools and join the program, and that it was a practice of the Rangers to solicit juveniles to commit murder because they received a lighter sentence if they were caught.

Of special interest was his testimony that the Rangers had offered to help the police, and, in fact, did outfit themselves in black uniforms, called themselves the police of the Blackstone Ranger Nation, policed their neighborhoods, and turned over to the police several non-Rangers in order to clear the name of their organization. He stated that the police accepted them at first, but then, "after we turned a couple of guys in and made it known that they weren't our guys, the police still started cracking our young fellows' heads, just because of the uniforms. They called us storm troopers because we had black jump boots, black pants tucked into the top of the boots. . . . They didn't like this at all. They called it mob action."

Rose also testified that after the Rangers were rejected by the police, Reverend John Fry advised them to begin extorting merchants. "Since we were being accused of it," he said, "there wasn't anything we could lose by doing it." Rose said that the Rangers got from $5000 to $8000 a week from tavern owners and various sums from shoe stores, clothing stores, food stores, and drugstores through threats of future violence against them.

Robert L. Pierson of the Chicago State's Attorney's Office told the Committee that the Rangers "are the beginning of a Black Mafia." He testified that the Rangers were, in fact, extorting merchants but that the merchants would not complain because of fear of retaliation from the gang. During the April days following the murder of Martin Luther King when the Rangers distributed signs to be displayed in the windows of neighborhood merchants, he said, they charged $50 for their protection.

Jeff Fort, who had assumed leadership of the gang after Hairston was convicted in May of 1968, was subpoenaed to testify before the Committee. He was sworn in but never sat down before Senator McClellan. Marshall Patner, Fort's lawyer, submitted a request that the Committee allow Fort to confront and cross-examine the witnesses who had testified against him. The request was refused by Senator McClellan under authority of the Committee Rules. After a heated exchange between Patner and Senator McClellan during which both the lawyer and Fort were reminded of the possibility of contempt charges if Fort refused to accept protection from the Fifth Amendment and proceed with his testimony, Marshall Patner turned to Fort, still standing beside him, and said: "We really must go." Then they walked out.

The Woodlawn, Kenwood, and parts of the Hyde Park areas of the South Side of Chicago are said to be Ranger territories. While the Rangers' presence in Hyde Park, especially in the area around the University of Chicago, is not very obvious to the casual observer, the walls of buildings in Woodlawn and Kenwood advertise their existence. It is impossible to pass a single block in Woodlawn without seeing the signs. Many of the buildings are being torn down, but most of the signs look fresh and bold and new; "Black P. Stone," "Stone Run It," "Almighty Black P. Stone Nation," "Don't Vote! B.P.S.," they read. The wind blows bits of dirt and plaster into the faces of the children who play among the bricks and rubbish in the lots where houses once stood.

Blackstone Rangers are shy these days. They do not talk to most strangers. Whenever Jeff Fort is arrested, and he has been arrested many times since the McClellan Committee hearings, the story is picked up by almost every major newspaper in the country. Perhaps it is because of determined harassment from the Gang Intelligence Unit that the Rangers have grown tight and uncommunicative. Whatever the cause, they are suspicious of strangers, and their meetings are held in secret. They no longer make much use of the First Presbyterian Church; they may meet there from time to time, but not regularly. Possibly their only facility open to the public is the Black P. Stone Youth Center on the corner of Sixty-seventh and Blackstone, in the heart of the Woodlawn community. The building was once a Chinese laundry, and at another time it was a poolroom. Now it seems to serve as the central point for most Ranger activities. The building is windowless, and it is painted black. Few non-Rangers go into the building uninvited; only those who have dealings with the Nation seem to feel free to enter. And perhaps this is because of the large black-and-red "All Mighty Black P. Stone" diamond-shaped symbol painted on the Blackstone Street side of the building. During the day adults hurry past the teen-age boys and men who may be standing outside the door. There is a bar a few doors away from the Center, and many of the older people who pass the building go in there to escape the wind, or into the barbecue house next to the bar, or else continue about whatever business they may have further down Sixty-seventh Street. The latch is broken, and the door is never really shut. Anyone can walk in, but for the most part only the children do.

Jeff Fort is the "Black Prince," the president, the "Chief" of the entire Blackstone operation. One cannot think of learning about the Nation without assuming that Jeff Fort is the key, the source of all information. To see Jeff, it is necessary to go to the Black P. Stone Youth Center and wait. It is necessary to wait a long time. Jeff Fort is extremely busy. Besides leading the Rangers, he is fighting a contempt of Congress conviction for walking out of the McClellan hearings last July (he was found guilty in November); awaiting certain cases pending against him in the Cook County courts; and, until he resigned in early December, working as a community organizer for the Kenwood-Oakland Community Organization (KOCO).

But waiting for Jeff Fort to come to the Center gives one the opportunity to observe some of the Rangers as they wander in and out of the smaller, first room of the place, which serves as an office. The room is painted black. There are two desks, a telephone, ancient magazines, a water cooler with no water, and a bulletin board. Tacked on the board are job announcements, pictures of Rangers who participated in *Opportunity Please Knock,* messages, and cartoons—including one by Jules Feiffer. It is not an impressive office, but the door never stops opening as the children come in. There is little in the office to suggest why they come, but sitting in the one big ragged chair in a dark corner of the office, one is able to observe a steady flow of children, boys and girls, ranging in age from seven to fourteen, walking in and out of the office as if in search of something.

Lamar Bell, the coordinator of the Black P. Stone Youth Center, does not mind my waiting. "The Chief is due here in a few hours," he always says. And he says it again, much later in the evening. It is obvious that he does not trust me. Finally he asks why I want to see the Chief. "I want to do a story on the Nation," I tell him. "I want to see how the Nation relates to the community and the police." Bell turns off completely. "Put *that* in your story!" he says, pushing a pink mimeographed sheet close to my face. "The trouble with Black Police in our community," it reads, "is not police brutality to blacks, it is that these men and women are afraid of the power structure. So they join it to save themselves from the misery of being Black and powerless. The only way they can prove themselves, to city rulers and world conquerors, with this so called authority is to take it out on their Brother's and Sister's, your Mother and Father and my Mother and Father, and our children. If they weren't police they would be in the same shape as any other oppressed Black man, Woman, or Child. God help them," it went on, "for they know not what they do. To them it's a job for money; to us it's our lives, home and children."

"This is just what I want to write about," I tell him.

Lamar Bell walks to the door between the office and the back room, which has been off limits to me during my past visits to the Center, and says, "You'll have to talk it over with the Chief. He'll be here in a couple of hours."

Every evening for at least three hours Lamar Bell and Carl Banks, one of the Center's teachers, conduct a percussion class for some of the younger boys who come there. Banks has been a Ranger for two years. He is twenty-one, and came to Chicago from New York two years ago. He wants to become a professional drummer and earns money from infrequent band engagements. The rest of his time he spends in the Center, teaching a percussion class for neighborhood children. He is friendly and talkative. "The kids are really interested in expressing themselves," he told me. "A lot of these kids are misunderstood. Drumming gives them a way to express themselves. If I had money for the course, I would get more equipment and books, take the kids to see other drummers perform. Try to work out a little drum and bugle corps."

From the chair where I sat in the office during my first visits to the Center, I could hear the music they made with their drums in the mysterious back room.

One Saturday night Bell informed me that there was an extra bongo drum and invited me to sit in on the session. He allowed me to enter the back room, a kind of auditorium with a small stage, and the three of us played drums, without speaking, for several hours. While we played, some of the older Rangers came in and watched us. They looked at me, and then at Bell, then at me again. It was obvious that I was not a Stone.

"You didn't give off the right vibrations," Art Richardson, the director of the Black P. Stone Youth Center, told me later that night. "That's why I was watching you. But you *could* be a Stone because you came into the Center and participated, on *our* level. That's what Stone is all about."

Art Richardson believes in vibrations as a method of determining the sincerity of people. Although he grew up on the South Side of Chicago, he has been a Ranger for only two years. He is not a member of the Main 21, but because he is articulate and extremely intelligent, he has been made a "head" and director of the Black P. Stone Youth Center. He is twenty-eight, married, and has served in the Army. He was given an Undesirable Discharge in 1965 because, he says, "I was just exposed to prejudice and reacted to it in the only way I knew." He has a police record. He also has a way with people. He would rather ride a bus than a cab because, he says, "You can't get vibrations from peoples in a cab." He never says *people;* the word always comes out *peoples,* with enough warmth and emphasis to suggest sincerity.

The Englewood Urban Progress Center, located at 839 West Sixty-Fourth Street in an area which is said to be Disciple territory, houses a

concentration of community service agencies. The building itself is a
Masonic Temple which has been converted into offices. Only the
ground floor is used for official purposes; the upper floors are essentially unused, although the second floor has a fairly large auditorium
with a stage and good seating capacity, and there are many other,
smaller rooms, all quiet and waiting to be put into use. In one of the
larger rooms on the second floor, the one with the stage, Darlene
Blackburn, an accomplished black dancer of considerable reputation in
Chicago, gives creative dance lessons to girls from the community.
Waiting for her in the semilighted room are children, boys and girls,
who come to participate in the class or to watch her dance. Art
Richardson and I wait with them. Art wants to ask her to dance at a
Thanksgiving show he is organizing for the Black P. Stone Youth
Center. While they wait, the children play at jumping off the stage and
onto the floor, a distance of some three or four feet. Sometimes they fall
on their faces, but they always laugh, and climb back onto the stage to
jump again. It is a game.

"Look at that," Art told me.

A boy was dropping onto the stage from a trap-door four or five feet
above. He landed on his knees, unhurt, and climbed up to jump again.

"That's energy," Art said. "We can't do that anymore."

I agreed.

Art walked over to the stage and watched the boy jump again. This
time he landed on his feet. "You know," he told me, coming back to
where I was sitting, "the young brothers represent a form of energy just
like any other energetic force in nature, just like the atom. If it could be
channeled, if it could be turned to constructive directions just like the
atom . . ." He began to walk about the room. "If I had a bigger place,
if I had a place like this, I could bring more of the little brothers in and
get that energy."

"What would you do with it?" I asked.

He looked up at the old Mason paintings on the walls and ceilings,
half-hidden in the darkness. "I'd like to have job-training programs, arts
and crafts workshops, adult workshops sort of like the P.T.A. to
assemble adults just to get them to talk and maybe close the generation
gap. Help them influence the kids in the necessary direction." He
paused. "As a matter of fact, I would do exactly what the other organizations are trying to do. But only I'd do it. Most of the other organizations can't reach the kids. We can. We can give them something to
relate to as theirs."

"What?" I asked him.

Art lowered his voice so that the children could not hear him.
"Stone," he said softly. Most of Englewood, and whatever energy there
is in it, still belongs to the Disciples.

No one really knows how many Rangers there now are in the South

Side area. The Gang Intelligence Unit estimates that they claim a membership of from 1500 to 3000, while the Rangers themselves claim a membership of from 5000 to 8000. Perhaps the difficulty in estimating their number lies in the fact that the gang, if it can presently be called that, is not well organized. Aside from the Main 21, there seems to be very little perceptible formal organization or control by leaders over individual gang members. If anything, the Rangers seem to represent a certain spirit in their community, a spirit which is adopted by young people. But whether this adoption is voluntary or forced upon young people is one of the major controversial questions that concern the Woodlawn, Kenwood, Oakland, and Hyde Park communities.

During the McClellan hearings there was a good deal of testimony that small children were being forced to join the Rangers and pay protection money. There is some evidence, some opinion, that the Rangers are still recruiting. But few black people in the areas in which most of the intimidation is supposed to be going on seem willing to talk about it, especially to a black like myself who is not known to them. At the hearings, charges were also made that the Rangers were using The Woodlawn Organization's federal funds to line their own pockets. Few private black citizens have much to say about this either.

In the proposal for the Black P. Stone Youth Center the Rangers state that "above all things or ideas of personal materialistic gain, we intend to cultivate our people spiritually, mentally, physically, and economically. To construct and develop our ideal of a new method of existence and behavior." The proposed program is a plea for community support. At present, few adults come to the Center. "Our P.," the statement of intentions goes on, "stands for people, progress, and prosperity." There is no mention of power in the statement.

"We're only interested in trying to develop our community services," Art Richardson told me, "so that it becomes obvious to the peoples that we only have the community's interest at heart and the development of ourselves. We're interested in all peoples as long as they are interested in our philosophy."

The Rangers have scheduled weekly Saturday night meetings at the Center for aults. Some adults do come out, but they are few in number; and those who come wait around nervously for other adults to show and attempt to make conversation with the older Rangers. For the Rangers have a community relations problem. They lack the vocal support of the majority of adults in the areas in which they have an obvious influence over young people. Perhaps it is because many of the adults are unwilling to recognize the Rangers as a legitimate force in a community crowded with "letter-name" organizations, all claiming a certain rapport with the grass roots.

Al Garrison, for example, is a twenty-five-year-old machinist. He is black, and he lives in the Woodlawn area. He grew up in Chicago, is divorced, and has two children. He is not so much concerned about the Rangers as he is about the present state of affairs in this country. He is afraid that his children will not live to reach his age. He believes that the country will not survive much longer, and he wonders why he continues to work every day. He believes that the Chicago police are corrupt beyond control. And he believes that the Mafia controls many members of the police force and the Blackstone Rangers.

"A friend of mine who used to be pretty big in the Rangers told me that white men run the gang," Garrison confides. "He said that they give the guys a new kind of dope that makes them want to kill people. They just go crazy when they take it," he says. "The whites are just using those boys."

Garrison is not bitter or militant. In fact, he cannot understand militancy at this late stage in what he believes to be the decline of America from causes still unclear to him.

The Rangers do not appear to be militant either, at least not in the contemporary sense of the word. They have refused to make a coalition with the Black Panthers. They do not seem to have any political philosophy. If anything, they believe only in themselves and in their motto: "Stone Run It!" But they are waiting too. Whether it is for more federal funds or for their presence and power to be recognized by the black community through their influence over ghetto youth, they are waiting. And their energy is at work.

"Just don't *do* it, put some *soul* into it! *I* got more soul than International Shoe Company!" the man says. His name is just "Buzz." He is a highly skillful pool player: he has beaten the great Minnesota Fats. But he is also a Blackstone Ranger, and for three hours every Monday afternoon, from 3 P.M. until 6 P.M., he is a disc jockey for a music program called *Stone Thang,* sponsored by the University of Chicago's student-run WHPK–FM radio station and the Black P. Stone Nation. Buzz takes his work seriously: he keeps time with his fingers, he sings along with the records, he makes spontaneous, soulful comments, he sweats and smokes, and he enjoys himself. The Rangers take the program seriously too: at least three of them assist him, tight-lipped and silent, in the little studio on the second floor of the university's student activities building. "If you got any soul at all," he announces to his FM audience, "give old brother Buzz a call." And the telephone keeps ringing for three hours, and Buzz keeps talking.

The station's program director, Tom Jacobson, is a senior at the university. He observed that since *Stone Thang* began in October, there has been an increase in the station's audience, and, he believes, some improvements in communications between the Ranger community and the University of Chicago-Hyde Park white community. The station, however, is a low-power operation, and only reaches FM sets in the Woodlawn, Hyde Park, and South Side areas. The students hope to expand the station's operations to AM sets in order to reach more people, but, Jacobson said, present expansion is doubtful because of lack of funds.

"We've been trying to do this type of show for months," Jacobson commented. "Finally we got Chuck Lapaglia from the First Presbyterian Church and Jeff Fort to help us set it up. The object of the show is to make the Black P. Stone Nation a part of the community."

Buzz and the Rangers who assist him are volunteers. Their only visible compensation lies in the plentiful opportunities Buzz has to say, "This is a *Stone Thang* presented by the All Mighty Black P. Stone Nation!" The other Rangers in the studio look solemn whenever he says this.

"The kids dig Stone," Carl Banks told me. "But the older people aren't sincere enough to come down and give help. We'd like to get to older people through their kids. In a sense, we're babysitting here because a lot of parents aren't interested in their kids and a lot of them don't trust the Stones. That's why we passed out a list of our intentions—to let them know that it's a peaceful thing. Some people in the area are skeptical because of the past, but they ought to come in and see us now."

The Rangers want money. They want to expand the range of activities presently offered in their Center and set up other Centers in the South Side area. They believe that they have the people, or at least the younger people, with them. Now they want money to put their programs into operation. Lamar "Bob" Bell, a former member of the Main 21, estimates that the Nation needs about $259,000 a year to put its present plans into operation. While his estimate may be far from conservative, it is obvious that for whatever cultural programs the Rangers may have in mind, the Sixty-seventh Street Center will not provide adequate accommodations. At present they have three rooms: the outer room, which serves as an office; the back room, with a small stage; and a sort of kitchen area, with a small bathroom. All of these rooms are in poor repair. For equipment they have a percussion set, two bongo drums, a Ping-Pong table, and about twenty-four metal chairs.

The Rangers are attempting certain ventures in business. The newly formed Kenwood-Oakland Community Organization, funded by a $100,000 grant from the Community Renewal Society of Chicago and headed by Reverend Curtis Burrell, has loaned the Rangers $3000 to open a restaurant on South Woodlawn Avenue. But there is a feeling, an old one, going back to the days of the OEO grant and the sponsorship of the Rangers by The Woodlawn Organization and Reverend Arthur Brazier, that a supposedly legitimate organization is subsidizing gang activities and allowing an already uncontrollable force to grow even larger and more powerful.

In 1968 there were two incidents which increased public interest and, perhaps, concern for the Blackstone Rangers. The first was their attempt to control the violence on the South Side of Chicago in the uncertain days in April after the assassination of Dr. Martin Luther King by passing out to neighborhood merchants hand-painted signs which read: "Do Not Touch . . . Black P. Stone . . . Jeff." They are said to have also set up a riot-control center in the First Presbyterian Church, where they received calls from troubled areas and directed Ranger leaders to the scenes of potential riotous activity. Finally, the Rangers and the Disciples called a truce on the Sunday following the assassination, during which some 1500 Rangers and 400 Disciples marched through the Woodlawn area and met in a park near the University of Chicago to negotiate the end of violence, or at least the immediate hostility, between the traditionally enemy groups. The march was covered by the local press, and the Rangers were given credit for preventing a riot on the South Side.

And in August, while the police and hippies rioted in the hotel area and in Lincoln Park, the South Side remained calm. Whether or not the Rangers were responsible for the calm remains an open question. There is some evidence that the F.B.I. had investigated certain threats, some of them alleged to have been made by Reverend John Fry, that the Rangers were planning to riot in the Loop, disrupt the Convention, and assassinate Eugene McCarthy and Hubert Humphrey.

Captain Edward Buckney, head of the Chicago Police Department's Gang Intelligence Unit and the ninth black police captain in the history of the Chicago Police Department, does not believe that the Rangers were responsible for keeping their neighborhoods cool during the April riots. "Fry will tell you that they were responsible for keeping things cool last April," he says, "but in our opinion that's a lot of hogwash. We just don't believe that's so. We believe that idea was a brand of hysteria created by the group to get credit for something they didn't do."

As an example of the hysteria, Buckney related that in August of 1968, just after Jeff Fort was jailed for probation violation and before the Democratic Convention, Reverend Brazier and other community people requested a meeting with the superintendent of police. "Their basic pitch was 'We can't guarantee what will happen with Jeff in jail.' They were pressuring the police to release him on the implication of the possibility of future violence. To me it's a means of bartering or dickering with the community for their own betterment," Buckney said. "There were no disturbances on the South Side, and the reason was basically because the black community did not want to become involved. If the Rangers claim credit for it, that's some more hogwash."

"In April," he said, "there were about 5000 United States troops, policemen, and many other agencies in the Kenwood-Woodlawn area. Historically, in Chicago there have never been riots on the South Side; they have always been on the West Side. The closest one was in April, and most of the damage there was done in Ranger-Disciple territory. Also, you have to consider the fact that over in the Ranger end there is little else to destroy because they have already destroyed most of it."

Buckney was promoted to captain last November, just after the election. He senses that his police position has made him unpopular in certain areas of the black community. But he believes that his role as a policeman is clearly defined. "Our approach is the hard-line police approach," he says. "We're not concerned with sociological approaches. As long as they don't violate the law, we don't concern ourselves with them." And as a policeman Buckney is in fact determined to break up the gang. He believes that this can be accomplished if most of the older members, possibly those who exert a bad influence over the younger members, are taken out of the area. He believes that 95 percent of the young people in the gang are there because they have no choice in the matter. "No one likes to be continually shot at because he's not a member of the gang," he said. "If we could divorce those who religiously believe in it from the community, the others would have a chance to get out. If the courts deal severely with a considerable number of them, if the courts deal severely in the cases pending against Jeff Fort and some of the other Main leaders, I think the Rangers could be broken up."

Like many other public officials in Chicago, Captain Buckney blames overzealous clergymen for the rapid growth of major gangs over the past two years. During the McClellan investigation, and later, in the Chicago papers and on television, he criticized Reverend John Fry and Reverend Brazier for supporting the activities of the Rangers and the Disciples. He was especially critical of Burrell's subsequent hiring of Jeff Fort as a community organizer. "From what we have seen already," he stated, "we can tell what kind of organizing he was doing. He used intimidation and fear to get young people to join the gang." He blames Reverend Fry's First Presbyterian Church for luring these youths away from the Boys' Clubs and into the church. Under Fry's guidance, according to Captain Buckney, the gang enjoyed a tremendous growth. He estimates the present membership of the Rangers to be between 1500 and 3000 youths, but indicates that Reverend Fry's estimation is closer to 4000. "But I doubt if you could find any more than 300 hard-core Rangers," he remarked.

The captain believes that the most notable achievement of the Rangers was the formation of an entertainment troupe, a major part of which was the "Blackstone Singers." "But you have to look at that with a jaundiced eye too," he cautioned me. "Most of them were high school kids, not hard-core Rangers." He feels that too much attention is being given the gang members to the exclusion of all the other poor children in the Woodlawn community. "If people keep pushing the bad things under the rug, at the rate they're going now they soon will become untouchable because they've already done almost everything attributable to organized crime.

"I believe in giving credit where credit is due," he says of the Rangers, "but they don't do anything constructive. All they're interested in is money in their pockets. If you have any dealings with them, the question always is what can *you* do for *them.* You won't get much out of them for nothing."

Buckney has been criticized for what some Chicagoans call his persecution of the Rangers. He is aware of this, and seems to be able to live with the constant criticism from community-minded whites as well as from some of his fellow blacks. "I'm often accused of persecuting the black community," he admitted. "But when I look at these homicides"—he picked up a pile of papers from his desk and dropped them before continuing—"when I look at these and see a minimum of 95 percent to 97 percent of them coming out of the black community— well, I believe you have to concentrate your men where the problem is." In 1968, the captain disclosed, there have been more than ten killings in Woodlawn.

"If they were so sincere about doing something constructive for the community and if they have knowledge of crime, why don't they turn it over to the police?" the captain asked. "There've been other gangs who have turned members over to the police for doing some wrong. But the Rangers have rarely if ever cooperated with the police and probably never will. If one of them is locked up, they'll try anything possible to spring him—bribing witnesses, even intimidation. They have a complete disdain for the law. They won't even show up for court appearances."

This sort of suspicion is reciprocated: the chief witnesses against the T.W.O. project and the Rangers before the McClellan Committee, George Rose and Annabelle Martin, are rumored to have been bribed by the police to testify as they did. Rose had been arrested for a narcotics violation, but charges were never brought; and the two sons of Annabelle Martin had been previously arrested for the murder of Leo McClure and were the principal witnesses in the case against Eugene Hairston. The charges against both the boys were dropped. Both Mrs. Martin and George Rose moved out of Chicago. Captain Buckney denies the bribery allegations: "Bribery is, point-blank, not true. In the case of George Rose, we got word that the Rangers wanted him killed. We got to him first. All we wanted was inside information on the Rangers. Mrs. Martin certainly wasn't bribed. She was merely asked by the senators if she wanted to go to Washington, and she agreed. We just arranged for her transportation out of the city."

Since its formation in March of 1967, the Gang Intelligence Unit has grown in power and importance in the Chicago Police Department. In 1968 there were only thirty-eight policemen, mostly black, assigned to the Unit; but since the first part of November, plans have been made to increase its strength to two hundred men. "We're striving for 100 percent integration of the Unit," Captain Buckney told me. It is highly probable that members of the Unit have infiltrated the gang; Captain Buckney seems well informed on Ranger activities. But it is also just as probable that the Rangers know a good deal about the activities of the Unit.

Some non-G.I.U. policemen, like Field Commander William B. Griffin, have attempted to work with the Ranger organization rather than against it. "Griffin's problems are different from mine," Buckney says. "He may have to do what is best for the community, while I, if I were in his place, might do something different. But the general consensus in the police department is the hard-line police approach."

Few uniformed policemen walk the streets in the Woodlawn area. Those who do are black. Most white policemen drive through the area in cars, usually accompanied by a black officer. Most of the policemen in the area seem to be young. They are, for the most part, polite, and a little cold. On occasion one notices a parked patrol car with two hard-faced white officers in the front seat and the barrel of a shotgun framed in the window between them. Only then does one remember the tension which is supposed to exist between the police and the black community. It is present, but it is not racial; at least not in the traditional—black-white—sense of the word.

Black people, if Blackstone Rangers can be called representative of black people, feel a tension between black policemen and themselves. It is a feeling of mistrust, of discomfort. Rangers do not seem to be under continual harassment from the police, but it is a fair assumption that they, or at least their leaders, are being watched by other blacks. If one sits too long in a restaurant with a Ranger of any status within the organization, he will eventually become aware of another black sitting in the next booth, sipping an eternal cup of coffee. Perhaps he is merely enjoying his coffee; perhaps he is a plainclothesman on the job. In any case, Rangers find it more relaxing to converse inside the Center or in one of their other meeting places.

"It shouldn't be called the Police Gang Intelligence Unit," says Mickey Cogwell, one of the Main 21 (the leadership of the Blackstone Rangers). "It should be called the Gang *Stupid* Unit because they are so stupid. If they really wanted to get us, they would wait until we commit crimes and then arrest us. Instead, they try to stop us from doing anything."

Mickey Cogwell is another busy man. Among the Main 21, he is recognized as the Ranger leader with the most business ability. For this reason Ranger president Jeff Fort put him in charge of West Side business operations of the Blackstone Nation. Cogwell is intelligent, and his directness suggests honesty and candor. He wears a black derby and a blue turtleneck sweater and talks very fast. He has had considerable experience with the Gang Intelligence Unit. He has been arrested more than sixty times.

"Every time people do things for us the G.I.U. tries to publicize it so that donators get bad publicity," Cogwell says. "It doesn't want the Rangers and Disciples to have a peace treaty because it threatens the security of their jobs. I feel that the G.I.U.—black men—use the Rangers and the rivalry between us and the D's to make their work more important to the system."

Cogwell believes that the members of the G.I.U. have extra-police powers. According to him, they can go into the Cook County Jail whenever they want; they have easy access to the press whenever they want to publicize stories about the Rangers; they have the help of the power structure in Chicago; and they can even influence judges. "Suppose one of the younger cats go out and does something and is put in the Cook County Jail. They will be offered a chance to get out if they swear that they were told to do something by one of the older Rangers, by one of the Main," he says. "The police have realized that they can't break up the Stones now. They might have done it four or five years ago, but now all they can do is arrest the Main. But Stone will still go on. In order to break us up, they will have to arrest everyone from the Main down to the peewees.

"If the police pick up a Stone, we take the number of the car, call a lawyer, and follow the car to the station," Cogwell states. "We wait in the halls until the lawyer comes. Then we try to find out what the bond is. If it's not too high, we try to raise it. But most bonds are set too high." He attributes the high bonds to intervention by members of the G.I.U. and the influence they seem to have over judges.

Cogwell denies that there was a payoff behind the November "Don't Vote" campaign. He says that it was an expression of the dissatisfaction of the Rangers with the local political structure. He observes that just after their campaign, G.I.U. chief Edward Buckney was promoted to captain and plans were made to increase the G.I.U. from 38 to 200 men. He believes that the campaign frightened the Chicago power structure. And the Rangers, he says, are now planning for 1971, the year of the next mayoralty election. Winston Moore, the black warden of the Cook County Jail and a critic of the Rangers, called the campaign "outright stupid," but whether or not the activity was politically naïve, it seems that the Chicago power structure is presently attempting to tighten up its control of the Blackstone Rangers.

Still, the Rangers appear to be growing, in both number and the scope of their business ventures. Besides the restaurant, they have obtained the use of a building from Humble Oil Company for $1 a year. The building, Cogwell says, will be used for Ranger businesses which will be operated by the eight Blackstone Rangers who are presently receiving training from the Chicago Small Businessmen's Association. Also, the Westinghouse Corporation has donated to the Rangers, through the University of Chicago's Firman House, fourteen washers and three dryers. The corporation will teach the Rangers how to operate them so they will be able to start their own laundromat. They have received two car-wash units from other sources, and have been given an interest in the Sammy Davis, Jr. Liquor Store, a pilot project owned by the famous entertainer and managed by the Rangers. The profits from the store go into a "slush fund" against the time when the Rangers are prepared to set up other businesses. Finally, an unnamed manufacturer has supplied them with 20,000 "All Mighty Black P. Stone" sweat shirts with the phrase "black is beautiful" printed on their backs in every major language. Lamar Bell, a Ranger leader, wears one with the phrase written in Greek.

"We want the Stones to be able to know something when they go into business," Mickey Cogwell says. He is not pleased with his attempts to run the West Side operation, he notes, because of what he calls attempts of the G.I.U. to stop Ranger business development by finding violations of the building and zoning codes, and reporting them to city agencies. At one point, he says, the Rangers had $800 worth of violations against them.

Mickey Cogwell claims that the Rangers made a genuine effort to keep the South Side cool during the April riots. "Jeff sent word out all over the Nation to keep peace," he says, "because King was killed and everybody was hurting. All the Main leaders went out into the streets to keep peace. Plus, the G.I.U. was out too, to provoke the Rangers into rioting. We feel that the city was out to get us to burn down our own community. But since we need the stores—our babies need milk—Jeff decided that all the stores in the area were part of the Ranger Nation."

I asked Mickey Cogwell if the Rangers would like to patrol their neighborhoods as a kind of community police force similar in some respects to the Black Panthers on the West Coast. "There is quite a difference between the power structure on the West Coast and the power structure in Chicago," he replied. "Mayor Daley is the most powerful man in America. He can tell the President what to do. On the Coast the Panthers can ride around in cars with guns, but not here. Mayor Daley is a powerful cat, very powerful. And dangerous, very dangerous."

While the Rangers can, in many instances, be considered a kind of spontaneous para-police force in their efforts to show the strength of their organization, there is another consideration to place in focus: are the police, specifically the members of the Gang Intelligence Unit, themselves a para-political force? This question is important in a very singular respect. It is evident that the Blackstone Ranger Nation is not interested in voluntarily *helping* the police: all of their activities which may be called helpful to the police seem to arise, unavoidably, from their efforts to keep the name of the Ranger organization safe from adverse publicity or else to demonstrate the tremendous power and community appeal, at least among the young, of the Blackstone Ranger Nation. In both of these areas the activities of the Gang Intelligence Unit seem to contribute the necessary pressure or motivation. The relative ease with which its members operate within the police department and the cooperation they receive from the State's Attorney's Office and the Cook County Jail, the influence they seem to have in the courts, and the easy willingness of the press to publicize incidents about the Rangers all suggest that members of the Unit have more than ordinary police powers.

For example, in December of 1968 after Jeff Fort was found guilty of contempt of Congress and released on $5000 bond, he was arrested by members of the G.I.U. on an old charge: failure to pay a $50 fine for a previous disorderly conduct arrest. The arrest warrant was issued on March 17, 1967. The eight G.I.U. officers who arrested Fort arrived at his home carrying axes, prepared to break down the door. They had no search warrant, but they searched his apartment and found a .22 caliber gun. Fort was charged with failure to register the gun.

Marshall Patner, the white Chicago lawyer who walked out of Senator McClellan's investigation of Poverty Program funding of a Ranger project with his client Jeff Fort last summer, has been in a position which enabled him to observe the activities of the Gang Intelligence Unit firsthand. "The question is," he says, "whether the police run the whole show. The G.I.U. can say 'no bond' to the judges, and no bond is given. Judges listen to them. State's attorneys listen to them."

Patner is paid by the Kettering Foundation to provide legal counsel for Rangers in general and Jeff Fort in particular. A 1956 University of Chicago Law School graduate, he quit his job as head of the appellate and test case division of the Legal Aid Bureau of Chicago to help William W. Brackett, who served as counsel for the Reverend John Fry before the McClellan Committee. Fry is a white clergyman whose church, the First Presbyterian, housed one of the Rangers' training centers funded by the Office of Economic Opportunity through a local grass roots group, The Woodlawn Organization (T.W.O.). The church thought Fort should have a black lawyer, but Fort preferred Marshall Patner.

"As a lawyer," Patner says, "I don't see my function as looking over a client to see what he's doing. I see these people as needing defense because they are being picked on for offenses which other people wouldn't be charged with, and subject to high bond just because they are Rangers." Since the McClellan hearings, Marshall Patner has received angry letters and telephone calls suggesting that he should be put into a concentration camp.

In Ranger cases, according to Patner, the judges set very high bonds. In one arrest for aggravated assault, the night judge set bond at $4000 and the morning judge reset bond at $5000. For a fight in the jail, Fort's bond was set at $10,000, and for a charge of resisting arrest, Jeff Fort's bond was again set at $10,000. He estimates that Fort has been picked up over one hundred and eighty times. Sometimes he will be arrested, processed, and released in a few minutes. Patner is bringing a suit in federal court for injunctive relief. The suit is against Mayor Daley, Captain Buckney, the State's Attorney, and certain judges, and is on behalf of Jeff Fort, Mickey Cogwell, and the Black P. Stone Nation.

Marshall Patner feels that the peacekeeping role of the Rangers is a "funny" one. "I would guess that as a matter of defiance and as a show of power the Rangers exert all the energy possible to see that police prophecies about them are not fulfilled. In contrast, they do this in areas where interests are common to their own. I believe that they keep a lot of ghetto kids out of trouble by giving them something with which they can identify."

"The police are definitely out to get the Stones," Carl Banks, a Ranger teacher, tells me at the Black P. Stone Youth Center, "especially since Nixon got in. Every time a black gets arrested, if he's from this neighborhood he's treated like a Stone. His bond is hiked up, he's harassed." Banks's voice changes to anger. "They don't want the Stones to have anything." He crushes a cigarette butt with his foot. "They want to keep us right down here on the ground."

"Why do you think they're out to get you?" I ask him.

Banks lights up another cigarette. "Some people in the area are still scared of us. This neighborhood used to be terrible, especially for strangers. Now all that's changed."

"How has it changed?"

"Stone run it," he says. "There's less fighting now. Stones are keeping dope and faggots out of the neighborhood. We even try to keep prostitutes out."

I follow Carl Banks over to the stage where the drums are assembled. It is time for his practice session. "We want to represent to the kids that this is our neighborhood," he continues; "we love it, it's all we got. We want the kids to feel the same way. We try to instill some dignity and pride in them. That's what the P. stands for."

"Are the kids forced to join?" I ask.

Carl considers this. He beats out a roll on one of the drums before answering. "It might have been that way in the old days," he admits. "But there's no pressure now. That's why we're going slow now. The older brothers aren't as active as they should be, some of them are drifting away. Having the peewees with us is OK, but we really need the adults to get our program going good."

"How do you get the kids to join?" I ask.

"They just come in," Banks says. "This is the only place open at night for kids to attend. There's nothing else in the area that's open except the Y.M.C.A. on Seventy-first Street."

Black children, at least those from the Woodlawn area, do come to the Center. They wander in and out of the broken door from the time it is unlocked in the morning until after ten every night. Except for the percussion class, there are few organized activities available for them. For the most part, they stand around the office, expectantly, waiting for something to develop; or else they wander back into the main room and sit in the metal chairs against the walls, under the painted faces of Marcus Garvey, Harriet Tubman, Malcolm X, Muhammad Ali, Martin Luther King, and Frederick Douglass. All of the walls in the main room are painted black. And the historical faces are on the right wall. On the left wall, also against a black background, there is a skillfully drawn mural of cosmic forces, the universe in motion, flaming comets, and the overall suggestion of pure energy.

The wall has its symbolic significance, although the children seem to favor the right side of the room and the faces on its wall, behind the metal chairs where they sit. Young people are only barred from the back room when the older Rangers come in—Jeff Fort, Edward Bey, Mickey Cogwell, and other Main leaders—and secret meetings are held. At these times the children wait in the small office, under orders to remain silent, or else they go outside. And whenever they do leave the Center, many of them, especially the younger ones, are quick to call back to anyone still standing in the room: "Stone Run It!"

Congressman Abner Mikva, a white reformer who has fought the Daley machine, was elected to his first term in Congress last November from the Second Congressional District of Chicago, which encompasses the Woodlawn part of the South Side. He is considered by many people in Chicago to be something of an expert on Ranger affairs. Over coffee in his home on South Kenwood Avenue, Mikva offers some of his impressions of the group.

"I'm not a pro-Ranger. If someone commits a crime in the area and if he is a kid, the victim will assume that he's a Ranger, but if the Rangers had committed all the crimes they have been charged with, there would probably have to be at least 100,000 of them, or they would have to be some of the most energetic criminals who ever lived," he says. "I don't think they are civic-minded young reformers. I think that many of them are so alienated that it will be a hard job trying to bring them back into the mainstream. But even if you could bust up the gang structure, it would cost more to keep these kids apart than it would cost to help them do something constructive."

Unlike most groups of young, organized blacks, the Rangers do not seem to be primarily racially oriented. If they believe in any form of black power at all, it's the physical energy which they are attempting to harness in the black community and the economic power which, they believe, will come through constructive uses of that energy. If they hold any political philosophy at all, it is truly a grass roots one: they want to wrest control of their community not so much from the power structure as from the control of an older generation of blacks. They have a large number of the young people; now they are attempting to expand their source of energy by moving into the black, middle-class neighborhoods. And it is in such areas that the limitations of the Ranger appeal are tested. It is within these areas that class lines become more apparent.

Abner Mikva admits the reality of these class lines which contribute to polarization in the black community. "In other neighborhoods they really are recruiting, but these are different kinds of kids. They're midldle-class, with two parents in the home—home-owning parents— not kids from broken families. The Rangers are scaring the daylights out of them. And unfortunately, some of the white churchmen are helping them. I get violent mail, more from the black community than from the white, asking: 'What are you doing defending the Rangers?'

"Some people in the South Woodlawn and Oakland areas would say that the police are too easy on the Rangers," he observes. "Some parents believe that they should crack some skulls. They're scared to death. And these are *black* people. This shows that it's not so much a color thing between the police and the Rangers. I can't recall any time over the last two years when I saw two white policemen alone in a car in the community. They're mostly black and white teams now. Or, if there are two white policemen, they don't respond to street calls. A good part of the G.I.U. is black, and some of these men have done community work in Woodlawn or with Operation Breadbasket. Some of them are militant, but they're against the Rangers because they're policemen and for obeying the law." Mikva feels, however, that the police do create a problem in the black community, in spite of the sameness of color. "The police insist on using direct, terrorist, violent methods and only succeed in polarizing people. They force people like myself to come out pro-Ranger because of their tactics. I come out saying more in defense of the Rangers than I would like to. Other people come out being more anti-Ranger than they would ordinarily be."

In spite of whatever constructive things they are attempting to do, Mikva says, the Rangers are unpredictable. He recognizes that the community has to deal with them, but, he says, "If they weren't here, I wouldn't invent them."

There was a birthday party given for Joyce Green at the Black P. Stone Youth Center one Saturday night in late November. The girls brought homemade cake and potato chips, a bowl of punch, balloons, some cookies, and a few records. Fifteen or so boys, ranging in age from nine to fourteen, sat on the metal chairs against the wall, under the pictures of Marcus Garvey, Malcolm X, Muhammad Ali, Martin Luther King, Du Bois, and the others, waiting for the party to start. They sat quietly, waiting for the girls to start the record player. And when the music finally began, the boys cut the lights out and proceeded to select dancing partners. Art Richardson, director of the Center, put the lights on. One of the boys cut them off again. "The lights have to stay on, little brother," Richardson told him.

"We want them out," some of the other boys said.

Richardson motioned for all the boys to come closer to him. "If it's not worth doing in the light," he said, "then it's not worth doing at all." Then he added: "That's what Stone is all about."

The boys considered this, and when Art left the room again one of them cut the lights off. Art came back into the room, put the lights on again, and stood next to the switch. All of the boys left the Center. And after gathering the cakes and the punch and the chips and records, and after breaking all the balloons, the girls followed them.

On Sunday morning before ten o'clock the boy who had made the last effort to darken the room leaned against the locked door of the Center, waiting for it to open. I waited with him.

"Art will be here in a while," I told him.

"I don't like Art," the boy said. "He's mean."

"Do you know what he was trying to tell you last night?" I asked him.

"Yeah," he said. "I know. But nobody wants to dance with girls with the lights on. If the other guys see it, they'll talk about you."

To get out of the wind, while we waited, we went across Sixty-seventh Street to a restaurant and played records and drank Cokes. The boy's name is Danny Jackson. He is in Carl Banks's percussion class. He is fourteen, an eighth-grader, has semi-processed hair, and he never smiles. He wants to be a musician because his father is a musician. He wants to finish high school and then work in a factory because his father works in a factory. He has never thought about college. He does not know much about what it means to be a Blackstone Ranger, but he knows that he is one because he is allowed to walk in and out of the Center whenever he wants. Asked why he likes being a Ranger and living in Woodlawn, he says, "Because Stone Run It!"

Youth Action, a Chicago youth organization funded by the Y.M.C.A. and the Chicago Boys' Club, opened the center on Sixty-seventh and Blackstone as an outpost early in 1968. There was a one-year lease taken on the building. Last September, according to Art Richardson, Youth Action abandoned the outpost. "In October," he says, "I just walked in the Center off the street, pulled the desks out of the basement, and got the Stones to clean up and paint the place. Then the kids started coming in."

Richardson believes that Youth Action abandoned the outpost because it could not reach the youth in the community. I asked Richardson why he thought the Center was more successful under his direction than it was under the administration of Youth Action.

"I'm a legitimate person from the community," he replied. "They were outsiders. The most important thing in this work is understanding the *needs* of the community. I don't profess to be able to *teach,* but I do come from the community. I know the needs. If I had the resources, I would be able to get peoples who are capable of carrying out my program. I'll always welcome agency peoples to come in, and I'll always welcome their ideas, but *we* have to run it."

"How do you know you *can* run it?" I asked him.

Art nodded toward the mural of the solar system on the left side of the main room. "That's energy," he said. "It only responds to the right vibrations. It's that way in nature. An outsider comes in projecting an outside vibration, communicating over the heads of the younger, grass roots brothers. That's wrong. You have to relate to young brothers simply, give off simple vibrations. Otherwise, the little brothers will not respond energetically."

I asked him if any black, and not just Rangers, could produce the right vibrations.

"No," he said. "A lot of Afro brothers don't know how to respond on the street level. So a lot of the little brothers here don't relate to and don't respect some of the outside brothers."

When Art Richardson speaks of "universal vibrations," he seems to imply that the Ranger Nation is not necessarily organized along racial lines; and the fact that many black residents of areas in which they operate condemn their activities serves to support this assumption. Subtle, almost imperceptible class lines are slowly being drawn. And the Rangers seem to be aware of this. "The Chief [Jeff Fort] wants to have white Stones and Mexican Stones and any other kind of person who has the ability to be a Stone," Richardson told me. "He's already extended the invitation."

The directors of the Center have worked out a "Performing Arts Program," with a selected schedule of classes running from Monday through Saturday. Among the classes listed are history, job training, dancing, speeches by interested religious leaders, businessmen, teachers, and entertainers, a class in percussion, boxing, current events, and a class in the importance of education. All these classes are still on paper. So far only one class, the percussion class taught by Lamar Bell and Carl Banks, has started. The others are waiting, like the children who come in every evening, perhaps for financial backing, perhaps for the trust and the enthusiasm of the adult community to grow.

In the middle of November Art Richardson and Lamar Bell began to make plans for the Ranger Thanksgiving show, to draw the interest of the Woodlawn community to the Black P. Stone Youth Center. The floors were cleaned, spotlights were rented or borrowed, posters were distributed over the Woodlawn, Hyde Park, Oakland, and Kenwood areas. Then they went out into the black community to recruit talent.

On the Friday evening just before Thanksgiving the Blackstone Rangers presented their show. It was well attended, but the young people in the audience far outnumbered the adults. A fair contingent of whites from the university areas came, and a TV newsman also came to film the first part of the show. Some of them, the whites, looked puzzled as they tried to comprehend the significance of the mural on the left wall of the auditorium room.

All of those who had volunteered to perform kept their promise. Darlene Blackburn even put on a small fashion show of female African clothing. And although Youth Action provided the microphone and helped the Rangers transport chairs from the Saint Ambrose Church, the show, for the most part, was an independent Ranger accomplishment. Visitors to the Center were asked, but not required, to make a contribution. Raffle tickets for a Thanksgiving turkey were given in exchange for the contributions. The Rangers collected almost seventy dollars.

During the late afternoon and evening there was a steady flow of people in and out of the Center. The Rangers estimate that they had between 300 and 400 people in the Center during the event. The whites who came in the early evening left, almost in a group, when the major part of the show was over. Jeff Fort, Edward Bey, Mickey Cogwell, all in leather jackets, came with some of the other older Rangers, some of them new faces in the Center. They walked, almost nervously, back and forth between the office and the auditorium during most of the show, watching. Occasionally they conferred together at the back of the auditorium, and occasionally they called Art Richardson aside and whispered to him.

Late into the evening, the real Ranger show began.

"We want to present now some Stones who have been on nationwide television," the M. C. said. "They've been on the Smothers Brothers. And they're here, back with us now: The *Blackstone Singers!*"

There were cries of Stone! Stone! from the young people in the audience. Most of the adults had already left.

"We haven't appeared much this year," the spokesman for the group began, "because of what went on in Washington, D.C., and because of what's going on with the Gang Intelligence Unit and with Uncle Toms and Aunt Sallys. And because of what Stones are like in the newspapers and radio and TV. We have not appeared."

The young people, who had been noisy all through the performance of a progressive jazz group some five or six minutes before, were silent as the spokesman finished his introduction. Then there were again cries of "Stone! Stone! Stone Run It!" And after the voices had subsided, the spokesman for the Blackstone Singers made the observation that: *"They're* in trouble, but we're together because Stone *is* going to run it!" Then he announced their first song, a variation of an old Temptations piece, rewritten by the Blackstone Singers. The song was called "You're In Trouble," and they asked everyone to sing along. Everyone did. The young people in the metal chairs, in the dark room, clapped their hands in time to the music and kept yelling "Stone! Stone!" or "Stone Run It!" during places in the song where they did not know the lyrics. The singing went on a long time.

When Jeff Fort moves around, people scatter to make connections with him. He is always moving. And when the word comes that he will eventually be at a certain place, a crowd of people—Rangers and non-Rangers alike—gather at that point to wait for him. He never arrives on time, but everyone waits. And when he does come, all activities and conversations and eyes stop moving and focus on him. Jeff Fort is a man completely aware of himself, and of what he represents. He is playful, full of laughter and good humor with his men. But there is a tenseness and a seriousness behind it all, and his men seem to guard their laughter and movements when he is about. It is obvious that each Ranger has great respect for him. Even the small boys, the "peewees," imitate his hair-style and the way he walks.

Fort may call a single man aside to converse in secret, but one is aware that, somehow, he is always conscious of the movements of everyone else in the room. He had been aware of me, of my movements in and out of the Center, for over four months. It was necessary to have his permission to talk with the Rangers. Then, when the talking was done and the Rangers who had spoken had read in type what they had said to me, I waited, patiently like the others in the Center, for Jeff to give me a few minutes of his time.

"What future plans have you made for the Nation?" I asked him when he walked close to me.

"Did you rap to him, Bop?" he said to Lamar Bell.

"Yeah, Chief," Bell said.

"How is it?"

"It's cool, Chief."

"You got everything I have to say," Jeff said to me.

Perhaps one of the few white men who can claim to have some close associations with the Blackstone Rangers is Charles Lapaglia, the youth worker whom McClellan called to testify to certain allegations made against him and the First Presbyterian Church where he is employed. He lives in Hyde Park and is planning to write a book about the Ranger Nation. Lapaglia is not an easy man to talk to because, like Reverend Fry, he has been subjected to adverse publicity and is suspicious of people who take notes of what he says. But when he begins to talk, he can relate a wealth of detail about the Rangers.

On Christmas Eve, in his home on Kimbark Street, Charles Lapaglia begins to talk. He is frequently interrupted by telephone calls from merchants who have unsold Christmas trees they want the Rangers to distribute in the area. He allows me to read something about the Gang Intelligence Unit he has written. "For both black militants and police," the paper states,

> the issue of who runs it [the black community] is both conscious and immediate. Traditionally, the black community has been controlled by white institutions who disguise the oppressive methods of control by their own institutional rhetoric. The black community has seen through the rhetoric and is attempting to escape oppression by those institutions by asserting their will to determine their own destiny. The order establishing the G.I.U. is the establishment's response to the black community's attempt to gain control of their own destiny. It gives the G.I.U. the direct authority to exercise political control in the black community. Its scope extends far beyond the generally accepted police functions of apprehending law violators. Nor is the intent primarily to control violence through aggressive police action. Its purpose is to maintain tight control over a potentially rebellious colony, and to eliminate all significant opposition. The order deals directly with who runs it. It gives the G.I.U. the power to determine what is good and bad for the community—what services should be subverted—what laws are to be enforced and what laws are to be ignored— what groups should exist and what groups should be destroyed.

Lapaglia claims that the alleged "raid" on the First Presbyterian Church and the firing of guns in the church vault by members of the G.I.U. were a publicity stunt. He maintains that the Treasury Department had asked the church to act as a repository for the Ranger weapons when it began its attempt, after the riots in the summer of

1966, to decrease the level of gun ownership in ghettos all over the country. "In that gun affair," he says, "we were actually a third party in gun-collection activities between the police and the Treasury Department and the Rangers."

A few of the older Rangers hang around the Black P. Stone Youth Center. There are no children. Lamar Bell is there. He is upset because, he says, since the first of December, just after the Thanksgiving show, policemen from the Gang Intelligence Unit have come into the Center at least six times. He says that they park in front of the building from time to time—four men in a car—or else they come in, searching for young boys or for certain of the Main leaders. Bell is worried about the new pop machine which the Center has acquired since the Thanksgiving show, and he says that the policemen have questioned him about it. Bell wants to go to Syracuse, New York, during the Christmas holidays to work with a band there and earn money, but he is reluctant to leave Carl Banks, who is not a union musician and who therefore cannot work with him. Jeff Fort is at home with his wife and two children on Christmas Eve. Some of the other Rangers are said to be out delivering baskets to the poor.

"They are quiet passing out Christmas baskets now," Marshall Patner told me. "At one time it was a famous thing. They solicited funds last year with a card that said 'Please Give to the Christmas Fund: Blackstone Rangers.' Some of them were arrested on an 1890 ordinance saying you can't solicit funds without disclosing the name of the organization. Their lawyer argued that signing 'Blackstone Rangers' was sufficient. The case was dismissed.

"In some areas the Rangers don't even want to take credit for the good that they do," Patner said. "They worry that it may be turned back on them."

Perhaps James Houtsma, a white, former Gang Intelligence Unit detective who gave damaging testimony against the Blackstone Rangers in Washington, was close to accurate in his assessment of the present dilemma of the group. "A lot of confusion is in their minds," he observed, "because of pressures on them from their affiliation with other groups. Organizations use them as guinea pigs in experimental projects and just brought them along too fast. They started as kids, but with all the pressures, they don't even know themselves now."

But again, perhaps the Rangers are now beginning to understand what they are, or better, the potentially creative power which they represent. Early this year Jeff Fort was invited, it is said by certain Illinois politicians, to attend one of the Inaugural Balls given for President Nixon in Washington. Characteristically, Fort did not go himself, but sent two of the Main leaders to represent the Blackstone Ranger Nation. One of the two men who dressed in tails and who mingled with political dignitaries was Mickey Cogwell. While Cogwell was having "a lovely time" at the Ball (as he later told Chicago reporters), detectives from the G.I.U. came to his house in Chicago to arrest him. After returning to Chicago, Cogwell was asked why the Rangers had accepted an invitation to celebrate the election of Richard Nixon, a man, it has been said, who did not actively court the black voter.

"*We* elected Nixon," Cogwell stated.

"What do you mean?" he was asked. "Do you mean that your 'Don't Vote' campaign helped him to beat Humphrey in Illinois?"

"No," said Mickey Cogwell, who talks very fast. "*We* are the ones who put crime in the streets."

part five
lies, fraud, and theft
as styles and
ways of life

13 | **Types of Jockeys** | Marvin Scott

The vital necessity for participant-observer studies of deviants is well illustrated by this essay. Although a great many Americans have attended horse races at some time in their lives, few are aware that certain race-track behavior, which they might consider immoral, is actually normal. Only someone who has been involved with the racing crowd for long periods of time would be able to recognize their deviant practices.

As Scott points out at the end of his essay, this study also demonstrates the importance of opportunities in producing deviance. It is a good illustration of Merton's famous theory that an individual's lack of legitimate opportunity to achieve societal goals provides a context in which he may seek illegitimate opportunity. It also shows what Cloward and Ohlin had argued in their book on Delinquency and Opportunity: *that is, "illegitimate opportunity" and a specialized knowledge of those opportunities are equally important in producing deviance.*

Horsemen recognize three categories of jockeys: "honest boys," "money jocks," and "businessmen."

To get the reputation of an honest boy (most jockeys are so categorized) a jockey must satisfy two conditions: he must accept all mounts offered him, and he must ride in strict accord to instructions.

If a jockey's services are called upon, he must not refuse, lest his reputation as "honest" be damaged. The only legitimate reason for not accepting a mount is to have already accepted a bid to ride some other trainer's horse. Given this cultural expectation, we might expect that all trainers would freely attempt to gain the services of the hottest jockeys, ensuring the best possible chance of their horses finishing in the money. Moreover, we might expect that given a choice between mounts, the jockeys will always choose the hot horse. In actuality, trainers will often call upon second-rate jockeys to ride their horses; and jockeys will

Reprinted from Marvin B. Scott, *The Racing Game* (Chicago: Aldine Publishing Company, 1968); Copyright © 1968 by Marvin B. Scott.

often choose to ride a second-rate horse. These anomalous choices deserve some explanation.

When a trainer has a horse whose expected performance for a particular event is highly uncertain, often he will prefer to call upon the services of a lesser known jockey. Should he choose a superior jockey and should the horse perform very poorly, then the superior jockey will—when given a choice in the future—choose to ride for another trainer. The trainer's disinclination to ask a hot jockey to ride an uncertain animal has the consequence of resolving the jockey's dilemma: to be "honest" he must accept all mounts—usually on a first-come, first-served basis—but to maintain a good winning record he needs a choice from among *hot* mounts. In sum, trainers in the pursuit of their own self-interest help jockeys maintain their reputation as being both "honest" and "hot."

From time to time, however, a trainer will call upon the services of a hot boy even when he knows for certain that his animal will do little running on a particular day. In the erratic horse's next race, where the winning effort is planned, the trainer may shift to a no-name jockey. This shifting from a hot jockey to a no-name boy is a maneuver to get better odds. The playing public reasons this way: "If hot jock Jones can't bring the animal home, the horse is a nothing." When the horse wins next time at a big price with the no-name jock, the public attributes the victory to some factor of racing luck and not to the manipulations of the man behind the horse. Naturally, the trainer can't pull this maneuver too often, for fear of alienating a good jockey. Moreover, each time the trainer employs this maneuver, he is tacitly indebted to "pay off" the jockey by furnishing him with a hot mount in the future.

As I have already suggested, the hot jock will sometimes choose to ride what he takes to be an inferior mount. Such decisions typically involve horses from the leading money-winning stables. The jockey "trades" a bad mount today for a good mount tomorrow. That is, the winning stable, when it has a hot horse, will go back with the boy who is willing to ride those horses whose performance is uncertain.

In general, a type of equilibrium is established whereby the leading trainers get the leading jocks to ride for them, and the leading jocks get the best mounts. But, as I indicated, this state of affairs is the result of many sorts of exchanges and tacit negotiations.

The second criterion of a jock's reputation as "honest"—strictly following instructions of the trainer—can be explained more briefly. Trainers, for reasons that will be made clear later, often have something to gain when their horses lose on a particular occasion. One way of making a horse lose or appear to be off form is to instruct the jockey to run the animal in a manner contrary to the horse's best efforts. If a horse runs best in front, the trainer who wants to lose will instruct the jockey to come from behind; if the horse runs best close to the rail, the trainer will instruct the jockey to keep the horse wide; if the horse responds only to energetic whipping, the trainer will instruct the jockey not to use the whip. The jockey may well realize that the instructions are contrary to the horse's best efforts; he might realize that by *not* following instructions he can win an otherwise losing race. However, he will *not* race in accord with his own best judgment, because what he has at stake is his reputation as an "honest boy."

The second type of jockey—the "money jock"—is not concerned with the number of mounts he receives but with getting the best mounts in the best races. If he had his way, the money jock would accept only mounts in the feature Saturday race. In receiving mounts, his agent is often instructed to demand a flat fee for his services. For instance, the stable demanding the services of the money jock must meet a set fee of, say, $250 (10 percent of the winning share in most ordinary races) on a win-or-lose basis. This demand usually means that the jock will get hot mounts, for owners are slow to put up a win-or-lose fee unless they have a hot horse and expect to win. By getting hot horses, the money jock will be on a mount where he can display his skills and character to best advantage. These are some of the backstage manipulations that make his onstage performance appear so stunning.

Money jocks are preferred by moneyed stables. The leading handicap and stakes horses are to be found in the barns of those owners who regard horse racing literally as a game. Being able to foot the bills, their concern is with the honor that goes with owning (and frequently breeding) the *winner.* Second- or third-place money is seldom a target for these owners.

The characteristic of the money jock is his in-and-out performance. When he is "in," it is frequently because he has—as a consequence of his coolness—staged a ride that saved the horse perhaps as much as five lengths. Many horsemen say that a money jock can give a horse a five-length advantage. They believe the money jock can remain cool in a pocket and plunge through on the inside rail when and if the opportunity comes, rather than taking a horse on the outside where the certainty of racing room may cost a horse five lengths. Since one length equals five pounds (by rule of thumb calculation accepted by racing secretaries), the right kind of ride can—in lay theory at least—make up for a deficit of 25 pounds spotted to the opposition. In short, the moneyed stables depend on the money jocks to bring home *first* money.

The third type of jockey—the "businessman"—is a boy who "gets what he can, any way he can," as one observer put it. This is the lay image most spectators have of all jockeys. Even Devereux, in his study of gambling, suggests that because the jockey's racing days are numbered, he will be inclined to conspire with gamblers in their betting coups. By entering into the plans of gamblers by, let us say, pulling a horse on orders (presumably to protect the bookies against a large loss), the jockey can solidify his relations with the gamblers who may be of help to him after retirement.[1]

Devereux's remarks represent an interesting theory of an activity that occurred in a real *past* or a *fictionalized* present. To begin with, jockeys —unlike most other athletes—are neither limited as to age nor do they believe they are. Unlike boxers, baseball players, and football pros who are called old men at 35 and are retired by 40, jockeys have been active and in fact won some of the richest handicap races while in their late fifties; two of the most prominent boys (jockeys are boys at any age) were Pat Remmilard and Johnny Longden, both of whom were racing until their sixtieth years. Asked when jockeys should retire, they respond not by mentioning an age, but say, "When you can't get any more mounts." Second, retirement funds and pension plans (for jockeys disabled in a spill) cushion the pressure of "getting it" while you can. Finally, and most important, the surveillance system (discussed later) of the various racing associations and the severity of sanctions (being ruled off the turf for misconduct) virtually have done away with the "businessman" who has conspired with gamblers to fix a race.

As the term is used today, "businessman" refers to the type of jockey whose overwhelming motivation is the profit motive. This motive is expressed in the jock's assertion, heard in the business world but seldom among the other jocks, "I'm not in business for my health." Further, businessmen believe that, at least for them, the way to make money is by betting on their mounts. So far as·possible, businessmen will seek mounts on horses they think are ready to win at a good price.

Among those jockeys who have no agents, by far the largest group are the businessmen. Preferring to hustle their own mounts, they seek out the small-time owner-trainer who stables "platers" (cheap claiming horses). This type of trainer can't pay the win-or-lose fee demanded by the money jocks, nor does he expect to get the hot jocks who are cultivating greener pastures. A more likely choice of rider is the businessman. Moreover, since the owner-trainer has to foot all the bills, he finds in the businessman an opportunity to cut corners. Frequently the businessman will exercise horses free or simply wait for payment until the stable is having some success. In exchange, the owner-trainer takes the jockey into his confidence and strategies are worked out together. Although not under contract to the owner-trainer, the jock often will travel the various circuits with him.

The owner-trainer with whom the businessman associates is invariably one who doesn't bet and often has the reputation of being poor but honest. This sets the stage for a mutually advantageous arrangement. A betting trainer would take great pains to conceal his intentions and limit the information flow; for a leak of intentions would affect the odds on the horse, and he wishes to get the most for his betting investment. Since the nonbetting trainer has little to lose by revealing his intentions to a jockey (even the nonbetting trainer has *something* to lose by revealing information about his horse, especially in claiming races, as we shall later see), he can get the services of a skillful jockey for little cost: namely, information concerning his intentions.

The businessman is quick to see the advantage in hooking up with the honest trainer. A brief explanation of the problems of putting over a coup will show why this is the case. When betting trainers manipulate horses for the purpose of winning bets, the investigative activities of the racing association quickly get wind of this and place pressure on the stable (just what pressures can be applied will be discussed later). To avoid such investigations, betting stables today engage in *partial* concealment of a horse's true form. A partial concealment, however, implies a partial disclosure of form, which legitimates a horse's winning (that is, nothing is incongruous about a horse winning if it has displayed a recent fair effort). On the other hand, the fact that form has been partly concealed helps assure a fair price (conceived typically at odds of about 4 to 1). Betting stables do not run "in-and-outers" or "sharp wakeups" that pay "boxcar mutuels" (winners with very big payoffs). Thus the gambling stables work to maintain the impression of simon-pure honesty. The known nonbetting, honest trainer, however, can run hot-and-cold horses and win at boxcar mutuels with impunity; officials will take for granted that the erratic performance of his horses is due to low-grade stock, thought to be naturally unpredictable. Also as long as the boxcar mutuels are coming from the horses of honest stables, in-and-out performances are tolerated—indeed, welcome—for they give variety in the payoffs. To the businessman jockey, one or two bets on one or two 40-to-1 shots during a 55-day racing meet are big dividends. Thus the betting jockey prefers to stick with the honest trainer. Indirectly, then, in the manner I have suggested, honesty is in the service of "vice."

When two or three businessmen are in the same race, the scene is set for possible chicanery. One may find here the closest thing to a fixed race, what is called a "jockeys' race." Here two or three boys, surveying the situation in the jocks' room before going to the paddock, will come to an understanding through a kind of tacit bargaining. The conversation among businessmen Tom, Dick, and Harry might run something like this:

Tom: How do you like your mounts today, fellers?

Dick: Well, I have a ready horse, but I'm not going to bet a dime. There's nothing that will keep up with the favorite.

Harry: My horse is pretty fair, too, but no use killing him for show dough. He'll be saved for next week. Think I'll bet him then.

Tom: You know, guys, my horse can turn it on in the stretch. If only something would go with the favorite for a mile and knock the wind out of him! You know, Dick, if your horse went with the favorite for half a mile and then you, Harry, picked him up at the far turn, the favorite would be a dead duck. And if I can get home with Slow Bones, I'll be glad to "save" with you boys.

That is all that need be said. The favorite is knocked out of competition by the top of the stretch, and Tom waltzes home on Slow Bones at 20 to 1. Next time, perhaps it will be Harry's turn to come home first.

A jockeys' race—when it occurs at all—takes place in the last race. One reason for this is that the cheapest race of the day is typically the last race, and here we would be more likely to find two or three businessmen in the same race. Second, the last race is almost always a distance race, at least 1$\frac{1}{16}$ miles. The longer distance is necessary for working out a strategy (however vaguely suggested). In a sprint race most of the horses are rushing from start to finish, and strategies to control the pace of the race are not easy to put into operation (unless the planning is highly deliberate and carefully worked out). The most important feature of the last race is that it is the *last* race. At this time the stewards tend to relax their usual vigilance, and the crowd is dispersing and is less likely to shout disapproval at what appears to be a jockeys' race. In fact, many fans assume that the last race will be a jockeys' race and will be stabbing for a long shot to get even on the assumption that a long shot has a better chance in the last race than it would otherwise. And when a long shot does suddenly pop home a winner the crowd—even when they haven't bet on the particular horse—voices a kind of approval. On homeward-bound buses and trains, the conversation will center on how the player bet or almost bet the winning long shot in the last race. On the other hand, a favored horse winning the last race is unpopular; the mass of players are betting long shots to get even. A subtle pressure is exerted on the stewards not to inquire too closely into the last race, since one of their jobs is to keep the public content. A jockey's race sometimes gives the appearance of a well-rehearsed performance, and yet there is nothing specific to put one's finger on. Nothing is, strictly speaking, illegal.

Another feature of the last race is that the riders, often having only one mount that day, have been sitting in the jockeys' room together for six hours, and as time has passed, eventually have turned their conversation to the race they will run. According to the rules of racing, the jockey—even if he has only one mount—must report to the jockeys' room one hour before the first race, and remain there until riding his last mount of the day. The sheer amount of time jockeys spend together is conducive to "discussing things."

Finally, the businessman is generally better informed than any other type of jockey about the condition of the animal he is to ride and the intentions of the stable. Moreover, since the businessman often has the trainer in his debt, he can get away with not running the race exactly to orders, which in any case will be something like: "You know what the horse can do. Just do your best."

The businessman jockey doesn't see anything wrong with the staging of a race and would probably be mildly shocked if accused of dishonest dealings. The cooperative arrangement is viewed as just another version of the traditional practice of "saving." During a race, a rider may try to make a bargain to share the purse. For instance, two horses may enter the stretch head and head, and one jock will call out: "How about saving?" The other might say: "You're on."

Although the practice of saving is frowned upon officially in most races, it is a mandatory practice among jockeys who ride as an entry in a stakes or handicap race. For example, a stable might enter two (or more) horses in a race, and the jockeys arrange a 60–40 split if one should win.

The bargaining arrangement that occurs among businessmen is to them but a form of the legitimate practice of saving. They legitimate the arrangements they make by referring to it as saving, just as trusted bank employees justify their embezzlement by referring to it as "borrowing."[2]

In sum, an analysis of the deviant practice of the jockeys' race involves the conditions typically thought to be relevant in the analysis of most kinds of deviance.[3] First the *conduciveness* and *opportunity* associated with knowing something about the trainer's intentions and being thrown into interaction together permitting the teaming up in a deviant act; the *strain* placed on the businessman who wins only a few races and has relatively few mounts and must make these count; the *legitimation* of the course of action through a "neutralization technique"[4] of saving; and finally, a *laxity of social control*—characteristic of the last race milieu—on the part of the racing officials.[5]

NOTES

1 Edward C. Devereux, "Gambling and the Social Structure—A Sociological Study of Lotteries and Horse Racing in Contemporary America" (Unpublished doctoral dissertation, Harvard University, 1949), p. 424.

2 Donald Cressey, *Other Peoples' Money* (New York: The Free Press of Glencoe, 1953).
3 Albert K. Cohen, "The Sociology of the Deviant Act," *American Sociological Review,* 30 (February 1965), pp. 9–14.
4 Gresham M. Sykes and David Matza, "Techniques of Neutralization," *American Sociological Review,* 22 (December 1957), pp. 667–669.
5 Taken together, these components of a deviant act constitute what Neil J. Smelser, *Theory of Collective Behavior* (New York: Free Press of Glencoe, 1963), calls a value-added process, which he uses in his explanatory model of all kinds of collective behavior.

14 | The Teen-age Shoplifter: A Microcosmic View of Middle-Class Delinquency |
Norman L. Weiner

One of the most common forms of deviance committed by both adults and adolescents is shoplifting. Many criminologists suspect that a majority of Americans have shoplifted at some time in their lives. This form of theft is not restricted to lower-class people, but rather is one of the most common forms of deviance among middle and upper-class adolescents and adults.

This report on the shoplifting of a middle-class adolescent is an unusual picture of middle-class deviance. It was made by an "undercover" researcher who had the rare opportunity to observe an adolescent involved in shoplifting and, more important, to observe what she later said about her behavior. The conflicting moral definitions of such activities and the ways in which adolescents (and adults) can interpret morality to justify their activities are also demonstrated here. As most students will probably recognize, the matter-of-fact justification offered for the shoplifting is an extremely common practice in our society. (It is an excellent example of what Sykes and Matza have called "Neutralization Processes.")

This form of theft is situational for most individuals—it is something they only do occasionally and generally only at one time in their lives. Only if the individual is arrested and, thereby, stigmatized for the activity is it likely to become a long-run problem for him. Moreover, businesses anticipate that a certain small percentage of their goods will "shrink" and, therefore, have shrinkage insurance. This form of theft has become quite normalized in our society and it seems unlikely that anything short of severe repression would eliminate it. Shoplifting has become one of the forms of crime that Daniel Bell referred to in his essay on "Crime as an American Way of Life." It is illegal and disreputable, but most people have a way of justifying it when they are involved in the situation.

This is an original essay prepared for this volume.

The area of deviant behavior abounds with participant-observation studies. Thieves, prostitutes, homosexuals, and drug addicts have all talked about themselves and their subcultures: we even have numerous first-hand reports about gangs of juvenile delinquents. But while much has been written about suburban youth, as yet we have no extensive participant-observation studies of middle-class delinquent practices. Thus, much of what we do know in this area is second-hand evidence and is largely unsupported by statements of participants. The reasons for this lack are fairly obvious. It would be impossible for a knowledge-able sociologist, who presumably is an adult, to unobtrusively observe middle-class teen-agers without disrupting their normal patterns of behavior.

Recognizing the need for participant-observation of middle-class youth, and possessing a youthful appearance, I returned to high school as a student. My purpose was known only to the board of education and to the school principal. To the best of my knowledge my attempt to pass as a student was successful since neither my teachers nor my fellow students ever displayed any signs of distrust or suspicion. I enrolled as a senior, explaining that my father had just been transferred to the area and that we were living temporarily with an aunt. The students had formed strong cliques by this stage of their high school careers, and it immediately became apparent that any attempt to become friendly with many groups would be fruitless. After about a week I decided to concentrate on the "nicest" kids—the smartest, the wealthiest, the leaders, the stars. It was not very long before I was able to establish myself as being unusually bright (being careful not to overdo things), and I was soon moving easily with the high school elite. In this crowd I met Karen.

Karen is eighteen years old. She is a very ordinary girl. She lives just outside the city in a well-manicured neighborhood, the sort of neigh-borhood that exists on the periphery of every city in the Uniited States. Only station wagons and delivery trucks drive up the well-lit streets. Trees grow tall and full. The atmosphere is one of quiet, comfortable affluence. Karen's father is a dentist. He comes home every night by seven o'clock, and stays home, except one night a week when he plays poker. That night her mother plays canasta. They own two cars, and they have three children, all girls. Karen is the oldest. She is an honor student and a cheerleader.

One Saturday morning early in November Karen called me, because she knew I was free, and asked me to take her shopping. I said that I would, and I picked her up about noon. She told me that she wanted to shop downtown, but I protested. There was a large shopping-center nearby with all the locally fashionable stores where parking was no problem. However, she insisted on going downtown, and so we went.

After I parked the car, she told me that she liked to shop at Hay's, a large, reasonably-priced store that carries quality merchandise of every imaginable type. We went down to the basement where the pet department was located, because she wanted to get something for her aquarium. To my surprise this vast basement was deserted; there was no one in sight. As I was looking around for hidden cameras, I glanced at Karen. She was putting a colored glass ball into her purse, believing that my back was turned. Suddenly she said, "They don't have what I want here. Let's go upstairs." As I passed the counter on which the glass balls were lying, I noticed the price: 49¢.

In the main store we went to the women's department. There, Karen bought a blouse, holding a long, cordial conversation with the young salesclerk. When the blouse was paid for, the clerk put it into a bag, folded the top of the bag, folded the sales slip over the top, and stapled it shut. This, of course, is a common practice in large stores today, to prevent potential shoplifters from putting merchandise into an open bag. Then we went to the dress department. Karen found her size on the racks and hurried through the merchandise, picking out, I noticed, four dresses. Four is the most this store allows a woman to take into the dressing room. She must show them to a clerk before she enters, which Karen did. This procedure is apparently based on the theory that the salesgirl will note how many dresses a woman takes into the dressing room with her, and will make sure she returns the same number. However, most clerks are not only busy, but also don't care; so they attend to this task with only token attention. That is, they merely make sure that a woman has no more than four items with her, and they see that she returns them to the rack. Clerks apparently feel that most women are honest, and that those who might be tempted are probably intimidated by the casual check.

Karen tried a dress on and came out of the dressing room to model it for me. She asked me if I liked it, and I said I did. She went back and tried on another one to show me. This elaborate show went on for about twenty minutes, with the salesgirl looking on with little interest and great amusement. Karen finally emerged from the dressing room with the dresses over her arm and the stapled bag with the blouse in her hand. She gave the dresses to the salesgirl and said, "No, I'm sorry. There's nothing I like." The salesgirl smiled and hung the dresses up. Karen had tried on only three dresses.

"This has really been a shitty day," she said. (Karen and her friends swear a lot. They believe that they do it nonchalantly, but it usually sounds self-conscious and strained.) "Let's look around." We wandered through the store for an hour or so, looking at shoes, televisions, records, and even a jacket for me. We bought nothing; just wandered. "Well, let's go home," Karen said. As we walked by the cosmetics counter near the entrance of the store, she stopped and said, "Oh, wait. I need some mascara." We approached the counter, which surrounded the cash register on four sides. She looked at the selection for a moment, and said, "I can't find the kind I use. See if you can find Revlon." I moved around to the other side of the counter and found her brand. I called to her, and she came over. After glancing up for a moment, she grabbed the mascara and put it into her purse. She looked up at me, standing beside her, watching her. She grinned.

We walked outside, and I asked, "Why'd you take that?"

"Didn't you ever take anything?"

I shrugged noncommittally. "No, really. Why'd you take it?"

"I needed it."

"But you could have paid for it. *I'd* have paid for it if you wanted it that badly."

"This is easier."

As we walked back to the car, she continued to talk. "Well, you know, I don't do it all the time. And I only get what I really need. Like that mascara. But not what I don't need, 'cause that's dumb. Nobody misses stuff in a store like that. I mean, everyone does it. It's easy to get things. Even like the dress."

"What dress?"

"Huh?" She seemed surprised I hadn't known. She opened the bag she had been holding, and there, along with the blouse she had paid for, was a dress.

"But the bag was stapled."

"I put it in the bag in the dressing room. With this." She opened her purse and showed me a stapler with a staple remover. She had opened the bag, put the dress in, and restapled it. "I thought you knew."

I replied, "No, not really." We dropped the subject, and, after brooding a moment on my innocence, she began to talk on as if nothing had happened. But she never told me about the glass ball she had taken.

Karen is not unusual. Her whole crowd steals. The same reasons are always heard: "I needed it; I only take from big stores." They only take what they "need," or, more precisely, what they claim they need. They never use the word "steal." It is always "get." They set up a vast web of rationalizations and excuses: "The large stores are impersonal and coldly efficient; they can stand the loss." This is merely an extension of the attitude that most people feel toward vending machines. To whom does one complain when a soda machine proffers a cup but no Coke? Thus, when a person gets back too much change from such a machine, he believes he is justified in keeping it. When these middle-class adolescents steal, they feel the same elation that most of us feel when we get something for nothing, especially if they think they have beaten the system.

Middle-class kids are smart. They manage to minimize the risks they run. This is why Karen had me drive her downtown. She and her friends know that many lower-class people shop there, and that store detectives and clerks pay little attention to clean, neat, well-mannered people downtown because they are so concerned with trouble from the poorer, more suspicious-looking shoppers. The personnel at the shopping center have mainly the well-to-do to concentrate on, and they are more on the alert for middle-class thefts.

The downtown stores are more lenient with shoplifters than are the suburban shopping centers. If a kid gets caught downtown, he is often let go because he is middle-class. Usually, the parents are called, but very rarely is the middle-class child prosecuted whereas a lower-class child would almost certainly be. This differential selection of offenders on the basis of socio-economic status occurs, I believe, for two reasons: 1) these children are seen as coming from "good" homes, and authorities feel that parents can best take care of their children's discipline once the wrong-doing has been brought to the parents' attention; and 2) parents of middle-class delinquents wield a great deal of economic power. Many stores are hesitant to risk the loss of business by prosecuting teen-age shoplifters. Karen knows all this. She knows that the risk is low, and that stealing is more fun than paying.

Skill at shoplifting does not necessarily confer status on a child from his peers, but abstinance is generally considered unique. Shoplifting seems to bother no one. Many parents reinforce their children's belief that stealing is a big game by assuring them that, if they return what they have stolen all will be well. And when stores fail to prosecute, this is usually the case. Parent and child alike seem to be unaware that shoplifting is a *crime*. It may be casual, like the mascara, or determined, like the dress. But it is common among the kids—too common to notice. So, when Karen went to cheerleading practice on Monday wearing her new dress, no one knew, and, had they known, they wouldn't have cared.

15 | **The Hustler** | Ned Polsky

Based on years of intimate involvement with hustling, this partici-
pant-observer report on pool-hall hustlers is the finest report
in the area of deviance. As Polsky shows in the beginning of the
essay, this kind of deviant behavior is not new. The cultural tech-
niques, ideas, and detailed strategies have been developed for
many decades and each new generation learns from the earlier
generation how to go about it.

Hustling is a style of deviance for those involved, rather than
a separate way of life. Most of them are only part-time hustlers;
the rest of the time they are perfectly "legitimate" citizens. More-
over, the things they do, while disreputable, are generally not
considered illegal by most people and certainly could not be
controlled.

Such a man spends all his life playing every day for small stakes.
Give him every morning the money that he may gain during the day,
on condition that he does not play—you will make him unhappy.
It will perhaps be said that what he seeks is the amusement of play,
not gain. Let him play then for nothing; he will lose interest and be
wearied. ■ *Blaise Pascal*

They talk about me not being on the legitimate. Why, lady, nobody's on
the legit when it comes down to cases; you know that. ■ *Al Capone*[1]

The poolroom hustler makes his living by betting against his opponents
in different types of pool or billiard games, and as part of the playing
and betting process he engages in various deceitful practices. The
terms "hustler" for such a person and "hustling" for his occupation
have been in poolroom argot for decades, antedating their application
to prostitutes. Usually the hustler plays with his own money, but often
he makes use of a "backer." In the latter event the standard arrangement is that the backer, in return for assuming all risk of loss, receives
half of the hustler's winnings.

The hustler's offense in the eyes of many is not that he breaks misdemeanor laws against gambling (perhaps most Americans have done so at one time or another), but that he does so daily. Also—and again as a necessary and regular part of his daily work—he violates American norms concerning (a) what is morally correct behavior toward one's fellow man and (b) what is a proper and fitting occupation. For one or another of these related reasons the hustler is stigmatized by respectable outsiders. The most knowledgeable of such outsiders see the hustler not merely as a gambler but as one who violates an ethic of fair dealing; they regard him as a criminal or quasi-criminal not because he gambles but because he systematically "victimizes" people. Somewhat less knowledgeable outsiders put down the hustler simply because gambling is his trade. Still less knowledgeable outsiders (perhaps the majority) regard hustlers as persons who, whatever they may actually do, certainly do not hold down visibly respectable jobs; therefore this group also stigmatizes hustlers—"poolroom bums" is the classic phrase—and believes that society would be better off without them. Hustling, to the degree that it is known to the larger society at all, is classed with that large group of social problems composed of morally deviant occupations.

However, in what follows I try to present hustlers and hustling on their own terms. The material below avoids a "social problems" focus; to some extent, I deliberately reverse that focus. Insofar as I treat of social problems, they are not the problems posed by the hustler but for him; not the difficulties he creates for others, but the difficulties that others create for him as he pursues his career.

This approach "from within" has partly dictated the organization of my materials. Some sections below are built around conceptual categories derived less from sociologists than from hustlers, in the hope that this may help the reader to see hustling more nearly as hustlers see it. The disadvantage for the scientifically-minded reader is that the underlying sociological framework may be obscured. Therefore I wish to point out that this framework is basically that of Everett Hughes's approach to occupational sociology.

I try mainly to answer three types of questions: (a) *The work situation.* How is the hustler's work structured? What skills are required of him? With whom does he interact on the job? What does he want from them, and how does he try to get it? How do they make it easy or hard for him? (b) *Careers.* Who becomes a hustler? How? What job risks or contingencies does the hustler face? When and how? What is the nature of colleagueship in hustling? What are the measures of success and failure in the career? In what ways does aging affect the hustler's job skills or ability to handle other career problems? What leads to retirement? (c) *The external world.* What is the place of the hustler's work situation and career in the larger society? What changes in the structure of that society affect his work situation or career?

Previous Research

A bibliographic check reveals no decent research on poolroom hustling, sociological or otherwise. Apart from an occasional work of fiction in which hustling figures, there are merely a few impressionistic accounts in newspapers and popular magazines. With a couple of exceptions, each article is based on interviews with only one or two hustlers. No article analyzes hustling on any but the most superficial level or provides a well-rounded description. The fullest survey of the subject not only omits much that is vital, but contains numerous errors of fact and interpretation.[2]

The desirability of a study of hustling first struck me upon hearing comments by people who saw the movie *The Hustler* (late 1961, re-released spring 1964). Audience members who are not poolroom habitués regard the movie as an accurate portrait of the contemporary hustling "scene." The movie does indeed truly depict some social characteristics of pool and billiard hustlers and some basic techniques of hustling. But it neglects others of crucial importance. Moreover, the movie scarcely begins to take proper account of the social structure within which hustling techniques are used and which strongly affects their use. *The Hustler* is a reasonably good but highly selective reflection of the poolroom hustling scene as it existed not later than the mid-1930's. And as a guide to today's hustling scene—the terms on which it presents itself and on which the audience takes it—the movie is quite misleading.

Method and Sample

My study of poolroom hustling extended over eight months in 1962 and 1963. It proceeded by a combination of: (a) direct observation of hustlers as they hustled; (b) informal talks, sometimes hours long, with hustlers; (c) participant observation—as hustler's opponent, as hustler's backer, and as hustler. Since methods (b) and (c) drew heavily on my personal involvement with the poolroom world, indeed are inseparable from it, I summarize aspects of that involvement below.

Billiard playing is my chief recreation. I have frequented poolrooms for over 20 years, and at one poolroom game, three-cushion billiards, am considered a far better than average player. In recent years I have played an average of more than six hours per week in various New York poolrooms, and played as much in the poolrooms of Chicago for most of the eight years I lived there. In the course of traveling I have played occasionally in the major rooms of other cities, such as the poolrooms on Market Street in San Francisco, West 25th Street in Cleveland, West Lexington in Baltimore, and the room on 4th and Main in Los Angeles.

My social background is different from that of the overwhelming majority of adult poolroom players. The latter are of lower-class origin. As with many American sports (e.g., baseball), pool and billiards are played by teenagers from all classes but only the players of lower-class background tend to continue far into adulthood. (And as far as poolroom games are concerned, even at the teen-age level the lower class contributes a disproportionately large share of players.) But such differences—the fact that I went to college, do highbrow work, etc.—create no problems of acceptance. In most good-sized poolrooms the adult regulars usually include a few people like myself who are in the poolroom world but not of it. They are there because they like to play, and are readily accepted because they like to play.

The poolroom I play in most regularly is the principal "action room" in New York and perhaps in the country, the room in which heavy betting on games occurs most often; sometimes, particularly after 1:00 A.M., the hustlers in the room well outnumber the non-hustlers. Frequently I play hustlers for money (nearly always on a handicap basis) and occasionally I hustle some non-hustlers, undertaking the latter activity primarily to recoup losses on the former. I have been a backer for two hustlers.

I know six hustlers well, and during the eight months of the study I talked or played with over 50 more. All are now usually based in New York, except for two in Chicago, two in Cleveland, one in Philadelphia, one itinerant hustler whose home base is Boston and another whose home base is in North Carolina. However, the hustlers based in New York are of diverse regional origins; almost a third grew up and started their hustling careers in other states.

It is not possible to demonstrate the representativeness of this sample because the universe (all U.S. pool and billiard hustlers) is not known exactly. But the hustlers I asked about the number of real hustlers in America, i.e., the number of people whose exclusive or primary occupation is hustling, generally agree that today the number is quite small. In response to my queries about the total number of poolroom hustlers, one hustler said "thousands" and another said "there must be a thousand," but the next highest estimate was "maybe 400" and somewhat lesser estimates were made by nineteen hustlers. Moreover, the three hustlers making the highest estimates have rarely been out of New York, whereas over half the others either come from other parts of the country or have made several road trips. It seems safe to assume that the sample is at least representative of big-city hustlers. Also, it is probable that it includes the majority of part-time hustlers in New York, and certain that it includes a good majority of the full-time hustlers in New York.

Poolroom Betting: The Structure of "Action"

Hustling involves betting against one's opponent, by definition. But the converse is not true. The majority of poolroom contests on which opponents bet do not involve any element of hustling. In order to understand how hustling enters the picture, one must first establish a perspective that encompasses all betting on poolroom games, hustled or not.

In pool or billiard games, the betting relationship has three possible modes: (1) player bets against player; (2) player against spectator; (3) spectator against spectator. In most contests only the first mode occurs, but combinations of the first and second are frequent, and slightly less so are combinations of the first and third. Combinations of all three are uncommon, but do occur when there is more "ready action" offered to the players by the spectators than the players can or wish to absorb. I have never seen the second mode occur alone, nor a combination of second and third. I have seen the third mode occur alone only twice—at professional tournaments. The betting relationship, then, involves the mode player-vs.-player, whatever additional modes there may be.

If two mediocre players are betting, say, upward of $15 per game, and at another table two excellent players are playing for only a token amount, the first table will invariably draw many more people around it. The great majority of spectators, whether or not they bet much and whatever their own degree of playing skill, are attracted more by the size of the action than the quality of the performance. (A visiting Danish billiardist tells me this is not so in Europe, and also that betting on poolroom games is far less frequent there than in America.)

There is an old American poolroom tradition that players should make some kind of bet with each other, if only a small one. This tradition remains strong in every public poolroom I know. (It is weak in the pool or billiard rooms of private men's clubs and YMCAs, weaker still in student unions, and virtually nonexistent in faculty clubs.) When one player says to another, "Let's just play sociable," as often as not he means that they should play for only a dollar or two, and at the very least means that they should play "for the time" (the loser paying the check). It is only some of the newer and least skilled players who refuse to bet at all (who want to "split the time"), and nearly always they rapidly become socialized to the betting tradition by a carrot-and-stick process—the stick being that it is often hard to get a game otherwise, the carrot that better players are always willing to give poorer ones a handicap (a "spot"). Most of the regular players will not even play for the check only, but insist on a little money changing hands "just to make the game interesting."[3] The player who claims that just playing the game is interesting enough in itself is regarded as something of a freak.

Few serious bettors, hustlers excepted, care for big action; but nearly all, including hustlers, want fast action. Although they may not want to bet much per game, they want the cash to change hands fairly quickly. Consequently, in an action room the standard games are redesigned for this purpose. Some are simply shortened: players gambling at snooker will remove all the red balls but one; or three-cushion billiard players will play games of 15, 20, or 25 points instead of the usual 30, 40, or 50. In straight pool (pocket billiards), where the standard game is 125 or 150 points, good players are usually reluctant to play a much shorter game because scoring is so easy—any really good player can occasionally run more than 50 balls—that shortening the game makes it too much a matter of chance. Therefore, in an action room one finds most of the pool players playing some variant of the game that not only requires high skill but also minimizes chance, and that therefore can be short (taking only 5 to 20 minutes per game). Today the chief of these variants are "nine ball" and "one pocket" (also called "pocket apiece"), although there are several others, such as "eight ball," "bank pool," and "rotation."

Every poolroom has at least one "No Gambling" sign on display, but no poolroom enforces it. The sign is merely a formal gesture for the eyes of the law (and in some cities required by law). It is enforced only in that the proprietor sometimes may ask players to keep payoffs out of sight—not to toss the money on the table after the game—if the room is currently "heaty," e.g., if an arrest has recently been made there. Police are hardly ever concerned to stop the gambling on poolroom games, and everyone knows it. (But police sometimes check to see that the minimum age law is observed, so proprietors will often ask youths for identification.) Betting is so taken for granted that in most poolrooms the proprietor—the very man who displays a "No Gambling" sign over his desk—will on request hold the players' stake money.

However, in no poolroom does the house take a cut of the action; the proprietor gets no fee for permitting gambling or holding stake money, and wouldn't dream of asking for one. His payment from bettors is simply that they comprise most of his custom in equipment rental. And hustlers, as he and they well know, count in this regard far beyond their numbers, for they play much oftener and longer than other customers; indeed, they virtually live in the poolroom.

The only non-bettor whose payment is somewhat related to the size of the action is the rack boy (if one is used), the person who racks up the balls for the players after each frame. The bigger the action, the larger the tip he can expect, and if one player comes out very much ahead he tips the rack boy lavishly. The rack boy's position is thus analogous to that of the golf caddie, except that a rack boy is used in only about half of hustler-vs.-hustler contests and in but a tiny fraction of other contests. Sometimes he is an employee (sweeper, etc.) of the poolroom, but more often he is a spectator performing as rack boy on an *ad hoc* basis.

Non-hustled Poolroom Gambling

Hustling is *not* involved when the games played for money are any of the following:

(a) *Non-hustler vs. non-hustler.* A "sociable" game in which the bet is a token one. The only betting is player vs. player.

(b) *Non-hustler vs. non-hustler.* A game for significantly more than a token amount. The players play even-up if they are fairly equal. If they are aware of a significant difference in skill levels, the weaker player is given an appropriate handicap. Usually the betting is just between players; rarely, one or both players will bet spectators; spectators do not bet each other.

(c) *Hustler vs. non-hustler.* The players are aware of the difference in skills, and this is properly taken into account via an appropriate spot. Usually the betting is only player vs. player, though sometimes spectators bet players or each other. The hustler tries to avoid this type of game, and agrees to it only when he has nothing better to do.

(d) *Hustler vs. hustler.* Each player knows the other's mettle, if only by reputation ("Minnesota Fats" vs. "Fast Eddy" in *The Hustler,* for example). The hustler, contrary to the impression given by the movie, does *not* prefer this type of game (though he does prefer it to the foregoing type) and does *not* regard it as hustling. But he plays it often because he often can't get the kind of game he wants (a true "hustle") and this alternative does offer him excitement—not only the greatest challenge to his playing skill, but the most action. The average bet between two hustlers is much higher than in any other type of poolroom contest.[4] And betting modes 2 and 3 (player vs. spectator, spectator vs. spectator) occur much more often.

Be that as it may, the hustler much prefers to hustle, which means to be in a game set up so as to be pretty much a sure thing for him, a game that "you're not allowed to lose" as the hustler puts it. In order to achieve this, to truly hustle, he engages in deception. The centrality of deception in pool or billiard hustling is perhaps best indicated by the fact that the poolroom hustler's argot originated that widespread American slang dictum, "never give a sucker an even break."[5]

The Hustler's Methods of Deception

The structure of a gambling game determines what methods of deception, if any, may be used in it. In many games (dice, cards, etc.) one can deceive one's opponent by various techniques of cheating. Pool and billiard games are so structured that this method is virtually impossible. (Once in a great while, against a particularly unalert opponent, one can surreptitiously add a point or two to one's score— but such opportunity is rare, usually involves risk of discovery that is judged to be too great, and seldom means the difference between winning and losing anyway; so no player counts on it.) One's every move and play is completely visible, easily watched by one's opponent and by spectators; nor is it possible to achieve anything via previous tampering with the equipment.

However, one structural feature of pool or billiards readily lends itself to deceit: on each shot, the difference between success and failure is a matter of a small fraction of an inch. In pool or billards it is peculiarly easy, even for the average player, to miss one's shot deliberately and still look good (unlike, say, nearly all card games, where if one does not play one's cards correctly this is soon apparent). On all shots except the easiest ones, it is impossible to tell if a player is deliberately not trying his best.

The hustler exploits this fact so as to deceive his opponent as to his (the hustler's) true level of skill (true "speed"). It is so easily exploited that, when playing good opponents, usually the better hustlers even disdain it, pocket nearly every shot they have (intentionally miss only some very difficult shots), and rely chiefly on related but subtler techniques of failure beyond the remotest suspicion of most players. For example, such a hustler may strike his cue ball hard and with too much spin ("english"), so that the spin is transferred to the object ball and the object ball goes into the pocket but jumps out again; or he may scratch (losing a point and his turn), either by "accidentally" caroming his cue ball into a pocket or by hitting his cue ball hard and with too much top-spin so that it jumps off the table; or, most commonly, he pockets his shot but, by striking his cue ball just a wee bit too hard or too softly or with too much or too little english, he leaves himself "safe" (ends up with his cue ball out of position, so that he hasn't another shot). In such wise the hustler feigns less competence than he has.

Hustling, then, involves not merely the ability to play well, but the use of a kind of "short con." Sometimes the hustler doesn't need to employ any con to get his opponent to the table, sometimes he does; but he always employs it in attempting to keep his opponent there.

The best hustler is not necessarily the best player among the hustlers. He has to be a very good player, true, but beyond a certain point his playing ability is not nearly so important as his skill at various kinds of conning. Also, he has to possess personality traits that make him "rock-like," able to exploit fully his various skills—playing, conning, others—in the face of assorted pressures and temptations not to exploit them fully.

The Hustler's Cardinal Rule

As the foregoing indicates, the hustler's cardinal rule is: *don't show your real speed.* Of course, an exception is permitted if by some miracle the hustler finds himself hustled, finds himself in a game with someone he thought would be easy but who turns out to be tough. But this is not supposed to happen, and it rarely does. For one thing, hustlers generally know each other, or of each other, and their respective skill levels. Secondly, any pool or billiard game is overwhelmingly a game of skill rather than luck—even in the chanciest type of poolroom game the element of skill counts for much more than in any card game whatsoever—and this means it is possible to rate the skill levels of various players (to "handicap" them) along small gradations with a high degree of accuracy. For example, if one has seen the three-cushion billiard players X and Y play various people over a period of time, it is possible to arrive at the judgment "On a 30-point game, X is two or three points better than Y" and to be dead right about it in at least eight out of ten contests between them.

The corollaries of the hustler's chief rule are: (a) The hustler must restrain himself from making many of the extremely difficult shots. Such restraint is not easy, because the thrill of making a fancy shot that brings applause from the audience is hard to resist. But the hustler must resist, or else it would make less believable his misses on more ordinary shots. (b) He must play so that the games he wins are won by only a small margin. (c) He must let his opponent win an occasional game.

It may be thought that once a hustler has engaged an opponent, a bet has been agreed upon and the stake money put up, and the game has started, the hustler might safely let out all the stops. This would be terribly short-sighted.

In the first place, as noted earlier, the typical non-hustler bets only a small amount on the game. The hustler's only hope of making real money, therefore, is to extend the first game into a series of games, entice his opponent into doubling up when he is behind, etc. If the hustler does this well, the opponent will hang on for a long time, may even come back after the first session to play him on another day, turn into a real "fish" (the poolroom term for an inferior opponent who doesn't catch on that he's outclassed, and keeps coming back for more). And when the opponent starts demanding a spot, as sooner or later he will, the hustler can offer him his (the hustler's) average winning margin, or even a little better, and still have a safe game.

Secondly, there are spectators to take into account. Some of them will bet the hustler if he offers the non-hustler a seemingly fair spot. More importantly, some of them are potential opponents. Nearly all poolroom spectators are also players. The hustler doesn't want to look too good to spectators either.

He knows that as he beats various opponents his reputation will rise, and that increasingly he'll have to offer spots to people, but he wants to keep his reputation as low as possible as long as possible with as many people as possible. He also knows that he has to play superbly on occasion—that he will play fellow hustlers when there's no other action around, and that then he must show more skill—but he wants to keep these occasions few. (It helps considerably, by the way, that because hustler-vs.-hustler games occur when hustlers give up hope of finding other action, these games usually take place after midnight when there aren't so many non-hustler potential victims around to watch.)

The sooner everyone in the poolroom knows the hustler's true speed, the sooner he exhausts the real hustling possibilities among the room's regular players. Such a situation constitutes one of the career crises that every hustler has to face. (For reasons which will become apparent below, he now has to face it earlier in his career than hustlers formerly did.) When it occurs, either he must move on to a poolroom where he's less known or, if he stays in the room, he has to take games he shouldn't take or else restrict his pickings to strangers who wander in.

Job-Related Skills and Traits

Although the hallmarks of the good hustler are playing skill and the temperamental ability to consistently look poorer than he is, there are other skills and traits that aid him in hustling. Some are related to deceiving his opponent, some not.

Chief of these is argumentative skill in arranging the terms of the match, the ability to "make a game." The prospective opponent, if he has seen the hustler play, may when approached claim that the hustler is too good for him or ask for too high a spot, i.e., one that is fair or even better. The hustler, like the salesman, is supposed to be familiar with standard objections and with "propositions" for overcoming them.

Another side of the ability to make a game reveals itself when the prospective opponent simply can't be argued out of demanding a spot that is unfair to the hustler, or can be convinced to play only if the hustler offers such a spot. At that point the hustler should of course refuse to play. There is often a temptation to do otherwise, not only because the hustler is proud of his skill but because action is his lifeblood (which is why he plays other hustlers when he can't find a hustle), and there may be no other action around. He must resist the temptation. In the good hustler's view, no matter how badly you want action, it is better not to play at all than to play when you are disadvantaged; otherwise you are just hustling yourself. (But the hustler often will, albeit with much argument and the greatest reluctance, agree to give a fair spot if that's the only way he can get action.)

The hustler, when faced, as he very often is, with an opponent who knows him as such, of course finds that his ability to make a game assumes greater importance than his ability to feign lack of skill. In such situations, indeed, his game-making ability is just as important as his actual playing ability.

On the other hand, the hustler must have "heart" (courage). The *sine qua non* is that he is a good "money player," can play his best when heavy action is riding on the game (as many non-hustlers can't). Also, he is not supposed to let a bad break or distractions in the audience upset him. (He may pretend to get rattled on such occasions, but that's just part of his con.) Nor should the quality of his game deteriorate when, whether by miscalculation on his part or otherwise, he finds himself much further behind than he would like to be. Finally, if it is necessary to get action, he should not be afraid to tackle an opponent whom he knows to be just about as good as he is.

A trait often working for the hustler is stamina. As a result of thousands of hours of play, all the right muscles are toughened up. He is used to playing many hours at a time, certainly much more used to it than the non-hustler is. This is valuable because sometimes, if the hustler works it right, he can make his opponent forget about quitting for such a "silly" reason as being tired, can extend their session through the night and into the next day. In such sessions it is most often in the last couple of hours, when the betting per game is usually highest, that the hustler makes his biggest killing.

Additional short-con techniques are sometimes used. One hustler, for example, entices opponents by the ancient device of pretending to be sloppy-drunk. Other techniques show more imagination. For example, a hustler preparing for a road trip mentioned to me that before leaving town he was going to buy a soldier's uniform: "I walk into a strange room in uniform and I've got it made. Everybody likes to grab a soldier."

One of the most noted hustlers of recent years, Luther "Wimpy" Lassiter, reports that in his own forays he has sometimes worn a wedding band and flashed a wallet (because the typical hustler is unmarried and, like dedicated gamblers generally and lower-class gamblers especially, carries his money loose in his pocket).

Finally, the hustler—the superior hustler at any rate—has enough flexibility and good sense to break the "rules" when the occasion demands it, will modify standard techniques when he encounters non-standard situations. An example: Once I entered a poolroom just as a hustler I know, X, was finishing a game with non-hustler Y. X beat Y soundly, by a higher margin than a hustler should beat anyone, and at that for only $3. Y went to the bathroom, whereupon I admonished X, "What's the matter with you? You know you're not allowed to win that big." X replied:

> Yeah, sure, but you see that motherfucking S over there? [nodding discreetly in the direction of one of the spectators]. Well, about an hour ago when I came in he and Y were talking, and when S saw me he whispered something to Y. So I had a hunch he was giving him the wire [tipping him off] that I was pretty good. And then in his middle game it looked like Y was stalling a little [missing deliberately] to see what I would do, so then I was sure he got the wire on me. I had to beat him big so he'll think he knows my top speed. But naturally I didn't beat him as big as I *could* beat him. Now he'll come back cryin' for a spot and bigger action, and I'll nail him.

And he did nail him.[6]

The Art of Dumping

As we saw, the structure of a pool or billiard game makes it virtually impossible for the hustler to cheat his opponent. By "stalling" (deliberately missing some shots, leaving himself out of position, etc.) and by "lemoning" or "lemonading" an occasional game in the session (winning in a deliberately sloppy and seemingly lucky manner, or deliberately losing the game), the hustler keeps his opponent on the hook and entices him into heavier action, but such deception falls short of outright cheating. However, in examining betting we saw that there is considerable variation in the interpersonal superstructure of the game, i.e., that there are several types of betting relationships between and among players and spectators. One of these varieties does lead to outright cheating by the hustler—not cheating his opponent, but cheating some spectators.

When two hustlers play each other, not only is the betting between players relatively heavy, but the betting of spectators against players is also, typically, at its height. Therefore, two hustlers sometimes will agree before their session that if, on any game, there is a good disparity between the amounts of action that each gets from spectators, the player with the most to gain from side bets with spectators will win the game and the palyers will later share the profits. The amount that spectators bet each other is of course irrelevant to such calculations, and in such circumstances the amount that the players bet each other automatically becomes a phony bet, strictly for deluding the spectators.

For example, one such game I know of went as follows: Hustler A played hustler B for $70. A's side bets with spectators totaled $100 and B's side bets with spectators totaled $380. Therefore A deliberately lost to B, paying him $70 and paying $100 to spectators, with B collecting $70 from A and $380 from spectators. Later, in private, B gave A $310 (the $70 that A had "lost" to B, the $100 that A had paid to the audience, plus $140 or one-half the overall amount won from the audience). Each player thus made $140 on the deal.

Sometimes the hustlers will set up the audience for such disparity in side betting, via previous games in the session. An example: Hustler X played hustler Y for $20 per game. By pre-arrangement, both players refused to make side bets with spectators on the first three games and player Y deliberately lost the first three games. At the end of the third game Y became enraged, claiming that bad breaks had beat him, that X was just lucky, etc.; he raised his bet with X to $50 and also offered to bet spectators. Naturally, he got lots of action from spectators—and just as naturally he won the fourth game.

More commonly, however, such setting up does not occur. Rather, the hustlers will agree before their session that they will play each other in earnest and the bets between them will be real, but that if there is a disparity in side betting with spectators on a given game and one player gives the other a prearranged signal (gives him "the office," as the hustler's argot has it), the player with the most side action will win.

In the hustler's argot, the above type of deliberate losing is called "dumping." It is always distinguished from "lemoning" (where deliberate losing is strictly a means of conning one's opponent). Though all hustlers use the verb "to dump" in referring to a game that the hustler deliberately loses for the purpose of cheating spectators, hustlers vary in the object they attach to the verb. Some hustlers would say that the hustler who lost "dumped the game," others that he "dumped to" his opponent, and others that he (or both players in collaboration) "dumped the bettors." Some hustlers on occasion prefer a nominal use: "the game was a dump."

Because dumping involves outright cheating and could lead to serious, in fact violent, reprisals if discovered, it is the aspect of hustling that hustlers are most evasive about. No hustler likes to own up to dumping, even in talk with other hustlers. One learns about dumping indirectly, via hustlers' comments on other hustlers, and only rarely via a hustler's direct admission that he has engaged in it. It is my impression that such reticence is always pragmatic rather than moral, i.e., that no hustler has strong compunctions about dumping and that every long-time hustler has dumped at least on occasion.

Although dumping is a possibility whenever two hustlers playing each other make unequal amounts of side bets with spectators, it actually occurs in only a minority of such situations.[7] For dumping is risky even when it is not literally discovered; sometimes the spectators' suspicions are aroused even though nothing can be proven, and hustlers can't afford to have this happen often, because it would kill their chances of side betting.

In this regard there are two kinds of spectator-bettors that the hustler distinguishes and takes account of: First, there are the ignorant majority of spectators who don't know about dumping; the hustler doesn't want talk, much less actual knowledge, of dumping to reach their ears. Second—and equally important to the hustler because, though they are in the minority, they bet more—there are some knowledgeable spectators (including other hustlers) who know about dumping but *also* know that it occurs in only a minority of hustler-vs.-hustler contests and therefore will often risk a bet. That is to say, just as some horse players assume that at certain tracks there probably will be one race per day that is fixed (one race "for the boys") and are willing to discount this because it's only one race out of nine or ten, similarly there are poolroom spectators who will bet on one hustler against another because they know that dumping occurs but seldom. (Among the knowledgeable spectators there are also, of course, some cautious types who refuse to make such bets because of a possible dump, even though they know the odds are against it.)

In sum, the fact that spectators will bet players in hustler-vs.-hustler games not only permits dumping but at the same time restrains its extent. Hustlers must severely limit their dumping, both to prevent it becoming known to the ignorant and, just as importantly, to prevent knowledgeable spectators from feeling that hustlers *generally* dump when they play each other. No hustler wants to get a reputation as a dumper; therefore he cautiously picks his spots. As a result, dumping provides only a small portion of his true hustling income, i.e., his "sure-thing" income. The great bulk of such income derives from his games with non-hustler opponents.

The Hustler and His Backer

The hustler frequently uses a backer, who pays the losses if the hustler loses and receives 50 percent of any winnings. A backer hardly ever assumes any managerial function. All he does is put up the hustler's stake money in return for a half share in the profits.

Once in a very great while, a hustler will work out a standing agreement for backing, that is, have someone agree to back him regularly. There is no time limit specified for such an arrangement; the deal lasts only as long as both parties consent to it.

But almost always the hustler has no standing agreement with a backer. Rather, he looks for backing on an *ad hoc* basis as the occasion for backing arises. The "occasion" is not that the hustler decides, in the abstract, to play on someone else's risk capital; it is a specific match with a particular opponent, whose handicap terms (if any) the hustler has already arranged or knows he can get. Indeed, even a top-notch hustler rarely can get backing without being able to tell the backer who the prospective opponent is and what the terms of the game are; the hustler has to convince the backer that the particular deal is a good one.

After tentatively arranging a game with his opponent, the hustler asks one of his acquaintances in the room to back him, and if he can't find backing in the room he phones a potential backer to hurry on down with some cash. Sometimes the hustler enters the poolroom with his backer in tow.

The backer specifies the maximum amount per game that he is willing to invest, but makes no guarantee about a total investment. That is, if the hustler starts to lose, the backer can pull out after any game. And if the hustler starts winning, he cannot then bet only his "own" money and dispense with the backer; the backer is in for 50 per cent of the profit made on the entire session.

Under what conditions does the hustler seek a backer? The obvious answer is that when the hustler is broke or nearly broke (as he very often is), he looks for backing, and when he has his own money to invest he plays with that. This is indeed how the average hustler operates. The superior hustler, however, figures more angles. As one of the most intelligent hustlers explained to me:

> If you've got lockup action [a game impossible to lose] and you're broke or maybe you need a bigger stake, you should first try like hell to *borrow* the dough. It's crazy to cut somebody in on action like that unless you have to. The other big thing—what some of these jerks don't understand —is that when you have a real tough game you should *always* look for a backer, even if you've got the dough. You should take out insurance.

The backer, then, should not assume he is being approached for backing because the hustler can raise stake money no other way (though this is usually the case), but has to consider the possibility that it's because the hustler has a very difficult game he wants to "insure."

Also, the backer must consider the possibility that he may be dumped by the hustler: If the hustler is playing a colleague, they may have agreed that one of them will win the good majority of games and that they will later split the profits. (When both hustlers making such an agreement are using backers, the decision as to which hustler will lose is more or less arbitrary. If one hustler is using a backer and the other is not, it is of course the former who agrees to lose.) Or, if the hustler is playing a non-hustler with whom no such collusion is possible, he may deliberately lose on the backer's money until the backer quits, and then, after the backer has left the room or on some other occasion, the hustler, playing with his own money, will slaughter the opponent he has set up on the backer's money.

All in all, it takes as much sophistication to be a good backer as to be a good hustler.

The Hustler as Con Man

As several parts of this study illustrate in detail, hustling demands a continuous and complicated concern with how one is seen by others. Attention to this matter is an ineluctably pervasive requirement of the hustler's trade, and is beset with risks and contradictions. The hustler has not only the concerns that one ordinarily has about being esteemed for one's skills, but develops, in addition to and partly in conflict with such concerns, a complex set of special needs or desires about how others should evaluate him, reactions to their evaluations, and behaviors designed to manipulate such evaluating.

The hustler is a certain kind of con man. And conning, by definition, involves extraordinary manipulation of other people's impressions of reality and especially of one's self, creating "false impressions."[8] If one compares the hustler with the more usual sorts of con men described by David Maurer in *The Big Con,* part of the hustler's specialness is seen to lie in this: the structural contexts within which he operates—the game, the setting of the game within the poolroom, the setting of the poolroom within the larger social structure—are not only more predetermined but more constraining. Structures do not "work for" the poolroom hustler to anywhere near the extent that they often do for other con men, and hence he must involve himself in more personal ways with active, continuous conning.

The point is not simply that the hustler can't find an ideal structural context, but that much less than the ordinary con man is he able to bend a structure toward the ideal or create one *ab ovo* (come up with an analogue of the con man's "store"). That is, the hustler is far less able to be a "producer" or "director" of ideal social "scenes." To a much greater extent he must work in poor settings, and to a correspondingly greater extent he must depend on being a continuously self-aware "actor."[9] (In this connection, note the ease with which many passages of this essay could be restated in dramaturgical or Goffmaniacal terms.)

There is another significant respect in which the hustler's conning differs structurally from the work of ordinary con men. The latter's work, according to Maurer, falls into one or the other of two structurally distinct types of con games: the short con, in which the mark is played for the money he happens to be carrying, or else the big con, in which an essential feature is that the mark is "put on the send" to withdraw much larger sums from his bank. (Some con men also on occasion "throw the send into" a short-con game, but this is unusual.) There is no analogous distinction made by pool hustlers in theory or practice. Virtually every hustle is in Maurer's sense a short con, i.e., the sucker is simply taken for the cash he has on him at the time, or as much of it as he will allow himself to lose.

There are two situations in which the hustler's conning involves his victim going on the send, but they are accidental and rare; the hustler doesn't expect them, though he is of course pleased when one or the other of them happens: (a) As we have noted, the ideal kind of sucker is the "fish" who doesn't realize he can never win and makes himself available on other days for return matches, much like the sort of mark whom con men call an "addict." In order to reinforce any propensity his victim might have for being or becoming a fish, the hustler tries to win the last game of a match by only a small margin even though he *knows* it is the last game, i.e., knows that after he beats the sucker the latter will quit because he is cleaned out or unwilling to risk the small amount he may have left. On very rare occasion, to the hustler's surprise and delight, when the sucker is thus cleaned out he may not end the match but instead become a sort of instant fish (my term, not used by hustlers): he may have the hustler wait while he (the sucker) runs out to get more cash and comes back with same. (b) As a result of having watched the hustler stall with some other opponent (or in solitary practice), the sucker may decide that before he challenges the hustler, or accepts the hustler's challenge, he should go get a bankroll so he can make bigger bets.

Although in both of the above situations the victim goes on the send as a result of the hustler's actions, such actions are not, strictly speaking, calculated to achieve that result. The sucker essentially puts himself on the send.

NOTES

1 The Pascal quotation is from *Pensées*, V. Al Capone's remark is quoted in Paul Sann, *The Lawless Decade* (New York: Crown Publishers, 1957), p. 214.

2 Jack Olsen, "The Pool Hustlers," *Sports Illustrated*, Vol. 14 (March 20, 1961), pp. 71–77. Jack Richardson's "The Noblest Hustlers," [*Esquire*, Vol. IX (September, 1963), pp. 94, 96, 98] contains a few worthwhile observations, but it is sketchy, ill-balanced, and suffers much from editorial garbling, all of which makes it both confusing and misleading for the uninitiated. One article conveys quite well the lifestyle of a particular hustler: Dale Shaw, "Anatomy of a Pool Hustler," *Saga: The Magazine for Men*, Vol. 23 (November, 1961), pp. 52–55, 91–93. Useful historical data are in Edward John Vogeler's "The Passing of the Pool Shark," *American Mercury*, Vol. 8 (November, 1939), pp. 346–51. For hustling as viewed within the context of the history of pool in America, see Robert Coughlan's "Pool: Its Players and Its Sharks," *Life*, Vol. 31 (October 8, 1951), pp. 159 ff.; although Coughlan's account of the game's history contains errors and his specific consideration of hustling is brief (p. 166), the latter is accurate.

   Among novels that deal with hustling, Walter Tevis's *The Hustler* (New York: Harper, 1959) has the most external documentary detail; but Don Carpenter's *Hard Rain Falling* (New York: Harcourt, Brace & World, 1963) is much superior in its exploration of a hustler's character, as well as more satisfying stylistically.

3 This attitude has of course existed among some regular players elsewhere. For example, see chapter 1 of Alexander Pushkin's novella *The Captain's Daughter* (1836).

4 When two high-rolling hustlers agree to play each other there is often a real race among poorer spectators to offer rack-boy services because, as previously noted, if one is engaged for such a session he can expect a good tip. I witnessed one six-hour session between hustlers in which the winning hustler came out $800 ahead and tipped the rack boy $50.

5 Its pool-hustler origin is noted by Vogeler, *op. cit.*, p. 347. It is recorded in none of the slang sourcebooks (Mencken, Mathews, Berrey and Van den Bark, *et al.*) except Harold Wentworth and Stuart Berg Flexner, *Dictionary of American Slang* (New York: T. Y. Crowell, 1960), p. 527. Wentworth and Flexner do not attempt to account for the phrase's origin. They claim that it dates to around 1835, but this seems impossibly early. The only source they cite is its use as the title of a 1941 W. C. Fields movie.

   Actually, Fields used the phrase earlier in his *Poppy* (1936), where it is his exit line and the last line of the movie. Fields's partiality to "never give a sucker an even break" is thoroughly in keeping with Vogeler's account of the origin of the phrase: Fields was the son of a Philadelphia poolroom owner, spent much of his boyhood in his father's poolroom, was an excellent player, and built his funniest vaudeville act around his poolplaying skill (at the act's climax he sank fifteen balls with one shot). Cf. Douglas Gilbert *American Vaudeville* (New York: Whittlesey House, 1940), pp. 273–74.

   Another of Fields's pool-playing vaudeville skits became the core of his first movie, a one-reeler of 1915 entitled *Pool Sharks*. Cf. Donald Deschner, *The Films of W. C. Fields* (New York: Citadel, 1966), p. 35.

6 This sort of situation is unusual. One part of the poolroom code, adhered to by nearly all regular players, holds that a player is supposed to watch out for himself in the matches he gets into, find out for himself whom he can and cannot beat. Ordinarily one does not warn a player about who is superior

or who the hustlers are, unless one is a close friend of that player. (And even if one is a friend, the code demands that such a warning be given only before any match is in prospect; that is, once a player has started to "make a game" with another, third parties are supposed to stay out.)

7 Under certain special circumstances, dumping can also occur when there are no bets with spectators or such bets are approximately equal on both sides; see below.

8 Of course, conning is only a matter of degree, in that all of us are concerned in many ways to manipulate others' impressions of us, and so one can, if one wishes, take the view that every man is at bottom a con man. This form of "disenchantment of the world" is central to Herman Melville's *The Confidence-Man* (one of the bitterest novels in all of American literature) and to the sociological writings of Erving Goffman. Its principal corollary is the view expressed by hustlers, by other career criminals, and by Thorstein Veblen, that all businessmen are thieves.

9 The kinds of structural problems faced today by the pool or billiard hustler are by no means all endemic; some are the result of recent social change. On the other hand, such change has not created structural problems for all types of hustling. Today the golf hustler, for example, finds that with precious little "acting" he can (a) get heavy action from non-hustlers, (b) lose the majority of the eighteen holes and still clean up, and at the same time (c) not be suspected as a hustler. The structure of the game of golf itself, the peculiar structurally predetermined variations in the betting relationship as one makes the round of the course ("presses," etc.), and the present setting of the game within the larger society—all these combine to create a situation that is tailor-made for hustling. But that is another story.

16 | **The Big-Con Games** | David Maurer

Big cons are almost always professional thieves. They identify themselves as such, and they see their activities as a separate way of life. Big con games have existed in American society for at least a century. Although there have been important creative contributions made to the con games at different times, all of the big con games seem to share basic similarities. The "wire" examined in this section by David Maurer shows the way in which these games generally operate.

As Maurer explains in his book, The Big Con, *con-men use the "larceny in the blood" of ordinary law-abiding citizens to defraud them of their money. Because the individuals taken in by con games are usually involved in some kind of illegal activity intended by the cons to get their money from them, they generally do not report the thefts to the police. Only Maurer's long association with con men allowed him to learn the details of this form of deviance.*

Unfortunately, few studies of professional thieves have been undertaken since Maurer's book was published in the 1940s. Professional thieves still continue to operate and to defraud the public of hundreds of millions of dollars per year. We are very much in need of modern studies of professional crime comparable to Sutherland's famous study of The Professional Thief *and Maurer's studies of professional thieves, especially* The Big Con *and* Whiz Mob.

The Wire*

Of the three modern big-con games, the rag, the wire, and the pay-off, the wire was invented first. Without it, the rag and the pay-off probably could not have developed. By 1910 it had spread all over the

* All names used in the explanation of this game are fictitious.

country, and scores of $200,000 and higher were being talked of. While it has now waned in popularity in favor of the rag and the pay-off, it is still played with very good success.

The name for the game is an abbreviated form of wire-tapping, from which the idea for the swindle was developed. During the late 1880's and the 1890's there were certain unemployed telegraph operators who traveled over the country looking for some gullible racing fan who could be induced to lay out rather large sums of money for the expensive equipment which they represented as being necessary to tap telegraph wires and obtain advance information on the results of a race, hold up these results until the fan had time to place a bet with a bookmaker, then advance the post time and forward the results—with very happy consequences for the fan who had meanwhile bet on the winner. No doubt some of them did do what they claimed to be able to do, in which case they shared the profits with the fortunate fan. But many more acted only in the rather crude capacity of tout. They studied the form sheets to find likely looking horses, convinced the fan that they *could* tap the wires, and hoped for the best. If the horse won, of course they shared in the profit; but most of them depended for their profit upon the exorbitant fees which they obtained from the fan in advance in order to buy tools and equipment necessary for wire-tapping. This was known as "expensing," and became a small-time racket. Because it lacked the professional touch, it might well have gone the way of many similar rackets.

However, at this time there were swarms of professional grifters who worked the country over with many types of confidence rackets, the immediate ancestors of the present-day big-time games. The idea of a big store, stimulated by old Ben Marks' original experiment and the subsequent success of the fight store, was being applied to many con games with great success. There were mitt stores and monte stores and fight stores and wrestle stores.* The big-time grifters of that day blinked in pleased surprise. Why hadn't someone thought of it before? Why not a *wire store?* In other words, why not apply the tried and proven principles of confidence work to the rather clumsy touting efforts of the telegraph operators? If an unemployed telegrapher could get the mark's confidence well enough to extort "expenses" from him, what could any expert insideman do? Once the mark was throughly convinced that the race results were being delayed for him, it was immaterial whether they really were or not—*provided he was played against a fake book-maker instead of a real one.* And so a fake horse-poolroom which took bets was set up, shills were used in place of real

---

* [Ed. note: These are all con games in which "stores," or phony establishments, with rigged games, are used by the con-men to take the mark by convincing him he is involved in real games of chance.]

bettors, fake races were called with convincing fervor, and the results were all that could be desired. Thus the wire store was born. Now it only remained for smart confidence men to study the idea, correct its weaknesses, refine its strong points, and develop its potentialities.

The modern wire store is operated by one regular insideman who poses as a Western Union official, a variable staff of shills, and a staff of several outsidemen or ropers. These ropers travel the country over looking for victims who have money and can be played for the wire. Some ropers depend largely on luck to enable them to find a mark and do very well by this haphazard method; others are more systematic, resorting to advertisements for "business opportunities" inserted in metropolitan newspapers, and carefully interviewing and sifting out the resulting clientele; the most enterprising have agents who locate prospective marks, investigate their financial standing, and compile a list from which the roper can select the fattest and juiciest. There is one restriction which, though it was formerly ignored, especially in New York, is now rigidly observed: the mark must not be a resident of the city where he is to be trimmed.

Wherever the roper finds his mark, he knows that each one is an individual problem and that the play must be varied somewhat for each victim. Consequently, in an account of the wire it has seemed best to simplify it in order to present the general principles of the game without confusing the reader by the infinite possible variations in the play.

In order to visualize the wire in operation, let us assume that a roper whom we shall christen Louis Sanborn has been told that one John Bates, owner of a small department store in Providence, is a prospect for the wire. So Mr. Sanborn visits Mr. Bates, represents himself as the agent for a large corporation which is buying up small stores, and gets his victim's confidence. Mr. Bates is pleased to find a buyer for the business because it has not been too profitable. The two spend several days going over the matter. Sanborn blows hot and cold, then finally decides to buy and makes Bates a very generous tentative offer, subject to the final approval of his superiors. Mr. Bates snaps it up. So Mr. Sanborn takes an option on the business and invites Bates down to New York to consummate the deal.

They arrive in New York around noon and take up quarters at the Fairdale. Mr. Sanborn phones his "main office" and reports that their attorneys are occupied with another deal and will not be available until the following day. Then he excuses himself and makes a private call from a phone booth to his insideman, whom we shall call Charley Maxwell.

"I have a businessman from Providence," he says. "What time can we play for him?"

Maxwell consults his appointment book. "How about half past two this afternoon?" he asks.

"Fine," says Sanborn. "We'll be there."

When he returns to the room he finds his victim ready for lunch. They go down to the dining room. There, during luncheon, Sanborn plants the first seeds for the play to come. He casually mentions the fact that his cousin is manager of the central office of Western Union here in New York.

"On my way up I tried to locate a friend in New London," he explains. "Charley wanted to see him about some kind of deal, but he was out of town."

Luncheon progresses. They talk of the pending sale of Mr. Bates' business. When it is time to depart, Sanborn picks up the check and again brings up his cousin. "We aren't in any hurry," he says, "and Charley's office is just around the corner from here. Would you mind walking around that way with me? I think you'll like Charley."

And Mr. Bates does like cousin Charley, for he has a dignified and attractive personality which puts Bates immediately at his ease. He is one of the best insidemen in New York. When they arrive, he is very busy directing the activities of a staff of telegraphers. In the midst of this wholesome hum and clatter the introduction is made.

"Where are you staying, Louis?" asks Charley.

"Over at the Fairdale," says Louis. "Mr. Bates is here on business with me and he is over there too."

"Why, you're just around the corner," observes Charley. "What about our man in New London? Have you talked to him?"

"Not yet," says Louis. "He was out of town."

Cousin Charley rolls up his sleeves another notch and adjusts his green eyeshade. "I want to talk to you about him later, but I can't entertain you here. The inspectors will be around any minute now and it wouldn't look good to have a couple of strangers loafing in the office. I think you understand the situation. Now you two go on down to the hotel and as soon as inspection is over I'll join you there in the lobby. It won't take long. Goodbye."

Little does Mr. Bates suspect that the Western Union office he has just been in is entirely fake, that the energetic whir of teletypes was for his benefit only, that as soon as he left it ceased entirely, the Western Union sign came down, and that cousin Charley put on his coat and dropped his manner of dignified, conscientious executive. The outward appearances have been so convincing, the stage set with such precision, that it does not occur to him to question its authenticity.

Half an hour later, in street clothes, Charley meets Mr. Bates and Mr. Sanborn in the hotel lobby. "It's all over," he remarks, "and they're gone. Now, Louis, how about Brown? You said that you'd find him and bring him along."

Louis explains that he learned that Brown is out of town for two weeks. He ventures to suggest tentatively that perhaps his friend here, Mr. Bates, could be persuaded to fill in on the deal. Cousin Charley looks somewhat shocked at this suggestion and gives Mr. Bates an appraising look.

"How long have you known this gentleman, Louis?" he asks.

"Not very long," answers Louis, "but long enough to know that he is a responsible man, with his own business in Providence. He is O.K. I feel sure that you can depend on him."

Mr. Bates' very natural discomfort in this situation is quickly allayed by cousin Charley, who turns upon him full force the benign rays of his personality and suggests that they talk the matter over confidentially. Mr. Bates begins to feel that he likes Mr. Maxwell even better than he does Mr. Sanborn. Charley Maxwell already "has his con."

They go up to Sanborn's suite and relax. Mr. Maxwell rises to the occasion and "tells the tale" with such dignified sincerity that even the cynical Mr. Sanborn is touched by his fine acting. He explains to Mr. Bates that he has worked for a heartless corporation for years; that he has had advancement, but never what he had been promised and assured; that the company has neglected him when it should have promoted him, and that he has decided to resign.

We must not assume that Mr. Bates is a fool. He has been about a bit himself, he manages his own business, and he flatters himself that he knows a good deal about people. If he ever saw character, there it is in Charley Maxwell. He is not so much touched by the facts which Maxwell has outlined, but by the manner in which they are presented. Instead of a dissatisfied, disgruntled employee, he begins to see before him a man with the makings of a fine executive who has been neglected and wronged.

"And," Mr. Maxwell adds, "I have decided that when I resign, I will not be poor. I know how to swing a deal by which I can make a very good profit without hurting my company in the least. But I must have the assistance of an honest and dependable man, one who is able to put up some funds in return for a share of the profits. Louis' friend, Mr. Brown, was the man I had in mind. Now he cannot be located. I must act quickly, for I may not have the opportunity a second time. Are you interested?"

Mr. Bates is chary. Is Maxwell trying to make a touch? What is this deal? Is it legitimate? How much would he have to invest? And, though he does not say so, the really serious question is: *how much is the profit involved?* He stalls for more information.

Mr. Maxwell drops the question of financing and tells him about the deal. He explains that through his central office pass the race results for all the bookmakers in the city, that the horse-poolrooms are growing fat on the profits from gambling on races, that rich men with inside information can win through the bookmakers, but that the poor fellow with only a form sheet to guide him always loses more than he makes. He says that he has worked out a system whereby he can beat the bookmakers at their own game by delaying the results long enough to phone them to his assistants who are to be stationed next door to the poolroom and who will bet on the races after they are run. Then the results will be released and, of course, their bets will pay a very neat profit. And no one will suffer but the rich and dishonest bookmakers.

Once the mark has gone this far, he seldom backs out. If he does, further pressure may be put on him or he may be dropped altogether. But we will assume that Maxwell's smooth voice and sincere manner have had their effect. Bates likes the proposition and sees in it a high profit with no risk. It is a sure thing.

"Now," says Mr. Maxwell, aside to Mr. Bates, "Louis doesn't understand much about this business and I will count on you to take the responsibility of seeing that everything goes all right. You and he go on down to this address on 48th Street and look the place over. Then go into the drugstore next door and wait for a call from me at three sharp. I'll give you the name of the winner and hold up the results just long enough for you to go next door and place your bet. I can't hold them for more than three or four minutes. That way we can see whether or not our system will work, and of course you and Louis can keep anything you win for yourselves. If it works out, we will want to try something bigger."

Mr. Bates and Louis follow the instructions they have received. They visit the poolroom and find there all the paraphernalia that go with a booking establishment. Races are chalked on the blackboard. The ticker is thrumming merrily. Prosperous gentlemen are winning and losing large bets nonchalantly. The caller calls the races with great zest. Bets of $10,000 to $20,000 are laid casually. Very large amounts of cash are changing hands like nickels in a crap game. Everywhere there is cash. The patrons peel off large bets from fat bankrolls or from bulging wallets. The cashier counts out $40,000 winnings without batting an eye. Louis and Mr. Bates are much impressed. A little of the fever of that atmosphere has worked its way into Mr. Bates' blood.

Three o'clock approaches. They return to the drugstore. Maxwell gives them, shall we say, Seabiscuit as winner. They hasten back and plunge into the thick and throbbing atmosphere. Both Mr. Bates and Louis put a ten-dollar bill on Seabiscuit to win. Mr. Bates feels a queer sensation of mingled guilt and triumph. It is a wonderful feeling to bet on a sure thing, even for ten dollars. They have hardly placed their bets when the caller says the magic words, "They're off!" Then he calls the race. Seabiscuit wins, at 4–1. Our pair of innocents collect fifty dollars each. The larceny in Mr. Bates' veins begins to percolate. He can already see a fortune stretching out ahead of him. Why, there is no limit—except the resources of the bookmaker—to what one could make out of this thing. And there are thousands of bookmakers.

They look about them while they await the next race. The same air of dignified, restrained feverishness prevails. No one seems to notice them. Mr. Bates looks the crowd over. It is not large, but it is sporty. Brokers with pasty faces. Sportsmen, tanned and casual. A financier with a Vandyke and highly tailored clothes. The thick blue haze wherein mingle the thin silver streams from a dozen fine cigars. They are betting, joking, absorbed in themselves.

Mr. Bates is a little taken aback at the nonchalant way in which these men handle money. He likes it, and would like to feel that he is a part of it. But he knows that he isn't. He turns to his friend Sanborn. The next race is coming up. They retire to the phone for more information. Then they bet fifty dollars each on War Admiral to win at 4–1. He does.

This nets them $250 apiece. "I think I'll shoot the works on the next race," says Mr. Bates. Sanborn counsels caution. After all, this thing is just starting. This is only an experiment to see if their plan will work. Charley knows what he is about, and perhaps they had better do as he says and place only small bets. But Mr. Bates is hooked. He returns to the telephone, awaits a horse, and comes back with the firm intention of placing the $250 on his nose. Louis cautiously refrains from betting this time.

Mr. Bates hurries to the window to place his bet. He has the $250 in his pocket, ready to be laid. But there are several men just ahead of him. They are laying down very big bets. He cannot help noticing the fat, sleek piles of fives, tens, twenties, fifties, and hundreds in the cashier's drawer. He sees the piles of bills on the shelf behind the cashier. He sees the deft hands swiftly paying out and taking in thousands of dollars. He grows impatient. Time is short. The race will be called any moment now. He pushes the line along, but it doesn't seem to move fast enough. He shifts his weight from one foot to the other and peers ahead. Only one man, now, laying a fifteen-thousand-dollar bet. Will he never get that money counted down? The man moves casually away, biting the end off a heavy cigar. Mr. Bates removes the wadded bills from his pocket. Challedon. Charley said Challedon to win.

"They're off!" shouts the caller.

Mr. Bates stands there, futilely fingering his money. Betting is closed. Challedon. . . . Where is Challedon? He lags to the rear. He is under wraps. The caller reads off the ticker with such animation that he might as well have been an eye-witness. Will Challedon never make his move? Here it is. They enter the stretch with Challedon moving up. He is booted home a winner. And at 6–1. Mr. Bates does a little sketchy mental arithmetic and wonders why he wasn't just one ahead in the line at the window.

He doesn't know it, but he has been given the "shut-out" or the "prat-out," a clever method of stepping up the larceny in the veins of a mark when the manager feels that he is not entering into the play enthusiastically enough. It may be repeated several times so that the mark is fully impressed with what he has missed. The shills who surround the mark at the window usually play for more than the mark is being played for; if the mark is being played for $25,000, the air is full of $50,000 bets; thus the mark always feels like a piker instead of a plunger. Furthermore, ambitious marks must not be allowed to get too much of the store's cash into their pockets.

Mr. Bates returns to Louis. "Tough luck," says Louis.

A suave-looking gentleman approaches them. He is quiet, polite, but authoritative. And just a little condescending. Mr. Bates doesn't know just why, but he feels embarrassed.

"Are you the gentlemen who have been placing these small bets?" he asks, waving a pair of slips.

"We just made a fifty-dollar bet, if you call that small," says Louis.

The manager looks at them with patronizing good nature. "Well, I'll have to ask you not to place any more small bets here," he says. "We have other poolrooms for working men. Small bets make too much bookkeeping for us." He smiles and gently starts them toward the door. Mr. Bates feels patronized. He doesn't like it.

"How much does a man have to bet here?" asks Louis.

"A thousand dollars is usually the lower limit," answers the manager, smiling. "Beyond that, you can go as high as you like. Come back, gentlemen, some other time."

As they pass the doorman, they see Maxwell coming down the street. "Did it work?" asks cousin Charley. "If it did, we can all make a fortune."

"We won a couple of hundred dollars apiece on two bets," volunteers Louis. "But we never got any further. They called us pikers because we didn't bet high enough."

"Never mind that, my boy," answers Charley. "When the time comes we will arrange to bet high enough to suit them. Let's go over to the hotel. I want to discuss this thing further with you in private."

Up in the suite at the Fairdale Mr. Bates hears what he wants to hear.

"This particular poolroom," says cousin Charley, "is the one that I have marked to work on. I know that they have very extensive financial backing. Their volume of business must be tremendous."

Mr. Bates, with a mind full of greenbacks, reflects that it certainly must be.

"They can lose a million and never miss it," continues Charley. "My plan is to take eight or nine hundred thousand in four or five days, then quit. What do you gentlemen say?"

Mr. Bates and Louis agree that it would indeed be a desirable course of action.

"But we have to have cash to finance it," says Charley. "That is why I was so concerned about Brown. He could dig up the cash we need. Let's see, I believe you were thinking that you might raise some for us?"

"How much would you need?" asks Mr. Bates, fearful of appearing too anxious.

"Do you think you would be willing to finance it?" asks Charley. "After all, you know, I haven't much except my salary, and Louis here is just getting a start. How much can you raise?"

Mr. Bates studies. He figures on an envelope. His mind is a whirl of mortgages, real estate, government bonds. It may take a couple of weeks to sell his business. Bonds would be the quickest. Government bonds.

"I think I could pick up twenty-five thousand within the next couple of days. Or maybe sooner," he adds, mindful of the potential Mr. Brown. "Is your friend definitely out?"

Mr. Maxwell is very cool and practical. "I hate to let Brown down," he muses. "But I think this arrangement will be fine. How much did you say you could raise? Twenty-five thousand? How is this money? In cash?"

"No, no," says Mr. Bates, "in bonds. Government bonds. I'll have to have my banker sell them and forward me a draft for the proceeds."

"That would be fine," says Charley.

"Now," says Mr. Bates, "how do you intend to split the profits? I would want to pay you whatever is right, but if I put up the money, I ought to get a good share of the profits. Otherwise it wouldn't pay me to get into it."

Mr. Bates suddenly feels important. All he needs is the information. He has the cash. That is the important thing. These men can be paid off at his own price if he finances it now, quickly, before someone else is cut in.

"I have thought that over," says cousin Charley. "Since the plan is mine, I think I ought to have at least fifty per cent. And we should cut Louis in for about twenty per cent for his co-operation. That would leave you thirty per cent, which would make you a very good return on your investment."

Mr. Bates doesn't like that arrangement. He wants to cut those men out of all he can. Of course they must have something, but why let Louis in on it at all? And Maxwell. Why, he would go to prison if this thing ever became known. He schemes and argues. As they dicker, Maxwell humors him by working out a compromise whereby he and Bates will split ninety percent of the profit, and Louis will get the remaining ten. Mr. Bates still feels that they have been too generous with Louis. He moves immediately to phone his banker in Providence. But Maxwell interposes.

"This deal must be kept absolutely secret," he argues. "If you phone in for money in a hurry, your banker may become suspicious. You know how bankers are. He may feel that you are making a mistake to dump a block of bonds like that on the market right now. It will be a little more expensive but much safer if you catch a train out of here this afternoon and talk to your banker personally tomorrow. Explain that you are buying some real estate here in the city and want to pay down that much cash."

"But," interposes Bates, turning to Louis, "what about that appointment with your lawyers?"

"Don't worry about that," says Louis. "I'll take care of everything for you. Just send me a telegram as soon as you know when you'll be back and I'll fix things up at the office."

"That's right," says Charley. "And you'd better add a note in that telegram which will let me know how much money you are bringing. But we don't want anyone to suspect you are bringing it. So let a thousand dollars equal, say, one 'bushel.' Then you can say, 'Bringing twenty-five bushels,' and I'll know you are prepared to go right ahead with the deal."

This stage of the game is known as "the send." It is a strange fact that, once a good insideman "tightens up" a mark, he can be sent anywhere for his money and will usually return despite all obstacles. For example, during the week of July 3, 1939, the metropolitan papers carried stories on the case of Mr. Leonard B. Reel, a public accountant of Beech Haven, New Jersey, who, with his wife, was put on the send from Mexico City. The couple flew to Philadelphia and brought back $74,000, which they lost on the rag to the Velvet Kid. They reported that they made the trip with some difficulty, having been forced down en route by storms four different times. If the con men think that they can get away with using the mails, they may not use "the send."

Mr. Bates agrees that it will be best to make the trip. There must be no slips. For a moment he fears what might happen if this scheme came to light. Then he remembers that he is only financing it. He feels better. Also, the $250 in his wallet will more than cover his expenses on the trip home. Mr. Bates watches his pennies. But on the other hand, is it safe to leave the deal open here? Suppose Brown—or someone else—turned up with the ready cash?

"You have decided definitely that I am to finance it?" he asks.

"Yes, indeed," says Charley. "Here is my hand on it. We'll shake hands all the way around. That swears us all to keep this deal absolutely secret."

They all shake hands, though having Louis cut in on the deal still sticks in Bates' craw. But after all, ten per cent isn't much, and Louis still holds the key to the sale of his store. Well, he'll get that ten percent back and more when Louis' company takes up that option.

Three days later he is back in New York with a draft for $25,000. He is at a high pitch of excitement. This business turns over a profit quicker than anything he has ever seen. And he gets a strange sense of elation—the same feeling, magnified a thousand times, that he felt when he had that first ten dollars on Seabiscuit and watched him romp home. He has a sure thing.

Maxwell takes him to a bank which has been fixed. Mr. John Bates endorses the check and now has $25,000 in cash. It burns holes in his pockets.

"This afternoon I think we can work," says Charley. "I'll find out what the best odds are, you stay near the phone booth, and I'll tell you what to bet just before each race. I'll get any last-minute change in odds as they come through over the wire, and we'll take all that into consideration. We'll work the same as we did the other day. Now hold on tight to that money." Then he goes back to directing the destinies of a minor province in the great empire of Western Union.

The next few hours are critical ones for the con men. Between now and post time the mark is most likely to have a "brain-blow" and lose his head. Marks have been known to go to the police with the whole story right at this point, and a "wrong" copper might lay a trap for the con men and get the mark to co-operate. Or the mark might worry about so large a gamble and look up some friend or acquaintance to consult about the matter; of course, any of these might tip the whole thing off. Occasionally the victim insists on seeking the advice of his wife, in which case wiser con mobs encourage such a move, for they have learned that such a consultation usually works in their favor. Some marks simply get cold feet at the last moment and go on about their business, or return home.

So a "tailer" is put on Mr. Bates during all the time that he is not with either of the con men. The tailer, a man of ample experience in such matters, can tell immediately by the mark's actions how he is getting along. If he consults the police, the tailer reports back immediately and the con men may simply not see him any more, or they may phone him and tell him that Western Union has become suspicious and that the deal must be postponed. However, if he has consulted a "right" copper or detective, the con men know that they are safe, for they can pay their way as soon as the score comes off. They go right ahead and play for him, knowing that the police will not "knock" him or tip him off to what is happening. If it seems necessary, the insideman himself or his fixer will go down and have a chat with the officer in order to be sure there will be no slips. Meanwhile, Mr. Bates, if he has had any traffic with the police, feels better in the knowledge that the officers of the law are not suspicious of the men with whom he is dealing or of the deal (if he lets that out) which he is contemplating.

Meanwhile, Louis stalls the victim along with the pending sale of his store, which, during the play, fades into the background. Some marks become so feverish that, during the period of the tie-up, they apparently forget all about the original reason for their coming to the city where the big store is located, or resent the roper's attempts to continue negotiations for the business while this big deal is in the air.

Post time finds Mr. Bates and Louis haunting the phone booth, awaiting the call which will come sometime during the afternoon. Bates hugs his $25,000. Louis handles his quarry skillfully, knowing just how to arouse his anticipations and how far to go in quieting the doubts which may be troubling his mind.

At last the phone jangles. Mr. Bates rushes into the booth. It is Maxwell.

"Hello," he says, "is that you, Louis?"

"No, this is John Bates."

"Well, I've got the winner. Hurry right on over and place the money on Flying Lill. Call Louis to the phone, will you?"

Louis talks briefly to Charley. "O.K.," he says. "I understand. Place it all on Flying Lill. Goodbye, Charley."

They hurry over to the poolroom and plunge into the atmosphere of synthetic excitement. There on the odds-board is Flying Lill, 5–1. Mr. Bates feels a momentary sinking in the pit of his stomach. His mouth is dry and his hands tremble. Louis takes the bills from his hands and pushes them through the cashier's window. "Flying Lill to win," he says. "Twenty-five thousand."

The cashier gives him his slip and begins to count the money. "They're off!" calls the announcer, and the next two minutes are hectic ones. It is Unerring by a length. Flying Lill second. Lady Maryland third.

Mr. Bates is stunned. *Unerring won.*

"Wait a minute," says Louis, "there must be something wrong. It isn't official yet." He looks with mingled sympathy and anxiety into Mr. Bates' ashen face.

But it is official. The announcement cuts through the smoke and clatter like a great somber gong. It is official.

"We've lost," says Louis, and they go out into the street.

It may occur to Mr. Bates that he has been betrayed. His mind is probably such a chaos that he cannot think at all. He may break into sobs immediately and wildly tear his hair. But we will assume that he is a gentleman and that he restrains his emotions and reserves his judgments until he learns what has happened. Louis has already solicitously begun the "cooling-out" process which will pave the way for Maxwell's smooth patter.

They meet Charley, who can only partly conceal his jubilation, a short distance from the Western Union office. He is talking in terms of winning $125,000. Mr. Bates tells him that Louis bet the horse to win, but that it placed and they lost. Charley turns on Louis in a fury. "Don't you know what the word *place* means?" he roars. Louis tries to justify his mistake on the basis of their misunderstanding of the word *place.* But Maxwell will have none of it. He rakes that young man over the coals until he hangs his head in red-faced shame and humiliation. Mr. Bates is very likely to come to Louis' defense, on the grounds that he, too, misunderstood. Then Mr. Maxwell turns on him and gives him also a piece of his mind. But finally he cools off.

"Well," he says, "we'll never make that mistake again." Then he takes Mr. Bates in hand in such a way that the "cooling-out" process is perfect and Mr. Bates lives only until he can raise enough money to give the plan a second trial. When Charley Maxwell cools a mark out, he stays cooled out. And if he has decided that the mark is good for another play—as about fifty per cent of them are—he will "feel him out" to see whether or not he can raise more cash; some marks have been beaten four or five times on the same racket. If he knows he has been swindled, or if he cannot raise any more money, he is "blown off" and disposed of as quietly as possible. Let us assume that Mr. Bates, being the perfect mark, is good for another play. Mr. Maxwell retains his confidence to such an uncanny extent that he will do almost anything he is told to do. So he is "put on the send" again for $20,000, which he borrows, using real estate as collateral.

The second play takes up just where the first left off. The only delay is caused by obtaining Mr. Bates' money. Louis knows how to handle the deal regarding Mr. Bates' business and assures him that everything is going along fine, but that his corporation is going to investigate the department store further before they sign the final papers. Usually, if the mark is good for a second play, he is by this time so wrapped up in the wire that he has practically dropped the legitimate deal. Some con mobs will send a tailer along home with the mark to see if he consults the police before returning. The tailer may pose as an agent for the corporation interested in the mark's business.

The big store, the boost, and all the necessary stage settings are again called into play. When the time comes to make the big bet, the sting is put in a little differently. Over the phone Mr. Maxwell gives the mark Johnny J. at 6–1 to win. Mr. Bates and Louis bet the $20,000, making sure that there is no misunderstanding this time regarding that tricky word *place*. The betting is heavy all around them, though Mr. Bates does not realize that those bank rolls have seen much service as props. The $50,000 in cold cash laid down by the bettor just ahead of him is real money; it makes an impression.

"They're off!" says the caller. The room quiets. The smoke drifts in swirls. The gamblers listen with polite eagerness. It is Johnny J. by a neck.

Mr. Bates feels a great exhilaration; his fingers and toes tingle; a warm wave of relief sweeps over him. His horse has won $140,000. Now to take his share and build it up into a fortune.

"Let's cash it right away," urges Louis, "before something happens to it."

Mr. Bates waves the ticket before the impassive cashier, who is imperturbably stacking big bills; Mr. Bates has never seen so much loose cash. It is everywhere. The cashier looks at him with polite indifference.

"Cash this, cash this, please," says Mr. Bates, pushing the ticket under the grating.

"Just a minute, sir," says the cashier. "I'm sorry, but those results are not yet official. Wait just a minute."

"Flash!" says the caller. "Flash! A mistake in colors. It was Silverette by a neck. Johnny J. second. Technician is third. This is official."

Mr. Bates vaguely hears a man beside him say to his friend, "I'm very glad that horse disqualified. I had $7,000 on Silverette."

"I'm not," says his friend, "that damned Johnny J. cost me just twenty thousand. . . ."

Mr. Bates is dazed. He remonstrates with the manager. He cries and curses his luck. He suspects that he has been swindled but doesn't know how. The manager is polite, firm, and impersonal. The heavy play goes right on for the next race. Louis, crying and complaining as if it were his $20,000 which went glimmering, leads him out into the street. The outside air only intensifies the terrible feeling of loss and despair in Mr. Bates' heart. To him money is a sacred thing. This is terrible.

Outside on the street they meet Charley. He looks tired and worried. He is nervous and distraught. He listens absently to the tale of woe. "Yes, that is terrible," he agrees. "But right now I am in terrible trouble myself. The Western Union detectives have been investigating the delay in race results and I'll be lucky if I only lose my job. If they pin anything on me, I'll go to prison. Maybe all three of us."

Mr. Bates hasn't thought of this angle since Charley first explained the deal to him. Fear now adds its agony to despair. They talk over the possibilities of arrest. Maxwell advises that Bates and Louis leave town as quickly and quietly as possible. They return to the hotel. Louis obligingly gets the time for the next train to Providence. It leaves at 10:00 P.M. Mr. Bates, worried, nervous, broken, agrees to take it. Charley promises that, if this thing blows over, he himself will raise enough money to play the game again and will give Mr. Bates all his money back, and some profit to boot. Then he leaves, so that he may not be picked up. Louis draws Mr. Bates aside.

"How much money do you have?" he asks.

Mr. Bates looks in his wallet. "Less than fifty dollars," he answers. "And I have to pay my hotel bill."

"Well," offers Louis, "I have nearly a hundred and fifty. You have had a bad break and I hate to see you stranded. You have been a fine sport to take it the way you do. Here, let me lend you seventy-five to get home on. You can pay it back any time. And remember," he adds, "our auditors will be at your place next week. Then I'll have everything in good shape at this end and we'll close the deal."

Mr. Bates takes the money which is pressed on him. He is surprised. Louis is a pretty nice fellow after all. He is ashamed of the way he has felt about him recently. Still in a daze, he shakes the proffered hand and Louis departs. "I'll be back about nine-thirty," he says, "to see that you get to the train safely. Wait for me in the lobby."

From now on, it is up to a local tailer to keep close tabs on Mr. Bates to see what he may do, reporting any tendency he may show to consult the police. Mr. Maxwell may have him paged to the telephone and continue the cooling process by phone. The tailer watches closely; if, after this conversation, Mr. Bates consults the house detective or a detective he has stationed in the lobby, the tailer reports immediately to Maxwell, who puts the machinery of the fix into operation. Or, Louis may deliberately delay his arrival at the hotel to see his victim off. As the time for departure approaches and Louis fails to appear, Mr. Bates may get nervous and make a phone call to the police, or consult a detective already stationed in the hotel. The tailer can predict the mark's reactions with a good deal of accuracy, for he has had ample opportunity to study at first hand the psychology of the trimmed mark.

Just before ten, at the tailer's signal, Louis appears with a good excuse for lateness, bundles Mr. Bates carefully into a cab, hurries him to the station, buys his ticket for Providence, and puts him on the train. He waits solicitously until the train pulls out.

As soon as the mark is safely on his way, Mr. Maxwell meets his roper, the manager, and the boost at the hangout. He is a meticulous bookkeeper. He gives each one a plain envelope containing his share of the score, and drops a word about an appointment for eleven-thirty on Wednesday. And so the big store goes on.

There is one fundamental weakness in the wire: the victim must furnish his own money.

part six
drugs as a deviant
style and way of life

17 | **White-Collar Pill Party** | Bruce Jackson

As most students know, in recent years many forms of drugs have become widely used among middle-class people; however, the great mass of illegal drug use is not publicly observable. It is well known, for example, that more than half the college students on many urban campuses have used marijuana at least once. We must realistically suspect that large numbers of "respectable" adults, like those in this article, are also doing so.

The striking thing about Bruce Jackson's report is the attitude toward drug use among this middle-class group, which is representative of the basic changes in attitudes toward drugs among middle-class people in our society. This change has brought the middle-class young, especially the college students, into growing conflict with the police, and this, in turn, has contributed to the so-called "generation gap." But an increasing number of adults are joining them and supporting them. This combination is bringing increasing pressure to change the laws.

There was a thing called Heaven; but all the same they used to drink enormous quantities of alcohol. . . . There was a thing called the soul and a thing called immortality. . . . But they used to take morphia and cocaine. . . . Two thousand pharmacologists and bio-chemists were subsidized in A.F. 178. . . . Six years later it was being produced commercially. The perfect drug. . . . Euphoric, narcotic, pleasantly hallucinant. . . . All the advantages of Christianity and alcohol; none of their defects. . . . Take a holiday from reality whenever you like, and come back without so much as a headache or a mythology.
■ *Aldous Huxley, Brave New World,* 1932

Drugs, like chewing gum, TV, oversize cars, and crime, are part of the American way of life. No one receives an exemption.

This was made particularly clear to me recently by my four-year-old son, Michael, who came into the kitchen one evening and asked me to go out and buy a certain brand of vitamin pills for him. Since he is quite healthy and not observably hypochondriac, I asked why he wanted them. "So I can be as strong as Jimmy down the block."

"There isn't any Jimmy down the block," I said, whereupon he patiently explained that the clown on the 5 P.M. TV program he watches every day had *told* him the pills would make him stronger than Jimmy, and his tone gave me to understand that the existence of a corporeal Jimmy was irrelevant: the truehearted clown, the child's friend, had advised the pills, and any four-year-old knows a clown wouldn't steer you wrong.

For adults the process is modified slightly. An afternoon TV commercial urges women to purchase a new drug for their "everyday headache" (without warning them that anyone who has a headache every day should certainly be consulting a GP or a psychiatrist); a Former Personality with suggestive regularity tells you to keep your bloodstream pure by consuming buffered aspirin for the headache you are supposed to have, and another recommends regular doses of iron for your "tired blood." (It won't be long before another screen has-been mounts the TV commercial podium with a pill that doesn't do anything at all; it just keeps your corpuscles company on the days you ate liver and forgot to have a headache.)

One result of all the drug propaganda and the appalling faith in the efficacy of drugs is that a lot of people take a lot more pills than they have any reason to. They think in terms of pills. And so do their physicians: you fix a fat man by giving him a diet pill, you fix a chronic insomniac by giving him a sleeping pill. But these conditions are frequently merely symptoms of far more complicated disorders. The convenient prescription blank solves the problem of finding out what the trouble really is—it makes the symptom seem to go away.

Think for a moment: how many people do you know who cannot stop stuffing themselves without an amphetamine and who cannot go to sleep without a barbiturate (over *nine billion* of those produced last year) or make it through a workday without a sequence of tranquilizers? And what about those six million alcoholics, who daily ingest quantities of what is, by sheer force of numbers, the most addicting drug in America?

The publicity goes to the junkies, lately to the college kids, but these account for only a small portion of the American drug problem. Far more worrisome are the millions of people who have become dependent on commercial drugs. The junkie *knows* he is hooked; the housewife on amphetamine and the businessman on meprobamate hardly ever realize what has gone wrong.

Sometimes the pill-takers meet other pill-takers, and an odd thing happens: instead of using the drug to cope with the world, they begin to use their time to take drugs. Taking drugs becomes *something to do.*

When this stage is reached, the drug-taking pattern broadens: the user takes a wider variety of drugs with increasing frequency. For want of a better term, one might call it the whlte-collar drug scene.

I first learned about it during a party in Chicago last winter, and the best way to introduce you will be to tell you something about that evening, the people I met, what I think was happening.

There were about a dozen people in the room, and over the noise from the record player scraps of conversation came through:

"Now the Desbutal, if you take it with this stuff, has a peculiar effect, contraindication, at least it did for me. You let me know if you . . ."

"I don't have one legitimate prescription, Harry, not *one!* Can you imagine that?" "I'll get you some tomorrow, dear."

". . . and this pharmacist on Fifth will sell you all the leapers [amphetamines] you can carry—just like that. Right off the street. I don't think he'd know a prescription if it bit him." "As long as he can read the labels, what the hell."

"You know, a funny thing happened to me. I got this green and yellow capsule, and I looked it up in the Book, and it wasn't anything I'd been using, and I thought, great! It's not something I've built a tolerance to. And I took it. A couple of them. And you know what happened? *Nothing!* That's what happened, not a goddamned thing."

The Book—the *Physicians' Desk Reference,* which lists the composition and effects of almost all commercial pharmaceuticals produced in this country—passes back and forth, and two or three people at a time look up the contents and possible values of a drug one of them has just discovered or heard about or acquired or taken. The Book is the pillhead's *Yellow Pages:* you look up the effect you want ("Sympathomimetics" or "Cerebral Stimulants," for example), and it tells you the magic columns. The pillheads swap stories of kicks and sound like professional chemists discussing recent developments; others listen, then examine the *PDR* to see if the drug discussed really could do that.

Eddie, the host, a painter who has received some recognition, had been awake three or four days, he was not exactly sure. He consumes between 150 and 200 milligrams of amphetamine a day, needs a large part of that to stay awake, even when he has slipped a night's sleep in somewhere. The dose would cause most people some difficulty; the familiar diet pill, a capsule of Dexamyl or Eskatrol, which makes the new user edgy and over-energetic and slightly insomniac the first few days, contains only 10 or 15 milligrams of amphetamine. But amphetamine is one of the few central nervous system stimulants to which one can develop a tolerance, and over the months and years Ed and his friends have built up massive tolerances and dependencies. "Leapers aren't so hard to give up," he told me. "I mean, I sleep almost constantly when I'm off, but you get over that. But everything is so damned boring without the pills."

I asked him if he knew many amphetamine users who have given up the pills.

"For good?"

I nodded.

"I haven't known anybody that's given it up for good." He reached out and took a few pills from the candy dish in the middle of the coffee table, then washed them down with some Coke.

The last couple to arrive—a journalist and his wife—settled into positions. The wife was next to me on the oversize sofa, and she skimmed through the "Product Identification Section" of the *PDR,* dozens of pages of pretty color photos of tablets and capsules. "Hey!" she said to no one in particular. Then, to her husband, "Look at the pretty hexagonal. George, get the Source to get some of them for me." George, across the table, near the fire, nodded.

I had been advised to watch him as he turned on. As the pills took effect something happened to the muscles of his face, and the whole assembly seemed to go rubbery. His features settled lower and more loosely on the bones of his head. He began to talk with considerably more verve.

A distractingly pretty girl with dark brown eyes sat at the edge of our group and ignored both the joint making its rounds and the record player belching away just behind her. Between the thumb and middle finger of her left hand she held a pill that was blue on one side and yellow on the other; steadily, with the double-edged razor blade she held in her right hand, she sawed on the seam between the two halves of the pill. Every once in a while she rotated it a few degrees with her left index finger. Her skin was smooth, and the light from the fireplace played tricks with it, all of them charming. The right hand sawed on.

I got the Book from the coffee table and looked for the pill in the pages of color pictures, but before I found it, Ed leaned over and said, "They're Desbutal Gradumets. Abbott Labs."

I turned to the "Professional Products Information" section and learned that Desbutal is a combination of Desoxyn (methamphetamine hydrochloride, also marketed as Methedrine) and Nembutal, that the pill the girl sawed contained 15 milligrams of the Desoxyn, that the combination of drugs served "to both stimulate and calm the patient so that feelings of depression are overcome and a sense of well-being and increased energy is produced. Inner tension and anxiety are relieved so that a sense of serenity and ease of mind prevails." Gradumets, the Book explained, "are indicated in the management of obesity, the management of depressed states, certain behavioral syndromes, and a number of typical geriatric conditions," as well as "helpful in managing psychosomatic complaints and neuroses," Parkinson's disease, and a hangover.

The girl, obviously, was not interested in all of the pill's splendid therapeutic promises; were she, she would not have been so diligently sawing along that seam. She was after the methamphetamine, which like other amphetamines "depresses appetite, elevates the mood, increases the urge to work, imparts a sense of increased efficiency, and counteracts sleepiness and the feeling of fatigue in most persons."

After what seemed a long while the pill split into two round sections. A few scraps of the yellow Nembutal adhered to the Desoxyn side, and she carefully scraped them away. "Wilkinson's the best blade for this sort of thing," she said. I asked if she didn't cut herself on occasion, and she showed me a few nicks in her left thumb. "But a single edge isn't thin enough to do it neatly."

She put the blue disk in one small container, the yellow in another, then from a third took a fresh Desbutal and began sawing. I asked why she kept the Nembutal, since it was the Desoxyn she was after.

"Sometimes I might want to sleep, you know. I might *have* to sleep because something is coming up the next day. It's not easy for us to sleep, and sometimes we just don't for a couple or three days. But if we have to, we can just take a few of these." She smiled at me tolerantly, then returned to her blade and tablet.

When I saw Ed in New York several weeks later, I asked about her. "Some are like that," he said; "they like to carve on their pills. She'll sit and carve for thirty or forty minutes."

"Is that sort of ritual an important part of it all?"

"I think it is. She seems to have gotten hung up on it. I told her that she shouldn't take that Nembutal, that I have been cutting the Nembutal off my pills. It only takes about thirty seconds. And she can spend a good half hour at it if she has a mind to. I told her once about the effect of taking a Spansule; you know, one of those big things with sustained release [like Dexamyl, a mixture of dextroamphetamine sulfate and amobarbital designed to be effective over a twelve-hour period]. What you do is open the capsule and put it in a little bowl and grind up the little pellets until it's powder, then stuff all the powder back in the pill and take it, and it all goes off at once. I'll be damned if I haven't seen her grinding away like she was making matzo meal. That's a sign of a fairly confirmed head when they reach that ritual stage."

Next to the candy dish filled with Dexedrine, Dexamyl, Eskatrol, Desbutal, and a few other products I hadn't yet learned to identify, near the five-pound box of Dexedrine tablets someone had brought, were two bottles. One was filled with Dexedrine Elixir, the other with Dexamyl Elixir. Someone took a long swallow from the latter, and I thought him to be an extremely heavy user, but when the man left the room, a lawyer told me he'd bet the man was new at it. "He has to be. A mouthful is like two pills, and if he was a real head, he'd have a far greater tolerance to the Dexedrine than the amobarbital, and the stuff would make him sleepy. Anyhow, I don't like to mess with barbiturates much anymore. Dorothy Kilgallen died from that." He took a drink from the Dexedrine bottle and said, "And this tastes better. Very tasty stuff, like cherry syrup. Make a nice cherry Coke with it. The Dexamyl Elixir is bitter."

Someone emptied the tobacco from a Salem and filled the tube with grass; he tamped it down with a Tinkertoy stick, crimped the tip, then lighted it and inhaled noisily. He immediately passed the joint to the person on his left. Since one must hold the smoke in one's lungs for several seconds to get the full effect, it is more economical for several people to turn on at once. The grass was very good and seemed to produce a quiet but substantial high. One doesn't notice it coming on, but there is a realization that for a while now the room has been a decidedly pleasant one, and some noises are particularly interesting for their own sake.

I leaned back and closed my eyes for a moment. It was almost 5 A.M., and in three hours I had to catch a plane at O'Hare. "You're not going to *sleep* are you?" The tone implied that this group considered few human frailties truly gauche, but going to sleep was surely one of them. I shook my head no and looked to see who had spoken. It was Ed's wife; she looked concerned. "Do you want a pill?" I shook my head no again.

Then, just then, I realized that Ed—who knew I was not a pill-user—had not once in the evening offered me one of the many samples that had been passed around, nor had anyone else. Just the grass, but not the pills. His wife suggested a pill not so that I might get high, but merely so that I could stay awake without difficulty.

"I'm not tired," I said, "just relaxing." I assured her I wouldn't doze off. She was still concerned, however, and got me a cup of coffee from the kitchen and offered some Murine from her purse.

The front door opened, and there was a vicious blast of winter off Lake Michigan. Ed kicked the door closed behind him and dumped an armful of logs by the fireplace, then went back into the kitchen. A moment later he returned and passed around a small dish of capsules. And this time it was handed to me. They looked familiar. "One a Days," he said. I had learned enough from the Book to see the need for them: the amphetamine user often does not eat for long periods of time (some days his only nourishment is the sugar in the bottles of soda which he drinks to wash down the pills and counter their side effect of dehydration of the mouth), and he not only tends to lose weight but also risks vitamin deficiencies. After a while, the heavy user learns to force-feed himself or go off pills every once in a while in order to eat without difficulty and to keep his tolerance level down.

Later, getting settled in the plane, I thought, What a wild party that was. I'd never been to anything quite like it, and I began making notes about what had gone on. Not long before we came into Logan, it suddenly struck me that there had been nothing wild about the party at all, nothing. There had been women there, some of them unaccompanied and some with husbands or dates, but there had been none of the playing around and sexual hustling that several years of academic and business world parties had led me to consider a correlative of almost any evening gathering of more than ten men and women: no meaningful looks, no wisecracks, no "accidental" rubbing. No one had spoken loudly, no one had become giggly or silly, no one had lost control or seemed anywhere near it. Viewed with some perspective, the evening seemed nothing more than comfortable.

There are various ways to acquire the pills, but the most common is also the most legal: prescriptions. Even though there is now a federal law requiring physicians and pharmacists to maintain careful records regarding prescriptions for drugs like Dexamyl, many physicians are careless about prescribing them, and few seem to realize that the kind of personality that needs them is often the kind of personality that can easily acquire an overwhelming dependency on them. Often a patient will be issued a refillable prescription; if the patient is a heavy user, all he needs to do is visit several physicians and get refillable prescriptions from each. If he is worried that a cross-check of druggists' lists might turn up his name, he can easily give some of his doctors false names.

There are dealers, generically called the Source, who specialize in selling these drugs; some give them away. They do not seem to be underworld types but professional people in various capacities who, for one reason or another, have access to large quantities of them. If one is completely without connections, the drugs can be made at home. One young man I know made mescaline, amphetamine, methamphetamine, LSD, and DET and DMT (diethyl- and dimethyl-tryptamine, hallucinogens of shorter duration and greater punch than LSD) in his kitchen. In small lots, dextroamphetamine sulfate costs him about 50 cents a gram; a pound costs him about $30 (the same amounts of Dexedrine at your friendly corner druggist's would cost, respectively, about $10 and $4200).

In some areas, primarily those fairly distant from major centers of drug distribution, the new law has begun to have some significant effect. In one medium-sized city, for example, the price of black-market Dexamyl and Eskatrol Spansules has risen from 15 cents to 50 cents a capsule, when one can connect for them at all.

In the major cities one can still connect, but it is becoming more difficult. The new law will inhibit, but there may be complications. It would be unfortunate if the price should be driven up so high that it would become profitable for criminal organizations to involve themselves with the traffic, as was the case with opiates in the 1940s and 1950s and alcohol in the 1920s.

There was talk in Manhattan last winter, just before the new law took effect, that some LSD factories were closing down, and I know that some Sources stopped supplying. For a short time the price of LSD went up; then things stabilized, competition increased, a new packaging method developed popularity (instead of the familiar sugar cubes, one now takes one's dose on a tiny slip of paper; like a spitball, only you don't spit it out), and now the price for a dose of LSD is about 20 percent *less* than it was a year ago.

Since most of the pillheads I'm talking about are middle-class and either professional or semi-professional, they will still be able to obtain their drugs. Their drugs of choice have a legitimate use, and it is unlikely that the government's attempt to prevent diversion will be more than partially successful. If our narcotics agents have been unable to keep off the open market drugs which have no legitimate use at all— heroin and marijuana—it hardly seems likely that they will be able to control chemicals legitimately in the possession of millions of citizens. I asked one amphetamine head in the Southwest how local supplies had been affected by the new law. "I heard about that law," he said, "but I haven't seen anybody getting panicked." Another user tells me prices have risen slightly, but not enough yet to present difficulties.

There are marked differences between these drug-users and the ones who make the newspapers. They're well educated (largely college graduates), are older (25 to 40), and middle-class (with a range of occupations: writers, artists, lawyers, TV executives, journalists, political aides, housewives). They're not like the high school kids who are after a kick in any form (some of them rather illusory, as one psychosomatic gem reported to me by a New Jersey teen-ager: "What some of the kids do is take a cigarette and saturate it with perfume or hairspray. When this is completely soaked in and dry, they cup the cigarettes and inhale every drag. Somehow this gives them a good high"), or college students experimenting with drugs as part of a romantic program of self-location. The kids take drugs "because it's cool" and to get high, but when you talk to them you find that most ascribe the same general high to a wide range of drugs having quite diverse effects; they're promiscuous and insensitive. There is considerable evidence to suggest that almost none of the college drug-users take anything illegal after graduation, for most of them lose their connections and their curiosity.

It is not likely that many of the thousands of solitary amphetamine abusers would join these groups. They take drugs to *avoid* deviance—so they can be fashionably slim, or bright and alert and functional, or so they can muster the *quoi que* with which to face the tedium of housework or some other dull job—and the last thing they want is membership in a group defined solely by one clear form of rule-breaking behavior. Several of the group members were first turned on by physicians, but a larger number were turned on by friends. Most were after a particular therapeutic effect, but after a while interest developed in the drug for its own sake and the effect became a cause, and after that the pattern of drug-taking overcame the pattern of taking a specific drug.

Some of the socialized amphetamine-users specialize. One takes Dexedrine and Dexamyl almost exclusively; he takes other combinations only when he is trying to reduce his tolerance to Dexamyl. Though he is partly addicted to the barbiturates, they do not seem to trouble him very much, and on the few occasions when he has had to go off drugs (as when he was in California for a few months and found getting legal prescriptions too difficult and for some reason didn't connect with a local Source), he has had no physiological trouble giving them up. He did, of course, suffer from the overwhelming depression and enervation that characterize amphetamine withdrawal. Most heads will use other drugs along with amphetamine—especially marijuana—in order to appreciate the heightened alertness they've acquired; some alternate with hallucinogens.

To the heroin addict, the square is anyone who does not use heroin. For the dedicated pillhead there is a slightly narrower definition: the square is someone who has an alcohol dependency; those who use nothing at all aren't even classified. The boozers do bad things, they get drunk and lose control and hurt themselves and other people. They contaminate their tubes, and whenever they get really far out, they don't even remember it the next day. The pillhead's disdain is some-times rather excessive. One girl, for example, was living with a fellow who, like her, was taking over 500 milligrams of amphetamine a day. They were getting on well. One night the two were at a party, and instead of chewing pills, her man had a few beers; the girl was furious, betrayed, outraged. Another time, at a large party that sprawled through a sprawling apartment, a girl had been on scotch and grass and she went to sleep. There were three men in the room, none of them interested in her sexually, yet they jeered and wisecracked as she nodded off. It was 4 or 5 A.M. of a Sunday, not too unreasonable a time to be drowsy. When they saw she was really asleep—breaking the double taboo by having drunk too much scotch and been put to sleep by it—they muttered a goddamn and went into another room; she was too depressing to have around.

There is an important difference in the drug-use patterns of the pillhead and opiate dependent: the latter is interested only in getting his drug and avoiding withdrawal; the former is also interested in perceiving his drugs' effects. I remember one occasion attended by someone who had obtained a fairly large mixed bag. In such a situation a junkie would have shot himself insensible; this fellow gave most of his away to his friends. With each gift he said something about a particular aspect of the drug which he found interesting. The heroin-user is far less social. His stuff is too hard to get, too expensive, his withdrawal too agonizing. But the pillhead is an experimenter. Often he seems to be interested as much in observing himself experiencing reactions as he is in having the reactions.

A large part of the attractiveness may be the ritual associated with this kind of group drug abuse: the *PDR* (a holy book), the Source (the medicine man whose preparations promise a polychromatic world of sensory and mystical experiences), the sharing of proscribed materials in a closed community, the sawing and grinding, the being privy to the Pythian secrets of colors and milligrams and trade names and contra-indications and optimum dosages. And, of course, using drugs is something of a fad.

But there are costs. Kicks are rarely free in this world, and drugs are no exception. One risks dysfunction; one can go out of one's head; one may get into trouble with the police. Though the users are from a socioeconomic class that can most likely beat a first offense at almost anything, there is the problem that legal involvement of any kind, whether successfully prosecuted or not, can cause considerable em-barrassment; an arrest for taking drugs may be negligible to a slum dweller in New York, but it is quite something else for a lawyer or reporter. And there is always the most tempting danger of all: getting habituated to drugs to such a degree that the drugs are no longer something extra in life but are instead a major goal.

One user wrote me, "Lately I find myself wishing not that I might kick the lunatic habit—but simply that our drug firms would soon develop something NEW which might refresh the memory of the flash and glow of that first voom-voom pill." I had asked him why take them at all, and he wrote, "I don't know. Really. Why smoke, drink, drive recklessly, sunbathe, fornicate, shoot tigers, climb mountains, gamble, lie, steal, cheat, kill, make war—and blame it all largely on our parents. Possibly to make oneself more acceptable to oneself."

Many of the pillheads are taking drugs not *only* to escape but also to have an experience that is entirely one's own. There is no one else to be propitiated, there are no explanations or excuses needed for what happens inside one's own head when one is turned on; words won't do, and that is as much a benefit as a disadvantage, because if you cannot describe, then neither can you discuss or question or submit to evaluation. The benefit and the risk are entirely one's own. Indiana University sociologist John Gagnon pointed out at a drug symposium held at Antioch College last year, "I'd like to argue that possibly in our attempt to protect people, we have underrepresented the real payoff for drug-taking as an experience, as a risk people want to run."

You select your own risks—that's what living is all about. For some of these drug-users, the risks currently being marketed do not have very much sales appeal: going South for the summer with SNCC is out because they feel that they are too old and that ofays aren't much wanted anyhow; going to Vietnam for Lyndon is absurd. So they go inside. A scarier place, but no one else can muddle around with it.

There is nothing *wrong* with using chemicals to help cope with life. That is one of the things science is supposed to do, help us cope, and the business of living can be rough at times. And we have the requisite faith: I am sure that far more Americans believe in the efficacy of a pill than believe in God. The problem arises when one's concern shifts so that life becomes an exercise in coping with the chemicals.

I think there has been an unfortunate imbalance in the negative publicity. For years the press has printed marvelous tales about all the robberies and rapes performed by evil beings whose brain tissue had been jellied by heroin. But it has rarely printed stories that point out that opiates make even the randiest impotent, or that alcohol, which has five hundred times as many addicts, is an important factor in sex offenses and murders.

Lately, attention has been focused on drug abuse and experimentation among college students. Yet all the college students and all the junkies account for only a small portion of American drug abuse. The adults, the respectable grown-ups, the nice people who cannot or will not make it without depending on a variety of drugs, present a far more serious problem. For them the drug experience threatens to disrupt or even destroy life patterns and human relationships that required many years to establish.

And the problem is not a minor one. Worse, it seems to be accelerating. As Ed advised one night, "You better research the hell out of it because I'm convinced that the next ruling generation is going to be all pillheads. I'm convinced of it. If they haven't dysfunctioned completely to the point where they can't stand for office. It's getting to be unbelievable. I've never seen such a transformation in just four or five years. . . ."

18 | **The Drug Takers** | James Mills

Narcotics are a normalized part of everyday life in some sections of our largest cities. Like the police, the people who live there know who the addicts are and understand their way of life, even when they do not accept that way of life.

Unlike what many people have believed, the life of the addict is not one of ecstasy and excitement. It is a dull and dreary existence in which the search for the drug consumes the addict's whole life. When he does get his normal dose, the drug does not fill him with ecstasy but simply enables him to continue without experiencing the pains of withdrawal.

From legal poppy fields in Turkey, by camel across the sands of Syria to the not-so-legal laboratories in Lebanon, then by ship to southern France for final refining, back to Italy and, courtesy of the Mafia, to New York's docks and airports—heroin comes to Harlem. And from Harlem the drug moves swiftly through the city of New York, as efficiently and regularly as milk from New Jersey or fish from Fulton Street. As it moves, the illicit stream swells into pools from which addicts in various parts of the city draw their daily needs. Addicts—and the police—are as aware of the selling locations as the housewife is of her neighborhood shopping center.

In the rush and confusion at 96th Street and Broadway, addicts gather on the corner to meet the pushers and buy their drugs—ignored by crowds of New Yorkers on their way to work. On the southwest corner of 82nd Street and Columbus Avenue, two blocks from Manhattan's Museum of Natural History and the expensive Central Park West apartments nearby, addicts spend thousands of dollars a day for heroin. In front of a drugstore at 47th Street and Broadway, within the chaotic glow of Times Square, unknowing tourists brush shoulder to shoulder with barbiturate addicts waiting stiff and zombielike for their connections. It's the same just two blocks south, among the honky-tonk bars and nightclubs, or down in Greenwich Village, where heroin and marijuana pass from hand to hand on the benches of Washington Square.

Of these hundreds of locations outside Harlem, one of the most typical is located at the corner of 71st Street where Broadway pushes through Amsterdam Avenue on its diagonal slice across Manhattan. To subway riders who use the stop there, the intersection is Sherman Square. To the drug addicts it is "Needle Park."

Needle Park, like the rest of the world of the big city narcotics addict, is peopled by a conglomeration of individuals who come from different backgrounds, have different ways of getting the money they need, and who prefer different combinations of drugs. Simply by hanging around Needle Park . . . you can meet a whole spectrum of addiction: Irene, a slight, wispy Lesbian addicted to "goofballs," barbiturates. Goofballs usually produce a quiet drowsiness, but also at times a tense aggressiveness that can be frighteningly unpredictable. Irene's behavior when she is high on GBs, which is most of the time, has created such havoc in the neighborhood restaurants that they no longer let her in. So sometimes she stands outside on the sidewalk and tries to shout at her friends through the window. After a while, she laughs uproariously and goes running on down the street with another girl.

There is Billy, who never stays around for long because he is trying desperately to stay clean. He just finished three years in Leavenworth for smuggling drugs from Mexico. Now he has had enough and wants to be square. He is trying to get a job, "but how can you explain three years out of your life? And no one in his right mind is going to hire a junkie."

Hank is a regular habitué. He is on *bombitas*—Spanish for "little bombs." In Harlem they cost a dollar; in Needle Park the price is $1.50 or $2. Hank has the customary symptoms of a *bombita* user. Because they are amphetamines, stimulants, he talks constantly, cannot sit still, and his arms and face are covered with sores where he has picked at the skin, sometimes with the illusion that bugs are crawling underneath.

And always, lurking in the shadows, haunting Needle Park, stands Mike, a tall, trench-coated Negro. Mike is a "take-off artist," and a man to keep away from. He supports his habit by taking off (robbing) connections, and almost anyone else in the junkie world who appears to have money.

When junkies meet, they talk incessantly about drugs. Which is better, heroin mixed with a *bombita* or with cocaine? Both cocaine and *bombitas* are stimulants, and either one combined with heroin, which is a depressant, produces a more pleasurable high than heroin alone. The mixture is called a "speedball." But cocaine is very expensive, so addicts agree that for the money, a *bombita*-and-heroin cannot be topped.

During one of these interminable conversations, someone said he had a friend who liked to shoot model airplane glue. No one else had heard of that. Sniffing glue, yes; but not shooting it. They had heard of people doing something to paregoric and shoe polish and then shooting it, but the high was reported to be no good. Heroin, of course, was the best. Heroin and a *bombita.* It gave the best high, completely relaxed, not a problem in the world.

But that's not really the best high, one addict said. Do you know what the best high *really* is? The voice was serious. Everyone turned and stayed very quiet to hear, maybe, of a new kind of high that was better than heroin, better than anything else. The best high—the voice was low and somber—is death. Silence. Man, that's outta sight, that's somethin' else. Yeah, no feelin' at all. Everyone agreed. The best high of all was death.

Junkies hang around Needle Park because it is surrounded by cheap hotels, needed by addict prostitutes; because three blocks away, a short walk for a sick junkie, are respectable neighborhoods which are good for burglary and "cracking shorts"—breaking into cars; and because, probably, a long time ago someone started selling dope there and the area just got to be known as a good place to make a connection—to "score."

Today much of the heroin in Needle Park comes from a man who lives in a very nice apartment on a pleasant East Side street. He buys heroin in "pieces" (ounces), cuts it and bags it, and hands it over on consignment to a handful of pushers—junkies themselves—who sell it for him. The pushers do not really have to push. It is a seller's market with heroin, and the junkies fight their way to any connection who has good stuff. The image of the sly pusher enticing nonusers into trying a free bag of heroin is pure myth.

The amount of payment the junkie pusher gets is the same anywhere in the city. Fifteen $3 bags are wrapped together with a rubber band (the package is called a half load). The pusher buys the package for $25, sells enough bags to recoup his investment, and uses the rest himself. Often the junkie pusher will deal "nickel bags" at $5 each, as well as $3 "Treys." These come in "bundles" similar to half loads, except that the package costs $75 and consists of 25 $5 bags. Sometimes a junkie pusher can get half loads or bundles on consignment. But if he decides to shoot up all the bags himself and beat the supplier for the money, his friends will soon be remarking that they haven't seen him around for a while. He usually keeps pushing until he is "busted" (arrested) or until he gets scared and decides to stop pressing his luck with the police, and return to less serious crimes to finance his habit.

From time to time the addict may voluntarily interrupt his life on the street to enter a hospital. (Several New York hospitals reserve beds for addicts.) His body has achieved such a high tolerance to heroin that he must shoot a huge number of bags—not just to get high, but to keep from getting sick. In the case of a prostitute, she may be getting so thin and sick-looking—so "strung out"—that she has been forced to reduce her price. In both cases the addict goes into a hospital to withdraw from the drug and get back to the point where just a bag or two will make him high.

The male junkie, when he isn't pushing, almost invariably turns to theft and burglary to support his habit.

Stringent search and seizure laws make it tough for detectives to produce much unshakable evidence against addicts and addict pushers. Merely being an addict is not a crime in New York; he must have drugs or a hypodermic needle in his possession. Many addicts—especially pushers—wear a rubber band on their wrists (a "dealer's band," some call it) which, if hooked properly around a deck of heroin, will send it flying if an approaching detective is spotted.

But when police are in a drug neighborhood they have no difficulty spotting addicts on the street. An experienced narcotics cop, or a longtime addict, can with surprising reliability spot a user in a group of 20 people, state with authority what kind of drug he is on, approximately how long it has been since his last fix, and whether or not he is at that moment "dirty," carrying drugs. Because heroin subdues appetite, the addict is almost always thin. He has a craving for sweets, and often carries a bottle of soda pop (although he may know that, to a detective, it is a badge of addiction). The backs of his hands are chronically puffed and swollen, from shooting in the veins there.

The addict is habitually dirty, his clothes filthy, and he stands slackly as if his body were without muscles. Waiting for a connection, he is nervous and intent, staring for minutes at a time in the direction from which he expects the pusher to come. Detectives know that when a group of addicts is standing around, talking, waiting, none of them is carrying heroin. But if you watch the group long enough suddenly it explodes, all the addicts walking off in different directions. The pusher has appeared and soon, one by one, they will make their roundabout way to him to "cop."

Once the addict has drugs on him, he keeps moving. He is about to achieve the one thing for which he lives, and he is not slow about it. His shoulders are hunched, his head is down, and he strikes out with what some detectives call a "leaving-the-set walk," as if he had just learned where a million dollars was hidden. When the heroin addict is high, his pupils are "pinned," constricted, and if the shot was sufficiently powerful he goes on a "nod"—his head drooping, eyelids heavy.

But though he appears terribly sleepy, he speaks coherently. His mind wanders, he daydreams, and everything he does, he does with maddening slowness. He can take 30 minutes to tie his shoelaces. But he always resists admitting that he is on a nod. He is very sleepy, he says, and if he stops talking in midsentence, he argues that he is not nodding, only trying to phrase the sentence properly. Once the addict has had his shot and is "straight," he may become admirably, though briefly, industrious, suddenly deciding to shine his shoes, brush his coat, comb his hair—all the while scolding himself bitterly for having slipped so far.

Even the seasons conspire to identify addicts. In winter, waiting to cop, they alone stand around in the snow and slush, apparently aimlessly. In summer, they alone wear long sleeves (to cover their "tracks" —needle marks). Because heroin users almost always feel cold, they wear piles of sweaters, even in hot weather.

When male and female addicts gather together, in a hotel room or public bathroom, the narcotics detective knows better than to suspect sexual activity. Heroin depresses sexual desire—men may become impotent, women often do not menstruate. (If a woman gives birth while she is addicted to heroin the infant also will be physically addicted and must live his first three days withdrawing from the drug). For most heroin addicts a sex crime would be impossible, and they are all contemptuous of stories about the "raging, dope-fiend, sex maniac."

Almost all heroin addicts are childishly immature; full of demands, empty of offerings. When they want something, they want it yesterday and they want it effortlessly. Nothing is their fault—their addiction, their degradation, their desperation. All are insecure, most dislike people, and—though the mechanics of obtaining and injecting drugs forces them into relationships with other people—most would prefer to be alone.

None can tolerate "changes." If the junkie goes looking for a connection and does not find him on the right corner at the right time, he grumbles about all the changes. Almost everything he is forced to do involves too many changes. He must go through changes to steal, to find a fence, to get a shot, to avoid police, but the addict is rarely violent. He wants heroin to get his fix with as few complications, as few changes, as possible, and be left in peace to shoot it. He prefers simple, nonviolent crimes—theft, burglary, prostitution.

When they are off heroin, addicts tend to be morose and restless. On heroin, when they are straight, they are pleasant, gentle, likable. Psychiatrists who have studied them over long periods know that most of them are extremely narcissistic, that their intense preoccupation with heroin is a surface manifestation of a more profound emotional preoccupation with themselves.

In pursuit of the drug they can bring to bear extraordinary cunning, nerve and acting ability. But once they have the fix in hand and the problem shifts from how to get drugs to how to avoid arrest, these qualities vanish. An addict who is arrested because a detective discovered heroin hidden in his pants cuff may, once he is released, immediately buy a deck of heroin and hide it in his pants cuff.

Perhaps the dominant emotional characteristic of the addict is his enormous compulsion to abdicate all responsibility for his own life. He craves to be told what to do. If he is encouraged to go to a hospital by someone he trusts, he will go; but soon, when he finds the hospital not to his liking, he will leave, and then blame the failure not on himself but on the person who urged him to go. An addict will walk along a street openly displaying a container of drugs, all but asking to be arrested. If a detective does spot the drug and arrests him, the addict will blame it on bad luck. He thus purges himself of the responsibility of choosing between jail and abstinence, or continued addiction on the street. He feels he has left the choice to fate.

Female addict prostitutes may, for the same reason, solicit men who are almost certainly detectives. One psychiatrist reported that when one of his addict patients saw another patient in an artificial lung, she became enraged and demanded the lung for herself, unconsciously demonstrating her wish to relinquish to the lung her ultimate responsibility—breathing.

19 | Exiles from the American Dream: The Junkie and the Cop | Bruce Jackson

Addicts and police live very close to each other. In fact, the police depend on addicts in various ways. The police are dependent for police to gain information that can be used to arrest and convict upon some addicts because the laws of evidence make it difficult users, or even pushers, without using informants. The police must therefore become a part of the addicts' world and must make extra-legal "deals" with its members, even when they hate that world. The police also use the addicts to justify their demands for more money and power.

In this essay Bruce Jackson has given a rare insight into this close involvement between police and addicts. It is a side of police work that most people know nothing about.

In the summer of 1966 I traveled around the country for a Cambridge research organization that had contracted with the President's Commission on Law Enforcement and Administration of Justice to study certain problems having to do with drug abuse and control in this country. The main part of my job was talking with and observing at work a spectrum of participants: police, judges, doctors, administrators, addicts, pushers, ex-addicts, rehabilitation personnel, and so on. We found early in the study that none of the sets of figures purporting to tell the numbers of drug abusers and their relationship to the economy were much good, and that almost everyone had The Answer. We spent the summer getting as many points of view as we could, then tried to make sense of those that were sufficiently rational and to evaluate those that seemed worth it.

After the report was written, I realized that many of my blacks and whites had gone to problematical gray, the burden of increased knowledge. I realized also that part of that knowledge was of a kind outside the numbers and specifics that fill government reports and sociological journal articles; it is composed of pieces of information that do not array themselves in nice neat patterns; they do not form pretty theses or admit nice tabular or verbal conclusions—but somehow I cannot help feeling that they are in many ways more important, more germane, than the figures and the charts. Art and science go around constructing and projecting coherences; the street does not think in coherences, it is just there.

An example: unlike police who deal with homicide or other major crimes, who have onetime or rare contact with their customers, the police who handle problems of morality rather than injury, crimes like prostitution and drug addiction, tend to develop a peculiar rapport with the people with whom they war. They do not deal in terms of single events, but in continuing relationships, some of which they must maintain in order to obtain information, others because there is no reason not to. This varies from city to city, but there is a clear level of consistency. The narcotics detective must live in the junkie's world, know his language, appreciate his pain; he may be—and often is—antagonistic to all of these, but he is rarely independent of them.

The sections that follow are from notes scribbled in police cars, in bars, on planes, on a beach, sitting in a park; they are some of those other pieces.

New York

Ray Viera is the larger, more volatile of the two. His hair is wavy with streaks of gray, and he tends to tap your shoulder when he is involved in a statement. Burt Alvins is smaller, wiry; most of his head is a short gray-flecked crew cut. Burt negotiates the green Lark around some construction on F.D.R. Drive; it doesn't feel much like a police car.

"Everybody lives outside the city now," one of them says.

"Not everybody," I say.

"I mean all the cops and firemen I know. Except for a couple of young single guys. Everybody else is out on the Island or up in Westchester. It's going to be just the poor and the illegal left in New York. People are moving out in droves. They're not doing it to escape the taxes. Taxes are just as high out there. They're doing it to keep their children together."

They complain about court decisions. "We've become robots. We can't think, we're mechanical men."

"Everybody I know quits at twenty years to the day. It's not the job he dislikes, it's the handcuffing."

"A thing a normal person would consider suspicious a policeman can't consider suspicious because we're robots."

"I'd give a month's pay to bring Earl Warren here and give him the tour I'm giving you."

"There's legitimate people here. They're suffering, they're in jail."

I ask how to break through the hostility, what you do about the reputation for brutality.

"You just count the days you have left."

We drive along 118th Street. The area crawls with big-city specialties: numbers, junk, whores. Garbage piles up in back, between the houses. The garbage men can't get in there because the backs are locked, so the stuff mounts and mounts, and every once in a while they make an assault and get some of it out, chasing away rats as big and careless as dogs.

"We have to go see somebody."

"One of our informers," Ray says. "This guy's not stupid. He's intelligent. He's a nice guy. Wait till you see him though."

We enter a building just above Central Park. Someone lives on the first floor. The second, up the narrow dark stairway that is even darker after the bright sun, is vacant. All the doors are open; one is unhinged and lies flat in the room, as if something walked right in without bothering to stop. Another door hangs at a grotesque angle, the top hinge ripped off. More rubbish in there. A few empty bottles. We go up another flight, and Ray goes to Elmer's door. It is unlocked, and he eases it open slowly. Elmer is sitting on the bed, a blanket over his knees. "Anybody here?" Ray asks.

"No. I'm alone."

Ray waves us in. The room is about twelve by twelve. A big, old TV is on a bureau by the wall. A new Sony is on another bureau, turned on to a talk show. Elmer tells us a prostitute friend bought it for him as a present.

"How are your legs, Elmer?" Ray asks.

Elmer moves the blanket from his thighs. On both are long running sores, about four or five inches long and a half inch or so wide; they look deep; something oozes.

"Jesus Christ," Burt says. "Why don't you let us get you in the hospital for a while?"

"Maybe next week."

"Those sores don't look so good."

"I can't go in this week. You know."

"How are your arms?"

"Feel a little better." He holds his forearms out and moves the fingers. A Popeye caricature: from the elbows up, the arms are the thin sticks of an old man; below the elbow, they are swollen like thighs. The fingers all look like oversize thumbs. Like his thighs, Elmer's arms are covered with scars that look like strip photos of the surface of the moon. There are too many of the dime- and quarter-size craters to count.

"This is Bruce, Elmer. He's a new man, and we're breaking him in."

Elmer looks up, noticing or acknowledging me for the first time. He nods and shrugs. They make a date to meet somewhere later in the week.

"You sure you don't want us to get you in a hospital, Elmer?" Ray asks.

Elmer says no.

For me, Ray asks, "Elmer, what you shooting now?"

"About eight bags."

"When did you start?"

"1955."

"And how old are you now?"

"Forty-eight."

There's a silence, directed to me. Elmer looks sixty-five or seventy, and they all know I'd thought him an old man. He folds the blanket over his thighs, and we go out. On the way, Burt gives Elmer a few bucks and says get some cigarettes.

Going down the stairs, Ray says, "If he tells you he's shooting eight bags, that means he's shooting twelve. That's sixty bucks a day. Seven days a week. Four hundred and twenty dollars a week. Almost what I make a month." Elmer, obviously, is in some business activities about which the police prefer not to ask.

Most New York addicts, I know, spend less than twenty dollars a day for narcotics. Few look as grim as Elmer. But enough do. And enough wind up dead because of infection or accidental overdose; many have TB. The physiological debilitation and destruction result from concomitants of drug taking: the junkie spends his money for drugs instead of food, his drugs are cut with quinine and other chemicals that often do him considerable damage, and worst of all, the material he injects and the instruments he uses are so unsanitary that he constantly risks the kinds of infection that have scarred Elmer. The junk itself, so long as it does not exceed the addict's tolerance, is not really as physiologically harmful as cigarettes or alcohol, but the life stye is vicious.

"Some of these guys," Burt says, "they get worse than Elmer. Ruin all the veins in the arms and legs, burn them out, and they shoot in the mouth. And when that goes, in the penis. Hurts like hell, they say, but they can find the vein."

I ask them if their visiting Elmer's apartment in daylight might not get him into trouble with other addicts. They say no, they spend a lot of time questioning addicts, most of whom are not informers, standard procedure.

"These people around here—they know who you are?"

"Sure, they know us. Even if they'd never seen us before, they'd know us. If you're white around here, you're either a bill collector or the Man. They maybe don't know which Man you are, but you're one of them."

"Or a trick looking for a whore," Burt says.

"You still get white tricks coming up here?"

"They'll always be coming up here."

We drive past a crap game. There are about fifty men standing around. Some of them yell.

They talk about Elmer. "I'm worried about him, Burt. Can't we get him into some hospital?"

"He doesn't want to go. We can't force him."

"Well, how about we get him some antibiotics for those sores? They're just awful."

"You have to have a prescription for that stuff."

"Maybe I can get somebody to let me have some."

"Heroin you can get; for penicillin you need a prescription."

We stop for a traffic light. A kid about five years old looks in the car, at me, says, "Fuck you, cop," and walks away.

We sit in the car by the 125th Street New York Central station. Two junkies they know hustle down 125th, counting money. We know where they are going, but there isn't sufficient cause to follow and arrest.

"I know what the courts are trying to do—protect the honest citizens. But you know something: in all the years we've been in this business, we've never hit one guy that was a square."

"The trouble with this job," Burt says, "is you take it home with you. We get together, and our wives say, why don't you talk about something else. They don't understand."

"You can't put it off at night," Ray says.

I look through their report book. They get two days off per week, but I notice that they work at least one, and sometimes both of them, either going out with an undercover agent or appearing in court. Many of the workdays run twelve to sixteen hours. I ask why they stick with it.

"I think it's a challenge," Burt says. "I like the work. But as my partner and I have told you a number of times, our hands are tied. To do this kind of a job I guess you have to have some dedication in you. It's a losing battle: for every one you arrest, there's five to take their place. But when you do make a good arrest, it can make the whole thing worthwhile."

I say something about Elmer.

"They ought to put a picture of him in the papers," Ray said. "Show some of these people."

"You could show them a picture of Elmer," Ray says. "Tomorrow they pick up a paper to see what the Giants did. That's it. As far as it goes."

Driving downtown we pass through Central Park. "It's like reverse shock treatment," Ray says. We see a spreading plume of black smoke over on the East Side, somewhere in the Eighties.

Burt: "Probably a junkie cooking up."

Ray: "Good-sized cooker."

And Burt: "You come back after a day off and hope maybe things are going to be a little different. Then it's not. There's still glass in the street. The same people."

Houston

Morning in the Narcotics Squad room. Captain Jack Renois and Don McMannes are the only ones in. Hooker, the secretary, does things and fetches coffee. The detectives come in around 11:00 or 11:30 and wait for the phone calls from informers. Things come alive around noon, after the addicts get up. One of the detectives is selling a shotgun; it is passed around and admired.

A phone rings. An addict snitching on another addict. For money, for a break on a case. Or maybe just talking for a while. I begin to appreciate the odd symbiosis. The addicts and the cops move in the same world, live the same hours, wait for deals to happen on the same streets. One addict had said something to me the week before, complaining about the hassles he was always in, and one police official had complained to me this morning about the difficulty he had getting adequate funds and equipment. Both used exactly the same sentence: "We got to scuffle for every fucking thing."

Don comes back into the room; he had been on the phone for about thirty minutes. "He just wanted to talk for a while," he tells me. "Somebody I arrested once." The addicts sometimes call up officers, not to snitch or bitch, but just to talk to someone who understands. For them, no one appreciates their hassles and their world better than the cop, who is so close they don't even consider him a square.

On Lieutenant Kennedy's desk: *"FIAT JUSTITIA, RUAT CAELUM."* And under it, in small letters, "Let justice be done, though the heavens may fall." "I saw it a long time ago and I liked it and it's been on my desk ever since," he says. "A reminder, I guess."

With one of the detectives, I go out to visit an informer. She is a slight pretty girl with dark eyes. Two children are in the house, and she says she can't stay in the car talking for very long. She talks about Joey, with whom she lives, currently in jail needing bond. "They say that county farm's a bad place. I don't know. Maybe I'll get him out."

She used to be a good booster, but no more. Shoplifting has become too dangerous: "I got too many children now. Nobody to take care of them if I go to the joint." A new connection had come by a few days ago and given her fifty dollars' worth of narcotics without asking for money.

"How come?" asks the detective. "He want some trim?"

"I don't know. Maybe. If Joey wasn't there." She tells us where the connection lives and who is with him, and the phone number.

"You hooked again?"

"No. I can't afford it. I shoot all the dope I can get, though."

"You high now?"

"No. I had two caps this morning. That's all."

Later the same day: riding with Mike Chavez and his partner, Charley. While Mike is at a phone booth, Charley tells me he has just been transferred into Narcotics from Vice. He says about every whore he knows is on some kind of drugs, that whenever they broke into a prostitute's apartment they found narcotics or pills.

"Did you ever file?"

"No."

"Why not?"

"Wouldn't stand up. Almost everything we would do is illegal. They know it, and we know it. Our job was mainly harassment. Make them uncomfortable enough to move on." Later he tells me it is as hard to make a prostitution case as a narcotics case. A few weeks earlier in Harlem, a New York policeman had told me the same thing.

Mike comes back. "Anything?" Charley asks.

"No."

Chavez has never taken the test for sergeant. Only one sergeant is permitted in the Narcotics unit, and if Chavez were promoted, he would be forced to change assignments. He likes the work and is very good at it.

He tells me that the talk and newspaper articles about violent addicts are nonsense; what bothers him is the crime associated with addiction. I mention the six million or so alcoholics, and all the damage they do. Chavez pulls up to a booth to make another call. While he is gone, Charley tells me what I said is irrelevant. Chavez comes back and says, "Funny, what you were saying. They have a bar in that store, and I could see that every stool was occupied." He says he would like to find some other way of handling the problem, but he doesn't know one that would work. He shrugs and says it bothers him sometimes. "But I'm a policeman, you know." He turns to Charley, sitting in the back, and says, "You got your gun?"

"Yeah."

I turn and see on the seat a .38 automatic. He tells me you need a holster for a revolver and everything bulges, but an automatic can be just tucked in the belt. I ask Mike it he has his.

"In the trunk."

Later that night, Donny tells me they almost never need weapons. No Houston addict would draw on a detective because the addicts know the detectives aren't going to shoot without a good reason. "Only time any of them ever does anything with a gun is to say, 'I got a gun.' I say, 'Where?' and he points, and I say, 'Put it on the table,' and he does. Or if he has one in his hand when we bust in, he just swings it around and hands it over. We all know each other."

Austin

I was in the homicide room of the police station waiting for Lieutenant Harvey Gann, the detective in charge of the Vice and Narcotics Squad. According to friends of mine in Houston and Huntsville, he is a very good policeman. Gann came in, laughing. He and his partner had just been out on a narcotics watch that didn't work out. They were using an old pickup truck and had stopped for a red light when two women walked over, and one said, "You want to have a good time?"

"How much?"

"Ten and three."

"What's the three for?"

"The room, baby."

Gann asked if the same applied for her friend and his friend. The other woman said yes. Gann noticed a tall Negro standing in a nearby doorway, and said, "Who's he?"

"Just an old nothing sonofabitch that hangs around."

Gann and his partner got out of the truck, took off their LBJ hats and lensless glasses.

"Goddamn, Lieutenant! It's you again!" The woman began laughing.

"You see," he told me, "I had arrested her four times before. And I put those hat and glasses right back on because we couldn't all fit in front, and I had to ride with them in the back of the pickup, and I'd be damned if I'd have anybody I know see me riding around town in a pickup truck with two old whores like that."

New York

The undercover man is late.

The two detectives, Al Koch and Ray Imp, lean against the phone booth they use for an office. The phone has an "Out of Order" sign on it that is phony. The two men are easily identifiable (one is about 6 feet 3 inches and has shocking red hair; the other is about 5 feet 10 inches and is shaped like a triangle but gives the feeling of a tank), and when they appear on the street, the dealers disappear, so they hover outside the Village perimeter, wait for a call from someone telling them a person they want to arrest is at a specific location, then go in and come out quickly.

The undercover man arrives at eight, an hour late. His name is Sam, and even though I know he is a police officer, I can't quite believe it—the first qualification of an undercover agent.

Al tells me it will be boring waiting with them. He suggests I go with Sam.

"But I know people in the Village."

"Do they know what you're doing in town?"

"No."

"O.K. You go with him. They'll think he's just some beatnik friend of yours. We'll just be standing here until he calls anyhow. But take that notebook and cigar and pen out of your pocket."

I hand over my things and go away with Sam.

We walk to the Rienzi, where we are to meet someone named Wilson, his informer. Wilson isn't there, and Sam curses him, saying he can't stand an unpunctual man. He tells me the statistics reporting 60,000 addicts in the United States are all wrong, there are hundreds of thousands of them. I must have looked incredulous because he says, "Yeah, man, I'm serious. Look around you. Half these people smoke weed."

"You don't get addicted to marijuana. They're not addicts."

"Goddamn right they are."

We walk down the street. Someone says hello to me, and I nod. Sam says, "I'll tell you who uses weed all the time: those folk singers. Bunch of addicts."

"Oh."

"You know any of those folk singers?"

"A few."

"They use weed."

We pass one place just as a four-man singing group is going in with their guitars. They pass in front of us. One of them sees me and waves; another says, "Hi, Bruce." I wave back. Sam looks at me queerly, then shrugs it off.

We go back to the Rienzi and talk about Court decisions.

"Those bastards. What this country needs is a Hitler for a while. Get these people off the streets. Should have elected Goldwater; he'd have straightened that Court out. You know why I hate addicts?" I shake my head. "I'll tell you why: I got a nice wife, over on Staten Island. She never heard a dirty word in her life. A nice girl." He says it with finality. I don't make the connection, but I decide to let it ride; it is too early in the evening to reveal my opacity.

We watch the teen-age girls in their carefully considered outfits.

We go into a bar, and over a beer he talks about his work. "Shouldn't we talk about something else? Someone might be listening."

"Nah. Nobody's listening. Nobody listens here." I don't tell him that when I go into bars like this, I always eavesdrop. Constitutional.

We go up the street to get something to eat, but on the way meet Wilson, the informer. With him is another man, who wears khakis, a white T-shirt, and a yellow sport shirt open all the way except for the bottom button. Wilson, the informer, goes off to talk with Sam.

The man in the yellow shirt says to me, "Who you with?"

"Huh?"

"I said who you with?"

"What are you talking about?"

"It's OK, man, I'm undercover too."

"A city cop?"

"No," he says, shaking his head.

"FBN?"

"No."

"Who?"

"FDA." He pauses, maybe to see if I'm going to make a wisecrack. When I don't, he says, "You city?"

I shake my head.

"Federal?"

I shake my head.

"Then who are you undercover for?"

"I'm not a cop."

"Come on, man."

A thin effeminate man in his twenties lopes up the street, walking sine waves. "My consciousness has expanded, expanded!"

"Man, is he drunk," the FDA man says.

"It might be something else." The thin guy weaves back. "What you on, man?" I ask.

"Five days on, five days off."

"Off and on what?"

"LSD, psilocybin off days. Little junk to keep the heebies away." He bumps into the FDA man and pats the shoulder of his yellow shirt. "Ain't it a bitch when your family's square?"

"Your family square?"

"You don't know. My father is——— [he names someone in city government whose name we know], and he is square."

On an off chance there's another celebrity with the same name, I ask, "Which————?"

"You know which one."

"Come on."

He pulls out his wallet and shows us his collection of identification cards, credit cards, and licenses; they all say————, Jr. Sam joins us. I look for Wilson, the informer, but he has disappeared. Thin says his family is down on him because he uses drugs.

"What else?"

"Drugs and because of the homosexual business."

"Are you queer?"

"Maybe a little."

He says he can get, in quantity, marijuana and pills. Sam and the FDA man try to stare one another down: if Thin produces grass, he is Sam's; if he produces pills, he is FDA's. Thin weaves in and out of the street. He goes to peer in a car window.

"I thought he'd pat my gun when he was tapping my shoulder just now," FDA says.

"You wearing a gun?" Sam says.

"Yeah. You?"

"I got a little .25."

"Ah. I got my .38 service."

"That cannon. You're crazy. If you ask me, you're better off with nothing."

Thin swings back to the sidewalk. Wilson, the informer, returns and points at someone, and Sam says, "Oh, oh, there's my man," and goes off down Bleeker. FDA wanders away with Thin, talking hippy.

"Come on," Wilson, the informer, says. "We got to stick with Sam."

"Where is he?"

"I don't know. Maybe he went into the park." We walk toward the park. "You new on the squad?"

"I'm not on the squad."

"Oho. A fed, huh?"

"What makes you think I'm a cop?"

"C'mon, man, it's OK. I'm an informer. We're all in this together. It's like I'm a half-cop, you know."

"Oh, all right, I'm working for the feds. But I'm not a cop. I'm a schoolteacher, and I'm doing a study."

"Hey, that's good. Say, what's your undercover name?"

"Bruce."

"What's your real name?"

"Bruce."

"You can't do that. You got to have an undercover name."

"I always use Bruce."

"OK, man, it's your *schtik*. We might meet someone, and I might have to introduce you or something. Where do you say you come from?"

"Cambridge."

"Come on, man, the Village is crawling with people from Cambridge."

"I *am* from Cambridge."

"Jesus Christ, man!"

We walk into Washington Square Park.

(Wilson stopped and talked with some characters he knew, and I stayed out of the light, which he seemed to appreciate. I knew several undercover agents had been exposed, "burned" in the argot, and badly beaten recently. I wondered what this nut was leading me into. I wondered what they were all leading themselves into. These people were so different from the cops uptown, the serious and competent Alvins and Viera, with whom I'd sat that afternoon in a car in the west Eighties, talking with an informer while pretty polished women and expensive fat ladies passed us by, seeing only four men in a car; that informer knew he was dead if he should be seen with us, and the conversation was serious. Here it seemed they'd adjusted to the madcap crowd, not only in appearance but in procedure, in thought. A crazy game world on both sides again, like Houston. But different.)

We walk on toward the arch. Wilson tells me he'd like to work for the FBI as an undercover man in the Communist Party. "They ever use people for anything like that?"

"I believe they have, on occasion."

"You think they'd hire me? It's not like I'm inexperienced. And I hate this amateur crap."

"I don't know."

"They wouldn't take me in the army. I would have been good in the army, but they wouldn't take me."

"Why not?"

"'Cause I'm an addict. Got a record. All that crap." He shrugs. "But I'd sure like to be an undercover man working on Commies. Man, I'm a natural. Who'd ever suspect."

We spot Sam. Wilson and I sit next to him on the bench. Sam tells us where the suspect is sitting. Wilson gets up, grabs my arm, and says, "Come on, man."

"Where we going?"

We walk behind the public toilets to a phone booth, and I wonder again about the setups. If even the police, who should know better, want to think I'm a cop, surely the other side would be willing to make the assumption. He calls the phone booth where Al and Ray wait. Wilson describes the suspect. "In the park, man, on Junkies' Row. Junkies' Row, I said." He hangs up, and we go back to watch the bust go down, but neither Sam nor the suspect is there. We rush out of the park, but see neither of them.

"You sit on that rail over there, and when Al comes by, you say, 'I don't know where the sonofabitch is.' Keep your head turned away. That way, if anyone is nearby, they'll think he asked you about someone and you wouldn't tell him anything; if no one is near, it won't look like you're talking to him at all. Everybody in the Village knows Al and Ray."

I sit on the rail, watching out of the corner of my eye for the two detectives to appear. I see them coming. As they near, I coolly turn away, waiting subtly to deliver my code message.

Several shoes stop in front of me, toes pointing my way. "Hey, Bruce," Al says. "Where'd they all go?"

"Shhh! We'll be spotted."

"Ah. Where'd they go?"

"Down McDougal."

They go down McDougal. I wait a tactful time, then follow. I see Al standing on the sidewalk across the street from Minetta's. I sit on a stoop about four doors away. Al comes over and sits next to me.

"Go away, Al. We'll be seen together." I feel as paranoid as a pusher.

"Ah, it's just the school kids. Nobody will notice."

A policeman with a walkie-talkie strapped to his body tells us to move on.

"In just a minute, officer," Al says. The policeman says make sure it's just a minute, and Al says we certainly will and thank you officer.

We watch the girls in their carefully considered outfits and the boys in their pageboys. "Bunch of kids," Al says. "Let's go back to the car."

"What if I get noticed walking with you?"

"Nah. Don't worry about it."

We walk back to the car.

After a while Ray comes with another detective, and we go back to the phone booth. It rings, and Ray answers. He listens for a moment, then sticks his head out. "Hey, Bruce: you're burned."

"I'm what?"

"You're burned. They saw you with Al, and they all know you're a cop."

"I'm not a cop."

"Tell *them*."

They all laugh. "Way it goes," one of them says.

It is almost 1 A.M., and the street is thinning as the action moves indoors and only the desperate are left. No business here. They adjust the "Out of Order" sign and decide to quit early for a change.

Los Angeles

Bill Sanderson and Jack White look like TV actors who are supposed to look like L.A. detectives: both are good-looking, young, bright detective sergeants; both have been attending college part-time and expect a degree this year; both have been on the police force for eight years, in narcotics for less than one year.

Like police everywhere, they complain about some of the Supreme Court decisions, but they do not seem to feel as hamstrung. It takes more work and more men, but still the jobs seem to get done. "I think the Supreme Court is trying to force the problems back on the community that created the problems," one of them says.

"I can see why some people go to heroin," the other says. "It is the ultimate: it puts you to sleep and keeps you awake."

In Watts, we stop at the intersection of Central and Vernon. Where a large drugstore used to be there is now a tremendous tent and a hand-painted sign: *You must see and hear Rev. Eugene Lewis. Evangelist who ministers like Christ.* Like the topless joints in San Francisco, Watts is one of those places visitors must see; one gets the same feeling of futility in both. White and Sanderson point out locations where they made interesting drug arrests, locations where they hope to make others, places where they were during the riot. We are supposed to be discussing narcotics, but during the early part of the afternoon it is the riot. They still do not understand it; no one seems to. The houses are a surprise to me: in the East it would be a lower-middle-class neighborhood in a residential town. Parks, lawns, some cars. If you don't have a car, I find out, it takes an impossible amount of time to get around out here. Still, it is so unlike Harlem. Had so overwhelming a riot occurred first in swelling and wretched Harlem, we might have dismissed what Watts said: a man could want and need more than a house.

Later, we have dinner in a Mexican restaurant around the corner from the temple Aimee Semple McPherson built; then we ride over to Hollywood. The radio gives Jack White a woman's phone number. The first booth cheats him out of two dimes, the second booth works.

White makes a date to meet her, and we race back to headquarters to pick up another car and some buy money. A lieutenant comes with us. We follow Jack to the bar, then drive down half a block and park in the shadows of a closed garage.

The lieutenant, just off vacation, says, "It gets harder and harder to generate enthusiasm for this kind of mess."

"Vacations do that," Bill says.

"It's not the vacation. Just getting a little tired of it."

After a while, Jack comes out of the bar with two women. One of them gets into the car with him, the other goes away. He U-turns and goes up the street, and we follow him at a distance.

Jack parks in front of an apartment house, and we park under a streetlamp fifty yards behind. There are three cars between us. With the light directly overhead, our car is not so suspicious: you can't see anyone inside unless you are quite close. I can't see anything in the other car, but Bill says Jack and the woman are still in it. He tells me they are probably arguing about whether or not Jack will be allowed to go inside with her. Jack isn't going to give her a chance to go out a back door with the money, and he wants to find out what apartment the man with the stash is in so we can move in later—if there is a man inside; it might be a phony deal.

It gets tense. If there is someone inside, there may be trouble: if Jack is recognized, he is unarmed and might not be near enough a window to call for help. We wait. Nothing moves in the car ahead, and after a while Bill wonders too. He gets out of our car, strolls down the block away from both cars, crosses in the dark somewhere below, walks up a side street, comes back down the opposite side, then retraces his steps. He gets back in. "They're still there."

Footsteps from down the block. A man approaches, reading a magazine in the dark. He slows down when he's under streetlamps, speeds up in the dark places between. He crosses directly in front of our car, his face buried in the magazine. "Now isn't that something," the lieutenant says. The man is reading *Startling Detective*.

More time passes. Jack's car lights up and U-turns, going back toward the bar. We duck, let it go a little bit, then do the same, going pretty fast. We come out of the U-turn, run a red light, and zip past a patrol car.

"Uh," I say.

"I guess they recognized me. Or the car," Bill says.

Jack is stopped at a red light a block ahead. He turns right, then stops in front of the bar. After a while the woman gets out and Jack drives away. We follow him and park both cars in a dark place.

He tells us the woman wouldn't let him come inside, and he refused to trust her with the money. "C'mon baby, take a chance," she said. "Everybody gets screwed sometimes in this business."

"Not me," he told her.

They tell me they've been having trouble nailing a couple of Cuban traffickers. The lieutenant says he liked the old days better. "I'd rather work a nice clean old Mexican dope peddler. You go boot his door in, take him down, and that's all there is to it."

I'll tell you something: it is not *just* a nitty-gritty world out there; it is a thing more unreal sometimes than the one we academics are usually accused of maintaining. You discover after a while that no one wears a white hat except the man who is talking to you right now; everyone spouts dogma except that single voice under that single white Stetson. Little Pavlovian mechanisms set junkies and cops in the same motions, day after day after day. The élan varies with the jurisdiction: in New York it is cold and faithless antagonism with exceptions, part of the general *Weltanschauung;* in Texas, where everyone has a gun, the policeman and criminal feel closer to one another.

It is little people, little, little people, playing out an ugly little game among themselves and taking it with precious and desperate seriousness, positing some lovely and fragile élan because both sides know that no one else in the world is willing to love them. Exiled from our American dream where everyman has his soporific and his weapon, the junkie and the cop find themselves bound to one another in one agonizing coil, and like Burton and Taylor in *Virginia Woolf,* they've learned the visceral lesson: people who bleed each other need each other.

20 | Involvement in the Drug Scene |
James Carey

*As is well known, the use of marijuana and other drugs has be-
come a common, taken-for-granted occurrence on many college
campuses. Most campus drug use is occasional and has not become part of the individual's way of life. But for many students
today taking drugs—especially smoking marijuana—has become
symbolic of a way of life that is in opposition to what they see as
the "straight" or "bourgeois" way of life. Marijuana use has become a symbol of alienation and attack. These symbolic meanings have become an important reason for the spread of drug use
among college students.*

*The different motives and patterns of drug use are well illus-
trated in James Carey's study of drug use in the Berkeley area,
one of the most important centers of college drug use in the country. But he also shows that there are certain basic patterns to the
process of becoming committed to drug use.*

*First, he shows that "everyone" begins with the feeling that
"something is wrong with society." Second, he then goes on to
show the details and stages of the commitment process. This
second part of his study adds greatly to the understanding of the
commitment process to drugs first revealed in Howard Becker's
classic work on marijuana users (republished in his book on Outsiders).*

Sense of Disillusionment

The beginning for everyone seems to be some critical awareness of
the way things are in society. A sense of disillusionment is strong. As a
24-year-old reformed head and laboratory technician put it:

> I guess it takes a dissatisfaction with—first you have to be dissatisfied
> with what you see around you in society. Because if you're satisfied with
> other people and yourself, and just whatever you see when you walk

From James T. Carey, *The College Drug Scene* (Englewood Cliffs, New
Jersey: Prentice-Hall). Reprinted by permission. Copyright © 1968.

> down the street or look out the window, then you'll probably never take
> it, because, because, if you're satisfied with it, then you accept all the
> norms. One of the norms is that you don't smoke pot. And, eventually,
> somebody is going to come along and offer you some. And, eventually if
> enough people offer it to you, you are going to take some.

Our questions focused on our respondents' situation prior to initial
use: the kind of scene in which they were moving, what their feelings
were about it, and so on. There are some problems in retrospective
reporting. Our respondents' replies may be inaccurate. They may not
remember or, more likely, their present situation may distort their recol-
lections. The critical stance of Colony* members might be much more a
function of later involvement in the drug scene than something which
existed prior to their first using drugs. Suffice it to say that they perceived themselves as more disillusioned with society than their peers,
prior to "turning on" for the first time. This usually went along with a
sense that they were defined by others as different—too "restless," or
"loners" or "too imaginative" by parents and school authorities. One 26-
year-old systematic user and part-time artist put it this way:

> I'd been drawing all my life, and scared my folks to death. They didn't
> like that at all. They didn't like the idea of me not adapting to the dog
> eat dog world, and being in what everyone calls a dream world.

A 27-year-old married woman who eventually became a hard-core user
linked up her own personal dissatisfaction with the shape of the large
society:

> I've always been dissatisfied and I think this holds true for my husband,
> too. With ourselves, as well as with things around us, the way we see
> things as being and how wrong-headed people are. And what in the hell
> is wrong with the world, and why do people have wars and that sort of
> thing?

The fundamental disillusionment comes because of society's hypocrisy—proclaiming one set of standards and doing something else. They
say we're interested in peace yet we are involved in a war against a
weak nation; they say we are interested in equality yet we have segregation; they say we're interested in freedom yet we suppress divergent
views. A 22-year-old user-dealer expressed this same view:

> [Society's] morality has had hassles with every other type of morality,
> you dig? They have suppressed people. They suppress right here in this
> country . . . The Indian was smoking grass, and hunting buffalo, having
> his little fights amongst himself, and all that, you dig? But the cat wasn't
> that bad, man to get to be damn near wiped out, so that there is only a
> population [of Indians] in the United States a population only big
> enough to fill Rhode Island. Man, that's terrible! And there were more
> than 900 different tribes of Indians on this continent, man.

* [Ed. note: "The Colony" refers to the area in Berkeley, California, where the
author did much of his research. This area is characterized by a drug-using,
nonconformist population.]

Not only is society hypocritical; it is rigid or "up tight." It is unable to be spontaneous, to let go. But more than that it doesn't want anyone else to, either. A 24-year-old hard-core user stated the case forcefully:

> (Speaking of reaction to beats) They're afraid of our place. They're afraid of our divergence from their solid norm, because they're so afraid to step out of theirs. You know they couldn't. They couldn't anymore go and turn around and grow a beard and wear dirty clothes and not wash for several days than . . . most of the hip people that I know are, have more, stand more on principle, than those people. It seems to me that those people aren't really taking their principles seriously, they're not taking too much at all seriously, . . . so that they really get an insane sick thing out of putting everything down, you know. Like an angry, drunk, clean slob, frat rat. He's angry at everything you know. He's angry at his next door neighbor. But it's a game there. . . . They call each other bad names all the time and they call some people on the street bad names all the time. Because that's their game—call everybody down you can.

The term "up tight" seems to point to a certain kind of wooden or martinet behavior exhibited by straight people. It refers to an inability to bend or to accept different ways of doing things or different notions of what constitutes right and wrong. The same young man continued:

> They feel that every action they do has to conform to a ritual, otherwise it's not right. You can't do anything that's spontaneous or from yourself. You make love like in the toothpaste ad, talk to your children like, like "Father Knows Best." . . . they've lost the natural ecstasy of living, man. Rigid as sort of a hollow block of wood so that you're kind of tight on the outside but if you konk it a couple of times,—sounds like a drum—like Is there anything going on inside of there?

Other themes are connected with the acute sense of the hypocrisy and rigidity of the straight world. One relates to the kind of status striving which does not permit any kind of enjoyment. An unemployed 21-year-old head voiced this criticism:

> Ah, knowing that "yes, you have to work, you know." But you don't have to work in order to buy a 1965 Buick for your wife. All you need is a 1953 Plymouth, man, to get you from here to there. . . . See, all these people are working for status. To build a house and live in—to build an image and live in it.

The sense of disillusionment leads to questioning the legitimacy of society's norms. Initial use of illegal drugs such as marihuana commonly occurs when structural circumstances favor it and when the novice is aware that ideas which neutralize its stigmatized character are known. The structural circumstances and the neutralizing ideas are so interrelated that little is gained by insisting on historical priority. A 24-year-old reformed head spoke about the gradual awareness of official deception about marihuana:

> I remember seeing movies when I was a kid, and they showed movies on drug addicts and everything, you know, little dramatizations of, of junkies and people that smoked marihuana and they painted a really bad picture like, look kids, don't ever get involved in this . . . this is what it's like, really bad people sitting around, shooting up dope, or smoking pot, really criminal type people. And they'd actually come out with lies, you know. They'd say "well marihuana was addicting and that if you take it twice, you automatically turn into a raving maniac, or something . . ." and then you find out, well these people lied to me, society in general has really lied to me, he said that, . . . They said a lot of things about drugs that weren't true.

A 19-year-old heavy user and part-time dealer further described the process:

> A person . . . can't have helped but hear that grass is, you know, when you're growing up that grass is, you know—marihuana and juvenile delinquency and all that. And . . . I think a person who tries it, having had all this knowledge about it before, suddenly he realizes something he has been told is wrong all his life is suddenly not wrong, that this can't help but lead him to think the same way about other things.

The claims society makes on its members to comply with norms relating to drug use cease to have meaning at this point. A 25-year-old graduate student much involved in the drug scene noted:

> . . . the thought of that when you take drugs you recognize that the frameworks don't have such absolute value as you had once seen . . . people who take marihuana are less concerned with the trivia of American values. In America as a country which spends more sometimes for the packaging of an article in the supermarket or an automobile than it does on the substance itself and it does the same with people and their characters and their attitudes and their jobs and their livelihood. . . . Often, much more attention is put to the packaging than to the content. People who smoke marihuana—this is usually one of their immediate reactions— they slow down a little. . . . They slow down and they say "hmm," they start noticing things in people's character that they have been moving too fast to see. . . .

Circumstances of First Use

While a profound state of dissatisfaction with the larger society and the values it proclaims usually precedes extensive experimentation with marihuana, the dissatisfaction by itself is not an explanation for use. Many alienated young people do not resort to drug use. Two other things must be present: the person must be in a setting where drugs are available and he must be introduced to drugs by someone he holds in esteem. [In a previous chapter we described the pattern of drug use as it has developed around large universities close to metropolitan areas.]

Drugs are now available to the student who is willing to experiment with them.

Commonly a person becomes aware of the possibility of using drugs when it comes to light that a friend is using them. If the novice is a girl, this person is likely to be a boyfriend; if a boy, a roommate or relatively long-time intimate. That a person standing in such a relationship to a novice takes drugs at all is a strong argument for the novice to take them as it dispels prior ideas that only "dope fiends" and "derelicts" of one kind or another would ever consider doing so. Perhaps other persons that he respects are considering the use of drugs, and this dispels some of the initial disfavor and apprehension.

A 23-year-old woman, an occasional user of marihuana, spoke of her boyfriend's reaction to his roommate's use:

> He was very willing to accept the fact that I didn't want to have anything to do with it so he just went along with his turning on (but not very much when you were around?) No, but doing it did effect me and, it made me—seeing him do it and suddenly realizing, you know, let's look at this again. You know, it's not hurting him and all this. Then my roommate, ah . . . who, she was much more interested in experimenting and "why not, let's try it." And she finally decided she was gonna try it and then, oh, another good friend was into the drug scene to a point that she rarely, but occasionally, had a joint and a lot of her friends were in it. And you know, I saw her and got into it thinking in terms of it being more widespread than I thought with her too. And I can't remember who influenced me to try it the first time. But it was a combination of either my roommate—she was gonna try it, you know "tonight," and that sort of thing. And my friend who I know as a perfectly sane person, you know, doing it and so, you know, then I tried it.

This is a situation of trust between a small group of friends which extends from introduction to drug use through the period of using occasionally as others make drugs available and therefore only periodic experimentation is possible.

Rationales for Using Marihuana

On occasion persuasion is involved in moving the novice to try drugs for the first time, but this persuasion takes the form of arguments which neutralize the effect of the customary restraints on using drugs instead of more straightforward directives to experiment. Such neutralization usually covers the following points: Marihuana is non-addicting and is, therefore, unjustly included under the narcotics laws. A 21-year-old part-time artist and systematic user observed:

> I think it should be legalized. I don't see any reasons why not. They have now a cruel and unusual punishment, and that's ridiculous, because it's not half as destructive as alcohol.

A 21-year-old heavy user-dealer and former student agreed:

> [this] is a misconception of the majority of the population . . . that it brings about a physical addiction. Ah . . . this is stupidity, it doesn't, because there is no addiction, no physical dependence on these particular drugs. I can stop, abruptly, not worry and whenever I feel like it.

Another statement that is rejected relates to drug dealing: drug dealers are wicked men who hang around playgrounds hoping to inject small children.

A 22-year-old woman, a casual user, agreed:

> I think a lot of fairy tales are passed down. I distinctly remember girl scout movies that I watched when I was a little girl. You know, along with ones, the one on the facts of life, they had one, about drugs and about alcoholism. There were 3 of them: sex, drugs, and alcohol. Quite a combination and, it started out with a scene—kind of a grubby city high school and a man in an overcoat with a package under his arm going through all sorts of little things and going down to the basements of their houses, or maybe in the stock of a grocery store they worked in, something like that.

A third statement concerns the ultimate consequences of using marihuana: that it will eventually lead to heroin. A 21-year-old heavy drug user thought the association between marihuana and heroin was misleading:

> . . . The best thing that could happen is that marihuana could be completely removed from its association with heroin. . . . No longer do they go hand in hand. Marihuana smokers won't become heroin addicted all the time, or in fact, as it goes on, most of the time. . . . You have all of these students becoming involved and in many cases the only things they are exposed to is the psychedelics—marihuana, LSD, occasionally peyote, because they've read about it so try to get it. Heroin in most cases isn't available to them and so there's nothing that will lead them on. You usually have to go looking and digging to find heroin up here in the Bay Area. It's just not that free.

A fourth point raises some questions about whose interests are involved when "non-addicting" drugs are included under the law. A 21-year-old hard-core user-dealer addressed himself to this point:

> Because of the nature of the drug the main groups that are against legalization you'll find are the tobacco and liquor interests. The people who have tremendous amounts of money involved in one of the two industries. These two lobbies are the main reason why the Federal government has not legalized it because they have tremendous amounts of money that they can throw in to the Senate to force them not to legalize it.

A fifth point compares marihuana and alcohol. Marihuana is held to be physically safe and much less debilitating than liquor and does not impair functioning so severely. A 25-year-old housewife and systematic user distinguished the effects of marihuana and alcohol:

> Getting high [on marihuana] is much, much better than getting drunk.
> . . . You have more control, . . . you're much happier than getting
> drunk. . . . That you have much more control, that you're much happier,
> that you come down much more gently, that your feelings are not wild, in
> short, even if you are very high you are still responsible for what you say
> and do.

The justifications which emphasize the positive reasons for using
marihuana consume a much larger proportion of the interviews and
conversations than do those rationales which seek to neutralize society's objections.

Marihuana is described as increasing a person's awareness, making
one more open to colors, sounds, and other people. It has a generally
relaxing effect and makes people feel peaceful, not violent. The effects
are sharply distinguished from alcohol. Marihuana sharpens your per-
ceptions, alcohol dulls them. If the person is engaged in some kind of
artistic or creative enterprise, it aids them. The freedom from anxiety
which marihuana induces enables the person to focus much more
clearly on the present. This makes immediate, natural responses possible. A 21-year-old systematic user and part-time artist described the
increased awareness attributed to marihuana:

> . . . you notice many things, you become very interested in the little de-
> tails. For instance, you may have noticed things like handles, or bottles, or
> pebbles, and children's attitudes, and you'd find that children aren't so
> young as you think and that you aren't as old as you think and that you
> don't become an adult if you don't understand that you aren't going to
> become any greater than a child.

In short, it enhances appreciation of sight, smell, taste, and sound
and is beneficial in many otherwise less-rewarding circumstances, e.g.,
movies and concerts.

Early Use

Early use is defended on intellectual grounds. It also continues to
offer the protective insulation of small friendship groups far from the
sources of supply. The fears that exist in these circumstances are not
those of the criminal more or less openly confronting hostile laws, as the
chances of being apprehended by the police are actually quite remote.
However, there are other sources of anxiety. As Becker notes, the
novice user will be concerned with whether or not he is able to control
disclosure of being high.[1] A 23-year-old woman who characterized her
use as occasional reported her own anxieties:

> I was petting the dog until all of a sudden I thought "I think I'm squishing
> him," you know . . . Oh, I was so frightened and I was sure that I was

going to squish this dog because my hands were so sensitive to it. But I thought I was doing very strange things and trying to get the composure to say something, just anything. I couldn't say hello because I was afraid it wouldn't come out right.

But, as Becker indicates, this passes and the marihuana user becomes more confident. He can be around straight people even while high and not suffer detection. A 21-year-old head described how he exhibits his own confidence:

I've learned to control most of the drugs that I take, on practically every experience that I have I end up going out and so I never have any worries at all along those lines. I have been confronted and sometimes I bring it on myself by asking directions or something and . . . other times I've been so crass as to walk into the Hall of Justice and visit a friend who had been arrested and in jail. . . .

A 23-year-old laboratory technician who saw himself as a weekender reported his own lack of concern about disclosure:

Oh, it's easy, people hardly ever know. I mean it's happened to me too. When I've been straight, people come in the house, or perhaps they come to a party, people, even on LSD, or something, they don't talk much. But they don't look glazed or don't do crazy things. And several times I've gone to straight parties and have turned on before I got there, or gone outside and turned on. And, I don't think anyone has any idea that was anything but booze. And sometimes I've even been in places where there wasn't even any booze, even, was completely straight, and I guess they just thought I was a very outgoing person or something, you know . . .

The beginning user is afraid that someone will inopportunely come into the surroundings of use unheralded, and will find some telltale sign of use like the butt of a marihuana cigarette. These feelings are largely directed toward other authorities than the police: parents, non-using friends who would become upset, school officials, and the like. These fears seldom act as a positive deterrent, but persons who are anxious about them will confine their use to "safe" circumstances within the confines of the friendship group away from prying eyes. They will not be likely, for example, to take the drug home with them when they return to their parents for a school holiday.

At this stage use is loosely ritualized. Special preparations are made for the occurrence: doors are locked, shades are pulled, foods are prepared, perhaps room lighting is altered, the drug is passed in a routinized fashion from one to another of the participants, and feeling states are commonly remarked upon. The presence and expectation of use of the drug provide a rationale for such a structured occasion. A 20-year-old student recreational user described the ritual connected with marihuana usage at this stage:

And the reason this all impressed me so much—I think this was the finest time I had on pot. He brought out a little box and he opened it up and he was extremely ritualistic about the whole thing only not in a phony way— just it was a medium of hospitality for him, it was like the same care with which one could pour a cordial for somebody or with which one would serve sandwiches or something—only better, you know . . . And it was great to watch this, this ah . . . very beautiful man ah . . . just in terms of his movements and his mannerisms, taking this pot, and, you know, just arranging it in the cigarette paper and very slowly and carefully . . . if it ever comes to a time when this is respectable, it is going to be an eminent mark on sophistication because so much is involved in preparing pot.

More Regular Use

If the novice passes more deeply into drug use, several important events occur. To regularize use (say, the use of marihuana several times a day), one must get closer to the source of illegal drugs, to information about the market and to the more public hazards associated with use. The user who wants to increase his use both in type of drug and in quantity must forsake the protection of the small group of friends. He must move into circles where users are *mutually known* as users but where not much else is known. This is nearer the relationship of acquaintanceship than friendship and may involve not even being acquainted but *known about*. The realization that this has happened, sometimes unwittingly, is a rude shock to persons who, for one reason or another, require secrecy.

The circumstances of introductory use are typically situations where someone was sometimes able to procure drugs from a third party that the others did not know personally and who did not know them. The situation from the point of view of the user is a relatively safe one. The circumstance of regularized use, however, puts the user into a broader arena of action. He tends to become a "known" figure, involving a reputation. Others may know about him but not know him intimately. This entails moving out of the small friendship group with all the protection that afforded. The discretion that holds between friends is not a feature of relationships between persons only known to one another. This observation is at odds with Becker's when he asserts that becoming a marihuana user necessitates tight information control. It involves just the opposite as the user tends to become known and dependent on the goodwill of persons he has no firm grounds for trusting. In short, the regular user loses control of the information that others have of him. A 30-year-old professional described the situation that caused him concern and limited his further involvement in the drug scene:

> I like to maintain a reasonable amount of discretion with people that I
> choose as friends, and I no longer had such a choice, 'cause I'd go over
> to somebody who was a friend and all kinds of outrageous types would
> show up. And, people I never knew, never saw before, would never see
> again but any one of them could have been a plant. So, I withdrew, it was
> time to move on.

Precautions are usually taken at this point to protect oneself from the
police. The concern shifts from being found out by straight friends or
school officials or parents to being found out by the police. The
strategy for dealing with this threat of police exposure is to exercise
discretion in buying or selling drugs, keeping drugs in one's possession, or "turning on" in public. One 21-year-old hard-core user-dealer
in reply to the question, "Have you ever supplied anybody that you
didn't know?," replied:

> No, first of all because ah . . . of the police aspect which is always prev-
> alent and second because ah . . . I like to know a person pretty well
> before I let them know I use.

Another 21-year-old part-time artist and part-time dealer discussed his
fears of the police:

> I'm always a little bit leary of it, and that's good, because it gives me
> caution. And, that's one of the penalties I pay. I've always had this little
> fear of having somebody knock on the door, just because it's illegal.

A 25-year-old housewife and systematic user spoke of her experiences with the police, which increased the precautions she took in
using drugs:

> Well, one time the police came into the house and busted everybody but
> me and my husband. We had [lived in] one room that was clean. And he
> had never made sales. In fact he had warned all the other occupants of
> this very large Victorian house that there was a lot, you know, that there
> was danger, that there were agents coming into the house, and he was
> yelling about this all the time, so we were clean. . . . And so they [the
> police] were constantly cruising by our house, and you know, several
> times our back door was broken down and nailed back up. In fact, it
> still happens to me every time I move, my back door is broken down, and
> what do you call the little frame that goes around the door is always
> nailed back up. Maybe 2 weeks after I move into a house, I look and I
> see that someone has broken in, the screen door latch has been rebored.
> But I never have anything in my house, never!

To progress into regular drug use it seems to be necessary to overcome the fear of giving oneself away while "high." The main fear now
is being caught in possession of the drugs by the law, either on the
streets or through undercover informants. Being caught in this position
is prima facie grounds for conviction or the opening wedge for being
compromised into the position of informer.

When one moves closer to the source of supply, several things may happen. Those persons who have developed attachments to the social order, primarily through occupational or professional commitments, will tend to withdraw. The more diffuse and serious dangers of apprehension by the law for persons in this condition highlight the hazards. They know that their career would be irremediably compromised by a drug conviction or endangered by rumors that they were users. This is the kind of diffuse sanction that Nadel[2] speaks of in a discussion of social control in closely knit primitive societies. Presumably, the more closely people are tied to and dependent upon the legitimate order, the more damaging is public disclosure of a delinquent act. For some of our Colony members such controls are much more thorough than simple legal threats. For such people, of course, other considerations may enter in. They may feel uncomfortable trying to conduct a day's work while "high." It may become too much of a strain to have to segregate the legitimate workaday world so radically from one's leisure pursuit, which is necessary if drug use is that leisure pursuit. A small number of persons who confronted this situation did not withdraw completely but reinstituted the earlier arrangement of casual, occasional use within a group of friends. This is safe and does not involve regular use of or wide experimentation with drugs of various sorts.

An important turning point is reached when the person starts to have his own supply. This decision calls for risking whatever dangers are involved in favor of more systematic use. It usually entails some striking out on one's own. Sources of supply may be identified by friends who know them. A 21-year-old unemployed hard-core user described this development:

> Students many times, will get turned on and won't buy anything but will come over to my house or the friend's house and turn on and smoke a little now and then when they visit you. So it's much slower. Sooner or later, most of them end up buying for themselves because they realize it costs you money and most of them like it. Some people take a very long time. I know one that still hasn't really begun.

An important code is observed in obtaining drugs. Questions are not asked about sources of supply. The information may be volunteered, but participants feel it is better not to know. Questions asked about where the stuff comes from arouse suspicion. This is the kind of question a plant might ask. Or the person asking the question might be an informer. No matter how intimate relationships are, there is the general recognition that pressures can be exerted to compel people to inform. This is an extremely sensitive area and Colony members were reluctant to discuss it. Several articulate observers of the drug scene admitted that they could visualize conditions under which they would become informers. The more a person had to lose in terms of reputation, or separation from family or job by prosecution, the more likely he would be to cooperate with the police in some kind of "set up." [The implications this has for social relationships within the Colony will be discussed later.] A 21-year-old heavy user-dealer described some of the precautions he takes:

> The only problem is for a new person, like walking into town and make a friend in one day and ask him for some grass. You can't because that's the way all the busts are made and people are really suspicious of people they don't know asking about grass . . . I've had no fears of getting it for other people who I think are pretty straight, as long as I know them. I don't like to have them come and say, "well I have a friend who wants to get some marihuana, will you get some for him, or will you sell him some?" I'll say: "well, I can get some for you, and you can give it to him. I don't want to have anything to do with him." Because I don't, I trust my own judgment, but I don't trust the judgment of other people. And, I think, that's pretty much what people sort of do. But, you know, once you have a circle of friends, then the number of people that become available as possible contacts, you know, becomes fantastic.

The pattern of scoring from strangers seems relatively rare. It's considered too dangerous. It only occurs when you hit a new place and have not had time to develop friends who use.

The progression into more regular use seems to be confirmed at the point the user decides to turn someone else on. If the initial experience with marihuana is pleasant then there seems to be a general impulse to share it with others. It is usually not possible to introduce another to the experience unless one is closer to the source of supply than the novice is. Introducing someone else is usually not done thoughtlessly— there is a certain ritual character to it. It is usually thought of as a minor rite of passage. Turning someone else on usually signifies to the person doing it that he has now become a regular user. The person turned on is usually a close friend of the first user. One is not interested in introducing strangers to drugs at this point. As a person moves further into the drugs scene, he may turn someone else on who is not a friend but who is known by someone he trusts. The same respondent who reported her concerns about scoring from strangers reported how this may work:

> It was usually a thing of where the person ah . . . was accepted by us all. That's the important thing, I guess, and you thought they were good people and groovy people and they had good ideas and liberal. I mean, open-minded is perhaps a better word. And you say "Have you ever heard of marihuana and would you like to try it?" you know. And, usually the answer is "I'm willing to try anything once," you know. Sort of the existentialist experience view type thing . . . and they would do anything once. Not for kicks. Just to see what it was like and ah . . . to see if it did add to their life sequence and things like that. . . .

A 21-year-old part-time model and hard-core user described how she ascertains that someone is to be trusted:

> You gotta be careful with the come on. You can't just walk up to somebody, . . . and say "Here, you want some grass?" Because, you know, it's a bad trip, so you know, you find out about it. You find out if they groove the same way you do . . . [if] that's what they consider wild at all, you know, or if they're directly within the law type thing. You find out more or less their values in life. You know, that type of thing. And, then, you can just tell 'em, "All right, I have used it in the past." You can sorta say it that way at first, you know. And, then they say "Well, I'd like to try it sometime." And then a little while later you say: "Well, I had one yesterday" or something. And then they'd say: "Really, you should have called me."—that type of thing and then—"Well, next time I get some."

NOTES

1 H. Becker, "Marihuana Use and Social Control," *Social Problems,* III (1955), 35–44.
2 S. F. Nadel, "Social Control and Self Regulation," *Social Forces,* XXXI (1953), 265–73.

21 | Heads and Freaks: Patterns and Meanings of Drug Use Among Hippies
Fred Davis with Laura Munoz

Hippies have been an important part of various deviant social movements in American society for a number of years now. Sociologists have done only a few excellent participant-observer studies of the hippie movement, and Fred Davis' studies have been among the best. As Davis and Munoz show in this essay, drug use among the hippies has profound ideological meanings and forms an integral part of their everyday life. It symbolizes attack not only on the normal society but also on the normal form of consciousness. Their opposition does not usually involve a specific attack on our society, but is rather a total withdrawal and rejection of the establishment's way of life. Hippies move in a world of their own, generally disregarding this world, except insofar as it occasionally impinges upon their lives. But even among hippies there are differences in the meanings of drug use, as this essay shows so clearly.

Regardless of whether the phenomenon is viewed in terms of a bohemian subculture, a social movement, a geographically based deviant community or some combination of these, there is substantial agreement among those who have studied hippies (Berger, 1967; Davis, 1967; Didion, 1967; Simon and Trout, 1967; von Hoffman, 1967) that drugs (or "dope," the term preferred by hippies)[1] play an important part in their lives. This generalization applies to nearly all segments of the hippie community for the reasons given below.*

From Fred Davis with Laura Munoz, "Heads and Freaks," *Journal of Health and Social Behavior* (June 1968), pp. 156–163; reprinted by permission of the American Sociological Association.

* We wish to acknowledge the substantial contribution of David A. Farmer, University of California, Davis, to this paper, both in its inception and through his valuable criticisms of an earlier draft. We also wish to thank Howard S. Becker for his comments and to express our profound indebtedness to Professor Frederick H. Meyers, University of California

First, the patent empirical fact of widespread and frequent drug use *per se*[2] is easily ascertainable through even a brief stay in San Francisco's Haight-Ashbury, New York's East Village, Los Angeles' Fairfax, Vancouver's Fourth Avenue or wherever else hippie colonies have sprung up.[3] Second—and this importantly distinguishes hippie drug use from that of other drug-using subcultures—there are pronounced ideological overtones associated with it. Not only is it frequently asserted by many hippies that there is "nothing wrong" with certain of the drugs favored by them (chiefly marijuana and LSD, along with a number of other hallucinogens), or that their use is less harmful than alcohol or tobacco,[4] but that these drugs are positively beneficial, either as a pleasant relaxant, as with marijuana, or as a means for gaining insight with which to redirect the course of one's life along inwardly more satisfying and self-fulfilling lines (LSD). Among other manifestations, this spirit of ideological advocacy expresses itself in the conviction of some hippies that their ultimate social mission is to "turn the world on"—i.e., make everyone aware of the potential virtues of LSD for ushering in an era of universal peace, freedom, brotherhood and love. The last, and perhaps most crucial, circumstance for making drug use important in the lives of hippies is the simple and stark matter of the drugs' illegality. As contemporary deviance theory of the symbolic interactionist persuasion has shown in so many differing connections (Becker, 1963; Davis, 1961; Freidson, 1965; Goffman, 1963; Kitsuse, 1961; Lemert, 1962), the act by a community of successfully labeling a particular practice deviant and/or illegal almost invariably constrains the "deviant" to structure much of his identity and activity (Strauss, 1959) in terms of such imputations of deviance and lawbreaking. Thus, the omnipresent threats of police harassment, of arrest and incarceration, as well as of a more diffuse social ostracism are "facts of life" which the hippie who uses drugs only occasionally must contend with fully as much as the regular user.

Beyond these rather global observations, all further generalizations concerning hippie drug use must be qualified carefully and treated as tentative. For not only are the actual patterns of drug use quite varied among individual hippies and different hippie sub-groups, but the patterns themselves are constantly undergoing change as the subculture evolves and gains greater experience with drugs (Becker, 1967). Further compounding the hazards of facile generalization are the following:

Medical Center, San Francisco, for having given us so unstintingly of his expertise in matters related to drugs, drug use and drug abuse. Partial support for the field study from which the paper derives was provided by the Academic Senate Research Committee, University of California, San Francisco Division, and the Center for the Study of Law and Society, University of California, Berkeley.

1. The apparent readiness of many hippies to experiment—if only once "to see what it's like"—with almost any drug or drug-like substance, be it Hawaiian wood rose seeds, opium or some esoteric, pharmacologically sophisticated psycho-active compound.
2. The periodic appearance on the hippie drug market of new drugs, usually of the hallucinogenic variety, which, like new fashions generally, excite a great flurry of initial interest and enthusiasm until they are either discredited, superseded or partially assimilated into a more "balanced" schedule of drug use. Thus, in the past year alone, for example, at least three new hallucinogenic type drugs have made much heralded, though short-lived, appearances in the Haight-Ashbury: STP (dimethoxymethyl-amphetamine), MDA (methylene-dioxy-amphetamine) and PCP, the "peace pill" (phencyclidine).
3. The vagaries, uncertainties, deceptions and misrepresentations of the illegal drug market as such. Not only is it hard for a buyer to be sure that he is getting the drug he thinks he is getting—indeed, that he is getting any drug at all and not some placebo—but dosages, strengths and purity of compounding, even when not knowingly misrepresented by dealers, are likely to be unknown or poorly understood by dealer and buyer alike.[5] Thus, the ubiquitous possibility of an untoward reaction in which the user, or a whole aggregate of users, becomes violently ill or severely disoriented.
4. The fact, to be discussed later, that the very same drug (LSD, for example) can, depending on the intent of the user, his mood, the setting and the group context, be used to achieve very different drug experiences and subjective states. Though this "choice of drug experience" is never fully within the control of even the experienced user (see 3, above), it does exist, and thus facilitates differential use by different users as well as by the same user at different times.

Obliquely, these circumstances point to what is perhaps the chief obstacle to making firm generalizations concerning hippie drug use, namely, that the subculture is not (at least as yet) of a piece, that it includes many disparate social elements and ideational tendencies (Davis, 1967; Simon and Trout, 1967) and that, to the extent that drug use constitutes something of a core element in it, this must be seen in the context of these varying and constantly shifting socio-ideational subconfigurations. As has been characteristic of almost any expressive social movement in its formative stages (cf. Blumer, 1946), this diversity in the midst of a search for common definition is reflected in the frequent discussions among hippies on who is a "real" hippie, who a "plastic" hippie, and what "genuine" hipness consists of. Moral, behavioral and attitudinal boundaries of inclusion and exclusion are constantly being assessed and redrawn. But, in the absence of any recognized leadership group capable of issuing ex cathedra pronouncements on these matters, one man's, or one underground paper's, definition is as good as the next's. These ongoing discussions, debates and polemics extend, of course, to the place and use of drugs in the "new community," as hippie spokesmen like to refer to themselves. Some take a very permissive and inclusive stance, others a more restrictive one, and still others shift their ground from one encounter to the next. Inconclusive as this dialogue may be from an organizational standpoint, it nonetheless is important for the influences, albeit variable, it exerts on drug practices and attitudes within the subculture.

With these reservations in mind we wish to sketch here a rough sociological atlas, as it were, of patterns and meanings of drug use among San Francisco's Haight-Ashbury hippies, at least insofar as these manifested themselves through the summer and well into the fall of 1967. The data were gathered by the methods of ethnographic field work as part of a broader study of the interaction of Haight-Ashbury's hippie community with the larger San Francisco community. Although informed by a close-in familiarity with the hippie community, the data are, strictly speaking, impressionistic inasmuch as time, resources and certain situational peculiarities connected with doing research among hippies[6] militated against any exhaustive study of drug use *per se*.

LSD and Methedrine

Since much of what follows deals with social psychological aspects of the use of the above two drugs, a few preliminary words are in order concerning the drugs themselves, their direct pharmacological effects, average dosages, modes of administration and frequency of use. No detailed description can be attempted here (see Blum, 1964; Kramer et al., 1967); rather, our aim is merely to touch on a few matters pertinent for the subsequent discussion of types of drug users. Inasmuch as we shall not be discussing marijuana, suffice it to say here that it is very widely used by all segments of the hippie community and constitutes the drug staple of the subculture. (Hashish, the purified and condensed forms of cannabis, though much preferred by those who have tried it, appears in the Haight-Ashbury only rarely and commands an exceedingly high price.)

The hallucinogenic LSD (lysergic acid diethylamide), one of a growing family of such drugs, is marketed in the Haight-Ashbury in tablet form. The shape, color and general appearance of tablets will vary considerably, from "well made" to "extremely crude," as new batches are produced by different illegal manufacturers. Taken orally, an average dose, usually one tablet, contains approximately 185 micrograms of LSD. Some users, though, are known to ingest considerably more than this amount, i.e., up to 1,000–1,250 micrograms, when they wish to "turn on." Street prices vary from about $2.50 per tablet in times of plentiful supply to $5.00 and $6.00 when supply is short. Typical users in the Haight-Ashbury "take a trip" once a week or thereabouts on the average; again, however, there is a considerable number who "drop acid" much more frequently, perhaps every three or four days, while still others resort to the drug only occasionally or episodically. The characteristic psychopharmacologic effects of the drug are described by Smith (1967:3) as follows:

> When someone ingests an average dose of LSD, (150–250 micrograms) nothing happens for the first 30 or 45 minutes, and then after the sympathetic response the first thing the individual usually notices is a change in the way he perceives things. . . . Frequently . . . he notices that the walls and other objects become a bit wavy or seem to move. Then he might notice colors . . . about the room are looking much brighter or more intense than they usually do and, in fact, as time goes on these colors can seem exquisitely intense and more beautiful than any colors he has seen before. Also, it is common for individuals to see a halo effect around lights, also a rainbow effect. . . . There is another kind of rather remarkable perceptual change, referred to as a synesthesia. By this I mean the translation of one type of sensory experience into another, so that if one is listening to music, for example, one can sometimes feel the vibrations of the music in one's body, or one can sometimes see the actual notes moving, or the colors that he is seeing will beat in rhythm with the music.

More pronounced effects of an emotional, meditative or ratiocinative kind can, but need not, follow in the wake of these alterations in sense perception. In any case, the direct effects of the drug last on the average for an eight to twelve hour span.

Methedrine (generic name, methamphetamine) is a stimulant belonging to the sympathomimetic group of drugs. Its appearance is that of a fluffy white powder, referred to commonly as "crystals." In the Haight-Ashbury it is sold mainly in spoonful amounts (1–2 grams, approximately) and packaged in small transparent envelopes, prices ranging from $15.00 to $20.00 an envelope. Frequently, a user or small dealer in need of cash will repackage the powder and sell it in smaller amounts. Until a few years ago most users of Methedrine took it orally in capsule form. Among Haight-Ashbury hippies, however, the primary and preferred mode of administration is intravenous injection. Hence, the paraphernalia employed is almost identical to that of the heroin user: hypodermic needle, syringe, spoon for diluting the powder in tap water, and candle for heating the mixture. Because needles and associated equipment are often unsterilized or poorly sterilized, cases of serum hepatitis are quite common among Methedrine users. The physiological effects of the drug are elevated blood pressure, increased pulse rate, dilation of pupils and blurred vision—these accompanied by such behavioral states as euphoria, heightened spontaneous activity, wakefulness, loss of appetite and, following extended use, suspicion and acute apprehensiveness ("paranoia").

Although there is some disagreement among experts on whether regular use of Methedrine leads to addiction as, for example, in the case of heroin, it is well-established that a fair proportion of users become extremely dependent on the drug. Thus, whereas the episodic user will inject 25–50 milligrams for a "high," those who get badly "strung out" on a two to three week Methedrine binge will by the end be "shooting" as frequently as six times a day for a total daily intake of some 1,000 to 2,000 milligrams (1 to 2 grams). Needless to say, were it not for the steep increase in body tolerance levels built up through continuous use of the drug, such high daily dosages might well prove lethal.

Heads and Freaks

A suitable starting point for our ethnographic sketch is those terms and references used by hippies themselves to distinguish certain types of drug users and patterns of drug use. Chief among these is the contrast drawn between "heads" and "freaks," sometimes explicitly, though more often implicitly with reference to a particular drug user or drug practice. While a whole penumbra of allusive imagery surrounds these terms, a "head" essentially is thought to be someone who uses drugs—and, here, it is mainly the hallucinogens that the speaker has in mind—for purposes of mind expansion, insight and the enhancement of personality attributes, i.e., he uses drugs to discover where "his head is at." For the "head," therefore, the drug experience is conceived of, much as during the first years of LSD experimentation by psychiatrists and psycho-pharmacologists (ca. 1956–1963), as a *means* for self-realization or self-fulfillment, and not as an end in itself. The term, "head," is, of course, not new with hippies. It has a long history among drug users generally, for whom it signified a regular, experienced user of any illegal drug—e.g., pot "head," meth "head," smack (heroin) "head." Although still sometimes used in this non-discriminating way by hippies, what is novel about their usage of "head" is the extent to which it has become exclusively associated with certain of the more rarified facets of the LSD experience.

By contrast, the term "freak" refers usually to someone in search of drug kicks as such, especially if his craving carries him to the point of drug abuse where his health, sanity and relations with intimates are jeopardized. Though used primarily in the context of Methedrine abuse ("speed freak"), the reference is frequently broadened to include all those whose use of any drug (be it Methedrine, LSD, marijuana or even alcohol) is so excessive and of such purely hedonistic bent as to cause them to "freak out," e.g., become ill or disoriented, behave violently or erratically, give evidence of a "paranoid" state of mind.

Whereas the primary connotative imagery of "head" and "freak" derives mainly from the subculture's experience with drugs, the terms themselves—given their evocative associations—have in a short course of time acquired great referential elasticity. Thus "head," for example, is extended to include any person (hip, "straight," or otherwise) who manifests great spontaneity, openness of manner, and a canny sensitivity to his own and others' moods and feelings. Indeed, hippies will claim that it is not strictly necessary to use hallucinogenic drugs—helpful though this is for many—to become a "head" and that, moreover, there are many persons in the straight world, in particular children, who are "really heads," but don't know it. Parenthetically, it might be noted that the concept of a *secret union* of attitude and sensibility, including even those ignorant of their inner grace, is a familiar attribute of expressive social movements of the deviant type; among other purposes, it helps to subjectively legitimate the proselytizing impulses of the movement. Homosexuals, too, are known to construct such quasiconspiratorial versions of the world.

Similarly, the term "freak," while much less fertile in its connotative imagery than "head," is also extended to persons and situations outside the immediate context of drug use. Hence, anyone who is too aggressive or violent, who seems "hung up" on some idea, activity or interactional disposition, might be called a "freak." Accordingly, abnormal phases (e.g., high anxiety states, obsessiveness, intemperateness) in the life of one customarily thought a "head" will also be spoken of as "freaking" or "freaking out."

The two terms, therefore, have acquired a quality of ideal-typicality about them in the hippie subculture and have, at minimum, come to designate certain familiar social types (cf., Strong, 1946). At this level of indigenous typifications, they can be seen to reflect certain ongoing value tensions in the subculture: a reflecting turning inward versus hedonism, Apollonian contentment versus Dionysian excess, a millennial vision of society versus an apocalyptic one. And that these generic extensions of the terms derive so intimately from drug experiences afford additional evidence of the symbolic centrality of drugs in the hippie subculture.[7]

Some Social Characteristics of Heads and Freaks

In the more restrictive, strict drug-using sense, who, then, are "heads" (LSD or "acid" users) and who "freaks" (Methedrine or "speed shooters")? Lacking accurate demographic data on the subject, our impression is that "heads" are found more often among the older, more established and less transient segments of the Haight-Ashbury hippie community, i.e., persons of both sexes in their mid-to-late twenties who, while not exactly holding down full time jobs of the conventional sort, are more or less engaged in some regular line of vocational activity: artists, craftsmen, clerks in the hippie shops, some hippie merchants, writers with the underground press, graduate students, and sometimes mail carriers, to mention a few. It is mainly from this segment that such spokesmen and leaders as the "new community" has produced have come. By comparison, "freaks" are found more often among the more anomic and transient elements of the community, in particular those strata where "hipness" begins to shade off into such quasi-criminal and thrill-seeking conglomerates as the Hell's Angels and other motorcyclists (known locally as "bikeies"), many of whom now frequent the Haight-Ashbury and have taken up residence in and around the area. Some observers even attribute the growing use of Methedrine to the fact that it and closely related stimulants (e.g., Benzedrine, Dexedrine) were popular with West Coast motorcycle gangs well before the origins of the hippie community in the Haight-Ashbury. Unlike "acid," which is widely used by both males and females, "speed" appears to be predominantly a male drug.[8]

As these observations would suggest, it is our further impression that "heads" are by and large persons of middle and upper-middle class social origins whereas "freaks" are much more likely to be of working class background. Despite, therefore, the strong legal and moral proscriptions against both LSD and Methedrine, their differential use by hippies reflects, at one level at least, the basic contrast in expressive styles extant in the American class structure; put crudely, LSD equals self-exploration/self-improvement equals middle class, while Methedrine equals body stimulation/release of aggressive impulses equals working class.

These characterizations, however, afford but a gross approximation of drug use patterns in the Haight-Ashbury. The actual demography of use is complicated considerably by a variety of changing situational and attitudinal currents, some of which were alluded to earlier. Two additional matters especially deserve mention here. The first is the existence of a large, socially heterogeneous class of mixed drug users: persons who are neither "heads" nor "freaks" in any precise sense, but who regularly sample both LSD and Methedrine, as well as other drugs. Shifting intermittently or episodically from one to another, they may, save for continued smoking of marijuana, even undergo extended periods of drug abstinence. Of such users it can, perhaps, best be said that the very absence of any consistent pattern is the pattern. Secondly, it should be noted that this non-pattern pattern of drug use (this secondary anomie within a more inclusive deviant life scheme) has grown more pronounced in the Haight-Ashbury in recent months. Whereas prior to the summer of 1967 a newly arrived hippie would in all probability have been socialized into the LSD users' culture of "trip-ping," "mind-blowing" and meditation—"heads" then clearly consti-tuted the socially, as well as numerically, dominant hippie group in the area—this kind of outcome became a good deal less certain following the publicity, confusion, congestion and increased social heterogeneity of recruits that attended the summer influx of youth from across the country (Davis, 1967). Not only did many of the settled hippies move away from the area in the wake of this massive intrusion, but new styles and tastes in drug use, notably "speed shooting," quickly established themselves. With the inundation and dispersal of the older "head" group, it became largely a matter of sheer fortuitousness whether a novice hippie turned to "acid" or "speed," to some other drug or a combination of several. Whose "pad" he "crashed" on arrival or who befriended him the first time he set foot on Haight Street could have as much to do with his subsequent pattern of drug use as anything else. This was conspicuously so in the instance of younger recruits, many of them runaways from home in the 14–17 age group, who, except perhaps for marijuana smoking, were completely naive to and inexperi-enced in drug use.

The Prestige Gradient of Drug Use

Nonetheless, to the extent that the hippie subculture has managed to conserve elements of a core identity and to develop something of a common stance vis-à-vis "straight" society, it is still the "head" pattern of drug use that is ideationally, if not necessarily numerically, dominant within it. Thus, to be spoken of as a "head" is complimentary, whereas to be termed a "freak" or "speed freak" is, except in certain special contexts, derogating. Similarly, the underground press is forever ex-tolling the virtues of "acid"; but, apart from an occasional piece of somewhat patronizing tone in which the author tries to "understand" what "gives" with Methedrine users (Strauss, 1967), it almost invariably condemns "speed." Numerous posters on display in the Haight Street print and funny button shops announce in bold captions "SPEED KILLS."

The perceived dichotomy between mind-expansion and body-stimulation represented by the two drugs is sometimes reconceptual-ized to apply to LSD users alone so as to draw a distinction between those who use the drug mainly for purposes of "tripping" as against "true" or "real" "heads" who purport to use it for achieving insight and effecting personality changes within themselves. While dosage levels of the drug seem to play some part in determining whether a "tripping" or "mind-expanding" experience will ensue—the larger the dose, the more likely the latter or, alternatively, a "bum trip," i.e., a panic reaction with severe disorientation—the intent and setting of the user also appear to have an important bearing on the outcome. Quiet surroundings, a contemplative mood and interesting objects upon which to focus (e.g., a mandala, a candle flame) are felt to be conducive to a mind-expanding experience; moving street scenes, an extroverted mood and the intense visual and auditory stimuli of the typical folk-rock dance and light show are thought conducive to "tripping." In any event, he who uses LSD only to "trip" (i.e., to intensify and refract his sensate experience of the environment) is regarded, at best, with a certain amused tolerance by "righteous acid heads." The latter, therefore, frequently counsel beginning users of LSD to move beyond mere "tripping" to where they can realize the higher meditative, revelatory and religious potentials of the drug. In this connection, a number of hippie groups, particularly those involved in the Eastern religions, advocate dispensing with LSD and other hallucinogens altogether following realization of these higher states; once the "doors of consciousness" have been opened, it is stated, it is no longer necessary to use drugs for recapturing the experience—newly discovered powers of meditation alone will suffice. Be that as it may, because the "head"—as both a certain kind of drug user and certain kind of human being—has emerged as the model citizen of the hippie movement, there are many who aspire to the status and aim to follow the true path that can lead them there.

Conclusion

In sum, drug use among Haight-Ashbury hippies reveals a number of contrary tendencies, the chief being the emergent social and symbolic contrast of the "head" and "freak" patterns—a contrast which, as we have seen, encompasses cultural elements well beyond the immediate realm of drug use *per se*. While the two patterns can, through several analytical levels removed, be traced back ultimately to certain historically persistent, subterranean expressive value strains in American society-at-large (see Matza, 1964), their surfacing and intimate co-existence within the hippie subculture serve to aggravate already difficult problems of member socialization, group integration and ideology that confront the community (Davis, 1967). Stated otherwise, the process of community formation is hindered, not wholly, or even primarily, by outside forces of repression—for, these will often solidify a social movement—but through the generation of anomie from within as well. If illegal and socially condemned drug use did not play so large a part in the subculture, these divisive tendencies could, perhaps, be better contained. As is, however, the pervasiveness of illegal drug use constantly opens up the subculture to a gamut of socially disparate, unassimilable elements and assorted predators, few of whom share the ethos of love, expressive freedom and disengagement from narrow materialistic pursuits that animated, and still animates, many within the movement. And, since it is highly unlikely that the drugs favored by hippies (again, possibly excepting marijuana) will soon be made legal, this situation is likely to get worse before it gets better.

As to the drug use patterns themselves, it can only be a matter of conjecture as to which—"head" or "freak"—if either, will come eventually to clearly prevail in the hippie community. Although the "head" pattern appears on the face of it to resonate more deeply with those broader philosophical and ideational themes that distinguish the movement,[9] it has, in the Haight-Ashbury at least, already lost much ground to the more exclusively hedonistic "freak" pattern. Should it continue to do so, what did have the earmarks of a culturally significant expressive social movement on the American scene could easily dissolve into little more than the sociologist's familiar "drug users' deviant subculture."

NOTES

1 As with earlier expressive social movements of a religious tendency, it is characteristic of hippies to employ, and thereby semantically reconstruct for initiates, a discredited term of pungent reference where, on purely denotative grounds, a more "acceptable" one would do as well or even better. The frequent public resort to sexual and scatological profanity by hippies (see Berger, 1967), most of whom were raised in homes where the use of such words would, to say the least, be frowned upon, is further evidence of this all but conscious tendency to linguistically celebrate the rejected and despised so as to cast them in a new moral light. Compare the remarks of Kenneth Burke (1954: 125–147) on "organized bad taste."

2 This, of course, is not to say that drug use (and abuse) is not widespread among Americans generally. Rather, the obvious point is that the alcohol, tranquilizers, barbiturates, stimulants and common pain-relievers used in conventional society have not, despite the known injurious effects of some of them, been officially declared illegal or detrimental to health and morals as have the drugs favored by hippies. Hence, they are, except in extreme instances of abuse, treated as part of the everyday, taken-for-granted world of pharmaceutical products and household remedies to which little, if any, stigma is attached. Hippies, naturally, are forever pointing this out in their continuing campaign for drug law reform. "Why condemn us, when so many of you are constantly turning to drugs for almost every conceivable contingency of daily life? What makes your drug 'abuse' any better than ours?"

3 Exception must be made for a small number of hippie communes and settlements, most of them in rural areas, where, according to reports in the underground press, the use of all mind and mood-altering drugs is disapproved of.

4 As far as tobacco is concerned, the point is largely gratuitous. Our impression is that a great many hippies are heavy cigarette smokers.

5 A useful discussion of the hippie drug market—manufacture of drugs, distribution, pricing, types of drug dealers, relations with buyers, etc.—would require a lengthy paper in itself. Two points in particular, however, deserve mention here for the special interest they hold for sociologists. 1) Much as in the legitimate drug trade, new drugs like STP and MDA are introduced selectively at first by manufacturers' and/or distributors' "detail men" making free samples available to the drug cognoscenti and opinion leaders in the hippie community (cf. Coleman et al., 1966). If favorably received in these élite circles, the drug is then put on the street market for "open" sale. 2) In line with the anti-hoarding sentiments of hippies, it is regarded as bad form not to share a "good thing," especially when one has a surplus on hand. It is not uncommon then, for hippie drug dealers, particularly non-commercial ones who only trade casually to earn a bit of extra cash, to give away gratis a fair portion of their stock to friends and favorities.

6 Above and beyond understandable sensitivities relating to illegal drug use, many hippies resent and deplore conventional modes of sociological inquiry—questionnaires, schedules, formal interviews, etc.—directed at them. These, they state, reduce the respondent to a "thing," a mere statistical instance in an artificially constructed class of events, thereby denying him his individuality and possibilities for creative being. In line with certain prominent strains in the hippie ethos, the feeling is that it is never humane or just to relate to another in these terms. Tied in with these sentiments is the not wholly unfounded conviction of certain, more sophisticated hippies that social science investigators who do research among them are interested primarily in furthering their own careers; they "take" from the "new community" and return nothing to it by way of aid or comfort. Much as these attitudes make for difficulties in conducting research among hippies, they have the virtue of posing in a sharp and decidedly concrete manner a number of largely unexamined ethical, and epistemological, issues underlying social science research on human groups. (See Bruyn, 1966; Seeley, 1967; Sjoberg, 1967.)

7 Similarly, hippie art, poetry and folk-rock music are after appraised frequently in terms of their "druggy" qualities, i.e., how nearly they evoke the moods and sensations associated with drug experiences.

8 Some preliminary survey data gathered by Professor Frederick H. Meyers of the University of California Medical Center, San Francisco, suggest, however, that the ratio of female Methedrine users (and abusers) among hippies is significantly higher than is commonly thought to be the case.

9 In this connection, a case could be made, and is by some hippies, that much which is distinctive about the hippie subculture (e.g., its music, aversion to physical violence, return to nature, communal sharing, etc.) are the product of the "acid" experience rather than psycho-cultural determinants of it. That is to say, the direct psycho-pharmacologic effects of LSD are such as to lead people to selectively reconstitute their inner world of memory, feeling, percept, attitude, etc. in a new and *particularistic* way—in this instance a kind of Apollonian reconstruction of social reality. If true this opens up the interesting, and frightening, Huxleyan possibility of drugs not merely regulating culture but, in an important sense, generating it as well. Also, if true, this would call for certain qualifications in Becker's (1967) proposed thesis that it is the users' subculture, and not the direct effects of the drug *per se,* which largely determine the meaning and ideational content of the drug induced experience.

REFERENCES

Becker, Howard S. *Outsiders.* New York: Free Press, 1963.
———. "History, Culture and Subjective Experience: An Exploration of the Social Bases of Drug-Induced Experiences," *Journal of Health and Social Behavior,* Vol. 8 (September 1967), pp. 163–176.
Berger, Bennett M. "Hippie Morality—More Old Than New," *Trans-action,* Vol. 5 (December 1967), pp. 19–27.
Blum, Richard H. and Associates. *Utopiates: The Use and the Users of LSD-25.* New York: Atherton, 1964.
Blumer, Herbert. "Collective Behavior," pp. 199–221 in Alfred McClung Lee (ed.), *New Outline of the Principles of Sociology.* New York: Barnes and Noble, 1946.
Bruyn, Severyn T. *The Human Perspective in Sociology.* Englewood Cliffs, New Jersey: Prentice-Hall, 1966.
Burke, Kenneth. *Permanence and Change.* Los Altos, California: Hermes, 1954.
Coleman, James S., Elihu Katz, and Herbert Menzel. *Medical Innovation, a Diffusion Study.* Indianapolis: Bobbs-Merrill, 1966.
Davis, Fred. "Deviance Disavowal," *Social Problems,* Vol. 9 (Fall 1961), pp. 120–132.
———. "Why All of Us May Be Hippies Someday," *Trans-action,* Vol. 5 (December 1967), pp. 10–18.
Didion, Joan. "The Hippie Generation," *Saturday Evening Post* (September 23, 1967).
Freidson, Eliot. "Disability as Social Deviance," pp. 71–99 in Marvin B. Sussman (ed.), *Sociology and Rehabilitation.* Washington: American Sociological Association, 1965.
Goffman, Erving. *Stigma.* Englewood Cliffs, New Jersey: Prentice-Hall, 1963.
Kitsuse, John I. "Societal Reaction to Deviant Behavior," *Social Problems,* Vol. 9 (Winter 1962), pp. 247–256.
Kramer, John C., Vitezslav S. Fischman and Don C. Littlefield. "Amphetamine Abuse," *JAMA,* Vol. 201 (July 31, 1967), pp. 305–309.
Lemert, Edwin. "Paranoia and the Dynamics of Exclusion," *Sociometry,* Vol. 25 (March 1962), pp. 2–20.
Matza, David. "Position and Behavior Patterns of Youth," in Robert E. L. Faris (ed.), *Handbook of Modern Sociology.* Chicago: Rand McNally, 1964.
Seeley, John. *The Americanization of the Unconscious.* Philadelphia and New York: International Science Press, 1967.
Simon, Geoffrey and Grafton Trout. "Hippies in College—From Teeny-boppers to Drug Freaks," *Trans-action,* Vol. 5 (December 1967), pp. 27–32.
Sjoberg, Gideon (ed.), *Ethics, Politics and Social Research.* Cambridge, Massachusetts: Schenkman, 1967.
Smith, David E. "Lysergic Acid Diethyamide: An Historical Perspective," *Journal of Psychedelic Drugs,* Vol. 1 (Summer 1967), pp. 2–7.
Strauss, Anselm L. *Mirrors and Masks.* Glencoe Illinois: The Free Press, 1959.
Strauss, Rick. "Confessions of a Speedfreak," *Los Angeles Oracle,* Vol. 1 (July 1967).
Strong, Samuel M. "Negro-White Relations as Reflected in Social Types," *American Journal of Sociology,* Vol. 52 (July 1946), pp. 23–30.
Van Hoffman, Nicholas. "Dope Scene—Big Business in the Haight," *San Francisco Chronicle* (October 31, 1967).

22 | The Hippie Ethic and the Spirit of Drug Use | Sherri Cavan

Nowhere has the intimate relation between the hippie ethic and drugs been better described than in this original essay by Sherri Cavan. To these hippies drugs are an integral part of a transcendental vision of life.

We see further in this essay why there is such a profound conflict—almost open combat at times—between the normal way of life in American society and the hippie way of life.

The Vision

For the hippies of the Haight, the world begins and ends with, literally, a vision.[1] Their ideology is, in a word, transcendental. One becomes aware of the world simultaneously with becoming aware of one's own psyche. One's psyche in this sense is constituted of the consciousness of possibilities, the ability to formulate images of things not given in the present moment of sensory awareness.

> Paul, in explaining what it is like to "really see" the world says, "You're looking at a glass of water and seeing it not just as a glass of water but as a glass of water *and* something to drink *and* crystal clarity *and* the seas *and* the rain *and* the rainbow."
>
> He goes on to say that once you have realized that all of those possibilities are always there, then you've "really" seen a glass of water for the first time.
>
> "I did it in the beginning [take acid for mind-expansion]. To see how far I could stretch my head. To see how far I could take an idea, and things like that . . . There's a whole period when you're just starting to take acid when you're getting used to it. Everytime you watch some different way of reacting to things. Every once in a while you watch yourself going through very egotistical patterns of behavior. And you kind of stand back and realize you've done this an awful lot, and you see it from an entirely different perspective. I never really got into using it that way."[2]

In a Cartesian sense, the consciousness of possibilities other than those of the present moment of sensory awareness are as "real" as the latter. The vision thus consists of the realization of the simultaneity of

This is an original essay prepared for this volume.

mind and matter (thought and sensory experience) as the reality of the here and now.

> A small group of hippies are sitting in the park, talking in general about the "straights," and the straights' lack of understanding about the world. At one point, one of the group says, of the straights, "They think that if you imagine something that you can't touch it's a hallucination . . . They'll never understand that ideas are real too."
>
> "After my first acid trip, I was overwhelmed with the importance of imagination. I suddenly saw how key imagination was to sanity. That in some ways you could define a problem as limited alternatives, all of which are unacceptable. But in reality, there are infinite alternatives . . . Everything is authentic. Everything is real. Human beings can invent unreal things, they can think of unreal things. It's all real. It's all right here."3

The "can" and the "could," the "is" and the "is not" are all elements of one's psychic consciousness. This is in effect the vision.

The sense of the vision—its meaning—is resolved into an unquestioned acceptance of "total reality" as the conjunction of the physical world and the psychic world. The physical world is, in Wittgenstein's terms, "all that is the case," and what is the case is the existence of sensate states of affairs.4 The psychic world is an attitude, a perspective, a particular choice of how to order and arrange the elements of the physical world. Thus, any particular "picture" one has of the physical world is dependent upon where one chooses to stand to look at what there is to see; how one chooses to arrange such "states of affairs."

> Bart says to me, "I want to be in control of my ideas instead of my ideas being in control of me. I am here [he puts out one hand] and my ideas are here [he puts out his second hand, a little away from the first one and a little in front of it]. If you look from here, it looks like this hand [the first one] is causing this hand" [the second one]. (The "here" is a perspective in which both hands appear to be part of the same continuous plane.)
>
> "But if you look from here, they are not the same at all." (This "here" is a perspective in which the hands appear to be located on separate planes and on points not coordinated between those planes.)
>
> "Everybody has their own frame. It's a big goddam planet. It includes every frame you can think of. Every tangent. Every opposite. Every travesty. Every permutation. Every practical joke. Every shade. Everything you want to talk about. That's not to say you can't see things clearly. I think you can."5

Man is thus seen to be "free" in the sense that he can transcend the immediate moment of sensate awareness of imagining alternative arrangements. The "necessity" of the world as it has always been apprehended dissolves into an open vista of possibilities. But it is equally important that man is free in the sense that he can act upon these imagined alternatives. And hence by his actions, man can bring about as sensate states of affairs any psychic possibility he can imagine.

> Howard and some others have been talking about what it is like to be on acid. At one point Howard turns to me and says, "I tried to play chess on acid one time. You can't. You see the board and there are a million possibilities [to make a move] and all of them are beautiful. I mean, you can move a piece, but you realize you could move any piece and play any number of games you want to."
>
> I ask him what he means by this and he goes on to explain that if you really wanted to you could play a conventional game of chess. But there is no necessity to it; you could also play a countless number of games which would be variations on the game of chess as it is customarily played.
>
> "You move around a lot. We're just out to turn everyone on. You're always up against the Man. You want to do beautiful things that you know are beautiful. You want to have a permit to have a fire in an open lot, so you can have a barbecue. You look at the ground, you look at the air where the fire would be. You know where the fire hoses are, you know there's no problem. Everyone knows it. But in comes the fire inspector, regulation twenty, you've got to have two exits. You don't have that. No fire . . . because of a foolish, obscene, ridiculous regulation that has nothing to do with the facts of the matter. You run into this all the time. You smoke marijuana, you know that marijuana is a good healthy thing for a human being to do. While you're doing this good healthy thing, you want to share it with your friend. [But] you've got this eye, this ominous presence, lurking around. It wants to put you in jail for doing what you know is a good thing to do . . . That's my day. Now somebody is going to say, 'Well, why don't you just obey the law?' Well, I don't know why it's there. What I do know is the Vietnamese are dying for what they believe In and all the technology and might and truth in the world isn't going to stop them."[6]

The vision and its concomitant realization of man's freedom is an individual event that occurs for individual men. No one can "give" the vision to another. At most, one can attempt to bring about the conditions under which it will be likely that another will have the vision too.[7]

> Michael and some others have been engaged in talking about the drug experience. It is one of the most constant topics of conversation. This evening the focus of the conversation has been how the drug experience results in the users "understanding" about what the world is "really like."
>
> I ask Michael if somebody could come to the same understanding about the world without drugs and he answers yes, citing some Yogis and other mystics who, he says, "understand the world in the same way after meditating." But then he goes on to add, "You know, it's a very personal thing. You have to see it yourself . . . Nobody can tell anybody else about it."
>
> When I ask why not he becomes a little impatient with me and says, "If you don't see it for yourself, you can never understand what somebody else is rapping [talking] about."
>
> "Like in music, like I always play flute on the street and stuff, and try

to turn the straight people on . . . 'Cause I know I'm doin' better'n them, and I would like to bring what I know is better—not better, but a different word . . ."[8]

The Given Situation

The circumstances of man's life are thus presented in the simultaneous presence of the physical world and the consciousness of the possibilities that exist within that world. Like the immediate moment of the sensory awareness of the physical world, the consciousness of the possible arrangements of that world are not a matter of some speculative future, but a matter of the present here and now.[9]

Insofar as the first cause and final basis of the given situation is one's psychic awareness, consciousness constitutes the crux of existence.

> Eric says, quite suddenly, "My mind is the most beautiful thing in the whole world because that's where the whole world is."
>
> The rest of the group respond by laughing, but it seems that they are laughing more at the sudden solemnity and awe of Eric's proclamation than at what he has said specifically.
>
> A few days later, someone who had been in the group that night, in talking about Eric, says, "Eric really knows where it is at."
>
> "If you don't want the world you're pushed into, you have to find another world. You can't sit back and say it's all going to work out. No exterior movement can function unless it's composed of people whose interior is fit . . . The first place that it has to happen is inside. You learn where you are. You learn if you want to make it here or in the trees. You learn if you want to make it with men or with women or play with yourself. You learn not because this is the way it's supposed to be, but truthfully, in yourself it's what you want."[10]

Yet consciousness does not exist without form and substance. The form of consciousness is embodied in action and the content of consciousness is embodied in sensate and psychic experience.

> Bart starts to tell the three of us about a rather serious accident he had some time ago, while he was on acid. He goes on and says, "On acid I had to learn to acknowledge vanity. I mean, I was all hung up on being vain—wanted to cleanse myself of it. That's when I fell out of the window. I saw [then] that you couldn't not be vain. That's you and if that isn't part of the world, then there's no world."
>
> Somewhat later he says, "I look at my feet. Beautiful. I love my feet. That's where I end. It's good to know where you end."
>
> "I'm very conscious of my social entity. The animal I am. I have needs: food, clothing and shelter. But I also have a desire to spread out my energies, to pour them into beautiful things, into beautiful people. Into raising their levels, and mine, because we all raise them together.
>
> "I frankly believe in the Haight . . . I live love, I live peace, I live beauty."[11]

Given the circumstances of life, a man will act only in ways that will not jeopardize his freedom. And by definition, such action cannot result in anything but aesthetic and spiritual beauty.

> Nora has been telling me about the changes which have taken place in her life in the past few years, particularly as they are related to the use of acid and peyote. At one point she says, "I saw so clearly that there's no point in trying to control your life."
> She goes on to expand this, explaining that if you just let yourself do what you feel intuitively is right, it will be right. But if you try to plan ahead and think it all out before you act—if you go against your intuition—you will probably make a mistake.

> Q: "You accept the idea that you have a right to be physically beautiful?"
> Ron: "Sure, [you] should be. Because everybody is. The more you're yourself, the more you really fill up and relax, listen, give. The more you're yourself, the more beautiful you are. And everybody is the most interesting person in the world. Every person is."[12]

The Psychic Community

Each individual's realization of the "true" circumstances of man's life can only result in action that is both free and beautiful. In this way, a spiritual community of visionaries is possible on the basis of each individual making the same discovery.

> David suggests that we go to the beach in Marin. I suggest that we might go to the one here in the city, since it is much closer. David says no, because the particular beach he wants to go to is the one which is in effect hippie territory and he says that "it can't help but be a good day with *them*." The implication that his remarks carry is that Hippies, by definition, are compatible and harmonious. This is a statement that I have heard from a variety of people in a variety of occasions. Sometimes it is put as "our people."
> "I feel that they're [the Haight-Ashbury] my people. Like when we were traveling . . . to see someone who was obviously a hippie was a marvelous thing, because it was instant communication, instant love, and helping . . . but when you're down on Montgomery Street walking and you see all the really poor people who are on their half-hour lunch break and are uptight, unhappy, in debt—the middle-class Montgomery Street employees . . . that their suits all look alike. And to see a hippie down there, as soon as you see one, there's this instant big smile and happy vibration, and wonderful communication, and it's like that all the time, except there are some kids who've got fouled up along the way, and that's to be expected in working things out, and all we can do is try to help them. There's people who're fouled up in every bunch of people, and all we can do is—try to help our own, you know."[13]

The love of one's self can no longer be separated from the love of others, insofar as there are no longer any perceivable differences

between self and other. Both self and other share the same consciousness and the same situation. Thus, the psychic community must be, by
definition, a utopia. Even though each individual member can construct
his personal world as he so desires, his actions can never jeopardize
the freedom of either himself or others, nor be anything but beautiful
for others, since the community is constituted in the first place by
individual men with the same vision and hence the same circumstances. It is a spiritual community of men that is not encountered as a
fact external to each individual man, but rather internal to each
member. It is a community constituted by individual psyches joined into
one.

The tribe exemplifies the spiritual community, for in the tribe, all
members know all there is to be known.[14]

> Five of us have been sitting around, listening to the radio and occa-
> sionally talking. I mention at one point Freuchen's *Book of the Eskimos,*
> saying that I find the way of life of the Eskimos very fascinating. Helen
> asks me what that way of life is like and I recount some ethnographic
> descriptions of it. When I am done, Stan says, "That's the way it should
> be. Everybody should know the same thing and then they would live in
> peace."
>
> I don't quite understand the relevance of Stan's remark at that point.
> When I bring it up again two or three days later, Stan says I said the
> Eskimos were a tribe, and that's the way people should live, although I
> did not in fact say anything about the Eskimos being a tribe, but only
> having organized their life in a particular kind of way.
>
> "Tribal identity comes because you want to trust each other. It's one of
> the things I realized at one of the [Be-Ins] in [Golden Gate] Park. There
> were a great number of people there that I could trust wtih my life. Be-
> cause they were people that belonged to me and I belonged to them. It's
> an instinctual, non-intellectual response. Now the tribal thing is very hard
> to define, because it's a very strange culture we're in. A lot of this stuff is
> camp. Like I don't think wearing a headband, and playing Indians, or any
> of these things means anything at all. Like it's a game. There's a lot of
> deadweight to it too. There's kids that are just playing for a while. They've
> run away from home, and they're going to go back home. I just hope that
> they carry with them what trust means, and what mutual care means.
> That's what the tribe is: people that are taking care of each other for
> real. Who care about each other. Who are mutually responsible for each
> other. Lovingly. Willingly. Who feel that sense of the tribe. You feel it
> when you know it. It doesn't come from the outside really."[15]

Reality is thus constructed by "cutting" the world in a horizontal
plane, rather than a vertical one. The community of man is not a
collectivity where the individual members share in common a psychic
life *and* a physical world. The latter collectivity is not a "spiritual"
community in that members perceive themselves separated by virtue of
the particular conjunction of the psychic-and-physical segment that is
"theirs."[16] Rather, the spiritual community of man is a collectivity

where the individual members all share in common the same psychic life vis-à-vis the same physical world differentiated only by where they are "at" in this conjunct.[17]

> Bev and a girl I have never met before have been arguing about their feelings about the present scene on the street. Bev seems to feel that the Community has been gradually deteriorating and the girl disagrees, saying that everyone on the street is after the same thing. Bev says to her, "That may be where you're at, but how do you know that's where they're at?"

The Universe

The apprehension of the true community of man as a spiritual community is made when the vision of imaginative possibilities is contrasted with the present conditions of mankind. The universe is thus a meta-realization, in which the original vision is seen from the perspective of the ultimate insight.

> It
> the thing for which I have no name
> completes the perfect circle perfectly
> just beyond the barricades of flesh
> called ego, encompassing the senses
> and the intellect in fierce imagination
> and mirage
> And I am paradoxed
> by matter Itself
> dromedary dream of the universe[18]

The ultimate insight—the insight of the "full realization of the insight of the first vision"—resolves all questions. There is nothing more to be known, although from this realization there is much to be concluded.

> Bart has been playing a kind of hide-and-go-seek with me (what Linda refers to, the next night, as "not really putting you on" even though it has the appearance of that). He "makes a point" by bringing two events together and once I have acknowledged them, he drops one of the original events and takes up a third, showing me that it is all really very different. I finally ask him, "What are you talking about?" He responds, "What do you mean, what am I talking about?" as though I should "surely" be able to see, as though it were all obvious.
> I try to explain that it will take me a while to figure out what he is talking about—that I know the world through the analysis of a series of discreet events. Bart responds that I am "not with it." He goes on to say that to "really understand" I would just "immediately understand"; I would just see it instead of having to break it into parts before I could

put it together to see "what it is." I ask how I can know that what I see right now (or at any given moment) will be the same as what he sees. But this is an irrelevant remark on my part; Bart treats it as a nonsense-noise, simply ignoring it and rapping on about something else.

On other occasions, when I have asked the same question, I have received the reply: "You just know, you're on the same wave length, getting the same vibrations and you know it."

"The common reaction of people who get high the first time is 'Wow! Is that real? Is that what's really happening? Wow! Did you see it? It's real!' Not a specimen world anymore. It's not a consumer-conveyor, consumer-conveyor-sit-in-a-slot-boom-boom-boom-boom-boom-boom-boom-boom-boom-boom-boom-FEED-boom-boom-boom-boom-SHIT-boom-boom-boom-SLEEP-boom-boom-boom . . . it's not like that. It's like sentences don't have so many periods, it's like getting more dashes and colons and commas and involutions."[19]

When the possibilities of how mankind's life is to be lived (as they are presented in the vision) are compared with any particular way of life (as it is presented in the given situation), some ways of life can be seen to be harmonious and others can be seen to be inharmonious. The true way of life is the way of life in which man and nature live in harmony; the false way of life is when man and nature live in conflict.

There's a very strong identification in the Haight-Ashbury [with the American Indians] as we play out our Karmic roles and go through our evolution in our previous incarnations . . . And the American Indian is the Indian-Human Being, brave warrior, non-killer, generally, coup-touch warrior, who had a good relationship with the land which we find missing today and which is a good part of the rebellion that was mentioned before . . .[20]

The ultimate insight is the ultimate insight because it is the final boundary of reason. Any insight concerning the insight concerning the insight of the vision resolves the universe into absurdity.

I have sent a friend in the Community a copy of an earlier paper I had been working on, on the analysis of the hippie beliefs about form and ritual. In the letter I receive from him in response, he comments on his impression of the activities of the hippies in the district and some of his own recent experiences, ending by writing: "Words seem almost impotent against such a profound sensual experience [such as that of acid]. Maybe it's a paradox to discuss the life of form since the act mitigates all discussion."

"Okay, so it's not new. So one day the universe might disappear into the wink of God's eye. And start all over again with some explosion. It doesn't concern me. The Communists say the root of everything is dialectical materialism, uh-huh. The Jehovah Witnesses say the root of everything is destruction by fire, uh-huh. Everybody has their own frame. It's a big goddamn planet. It includes every frame you can think of. Every tangent. Every opposite. Every travesty. Every permutation. Every practical joke. Every shade. Everything you want to talk about. That's not to say you can't see things clearly. I think you can."[21]

In effect, the three-valued logic can be carried out only to two places in the search for final truth, for final truth, to be both final and true, must be stable. One can know (have the vision); one can know that one knows (have the insight of vision); but to know that you know that you know tumbles into an infinite regress for which there is no stop-rule.[22]

The Beliefs About Drugs

For the hippies of the Haight, drug use takes place within the context of what they consider to be normal, everyday life. Their understandings of the world-in-general and their understandings about hallucinogenic drugs in particular coincide in a mutually supportive manner. Hence for members, the use of drugs is both a sensible and a sanctioned course of action, despite the perceivedly irrational and censured status that such activity has for members of the conventional community.

The actual beliefs about hallucinogenic drugs in the hippie community have two sanctioned interpretations. According to both interpretations, drugs are important in that they "expand" one's consciousness, and hence create a situation where one becomes not only aware of his psyche as a part of himself, but also aware of the potential of that psyche. The interpretations differ essentially on whether drugs are believed to be necessary and sufficient for this expansion of the consciousness or whether they are believed to be only a tool to effect it.[23]

In one interpretation, the hallucinogenic effects of drugs (particularly LSD, but also peyote, psilocihine, mescaline, marijuana, STP, DMT) are the direct and essentially the only cause of the initial vision.

Statements such as these from *Voices of the Love Generation* are illustrative of this interpretation:

> LSD puts you in touch with your surroundings. You take LSD and your surroundings are there. Feelings about your surroundings are there. The onion is peeled and peeled and peeled, and in the center we have something that is really an incredible thing. It's where we're able to see from more accurately, and more honestly, and without a great deal of incredible amounts of efforts . . . [the use of these drugs] automatically puts people in a different frame of reference. It points out a lot of inequities in the system. Just by their existence; by the fact that they are suppressed.[24]

> I went to a psychiatrist when I was twenty-three . . . I took some LSD. I took quite a lot of it before I went to the psychiatrist, but one time I took it when I went down the coast and I ended up running naked on the highway and really flipped out. My mother had to come down and take me . . . My mother said "You have to go to a psychiatrist." . . .
> "What about the acid trip? Wasn't that supposed to help?"
> "Yeah, it did. I could never have gotten where I am now without the acid."[25]

Within the framework of such an interpretation, no one not having fully experienced the drug experience can fully understand and acknowledge the truth of the ideology since the vision upon which it is built is missing.

Furthermore, anyone who has utilized drugs is destined to see the vision in its ideologically postulated form. "Freaking-out" and to a lesser extent "bad trips" are thus to be understood in terms of the user being in a bad situation: either not prepared to understand the meaning of the vision; too caught up in the conventional world to accept the implications of the vision even if he understands them; or surrounded by incongruent elements, so that there is no opportunity for the drugs to "properly" affect him.

The first example below comes from *Voices of the Love Generation;* the second from field observations:

> "I've had silocybin, mescaline, peyote, and datura and methedrine. I'm going to take STP. I'm kind of afraid of it but I'm going to take it . . . I feel my fear is that there'll be a revelation of something that I'm not yet willing to accept the consequences of. I feel I must if it's the truth. So I'm going to take it."[26]

> Carol is telling Nora and me about the "bad trip" her roommate had recently experienced. Carol explains that some friend of Anne, her roommate, brought Anne home "high and screaming." The evening was spent with the roommate sitting naked on the bed. Carol goes on to say "she screamed all night—terrible cries. I thought she would never stop."
> Nora asks if it was the roommate's first trip and Carol replies, "No, I don't know how many times she's dropped acid before. But it's a lot." I ask why this was such a bad trip for her and Carol answers, "It was the situation she was in," although she cannot explain what the situation was like, other than to say, "It was a bad scene. She shouldn't have dropped it (taken acid) there."

In the second interpretation, drugs are not central but only a means— a tool—to assist the user in breaking the bonds of the perspective of the world and the accompanying ideology that he has accepted all his life.

> "What makes you reach for a drug and what's in it for you? You personally."
> "It's always different. Sometimes maybe to disguise feelings. Sometimes to blow them up, sometimes maybe not to think. A lot of reasons, a lot of different drugs."
> "Is there no moral imperative in acid?"
> "I don't think so. Look at acid dealers. Acid dealers carry guns around. They take it.
> They've had it."[27]

The following excerpt from the introduction to a guide for "successful" drug experience sums up this interpretation rather succinctly:

> Acid-LSD: Although acid has no value in and of itself will not make you holy or good or wise or anything else except high—it can be used in a valuable way. It can be an educational tool; you can learn something from it.[28]

For those employing this interpretation, there are means other than drugs that can be used to attain the vision: meditation, Eastern religions, and to some extent, Western religion. Therefore, since the hallucinogenic drugs are only a tool for bringing about the vision, they may be put to other uses as well. One of the Community members notes in *Voices of the Love Generation:*

> I think drugs are being used for everything . . . I think I see drugs being used . . . to open up the sexual synapse in the head and to get some of that conditioning out of the way. Acid is a great deconditioning agent . . . I think that perhaps drugs are being used for every possible reason . . . the same reasons that cars are used. Some people fuck in their cars. Some people use their cars to take them to and from work. Some people just go for a ride in their cars to be alone. Some people take a car only to use once in a while. It's a tool.[29]

Within this interpretation of the role of drugs, what the user will "find" during the course of this use is not guaranteed. He may find the vision that is at the basis of the ideology, but he may also encounter visions that are in no way compatible with the ideology.

> We have been sharing a table in the café with some members of the Hell's Angels, chatting idly about what their "scene" is like. At one point, one of them begins to recount what he describes as "one of the best experiences I've ever had." The nature of the experience was essentially a rumble between himself and some other Angels and some negro males. At the conclusion of the account, he says, "Those Hippies say that if you fight or something like that on acid you'll freak out. They don't know what they're talking about. It was the best fight I was ever in, that fight when I was on acid. Beautiful. Just beautiful."[30]

However, regardless of which particular interpretation of the drug experience a member uses, the hippies of the Haight in general acknowledge the relationship of drug use to the recognition and implementation of the ideologies that justify the community in the first place. Drug use as a course of action on the part of the members is comprehensible, perceived as legitimate, and frequently undertaken. Within the hippie community, then, the smoking of marijuana is a regular and recurrent activity for "good reasons" that members can and will provide.

Since the beliefs about drugs and the beliefs about the world in general are mutually supportive, each may serve to independently justify the other. That is, members can begin with their understanding of the world in general as a method of justifying their use of drugs or they may begin with their understanding of drugs as a method of justifying their allegiance to the ideology. Thus, in the normal course of events in the Haight, drug users may become ideological converts and ideological converts may become drug users.[31]

NOTES

1 The role of the supernatural vision as the basis for belief systems is similarly noted in Weston LaBarre, "Primitive Psychotherapy in Native American Cultures: Peyotism and Confession," *Journal of Abnormal and Social Psychology*, v. 42 (1947), pp. 294–308.
2 Leonard Wolf, *Voices of the Love Generation* (New York: Little, Brown and Co., 1968), pp. 197–198.
3 *Ibid.,* pp. 114–139.
4 Ludwig Wittgenstein, *Tractatus Logio-Philosophicus* (London: Routledge and Kegan Paul, 1961), p. 7.
5 Wolf, *op. cit.,* p. 140.
6 *Ibid.,* pp. 122–123.
7 The importance of the role of the guru is found essentially in this context: the guru teaches by example, structuring the situation so that the student will learn on his own whatever there is for him to learn.
8 Wolf, *op. cit.,* p. 175.
9 Time is in effect foreshortened. In contrast with the conventional formulation of time, primary emphasis is placed on "now"—the immediately present moment. The role of time per se is addressed in greater detail in S. Cavan, *The Hippie of the Haight* (unpublished dissertation).
10 Wolf, *op. cit.,* p. 28.
11 *Ibid.,* p. 10.
12 *Ibid.,* p. 220.
13 *Ibid.,* p. 89.
14 Cf. Émile Durkheim, *The Division of Labor in Society* (Glencoe, Ill.: The Free Press, 1960) on mechanical and organic solidarity; and Karl Mannheim, *Essays on the Sociology of Knowledge* (London: Routledge and Kegan Paul, Ltd., 1959), on the social distribution of knowledge.
15 Wolf, *op. cit.,* p. 32.
16 For a discussion of the locating of individuals in terms of segments of their lives socially shared with others see George Simmel, *The Sociology of George Simmel* (Glencoe, Ill.: The Free Press, 1949), pp. 26–39.
17 In somewhat different terms, the community is not composed of individual-man-in-relationship-to-individual-man, but of men's consciousness-in-relationship-to-men's-physical-conditions.
18 From Steve Levine, "Fifth Song," *San Francisco Oracle* (February 1967).
19 Wolf, *op. cit.,* p. 261.
20 *Ibid.,* p. 55.
21 *Ibid.,* pp. 139–140.
22 Gilbert Ryle, "Categories," in A. Flew, ed., *Logic and Language* (Garden City, New York: Doubleday Anchor), pp. 281–298.
23 Whether the interpretation is one that prescribes drug use or accepts drug use, drug use as such constitutes a sanctioned means for what stand as the culturally valued goals of the hippies of the Haight. Thus, at least within the hippie community, those who use drugs are conforming members. Cf. Robert Merton, *Social Theory and Social Structure* (Glencoe, Ill.: The Free Press, 1957), pp. 131–160.

24 Wolf, *op. cit.,* pp. 207–208.
25 *Ibid.,* pp. 145–146.
26 *Ibid.,* p. 74.
27 *Ibid.,* pp. 134–135.
28 Chester Anderson and Lorraine Glennby, "Flight Plans" in Jerry Hopkins, ed., *The Hippie Papers* (New York: Signet Books, 1968), p. 68.
29 Wolf, *op. cit.,* p. 51.
30 A similar example of variant interpretations of "good music" can be found in Anthony Burgess, *The Clockwork Orange* (New York: Signet Books, 1965), where the protagonist recounts how he would listen to Beethoven as a means of evoking fantasies of fights, bloodied bodies, and general violent destruction.
31 There is no way to estimate what proportion of the members of the Community use drugs, in part because there is no precise way to determine the actual population of the Community: members come and go quite frequently. When members of the Community talk about themselves, one of the things they say is "We all use drugs." This may be a matter of members' perception of their own beliefs, or a matter of members perception of their own practices, or both. However, since the ideologically sanctioned vision need not be obtained by means of drugs, drug use need not be a universal in the community. My own observations have included at least two dozen acknowledged members who do not use drugs. But there is no reasonable way to use this figure as a sample of abstinence for the community-at-large.

23 | Focus on the Flower Children: Why All of Us May Be Hippies Someday | Fred Davis

Deviant groups often serve as social experiments *for the larger society. They become trials of a new way of life that other members of society, who are, perhaps, less willing to give up their ordinary way of life, can observe to see what it would be like to live in a different social world. Most deviant groups lead ways of life which prove to be "failures," from the standpoint of most members of society. As most members see those ways of life, they would not be willing to join in.*

Many people have asked these questions: Is the hippie way of life a valid vision of the way in which our whole society is moving? Is it a viable response to something basic and lasting in our society that would lead us to suspect that all of us may someday become hippies, or that our children may become hip? While there are grounds for tremendous disagreements over the answer to this question, and while I, for one, do not believe that the hippies in any way represent what our society will become, these are questions that should be seriously examined, not only for hippies, but for any group that leads a coherent but different way of life within our society. Nowhere has this question been examined more pertinently for hippies than in this essay by Fred Davis.

And thus in love we have declared the purpose of our hearts plainly, without flatterie, expecting love, and the same sincerity from you, without grumbling, or quarreling, being Creatures of your own image and mould, intending no other matter herein, but to observe the Law of righteous action, endeavoring to shut out of the Creation, the cursed thing, called Particular Propriety, which is the cause of all wars, bloudshed, theft, and enslaving Laws, that hold the people under miserie. ∎
Signed for and in behalf of all the poor oppressed people of England, and the whole world. ∎ *Gerard Winstanley and others* ∎ June 1, 1649

This quotation is from the leader of the Diggers, a millenarian sect of communistic persuasion that arose in England at the time of Oliver

Cromwell. Today in San Francisco's hippie community, the Haight-Ashbury district, a group of hippies naming themselves after this sect distributes free food to fellow hippies (and all other takers, for that matter) who congregate at about four o'clock every afternoon in the district's Panhandle, an eight-block strip of urban green, shaded by towering eucalyptus trees, that leads into Golden Gate Park to the west. On the corner of a nearby street, the "Hashbury" Diggers operate their Free Store where all—be they hip, straight, hostile, curious, or merely in need—can avail themselves (free of charge, no questions asked) of such used clothing, household articles, books, and second-hand furniture as find their way into the place on any particular day. The Diggers also maintained a large flat in the district where newly arrived or freshly dispossessed hippies could stay without charge for a night, a week, or however long they wished—until some months ago, when the flat was condemned by the San Francisco Health Department. Currently, the Diggers are rehabilitating a condemned skid-row hotel for the same purpose.

Not all of Haight-Ashbury's 7500 hippies are Diggers, although no formal qualifications bar them; nor, in one sense, are the several dozen Diggers hippies. What distinguishes the Diggers—an amorphous, shifting, and sometimes contentious amalgam of ex-political radicals, psychedelic mystics, Ghandians, and Brechtian avant-garde thespians—from the area's "ordinary" hippies is their ideological brio, articulateness, good works, and flair for the dramatic event. (Some are even rumored to be over 30.) In the eyes of many Hashbury hippies, therefore, the Diggers symbolize what is best, what is most persuasive and purposive, about the surrounding, more variegated hippie subculture—just as, for certain radical social critics of the American scene, the hippies are expressing, albeit elliptically, what is best about a seemingly ever-broader segment of American youth: its openness to new experience, puncturing of cant, rejection of bureaucratic regimentation, aversion to violence, and identification with the exploited and disadvantaged. That this is not the whole story barely needs saying. Along with the poetry and flowers, the melancholy smile at passing and ecstatic clasp at greeting, there is also the panicky incoherence of the bad LSD trip, the malnutrition, a startling rise in V.D. and hepatitis, a seemingly phobic reaction to elementary practices of hygiene and sanitation, and—perhaps most disturbing in the long run—a casualness about the comings and goings of human relationships that must verge on the grossly irresponsible.

But, then, social movements—particularly of this expressive-religious variety—are rarely of a piece, and it would be unfortunate if social scientists, rather than inquiring into the genesis, meaning, and future of the hippie movement, too soon joined ranks (as many are likely to, in any case) with solid burghers in an orgy of research into the "pathology" of it all: the ubiquitous drug use (mainly marihuana and LSD, often amphetamines, rarely heroin or other opiates), the easy attitudes toward sex ("If two people are attracted to each other, what better way of showing it than to make love?"), and the mocking hostility toward the middle-class values of pleasure-deferral, material success, and—ultimately—the whole mass-media-glamorized round of chic, deodorized, appliance-glutted suburban existence.

The Hip Scene Is the Message

Clearly, despite whatever real or imagined "pathology" middle-class spokesmen are ready to assign to the hippies, it is the middle-class scheme of life that young hippies are reacting against, even though in their ranks are to be found some youth of working-class origin who have never enjoyed the affluence that their peers now so heartily decry. To adulterate somewhat the slogan of Marshall McLuhan, one of the few non-orientalized intellectuals whom hippies bother to read at all, *the hip scene is the message,* not the elements whence it derives or the meanings that can be assigned to it verbally. (Interestingly, this fusion of disparate classes does not appear to include any significant number of the Negro youths who reside with their families in the integrated Haight-Ashbury district or in the adjoining Negro ghetto, the Fillmore district. By and large, Negroes view with bewilderment and ridicule the white hippies who flaunt, to the extent of begging on the streets, their rejection of what the Negroes have had scant opportunity to attain. What more revealing symbol of the Negro riots in our nation's cities than the carting off of looted TV sets, refrigerators, and washing machines? After all, aren't these things what America is all about?)

But granting that the hippie scene is a reaction to middle-class values, can the understanding of any social movement—particularly one that just in the process of its formation is so fecund of new art forms, new styles of dress and demeanor, and (most of all) new ethical bases for human relationships—ever be wholly reduced to its reactive aspect? As Ralph Ellison has eloquently observed in his critique of the standard sociological explanation of the American Negro's situation, a people's distinctive way of life is never solely a reaction to the dominant social forces that have oppressed, excluded, or alienated them from the larger society. The cumulative process of reaction and counterreaction, in its historical unfolding, creates its own ground for the emergence of new symbols, meanings, purposes, and social discoveries, none of which are ever wholly contained in embryo, as it were, in the conditions that elicited the reaction. It is, therefore, less with an eye toward explaining "how it came to be" than toward explaining what it may betoken of life in the future society that I now want to examine certain facets of the Hashbury hippie subculture. (Of course, very similar youth movements, subcultures, and settlements are found nowadays in many parts of the affluent Western world—Berkeley's Telegraph Avenue teeny-boppers; Los Angeles' Sunset Strippers; New York's East Village hippies; London's mods; Amsterdam's Provos; and the summer *Wandervögel* from all over Europe who chalk the pavement of Copenhagen's main shopping street, the Strøget, and sun themselves on the steps of Stockholm's Philharmonic Hall. What is culturally significant about the Haight-Ashbury hippies is, I would hazard, in general significant about these others as well, with—to be sure—certain qualifications. Indeed, a certain marvelous irony attaches itself to the fact that perhaps the only genuine cross-national culture found in the world today builds on the rag-tag of beards, bare feet, bedrolls, and beads, not on the cultural-exchange programs of governments and universities, or tourism, or—least of all—ladies' clubs' invocations for sympathetic understanding of one's foreign neighbors.)

What I wish to suggest here is that there is, as Max Weber would have put it, an *elective affinity* between prominent styles and themes in the hippie subculture and certain incipient problems of identity, work, and leisure that loom ominously as Western industrial society moves into an epoch of accelerated cybernation, staggering material abundance, and historically-unprecedented mass opportunities for creative leisure and enrichment of the human personality. This is not to say that the latter are the *hidden causes* or tangible *motivating forces* of the former. Rather, the point is that the hippies, in their collective, yet radical, break with the constraints of our present society, are—whether they know it or not (some clearly do intuit a connection)—already rehearsing *in vivo* a number of possible cultural solutions to central life problems posed by the emerging society of the future. While other students of contemporary youth culture could no doubt cite many additional emerging problems to which the hippie subculture is, willy-nilly, addressing itself (marriage and family organization, the character of friendship and personal loyalties, the forms of political participation), space and the kind of observations I have been able to make require that I confine myself to three: the problems of *compulsive consumption,* of *passive spectatorship,* and of the *time-scale of experience.*

Compulsive Consumption

What working attitude is man to adopt toward the potential glut of consumer goods that the new technology will make available to virtually all members of the future society? Until now, modern capitalist society's traditional response to short-term conditions of overproduction has been to generate—through government manipulation of fiscal devices—greater purchasing power for discretionary consumption. At the same time, the aim has been to cultivate the acquisitive impulse—largely through mass advertising, annual styling changes, and planned obsolescence—so that, in the economist's terminology, a high level of aggregate demand could be sustained. Fortunately, given the great backlog of old material wants and the technologically-based creation of new wants, these means have, for the most part, worked comparatively well—both for advancing (albeit unequally) the mass standard of living and ensuring a reasonably high rate of return to capital.

But, as Walter Weisskopf, Robert Heilbroner, and other economists have wondered, will these means prove adequate for an automated future society in which the mere production of goods and services might easily outstrip man's desire for them, or his capacity to consume them in satisfying ways? Massive problems of air pollution, traffic congestion, and waste disposal aside, is there no psychological limit to the number of automobiles, TV sets, freezers, and dishwashers that even a zealous consumer can aspire to, much less make psychic room for in his life space? The specter that haunts post-industrial man is that of a near worker-less economy in which most men are constrained, through a variety of economic and political sanctions, to frantically purchase and assiduously use up the cornucopia of consumer goods that a robot-staffed factory system (but one still harnessed to capitalism's rationale of pecuniary profit) regurgitates upon the populace. As far back as the late 1940s sociologists like David Riesman were already pointing to the many moral paradoxes of work, leisure, and interpersonal relations posed by a then only nascent society of capitalist mass abundance. How much more perplexing the paradoxes if, using current technological trends, we extrapolate to the year 2000?

Hippies, originating mainly in the middle classes, have been nurtured at the boards of consumer abundance. Spared their parents' vivid memories of economic depression and material want, however, they now, with what to their elders seems like insulting abandon, declare unshamefacedly that the very quest for "the good things of life" and all that this entails—the latest model, the third car, the monthly credit payments, the right house in the right neighborhood—are a "bad bag." In phrases redolent of nearly all utopian thought of the past, they proclaim that happiness and a meaningful life are not to be found in things, but in the cultivation of the self and by an intensive exploration of inner sensibilities with like-minded others.

Extreme as this antimaterialistic stance may seem, and despite its probable tempering should hippie communities develop as a stable feature on the American landscape, it nonetheless points a way to a solution of the problem of material glut; to wit, the simple demonstration of the ability to live on less, thereby calming the acquisitive frenzy that would have to be sustained, and even accelerated, if the present scheme of capitalist production and distribution were to remain unchanged. Besides such establishments as the Diggers' Free Store, gleanings of this attitude are even evident in the street panhandling that so many hippies engage in. Unlike the street beggars of old, there is little that is obsequious or deferential about their manner. On the contrary, their approach is one of easy, sometimes condescending casualness, as if to say, "You've got more than enough to spare, I need it, so let's not make a degrading charity scene out of my asking you." The story is told in the Haight-Ashbury of the patronizing tourist who, upon being approached for a dime by a hippie girl in her late teens, took the occasion to deliver a small speech on how delighted he would be to give it to her—provided she first told him what she needed it for. Without blinking an eye she replied, "It's my menstrual period and that's how much a sanitary napkin costs."

Passive Spectatorship

As social historians are forever reminding us, modern man has— since the beginnings of the industrial revolution—become increasingly a spectator and less a participant. Less and less does he, for example, create or play music, engage in sports, dance or sing; instead he watches professionally-trained others, vastly more accomplished than himself, perform their acts while he, perhaps, indulges in Mitty-like fantasies of hidden graces and talents. Although this bald statement of the spectator thesis has been challenged in recent years by certain social researchers—statistics are cited of the growing numbers taking guitar lessons, buying fishing equipment, and painting on Sunday— there can be little doubt that "doing" kinds of expressive pursuits, particularly of the collective type, no longer bear the same *integral* relationship to daily life that they once did, or still do in primitive societies. The mere change in how they come to be perceived, from what one does in the ordinary course of life to one's "hobbies," is in itself of profound historical significance. Along with this, the virtuoso standards that once were the exclusive property of small aristocratic elites, rather than being undermined by the oft-cited revolutions in mass communications and mass education, have so diffused through the class structure as to even cause the gifted amateur *at play* to apologize for his efforts with some such remark as, "I only play at it." In short, the cult of professionalism, in the arts as elsewhere, has been institutionalized so intensively in Western society that the ordinary man's sense of expressive adequacy and competence has progressively atrophied. This is especially true of the college-educated, urban middle classes, which—newly exposed to the lofty aesthetic standards of high culture—stand in reverent, if passive, awe of them.

Again, the problem of excessive spectatorship has not proved particularly acute until now, inasmuch as most men have had other time-consuming demands to fill their lives with, chiefly work and family life, leavened by occasional vacations and mass-produced amusements. But what of the future when, according to such social prognosticators as Robert Theobald and Donald Michael, all (except a relatively small cadre of professionals and managers) will be faced with a surfeit of leisure time? Will the mere extension of passive spectatorship and the professional's monopoly of expressive pursuits be a satisfactory solution?

Here, too, hippies are opening up new avenues of collective response to life issues posed by a changing sociotechnological environment. They are doing so by rejecting those virtuoso standards that stifle participation in high culture; by substituting an extravagantly eclectic (and, according to traditional aestheticians, reckless) admixture of materials, styles, and motifs from a great diversity of past and present human cultures; and, most of all, by insisting that every man can find immediate expressive fulfillment provided he lets the socially-suppressed spirit within him ascend into vibrant consciousness. The manifesto is: All men are artists, and who cares that some are better at it than others; we can all have fun! Hence, the deceptively crude antisophistication of hippie art forms, which are, perhaps, only an apparent reversion to primitivism. One has only to encounter the lurid *art nouveau* contortions of the hippie posters and their Beardsleyan exoticism, or the mad mélange of hippie street costume—Greek-sandaled feet peeking beneath harem pantaloons encased in a fringed American Indian suede jacket, topped by pastel floral decorations about the face—or the sitar-whining cacophony of the folk-rock band, to know immediately that one is in the presence of *expressiveness* for its own sake.

In more mundane ways, too, the same readiness to let go, to participate, to create and perform without script or forethought is everywhere evident in the Hashbury. Two youths seat themselves on the sidewalk or in a store entranceway; bent beer can in hand, one begins scratching a bongo-like rhythm on the pavement while the other tattoos a bell-like accompaniment by striking a stick on an empty bottle. Soon they are joined, one by one, by a tambourinist, a harmonica player, a penny-whistler or recorder player, and, of course, the ubiquitous guitarist. A small crowd collects and, at the fringes, some blanket-bedecked boys and girls begin twirling about in movements vaguely resembling a Hindu dance. The wailing, rhythmic beating and dancing, alternately rising to peaks of intensity and subsiding, may last for as little as five minutes or as long as an hour, players and dancers joining in and dropping out as whim moves them. At some point—almost any—a mood takes hold that "the happening is over"; participants and onlookers disperse as casually as they had collected.

Analogous scenes of "participation unbound" are to be observed almost every night of the week (twice on Sunday) at the hippies' Parnassus, the Fillmore Auditorium, where a succession of name folk-rock bands, each more defeaning than the one before, follow one another in hour-long sessions. Here, amidst the electric guitars, the electric organs, and the constantly metamorphizing show of lights, one can see the gainly and the graceless, the sylph bodies and rude stompers, the crooked and straight—all, of whatever condition or talent, *dance* as the flickering of a strobe light reduces their figures in silhouette to egalitarian spastic bursts. The recognition dawns that this, at last, is dancing of utterly free form, devoid of fixed sequence or step, open to all and calling for no Friday after-school classes at Miss Martha's or expensive lessons from Arthur Murray. The sole requisite is to tune in, take heart, and let go. What follows must be "beautiful" (a favorite hippie word) because it is *you* who are doing and feeling, not another to whom you have surrendered the muse.

As with folk-rock dancing, so (theoretically, at least) with music, poetry, painting, pottery, and the other arts and crafts: expression over performance, impulse over product. Whether the "straight world" will in time heed this message of the hippies is, to be sure, problematical. Also, given the lavish financial rewards and prestige heaped upon more talented hippie artists by a youth-dominated entertainment market, it is conceivable that high standards of professional performance will develop here as well (listen to the more recent Beatles' recordings), thus engendering perhaps as great a participative gulf between artist and audience as already exists in the established arts. Despite the vagaries of forecasting, however, the hippies—as of now, at least—are responding to the incipient plenitude of leisure in ways far removed from the baleful visions of a Huxley or an Orwell.

The Time-Scale of Experience

In every society, certain activities are required to complete various tasks and to achieve various goals. These activities form a sequence—they may be of short duration and simple linkage (boiling an egg); long duration and complex linkage (preparing for a profession); or a variety of intermediate combinations (planting and harvesting a crop). And the activity sequences needed to complete valued tasks and to achieve valued goals in a society largely detemine how the people in that society will subjectively experience *time.*

The distinctive temporal bent of industrial society has been toward the second of these arrangements, long duration and complex linkage. As regards the subjective experience of time, this has meant what the anthropologist Florence Kluckhohn has termed a strong "future orientation" on the part of Western man, a quality of sensibility that radically distinguishes him from his peasant and tribal forebears. The major activities that fill the better part of his life acquire their meaning less from the pleasure they may or may not give at the moment than from their perceived relevance to some imagined future state of being or affairs, be it salvation, career achievement, material success, or the realization of a more perfect social order. Deprived of the pursuit of these temporally distant, complexly modulated goals, we would feel that life, as the man in the street puts it, is without meaning.

This subjective conception of time and experience is, of course, admirably suited to the needs of post-18th century industrial society, needs that include a stable labor force; work discipline; slow and regular accumulation of capital with which to plan and launch new investments and to expand; and long, arduous years of training to provide certain people with the high levels of skill necessary in so many professions and technical fields. If Western man had proved unable to defer present gratifications for future rewards (that is, if he had not been a future-oriented being), nothing resembling our present civilization, as Freud noted, could have come to pass.

Yet, paradoxically, it is the advanced technology of computers and servo-mechanisms, not to overlook nuclear warfare, that industrial civilization has carried us to that is raising grave doubts concerning this temporal ordering of affairs, this optimistic, pleasure-deferring, and magically rationalistic faith in converting present effort to future payoff. Why prepare, if there will be so few satisfying jobs to prepare for? Why defer, if there will be a superabundance of inexpensively-produced goods to choose from? Why plan, if all plans can disintegrate into nuclear dust?

Premature or exaggerated as these questions may seem, they are being asked, especially by young people. And merely to ask them is to prompt a radical shift in time-perspective—from what *will be* to what *is,* from future promise to present fulfillment, from the mundane discounting of present feeling and mood to a sharpened awareness of their contours and their possibilities for instant alteration. Broadly, it is to invest present experience with a new cognitive status and importance: a lust to extract from the living moment its full sensory and emotional potential. For if the present is no longer to hold hostage to the future, what other course than to ravish it at the very instant of its apprehension?

There is much about the hippie subculture that already betokens this alteration of time-perspective and concomitant reconstitution of the experienced self. Hippie argot—some of it new, much of it borrowed with slight connotative changes from the Negro, jazz, homosexual, and addict subcultures—is markedly skewed toward words and phrases in the active present tense: "happening," "where it's at," "turn on," "freak out," "grooving," "mind-blowing," "be-in," "cop out," "split," "drop acid" (take LSD), "put on," "uptight" (anxious and tense), "trip out" (experience the far-out effects of a hallucinogenic drug). The very concept of a happening signifies immediacy: Events are to be actively engaged in, improvised upon, and dramatically exploited for their own sake, with little thought about their origins, duration, or consequences. Thus, almost anything—from a massive be-in in Golden Gate Park to ingesting LSD to a casual street conversation to sitting solitarily under a tree—is approached with a heightened awareness of its happening potential. Similarly, the vogue among Hashbury hippies for astrology, tarot cards, I Ching, and other forms of thaumaturgic prophecy (a hippie conversation is as likely to begin with "What's your birthday?" as "What's your name?") seems to be an attempt to denude the future of its temporal integrity—its unknowability and slow unfoldingness—by fusing it indiscriminately with present dispositions and sensations. The hippie's structureless round-of-day ("hanging loose"), his disdain for appointments, schedules, and straight society's compulsive parceling out of minutes and hours, are all implicated in his intense reverence for the possibilities of the present and uninterest in the future. Few wear watches, and as a colleague who has made a close participant-observer study of one group of hippies remarked, "None of them ever seems to know what time it is."

It is, perhaps, from this vantage point that the widespread use of drugs by hippies acquires its cultural significance, above and beyond the fact that drugs are easily available in the subculture or that their use (especially LSD) has come to symbolize a distinctive badge of membership in that culture. Denied by our Protestant-Judaic heritage the psychological means for experiencing the moment intensively, for parlaying sensation and exoticizing mundane consciousness, the hippie uses drugs where untutored imagination fails. Drugs impart to the present—or so it is alleged by the hippie psychedelic religionists—an aura of aliveness, a sense of union with fellow man and nature, which—we have been taught—can be apprehended, if not in the afterlife that few modern men still believe in, then only after the deepest reflection and self-knowledge induced by protracted experience.

A topic of lively debate among hippie intellectuals is whether drugs represent but a transitory phase of the hippie subculture to be discarded once other, more self-generating, means are discovered by its members for extracting consummatory meaning from present time, or whether drugs are the *sine qua non* of the subculture. Whatever the case, the hippies' experiment with ways to recast our notions of time and experience is deserving of close attention.

The Hippies' Future

As of this writing, it is by no means certain that Haight-Ashbury's "new community," as hippie spokesmen like to call it, can survive much beyond early 1968. Although the "great summer invasion" of émigré hippies fell far short of the 100,000 to 500,000 forecast, the influx of youth from California's and the nation's metropolitan suburbs was, despite considerable turnover, large enough to place a severe strain on the new community's meager resources. "Crash pads" for the night were simply not available in sufficient quantity; the one daily meal of soup or stew served free by the Diggers could hardly appease youthful appetites; and even the lure of free love, which to young minds might be construed as a substitute for food, tarnished for many— boys outnumbered girls by at least three to one, if not more. Besides, summer is San Francisco's most inclement season, the city being shrouded in a chilling, wind-blown fog much of the time. The result was hundreds of youths leading a hand-to-mouth existence, wandering aimlessly on the streets, panhandling, munching stale doughnuts, sleeping in parks and autos and contracting virulent upper-respiratory infections. In this milieu cases of drug abuse, notably involving Methedrine and other "body-wrecking" amphetamines, have showed an alarming increase, beginning about mid-summer and continuing up to the present. And, while the city fathers were not at first nearly so repressive as many had feared, they barely lifted a finger to ameliorate the situation in the Haight-Ashbury. Recently, however, with the upcoming city elections for Mayor and members of the Board of Supervisors, they have given evidence of taking a "firmer" attitude toward the hippies: Drug arrests are on the increase, many more minors in the area are being stopped for questioning and referral to juvenile authorities, and a leading Haight Street hippie cultural establishment, the Straight Theatre, has been denied a dance permit.

It has not, therefore, been solely the impact of sheer numbers that has subjected the new community to a difficult struggle for survival. A variety of forces, internal and external, appear to have conjoined to crush it. To begin with, there is the hippies' notorious, near-anarchic aversion to sustained and organized effort toward reaching some goal. Every man "does his own thing for as long as he likes" until another thing comes along to distract or delight him, whereupon the hippie ethos enjoins him to drop the first thing. (Shades of the early, utopian Karl Marx: ". . . in the communist society it [will be] possible for me to do this today and that tomorrow, to hunt in the morning, to fish in the afternoon, to raise cattle in the evening, to be a critic after dinner, just as I feel at the moment; without ever being a hunter, fisherman, herdsman, or critic." From *The German Ideology*.) Even with such groups as the Diggers, projects are abandoned almost as soon as they are begun. One of the more prominent examples: An ongoing pastoral idyll of summer cultural happenings, proclaimed with great fanfare in May by a group calling itself the Council for the Summer of Love, was abandoned in June when the Council's leader decided one morning to leave town. Add to this the stalling and ordinance-juggling of a city bureaucracy reluctant to grant hippies permits and licenses for their pet enterprises, and very little manages to get off the ground. With only a few notable exceptions, therefore, like the Haight-Ashbury Free Medical Clinic, which—though closed temporarily—managed through its volunteer staff to look after the medical needs of thousands of hippies during the summer, the new community badly failed to provide for the hordes of youth drawn by its paeans of freedom, love, and the new life. Perhaps there is some ultimate wisdom to "doing one's own thing"; it was, however, hardly a practical way to receive a flock of kinsmen.

Exacerbating the "uptightness" of the hippies is a swelling stream of encounters with the police and courts, ranging from panhandling misdemeanors to harboring runaway minors ("contributing to the delinquency of a minor") to, what is most unnerving for hip inhabitants, a growing pattern of sudden mass arrests for marihuana use and possession in which as many as 25 youths may be hauled off in a single raid on a flat. (Some hippies console themselves with the thought that if enough middle-class youths get "busted for grass," such a hue and cry will be generated in respectable quarters that the marihuana laws will soon be repealed or greatly liberalized.) And, as if the internal problems of the new community were not enough, apocalyptic rumors sprung up, in the wake of the Newark and Detroit riots, that "the Haight is going to be burned to the ground" along with the adjoining Fillmore Negro ghetto. There followed a series of ugly street incidents between blacks and whites—assaults, sexual attacks, window smashings— which palpably heightened racial tensions and fed the credibility of the rumors.

Finally, the area's traffic-choked main thoroughfare, Haight Street, acquired in the space of a few months so carnival and Dantesque an atmosphere as to defy description. Hippies, tourists, drug peddlers, Hell's Angels, drunks, speed freaks (people high on Methedrine), panhandlers, pamphleteers, street musicians, crackpot evangelists, photographers, TV camera crews, reporters (domestic and foreign), researchers, ambulatory schizophrenics, and hawkers of the underground press (at least four such papers are produced in the Haight-Ashbury alone) jostled, put-on, and taunted one another through a din worthy of the Tower of Babel. The street-milling was incessant, and all heads remained cocked for "something to happen" to crystallize the disarray. By early summer, so repugnant had this atmosphere become for the "old" hippies (those residing there before—the origins of Hashbury's new community barely go back two years) that many departed; those who remained did so in the rapidly fading hope that the area might revert to its normal state of abnormality following the expected post-Labor Day exodus of college and high-school hippies. And, while the exodus of summer hippies has indeed been considerable, the consensus among knowledgeable observers of the area is that it has not regained its former, less frenetic, and less disorganized ambience. The transformations wrought by the summer influx—the growing shift to Methedrine as *the* drug of choice, the more general drift toward a wholly drug-oriented subculture, the appearance of hoodlum and thrill-seeking elements, the sleazy tourist shops, the racial tensions—persist, only on a lesser scale.

But though Haight-Ashbury's hippie community may be destined to soon pass from the scene, the roots upon which it feeds run deep in our culture. These are not only of the long-term socio-historic kind I have touched on here, but of a distinctly contemporary character as well, the pain and moral duplicity of our Vietnam involvement being a prominent wellspring of hippie alienation. As the pressures mount on middle-class youth for ever greater scholastic achievement (soon a graduate degree may be mandatory for middle-class status, as a high-school diploma was in the 1940s), as the years of adolescent dependence are further prolonged, and as the accelerated pace of technological change aggravates the normal social tendency to intergenerational conflict, an increasing number of young people can be expected to drop out, or opt out, and drift into the hippie subculture. It is difficult to foresee how long they will remain there and what the consequences for later stages of their careers will be, inasmuch as insufficient time has passed for even a single age cohort of hippies to make the transition from early to middle adulthood. However, even among those youths who "remain in" conventional society in some formal sense, a very large number can be expected to hover so close to the margins of hippie subculture as to have their attitudes and outlooks substantially modified. Indeed, it is probably through some such muted, gradual, and indirect process of social conversion that the hippie subculture will make a lasting impact on American society, if it is to have any at all.

At the same time, the hippie rebellion gives partial, as yet ambiguous, evidence of a massiveness, a universality, and a density of existential texture, all of which promise to transcend the narrowly-segregated confines of age, occupation, and residence that characterized most bohemias of the past (Greenwich Village, Bloomsbury, the Left Bank). Some hippie visionaries already compare the movement to Christianity sweeping the Roman Empire. We cannot predict how far the movement can go toward enveloping the larger society, and whether as it develops it will—as have nearly all successful social movements—significantly compromise the visions that animate it with the practices of the reigning institutional system. Much depends on the state of future social discontent, particularly within the middle classes, and on the viable political options governments have for assuaging this discontent. Judging, however, from the social upheavals and mass violence of recent decades, such options are, perhaps inevitably, scarce indeed. Just possibly, then, by opting out and making their own kind of cultural waves, the hippies are telling us more than we can now imagine about our future selves.

REFERENCES

It's Happening by J. L. Simmons and Barry Winograd (Santa Barbara, Calif.: Marc-Laird Publications, 1966).

Looking Forward: The Abundant Society by Walter A. Weisskopf, Raghavan N. Iyer, and others (Santa Barbara, Calif.: Center for the Study of Democratic Institutions, 1966).

The Next Generation by Donald N. Michael (New York: Vintage Books—Random House, 1965).

The Future as History by Robert L. Heilbroner (New York: Grove Press, 1961).

About the Editor

Jack D. Douglas, Associate Professor of Sociology at the University of California at San Diego, received his B.A. from Harvard University and his Ph.D. from Princeton University. He has previously taught at Dartmouth College, Wellesley College, U.C.L.A., Princeton University, and Syracuse University. Professor Douglas is the author of *The Social Meanings of Suicide* and the editor of *The Relevance of Sociology, The Impact of Sociology and Other Social Sciences,* and *Deviance and Respectability.* Two other forthcoming books edited by Professor Douglas are *Crime and Justice in American Society* and *Freedom and Tyranny in a Technological Society.*